ISSUES AND RESPONSE

SECOND EDITION

Edited by

Lee A. Jacobus

University of Connecticut

Harcourt Brace Jovanovich, Inc.

New York   *Chicago*   *San Francisco*   *Atlanta*

Cover Art by Robert J. Saunders.
Puzzles reproduced courtesy of Springbok Editions,
a division of Hallmark Cards, Inc.

ISBN: 0–15–547151–1

Library of Congress Catalog Card Number: 73–187572

Printed in the United States of America

PREFACE

In ages past the issues of the day generally remained the same; most of the social problems confronted by Rome had also plagued Athens and earlier cultures. Today the issues that demand our attention arise more rapidly, and identifying the most important ones has in itself become a major problem. This collection attempts to picture the state of America in the early 1970s by focusing on those issues that seem the most long-lasting and the most likely to involve basic changes in the national temperament.

Our individual response to these issues is a primary concern of this book; each essay will stir strong feelings in the reader. For example, although a range of reactions is possible, it is hard to imagine any of us remaining indifferent to Christopher Chandler's account of the killing of Black Panthers by Chicago police, or unmoved by Ralph Guzman's description of the militancy growing among Mexican-Americans. Similarly, all of us should find cause to worry in reading the essays by Richard Hofstadter and Irving Howe, for they suggest that violence is becoming a dominant feature of American politics.

Our response to violence of all kinds has become much more complex in recent years. In the section on war and peace, biologist George Wald denounces the new military tactics that have killed countless noncombatants and devastated large tracts of land in Southeast Asia; Michael Herr presents a picture of the Vietnam war as it appears to the news correspondent on the scene; and Richard Barnet discusses the power of the military-industrial complex and the role war plays in America's economic prosperity. Many social critics see a connection between our involvement in the war abroad and the high domestic crime rate, especially as it relates to narcotics; the section on crime includes the alarming story of a neighborhood overrun by junkie-thieves, and an article by the editors of *Forbes*—a magazine considered one of the bibles of big business—offers a very businesslike analysis of the narcotics trade. Whether it is possible and desirable to teach students to cope with our increasingly violent world is the subject of Douglas Heath's essay in the section on education. Heath's underlying theme, the need to apply the realities of our times to our educational system, is suggested by several of the other essays in that section as well: Barbara Goodheart's article on sex education courses in the schools; the divergent views on black studies courses provided by Charles V. Hamilton and Kenneth Clark; Sidney Simon's argument for the elimination of academic grading; and Peter Schrag's essay on the education-for-failure received by most working-class whites.

Ecology and women's rights are two of the "new" issues that have attracted recent attention. The essay by William Murdock and Joseph Connell and the one by Kenneth Watt are both good introductions to the environmental issue; the specific problem of feeding the world's growing population is analyzed in essays by Anne Funkhouser and Margaret Mead. The goals of the Women's Liberation Movement, which have prompted both mockery and serious controversy, are carefully examined here in essays by Caroline Bird, Cynthia Ozick, and Shirley Chisholm. Like these two issues, the consequences of landing on the moon have become a major public concern only in the last decade. In the section on science, C. P. Snow takes a look at the philosophic implications of man's exploration of space and concludes that reaching the moon may ultimately do mankind more harm than good. Equally apprehensive of "progress" are James Moriarity in an essay on the increasing use of scientific devices in political campaigning, and Francis Wormuth on the relationship between science and elected government.

These essays employ several modes of exposition in getting their points across, and the student can readily use them as models of good writing. The selections by Baraka, Stegman, and Watt all show how enumeration can help a writer structure his material and clarify his major ideas. Tom Wicker's patient reply to those who attack the press for a lack of objectivity and Anne Funkhouser's essay on population are fine examples of simple, direct narrative used to explain personal feelings on a serious issue. Similarly, the sensitive reportorial styles of William Laurence on the first A-bomb test and Michael Herr on the Vietnam war should aid students who need to build their powers of observation and their skill in reporting what they have witnessed.

Questions and suggestions for writing follow each essay to stimulate the reader who may not immediately form his own personal reactions to the material; however, they are not intended as substitutes for the reader's thoughts on these issues. Personal response is the key in this book; when it is present the job of learning to write is more obviously useful, more personally involving, and more likely to produce long-lasting results.

Lee A. Jacobus

CONTENTS

POLITICS

CRIME IN AMERICA AND ABROAD

THE ECONOMY OF DEATH

Richard Barnet

War, all war, is expensive; more than one great nation
has come to financial grief because of war. The sums the
United States has spent on war and defense in recent
years are mind-boggling. Richard Barnet thinks a reordering of priorities is necessary if American society is
to survive.

Since 1946 the taxpayers have been asked to contribute more
than one trillion dollars for national security. Each year the federal
government spends more than 70 cents of every budget dollar on
past, present and future wars. The American people are devoting
more resources to the war machine than is spent by all federal, state
and local governments on health and hospitals, education, old-age
and retirement benefits, public assistance and relief, unemployment
and social security, housing and community development, and the
support of agriculture. Out of every tax dollar there is about 11 cents
left to build American society.

The result of this gigantic investment in security has been to make
the American people among the most insecure on the planet. Perhaps
the most important index of this fact is that Americans are more
afraid to walk the streets of Washington than the streets of Saigon.
These feelings are a direct reflection of an increasingly violent society.

The pattern is tragically familiar. The world historian Arnold
Toynbee, who has traced the fate of the great empires of the past,
finds that most have gone down to defeat not by invasion from without but because of social dissolution within. Mighty nations that do
not respond to the needs of their own people have traditionally tried
to solve problems and overcome frustration through violence abroad
and repression at home. In the process, they have hastened their

THE ECONOMY OF DEATH   Reprinted from the May 1970 issue of *Journal of
the American Association of University Women* by permission of the author and
Journal of the American Association of University Women.

own exit from center stage. The greatest security problems for a nation are the hostility and frustration of its own citizens.

A nation that puts its trust in military power to solve its problems weakens itself in many ways. The most disastrous consequence of building the power of military institutions at the expense of the rest of the society is to turn that society into a warrior state ready to sacrifice its most precious values, including freedom itself, to defense against foreign enemies real and imagined. The United States has sought to find national security by accumulating more military power than any other nation in history, but the result has been increasing powerlessness. We are unable to solve the nation's problems at home because we have allocated our resources to our war machine, and we find that the machine, no matter how great its killing power, cannot solve political problems such as the future of Vietnam.

There is no way to fix a rational limit to defense spending other than by the application of old-fashioned political judgment and moral insight. Unless the American people begin to ask and keep asking what real security they are buying, there is no hope of stopping the mindless expansion of the war machine. For a generation these questions have not been asked. Until the Vietnam war and the fight over the anti-ballistic missile, no significant interest group in or out of Congress challenged the basic assumptions behind any project of the military, no matter how massive the investment. Every new weapons system has been presented to the public doubly wrapped: an inside wrapping of baffling technical detail, and on the outside, the flag. When the Joint Chiefs of Staff proclaim a new military "requirement" based, as they like to point out, on their 178 years of collective military experience, the taxpayer is expected to say thank you for being taken care of so handsomely.

The central task of American society is to free ourselves from the economy of death. Whether we shall have the money, energy or will to turn back the rising tide of violence at home, whether we can rouse ourselves from the dream of Pax Americana abroad, are equally dependent on the same critical question: are the American people capable of reordering national priorities so that their children can live as free men and in peace?

Any effort to rescue the American people from the economy of death has two principal tasks. First, it must persuade enough Americans that neither peace nor security is to be achieved through the endless preparation for war. Second, it must hold up an alternative vision of an American economy that can function without a spiraling military budget and an American society that does not feel compelled to seek security through violence.

The task of shifting American priorities is primarily a political rather than an economic problem. The federal government must play an active role in redirecting investment into essential areas of the public economy and in helping individuals and communities now dependent upon war industry to play a productive role in a life-oriented society. Most economists are confident that the economics of conversion could be successfully managed and that the nation as a whole would emerge from the process richer and better equipped to solve its problems. Indeed, as the United States government economist, S. M. Greenhouse, points out, high military spending contributes substantially to the dangerous combination of recession and inflation which now threatens the economy.

The problem is one of will and incentive. The Department of Defense and its captive industry have achieved a privileged position in American life, enjoying substantial exemptions from the rules that govern the rest of us. They need not explain what they do. There is no great necessity to tell Congress or the public the truth. "Promise anything and charge twice as much" has been the operating creed in defense procurement. Generals and Pentagon administrators do not look forward to the day when others will decide how to spend the money that they have so long controlled. It is too much to expect giant bureaucracies to greet their own liquidation with enthusiasm. One should not expect to see the executives of General Dynamics at Quaker peace vigils.

How then can the hold of the military-industrial complex on American society be broken? What can the citizen do?

First, he can educate himself about the issues of military spending and the role of the military-industrial complex. He can do some of this on his own through reading and listening. He should hound his congressman if the congressman is not alert to the dangers of militarism, and give him active support if he is. He should work at the precinct level in persuading local political organizations to take forthright positions against the economy of death, on both national and local issues. Individual citizens can help persuade city and town councils to continue the practice begun in the Vietnam war of taking positions on foreign-policy and defense questions. They can also organize or assist door-to-door educational campaigns to discuss issues of security and military spending. Only when the public is sufficiently informed so that it can no longer be stampeded into supporting whatever the Pentagon asks will our leaders abandon this easy tactic.

One method of forcing congressmen to educate themselves and to avoid ducking fundamental issues of national security is the local hearing. Some congressmen, in connection with the Vietnam war and the ABM fight, have conducted such hearings in their districts to which constituents come to ask questions, to make their views known, to press the congressman to commit himself on issues, and to be educated on foreign and defense policy. These hearings are a good vehicle for increasing democratic participation and control on these issues. Each year the defense budget should be discussed at a series of such hearings in each Congressional district. Congressmen themselves should take the initiative to set them up. Where they don't, local citizen groups should organize them and invite the congressman to appear. If a congressman refuses, the group should organize immediately to defeat him at the next election or even to have him recalled if the state constitution has such a provision, for it is unthinkable for an elected representative to refuse to discuss life-and-death issues of war and peace with his constituents.

Such hearings would educate the public to the reality that the decisions on defense and foreign policy are matters of political rather than technical judgment. They are no easier but probably no harder than many other public policy decisions that have to be made in a complex modern society. Only the stakes are higher. Technical and secret information play a minor role in the fundamental decisions on how large the defense budget should be. In the Kennedy administration, for example, the decision to buy 1000 Minuteman missiles was based not on McNamara's computers but on a political compromise between the Joint Chiefs of Staff, who wanted 2000, and the White House staff, who thought a few hundred were quite sufficient. There are very few magic numbers or critical secret facts that are not printed in *The New York Times* a few weeks after they appear in top-secret memoranda. The most closely guarded secrets concern the details of intelligence-gathering operations. They play only a marginal role in the basic strategic choices of the top national security managers and *are not essential for an informed analysis of those decisions by an intelligent citizen.*

Congressmen have an obligation to become sufficiently informed themselves to be able to discuss intelligently with their constituents what they can know about military spending, what they can't know and what difference it makes. Only when the issue of secrecy and technical information is confronted directly will the citizen be able to come to a better judgment than "The President knows best." The "If you only knew what I know" mystique undermines the very principle of democratic government. *Unless it is publicly and consistently challenged, the American system is threatened.*

The burden should now be placed on a congressman to explain why he votes to increase America's overkill power, why he supports the maintenance of 1,222,000 U.S. servicemen overseas in 399 major military installations and a five ocean navy. In short, the citizen should demand to know why he thinks America's national security can be achieved through militarism and empire. Does he understand that America's youth do not consider it patriotic to kill people of other nations and other races who have not harmed and could not harm this nation? Does he realize what it will do to this country to force our young people to kill in violation of their own convictions and the best traditions of the country? Why does the national security of the United States depend upon whether revolutions in Cuba or Thailand succeed or fail? Why must we spend most of the money and energy we allot to America's relations with the outside world on instruments of death?

The congressman should understand that a growing part of the new generation of Americans does not accept the assumptions of the economy of death. Several thousands of our best youth have gone to prison because of such conviction. The congressman should be told that he will be held accountable for his continued support of the mindless expansion of the military budget or for his silent acquiescence. His duty is to use the power that still remains to him to reverse the national crisis of militarism. This means pressing for a serious redefinition of America's role in the world and a drastic cutback in military spending.

We cannot much longer have both an economy of death and a free society. One will overwhelm the other. Which one?

STUDY QUESTIONS

1. What does Barnet mean when he says the streets of Washington are more dangerous for Americans than the streets of Saigon? How does this relate to the economic situation?
2. What are the greatest security problems for a nation?
3. What is the real expense of a warrior state?

4. How have weapons systems been "wrapped" when being presented to Congress for approval?
5. How much say have the American people had in approving the expenses they have financed?
6. In Barnet's opinion, what is the central task of American society?
7. What are the economic results of high military spending?
8. What are some of the things a society can do to get out of the grip of a military economy?
9. How well informed are our congressmen on the issues of war and peace?
10. How secret are our military secrets?

SUGGESTIONS FOR WRITING

1. Consider the nature of this essay. Do you find it convincing? Does it change your thinking in any way? Write a brief analysis of the approach Barnet uses and how well it works.
2. If you wanted to follow up on the ways Barnet suggests a citizen can influence his government, what would you do? Detail the steps you would take and give some suggestion of the way in which your efforts would probably be rewarded. Do you think your own legislators would listen to you?
3. Describe what you think would be the average American's reaction to the information Barnet supplies here. In preparation for writing such an essay, you might memorize a few of the more pertinent details and statistics and bring some of them up in conversation with people whose views are somewhat different from yours.
4. Using as many details as possible from the essay, either defend or attack the statement: "Unless it is publicly and consistently challenged, the American system is threatened."
5. Write an essay that attacks Barnet's views. Be sure to go to the heart of the essay and pinpoint its basic assumptions. Analyze them, suggest alternative views, and write a position paper that effectively contradicts Barnet's.

THE LEAVES FALL, THE BLOOD FLOWS

George Wald

Despite all the campaign promises of 1968, the war in Vietnam continues. Our troop involvement has changed but our modern fighting methods are still destroying noncombatants and ravaging the land. Biologist George Ward, one of the most eloquent and convincing voices in opposition to the war, speaks about American military policy and the suffering it brings to Vietnamese civilians.

During World War I, all Americans learned the German word *Schrecklichkeit*—frightfulness. We were told that *Schrecklichkeit* was a deliberate aspect of German military policy. Its point was to direct military operations in large part against civilians—to terrorize and starve civilian populations in the theater of war. All Americans felt that civilization needed to be defended against such practices.

It is hard for Americans to realize that our own Armed Forces now pursue such policies. It is now we who practice frightfulness. In our present methods of warfare, civilians are among the principal victims. Our operations are not intended to spare them, and the civilians, of course, most often lack the means of self-defense.

If our Department of Defense or our Armed Forces at present exercise any restraints in the procedures and weapons they have prepared for use, on the grounds of humanity or sparing noncombatants, I would be happy to know of them. There still seems to be some compunction about shooting civilians while looking at them; a number of soldiers and ex-soldiers are about to be court-martialed for allegedly having done that. But if noncombatants are killed from the air, or with artillery, or by some indirect means so that they are not

THE LEAVES FALL, THE BLOOD FLOWS   Reprinted from the June 6, 1970 issue of *Saturday Review* by permission of the author and *Saturday Review*. Copyright 1970 Saturday Review, Inc.

visibly and individually identifiable as civilians, that seems altogether
acceptable.

However, the military mustn't be blamed for all of this. Much of
it was started and is fostered by civilians.

Our use of defoliation and herbicides in Vietnam is a case in point.
A major change in U. S. policy occurred in November 1955, when
Secretary of the Army Wilbur M. Brucker approved the report of a
civilian advisory committee that urged the development of instruments of chemical, biological, and radiological warfare "to the fullest
extent the human mind can encompass" (*The New York Times,*
November 7, 1955). That decision marked the beginning of our modern CBW establishment. In the fifteen years since, the CBW community seems to have been engaged in fulfilling this program to the
letter.

At the heart of the American system is civilian control of the military. Among the major instruments of that control should be the
House Armed Services Committee and the Senate Military Affairs
Committee. Those committees, however, rather than restraining the
military, goad them on, particularly in the expenditure of military
equipment and funds, and in the expansion of defense contracts. As
the whole world looks with hope to the Strategic Arms Limitation
Talks (SALT) in Vienna, Representative L. Mendel Rivers (D–S.C.),
Chairman of the House Armed Services Committee, calls those talks
a meaningless exercise (the *Times,* April 29, 1970). So, it wouldn't
be fair to blame these things entirely on the military.

Always the excuse made for acts of atrocity, such as in the Mylai
massacre, is that our men are fighting for their lives in a war in which
civilians do take part. Often I am asked: What would you do? I
think the point is that, if one finds oneself fighting old men, and
mothers, and five-year-old children, then one is in the wrong war,
and had better get out of it.

Students in Santa Barbara recently burned down a bank, and here
and there other students are breaking up ROTC offices. I abhor violence in all its forms, wherever it happens. Student violence, like
black violence, is a symptom of despair, of hopelessness. Give the
students and black people, and red and yellow and brown people,
some grounds for hope, and they will turn from violence to working
to fulfill that hope.

But, of course, the big violence in the world occurs under official
auspices. Student violence usually stops at breaking windows; but
"law and order" begins with breaking heads.

In the case of our intervention in Cambodia, we are told that the internal conflict there is in no sense a civil war, but a matter of foreign aggression. The penetration by American troops twenty miles into the country is "not an invasion." It took only twenty-four hours for that noninvasion to turn from a South Vietnamese force accompanied by American advisers to an American force accompanied by South Vietnamese auxiliaries.

Every killing that we know about anywhere in the world we share in, we well-behaved civilians trying to live decent lives. We share responsibility for every maiming, burning, and starving out of civilians, of innocent and helpless persons, and for every child who is hurt, orphaned, sick, or hungry. That is true if only because, knowing of these things, one grows used to them, one ceases to respond.

Our country took the lead in drafting the Geneva Protocol of 1925, which banned the use in war of all "asphyxiating, poisonous, or other gases" and of "bacteriological methods of warfare," but the Protocol was never ratified by the Senate.

Why have we not even now ratified the Geneva Protocol? A curious consideration keeps this from happening. Virtually all the rest of the civilized world includes among the gases mentioned the so-called incapacitating gases—tear gas and CS, really a lung rather than a tear gas—as well as herbicides and defoliants. Our government from the beginning has wanted the "incapacitating gases" excluded from the Protocol on the curious ground that we should not refuse to use on an enemy what we use on our own people. We speak of the tear gases and CS as "riot control agents." There are two major difficulties with this view. As riot control agents, these materials are used in the open, and their purpose is to make people move away from the area of application. In Vietnam, however, they have frequently been used on underground shelters, where their concentration rises to such levels as to become lethal, particularly to children. The main object of their use in underground shelters is to drive persons out from under cover so as to expose them to attack by other means, by bombing or artillery fire. So what are "riot control agents" here become lethal weapons under combat conditions, as in Vietnam.

It is much the same with the use of defoliants and herbicides. Our government stands almost alone in insisting on exempting these agents from the terms of the Geneva Protocol. Apparently, at the Geneva Conference in 1925, everyone else agreed that the Protocol included among the chemical weapons it intended to ban both tear gases and herbicides.

Defoliation and herbicides kill not only plants but men. The most widely used agent of defoliation in Vietnam has been a 50-50 mixture of 2,4-D and 2,4,5-T. The latter has been shown to cause a high incidence of birth deformities—teratogenic effects—in pregnant rats and mice, when fed in extraordinarily small amounts, such as might easily be reached by drinking water in the sprayed areas. We have as yet no definite information of its effects on man. Yet, at least four newspapers in South Vietnam reported last summer a remarkable rise in the incidence of deformed babies in areas that had been sprayed with 2,4,5-T. The newspapers were promptly closed by the Thieu government for "interfering with the war effort" (*New York Post*, November 4, 1969). Further, 2,4-D has been reported to cause a significant rise in birth abnormalities in experimental animals. These chemicals have been in common use in the United States for weed control, but under carefully restricted conditions. They have been sprayed in Vietnam without those restrictions, and at more than ten times the concentrations employed here.

Herbicides also, as used in Vietnam, are lethal weapons. In that poor country, where most of the population is never far above the subsistence level, they are used to destroy food crops. Our food destruction programs in Vietnam—and now also in Cambodia—are almost exclusively directed against civilians. The point is simple enough. When food is scarce, soldiers take what they want. It is the weak and defenseless who do without: the aged, infirm, the women, and most of all the children.

Why do we do such things? One major objective of our herbicide and defoliation programs in Indochina is to make large sections of the countryside uninhabitable, and so to drive the farmers and peasants into the cities. Wars of national liberation have their principal base in the peasantry. Destroy the peasantry by destroying the countryside, and the base has been removed.

The major villain in the piece is, of course, the concept of total war. War itself is an atrocity, and by now has become so dangerous that we cannot live with it much longer. Total war is altogether depraved and brutalizing. It leaves one nothing with which to continue. The vanquished are hardly more injured than the victors. Even the spectators are maimed irretrievably. For they grow used to the atrocities and cease to respond, and so forgo their common humanity.

All the chickens are coming home to roost. A few months ago, CS was sprayed by helicopter upon a penned-in crowd of students and faculty on the Berkeley campus. Within the space of a few days, four unarmed white students have been shot dead at Kent, Ohio; two black students at Jackson, Mississippi; and six alleged black looters in Augusta, Georgia. The Bill of Rights is under fire, the news media are harassed by the administration, and construction workers beat up peace demonstrators while members of the financial community and the police look on. Having been stopped by the Senate from degrading the Supreme Court, the President seems bent on subverting and humiliating the Senate. We have supported military dictatorships in so many places—Spain, Greece, Brazil, South Vietnam, now Cambodia, to name a few—is dictatorship also coming home to roost?

That is now our problem.

STUDY QUESTIONS

1. What are the most distressing aspects of *Schrecklichkeit?*
2. Who are the principal victims in our present method of war?
3. What kinds of civilian killings seem acceptable to the Army? Does American society also accept those kinds of killing as blameless?
4. What kinds of chemical and biological warfare are being practiced in Vietnam?
5. How long has there been a CBW program in Vietnam?
6. Does Wald hold the military completely responsible for what is going on in Vietnam?
7. What kinds of distinctions does Wald make between violence of a private nature and governmental violence?
8. In Wald's view, what responsibility do the American people have for the suffering of civilians in Southeast Asia?
9. Why has the United States not ratified the Geneva Protocol banning the use of gases and bacteriological warfare?
10. How are herbicides lethal to human beings? What makes their effects particularly long-lasting?

SUGGESTIONS FOR WRITING

1. Analyze the allegations that Wald makes in the last paragraph of the essay. Is there any current evidence to support or refute his claims? Amplify your discussion with details from current news releases and your general knowledge.
2. In a brief essay that uses the facts the article provides and any information you may be able to add, show the relationship be-

tween American policies in Vietnam and American policies at home.

3. Wald's ultimate assertion is that there is likely to be a dictatorship in America. He points out that civilian despair gives way to violence and that violence is met with repression. How serious is the threat of repression in America? Do you feel that your own freedoms are being threatened?

4. Using the information provided in the article, describe the attitude of the U. S. Government toward its own citizens. Is there any evidence that clearly points toward a new pattern of behavior and a changing concern?

5. How would you defend this article against someone who claimed that Wald doesn't realize the threat America faces and that wars not fought abroad will be fought on American soil?

THE MILITARY ATOM: DISARMAMENT PROBLEMS

Hans A. Bethe

Universal disarmament has long been a goal to which
heads of state paid lip service while escalating their nation's arsenals. Meaningful talks on limiting arms are
finally under way between the United States and the
Soviet Union. But, even if they end with some practical
agreement, they may prove to be too little, too late.

Disarmament is a more lively topic today than it has been for
the past six years. There is both hope of success, and fear of failure—
of any agreement being too late.

The hope is kindled by the SALT talks: the negotiations between
the United States and the Soviet Union for a strategic arms limitation treaty. The preliminary talks at Helsinki, concluded in December, were apparently successful. The substantive talks then started
on April 15 in Vienna. According to the newspaper reports, both sides
were satisfied with the progress; Vladimir Semyenov, the chief Russian negotiator, described the atmosphere with the words, "You give
a little, and you take a little."

This is the spirit in which one can hope for progress, and it differs
favorably from the Russian attitude during most of the negotiations
on the Test Ban Treaty in 1958–61. In those negotiations, the USSR
seemed unwilling to trade one concession for another. Often, the
United States would make concessions without getting any response,
and then occasionally and suddenly, the Russians would make a concession without any apparent preparation leading up to it. It is to be
hoped that the SALT talks will indeed be more give and take, more
direct and transparent bargaining.

Another hopeful point is that, again according to newspaper re-

THE MILITARY ATOM: DISARMAMENT PROBLEMS   From the June 1970 issue of
Bulletin of the Atomic Scientists. Reprinted by permission of Science and Public
Affairs, the Bulletin of the Atomic Scientists. Copyright © 1970 and 1971 by
the Educational Foundation for Nuclear Science.

ports, both sides put their specific concerns on the table, so that in the interval between the end of the Helsinki talks and the Vienna meeting, they could react to each other's ideas and formulate concrete proposals.

But there is also a great fear that SALT may be too late to stop the triple escalation of the arms race which is in progress: ABM, MIRV, and the increase in total "throw-weight." All three of them tend to destabilize the strategic situation, and to give an advantage to the one who launches his missiles first. Much has been written on ABM, in the *Bulletin*, for example, and especially Wiesner's and Chayes' book, "ABM: An Evolution of the Decision to Deploy an Antiballistic Missile System." But it may be useful to summarize a few points about MIRV.

The "multiple independently targeted re-entry vehicles" (MIRVs) can have very different functions and different effects on strategic stability. One function is the penetration of possible enemy ABM. Multiple re-entry vehicles (MRVs) are most effective in doing this, presenting a "traffic handling" problem to the enemy radar, and increasing the difficulty of distinguishing warheads from decoys. Fear of Soviet ABM deployment was one of the initial reasons for U. S. development of this weapon. However, for penetration of city ABM defenses, no great accuracy in guidance of the MRVs is needed; a few miles is sufficient. Nor is independent targeting required. The yield of each warhead can be quite small, e.g., of the order of 100 kilotons. This use of MIRV—or rather MRV—is stabilizing in offsetting the de-stabilizing ABM.

A second use of MIRV is to make better use of one's firepower (throw-weight) for the destruction of cities and other soft targets. Only big cities require megaton or multi-megaton yields; the large number of medium-sized cities can be destroyed by smaller weapons. Thus one missile can destroy several cities. This requires independent targeting of the re-entry vehicles, but still only moderate accuracy in guidance. This possibility of destroying several targets with one missile is much more important than the fact, sometimes stated—by Eugene Wigner, for example—that the total area which can be destroyed by all warheads is less with multiples than with single warheads. (In a talk at the ABM symposium of the American Physical Society, April 1969, Wigner wished to show that the Russian ABM, by inducing us to use MIRV, had forced us into reducing the area of an enemy country that we can destroy, thus reducing our striking force. On the latter point, this is of course at variance with the opinion of both the former and the present Secretary of Defense.) But it is not really very important, because both Russia and the United States possess far more missiles than are necessary to destroy the other's cities. MIRVs in this mode have no appreciable effect on strategic stability.

The third use of MIRV is in an attack on the enemy missile force. The aim here is, of course, to destroy several of the hard missile silos of the enemy with the multiple warheads on one of your own missiles. For this use, both independent targeting and extreme guidance accuracy are essential. In fact, whether this use of MIRV is at all possible, depends on (1) the hardness (in psi) of the enemy silos; (2) the yield of your own warheads; and, most important, (3) the guidance accuracy, measured by the CEP, the "circular probable error" of hitting the target. If the CEP is about equal to the "kill radius" (for hardened silos) of a single warhead on your missile, then not much is gained, or possibly something is lost, by going to MIRV. But if the CEP is substantially smaller, then "MIRVing" makes the attackers' force more effective. Unfortunately, it is extremely difficult to get reliable data on another country's CEP, and a factor of two here will make all the difference between a highly effective and an essentially unimportant MIRV force.

The fear that the Russian MIRV, whose testing we have observed, may be intended to be used against our hard Minuteman silos was uppermost in the minds of President Nixon and Secretary Laird when they advocated deployment of ABM to defend our Minuteman sites. Whether their fear is justified or not is very difficult to tell because it depends so much on the poorly known guidance accuracy of the Russian SS-9 missile and of their MIRV. However, if their fear is justified, then the Russian MIRV would indeed be highly de-stabilizing. The great point in the strategic stability provided by missiles in hard silos, deployed at appreciable distance from each other, was that one enemy missile (even of extremely high yield) could destroy at most one of ours, thus making an enemy attack on the silos very unattractive, at least between two nations possessing about the same number of missiles. This is completely changed if there are MIRVs of high accuracy and high yield; then a surprise attack by one side on the missile silos of the other may give the attacker complete missile superiority, and thus may "win" the war for him.

Or at least, this would be so in the absence of missile-carrying submarines. Actually, an effective "counter-force" MIRV of one side will only make the land-based missiles of the other ineffective. Even here, there are possible counter-measures, such as super-hard silos, mobile missiles or ABM defense of the missile silos. But all of these are expensive and only partially effective. If one then has to fall back on submarine-carried missiles, there is the worry that some other technical development, especially improved methods of submarine detection (however unlikely), may erode the security of this weapon. Thus the counter-force MIRV, like any counter-force weapon, is clearly de-stabilizing.

It is obvious that the Soviet MIRV is far more dangerous in this respect than any of ours. This is because the basic Soviet missile, the SS-9, is reported by the U. S. Defense Department to carry a warhead of about 20 megatons, while our Minuteman is in the one megaton class. Thus, assuming that the Russian silos are about as hard as ours, we would have to achieve about three times greater guidance accuracy than the Soviets to make our Minuteman effective against Soviet silos. Moreover, once you get to submegaton yields, such as our Minuteman MIRV would have, the errors due to re-rentry into the atmosphere become appreciable compared with the guidance errors. Hence our MIRV is presumably less of a counter-force weapon, and thus less de-stabilizing, than the Russian.

This brings us to the third escalation, the rapid increase of the "throw-weight," the total weight of payload which can be launched by missiles. The most worrisome fact here is the rapid deployment, by the Soviet Union, of further large SS-9 missiles. The total number of land-based missiles of the USSR is probably by now comparable with ours, but their throw-weight is much higher. Because of the possibility of MIRV, it no longer seems fair to compare missiles simply by number; a disarmament agreement should take the size into account as well. The formula which has always appealed to me most is to compare the gross weight of the missiles. This gives, for example, less weight to IRBM (intermediate-range ballistic missiles) than to ICBM (inter-continental ballistic missiles), and yet counts IRBM to some extent. Moreover, gross weight is easiest to estimate by unilateral intelligence.

According to the newspaper reports, the increasing number of Russian SS-9s is one of the chief concerns of our SALT negotiators. Conversely, our MIRV-equipped successor to Polaris, the Poseidon, appears to be a major concern to the USSR, and this also represents an increase in throw-weight, over and above the introduction of MIRV.

The fear of escalation of the arms race—by MIRV, ABM and increase in throw-weight—is probably the main argument which has brought Russia and the United States to the conference table. Both sides appear to have recognized that there is no increased security for themselves in any of this escalation, as there has not been increased security in any previous escalation: A-bombs, H-bombs, ICBM, etc. At best, escalation adds to the expense of armaments; more often, it further reduces the already tenuous security of each of the powers. It is futile for either America or the Soviet Union to hope to gain an important technical advantage over the other. In every case in the past, these technical advantages have been very transient, and we have then returned to the same insecurity that we had before, relying only on the good sense and self-interest of the other side to avoid nuclear war.

After the fear of escalation, there is hope again: The problem of monitoring a disarmament agreement is immensely simpler now than in 1958–61 when we negotiated the Test Ban for nuclear weapons. At that time, our primary concern was with inspection for possible violations of the agreement, and many ingenious methods of inspection were devised, such as the zonal inspection of Louis Sohn. Nevertheless, the Russians remained opposed to inspection, although they yielded in principle by allowing a maximum of three inspections per year of suspected nuclear explosions on their territory.

The present hope is that monitoring can be accomplished entirely (or almost entirely) by unilateral intelligence, chiefly by satellite photography. Our Defense Department has confidently announced the numbers and types of ICBMs deployed by the USSR, and gives estimates of the size of the warhead carried by the SS-9. It is almost certain that the Russians have a similar satellite capability to find out our ICBM deployment. Thus both sides can rely on their unilateral capability to monitor the agreed number and size of missiles on the other side. Similar capabilities exist concerning submarines.

However, no satellite photography is likely to tell us what is inside the deployed missiles, in particular whether there is a single warhead or many. On the other hand, the hope has been expressed that the testing of MIRV can be observed; according to newspaper reports, Presidential adviser Lee DuBridge has expressed some confidence that this can be done (I tend to agree). Thus an agreement to stop the de-stabilizing MIRV may have to rely chiefly on prohibition (or at least severe restriction) of testing this device.

And here again we come to a fear: It may be too late. Both we and the Russians have made numerous tests of MIRV. Are they enough for deployment? It is most unfortunate that the SALT talks have been so much delayed. Early in 1967, President Johnson proposed such talks, chiefly on prohibiting ABM. Late that year, the

USSR accepted this idea, provided the talks would cover both offensive and defensive strategic weapons, and this proviso was accepted by the United States. In August 1968, these talks were agreed to and imminent, and at that time no MIRV had been tested by either side. But then came the Russian invasion of Czechoslovakia, and it was clear that the Americans could not begin talks immediately thereafter. Then came the U. S. election, after which President Nixon understandably wanted to have his own team develop a posture on the forthcoming talks. After more delay by the Russians, the preliminary meeting started in Helsinki in November. In spite of its friendly atmosphere, that meeting set the date for the definitive meeting rather late, for April. In the meantime, MIRV tests are proceeding apace, and perhaps MIRV deployment.

Is it too late to stop MIRV testing? I don't believe so, judging from the experience with hydrogen weapons. After having established the principle in 1952, we (or at least I) believed that the test series of 1954 gave us all the essential knowledge on these weapons, namely, how to design multi-megaton weapons. But the later test series, of 1956 and 1958, opened completely new perspectives, particularly on smaller weapons which have proved most useful in connection with ICBM, and are indeed essential for our MIRV. Thus while a weapon may seem to have been established by one series of tests, later tests may greatly increase its capabilities. Thus for arms control, it should be quite useful to stop testing of a new weapon after a limited number of tests, and thus to prevent increased sophistication.

SALT is, of course, not the only possible arms control treaty. Many people, both in the U. S. and abroad, still would like to extend the test ban to underground tests. It is generally agreed that our capability of monitoring such tests has improved greatly since 1963, the year when the limited test ban was concluded. But the extension to underground tests now seems quite unimportant as a disarmament measure. The three original nuclear powers—America, Russia and Great Britain—have little more to learn in weapons development that is of military importance. The two newer nuclear powers—France and Communist China—have not signed and do not obey the Test Ban Treaty anyway. Any possible future nuclear power would probably find underground tests rather unsatisfactory since it is difficult to determine the yield of the device with any accuracy, unless one is able to calibrate this with a device previously tested in the air.

Perhaps a treaty limiting the yield of underground tests could be concluded, such as that proposed by President Eisenhower in 1960, in which tests would be limited to a maximum earthquake equivalent of magnitude 4.75 on the Richter scale. This could now be easily monitored without inspection.

However, because of the relative lack of importance of the comprehensive (or Eisenhower type) test ban as a disarmament measure, I would argue against even attempting such a ban. It would arouse opposition from many military quarters, probably both in the United States and the Soviet Union, and it would divert our energies from the problem which really matters, the SALT talks.

It is likely that any agreement we may reach on SALT will be imperfect. "Give a little, take a little" implies that neither side will get all it wants, that each party will have to reduce its weapons plans, and that each will think the other side has not made enough reductions. Moreover, the monitoring system will probably also be imperfect. Still, I believe that such an agreement is preferable to none. (Of course, this depends on the degree of imperfection.) Let us remember once more the negotiations on the test ban: We could probably have had an agreement on this in 1959, with an admittedly imperfect monitoring system. By insisting on perfection we got no agreement, and we got the Russian test series of 1961–62. This was a tremendous series. It gave the Soviet Union their jumbo device of 60 megatons, and more important, their big warhead for the SS-9. It permitted them to equal (for all intents and purposes) our capability in weapons over one megaton, which they had not been able to do yet in 1958. We were looking, in the negotiations of 1958–61, for certainty of detection of small weapons tests of a few kilotons, and paid no attention to the fact that the USSR had a great deal to learn in the megaton range, a range in which test detection is extremely easy. True, we also learned a lot from our test series of 1962, but in my opinion this was less vital to our present weapons systems than the Russian series was to theirs.

Therefore I believe we should be prepared to accept a somewhat imperfect agreement. And we must remember that time is of the essence if we wish to prevent an irreversible major escalation of armaments.

STUDY QUESTIONS

1. What are the SALT talks?
2. Why is it possible that the SALT talks may be "too little, too late?"

3. What are the principal characteristics of MIRV missiles?
4. What are the three specific uses of MIRV missiles?
5. How accurate are the MIRV vehicles?
6. Is the question of accuracy or probability of a strike very important with the multiple warhead vehicles? What are the variables?
7. What is the role of missile-carrying submarines in determining the effectiveness of MIRVs?
8. Why is the Russian MIRV more effective than the American MIRV?
9. What is "throw-weight"?
10. Why is technical advancement not the key to avoiding nuclear war?

SUGGESTIONS FOR WRITING

1. In view of the information presented in this article, how serious do you think efforts have been on each side to promote disarmament? What are some of the factors that have caused delay so far, and how valid do you think they have been? Do they indicate bad faith on the part of either power?
2. How practical is the entire program of disarmament? In a short essay, evaluate the problems that each side faces in disarmament, or even in control of armaments, and decide whether or not the possible outcome will be worth the efforts.
3. Do you favor disarmament treaties? If so, write a persuasive article that is designed to convince someone who does not agree with you. Or, if you do not favor such treaties, write a statement that gives your reasons. Again, assume you are trying to convince someone who does not agree with you.
4. As far as you can tell, what are the most important and likely threats to disarmament? Use the information in the article as much as possible, but do not hesitate to use any other information you may have available. Evaluate each threat with care to determine how serious it is.
5. How do you account for the cautious tone of this article? Considering how much is at stake, and how serious the time problems are, shouldn't Bethe be more excited, more startling? Defend or attack his tone in this article.

THE WAR CORRESPONDENT: A REAPPRAISAL

Michael Herr

In former wars the derring-do of the correspondents was
taken for granted. In the Vietnam war there is probably
no less derring-do, but there is a very different atmosphere, one in which such actions seem unreal. Correspondent Michael Herr recreates that unique atmosphere almost too painfully.

*There's a candle end burning in a corner of the bunker, held
to the top of a steel helmet by melted wax, the light guttering
over a battered typewriter, and the Old Guy is getting one off:
"Tat-tat-tat, tatta-tatta-tat like your kid or your brother or your
sweetheart maybe never wanted much for himself never asked
for anything except for what he knew to be his some men
have a name for it and they call it Courage when the great
guns are still at last across Europe what will it matter maybe
after all that this one boy from Cleveland Ohio won't be coming back-a-tat-tat." You can hear shellfire landing just outside,
a little gravel falls into the typewriter, but the candle burns on,
throwing its faint light over the bowed head and the few remaining wisps of white hair. Two men, the Colonel and the
Kid, stand by the door watching. "Why, sir?" the Kid asks.
"What makes him do it? He could be sitting safe in London
right now." "I don't know, son," the Colonel says. "Maybe he
figures he's got a job to do, too. Maybe it's because he's somebody who really cares. . . ."*

I never knew a member of the Vietnam press corps who was
insensible to what happened when the words "war" and "correspondent" got joined. The glamour of it was possibly empty and lunatic,

THE WAR CORRESPONDENT: A REAPPRAISAL   Reprinted by permission of Lantz-
Donadio Literary Agency, first published in the April 1970 issue of *Esquire
Magazine*. Copyright © 1970 by Michael Herr.

but there were times when it was all you had, a benign infection that ravaged all but your worst fears and deepest depressions. Admitting, for argument's sake, that we were all a little crazy to have gone there in the first place, there were those whose madness it was not to know always which war they were actually in, fantasizing privately about other, older wars, Wars One or Two, air wars and desert wars and island wars, obscure colonial actions against countries whose names have since changed many times, punitive wars and holy wars and wars in places where the climate was so cool that you could wear a trench coat and look good; in other words, wars which sounded old and corny to those of us for whom the war in Vietnam was more than enough. There were correspondents all around who could break you up with their bad style and self-consciousness, but those aberrations were hardly ever beyond your understanding. Over there, all styles grew in their way out of the same haunted, haunting romance. Those Crazy Guys Who Cover The War.

In any other war, they would have made movies about us too, *Dateline: Hell!*, *Dispatch From Dong Ha*, maybe even *A Scrambler to the Front*, about Tim Page, Sean Flynn and Rick Merron, three young photographers who used to ride in and out of combat on Hondas. But Vietnam is awkward, everybody knows how awkward, and if people don't even want to hear about it, you know they're not going to pay money to sit there in the dark and have it brought up. (*The Green Berets* doesn't count. That wasn't really about Vietnam, it was about Santa Monica.) So we have all been compelled to make our own movies, as many movies as there are correspondents, and this one is mine. (One day at the battalion aid station in Hué a Marine with minor shrapnel wounds in his legs was waiting to get on a helicopter, a long wait with all of the dead and badly wounded going out first, and a couple of sniper rounds snapped across the airstrip, forcing us to move behind some sandbagging. "I *hate* this movie," he said, and I thought, "Why not?") My movie, my friends, my colleagues. But meet them in context:

There was a ridge called Mutter's Ridge that ran the crest of one of the hills below the DMZ which the Americans usually named by height-in-meters, Hill Three Hundred Whatever. The Marines had been up there since early morning, when Kilo Company and four correspondents were choppered into a sparse landing zone on the highest rise of the ridge. If this had been an Army operation, we would have been digging in now, correspondents too, but the Marines didn't do that, their training taught them more about fatal gesture than it did about survival. Everyone was saying that Charlie was probably just over there on the next hill scoping on us, but the Grunts were keeping it all in the open, walking out along the ridge "coordinating," setting up positions and cutting out a proper landing zone with battery-powered saws and chunks of explosives. Every few minutes one or another of them would shag down to the spot below the lz where the correspondents were sitting and warn us indifferently about the next blast, saying, "Uh, listen, there's fire in the hole, so you guys wanna just turn your backs and sort of cover over your heads?" He'd hang in there for a moment to give us a good look, and then run back up the lz site to tell the others about us.

"Hey, see them four guys there? Them're reporters."

"Bulls - - - , reporters."

"Okay, motherf - - - er, go on down and see next time we blast."

There were some Marines stretched out a few feet from us, passing around war comics and talking, calling each other Dude and Jive, Lifer and S - - - kick and Motherf - - - er, touching this last with a special grace, as though it were the tenderest word in their language. A suave black Grunt, identified on his helmet cover as Love Child, was studying an exhausted copy of *Playboy*, pausing to say "Oh . . . *man*! She can sure come sit on my face *any*time. Any . . . time . . . at . . . all." But none of them were talking to us yet, they were sort of talking for us, trying to make us out, maintaining that odd delicacy of theirs that always broke down sooner or later. It was like a ritual, all the preliminary forms had to be observed and satisfied, and it wasn't simply because they were shy. As far as any of them knew, we were crazy, maybe even dangerous. It made sense: They *had* to be here, they knew that. We did *not* have to be here, and they were sure enough of that, too. (The part that they never realized until later was that our freedom of movement was a door that swung both ways; at that very moment, the four of us were giving each other that Nothing Happening look and talking about getting out.) A G.I. would walk clear across a fire base for a look at you if he'd never seen a correspondent before because it was like going to see the Geek, and worth the walk.

Besides, there were four of us sitting there in a loose professional knot, there was another one flying in the command helicopter trying to get a long view of the operation, and a sixth, A.P. photographer Dana Stone, was walking up the hill now with a platoon that had been chosen to scout the trail. It was one thing for a lone reporter to join an outfit before an operation; if the outfit was company-size or larger, it could absorb him and the curiosity that his presence always set working, and when the operation was over most of the troops would never even know that he'd been along. But when six correspondents turned up on the eve of an operation, especially when it fell during a long period of light contact, the effect was so complicated that the abiding ambivalence of all troops and commanders toward all reporters didn't even begin to explain it. Everyone from the colonel to the lowest-ranking Grunt felt a new importance about what he was going into, and to all appearances, as far as they were in touch with it, they were glad to see you. But our presence was also unnerving, picking at layers of fear that they might never have known about otherwise. ("Why us? I mean, *six* of those bastards, where the hell are we *going?*") When it came all the way down to this, even the poorest-connected free-lancer had the power on him, a power which only the most pompous and unfeeling journalists ever really wanted, throwing weird career scares into the staff and laying a cutting edge against each Marine's gut estimates of his own survival. Then, it didn't matter that we were dressed exactly as they were and would be going exactly where they were going; we were as exotic and as fearsome as black magic, coming on with cameras and questions, and if we promised to take the anonymity off what was about to happen, we were also there to watchdog the day. The very fact that we had chosen *them* seemed to promise the most awful kind of engagement, because they were all certain that war correspondents never wasted time. It was a joke we all dug.

It was August now, when the heat in I Corps forgave nothing. That year the northern monsoons had been almost dry (so many stories had run the phrase, "Grim reminders of a rainless monsoon," that it became a standard, always good for a laugh), and across the raw spaces between hills you could see only the faintest traces of green in the valleys and draws, the hills rising from pale brown to sun-bleached yellow and gaping like dark, dried sores wherever the winter air strikes had torn their sides out. Very little had happened in this sector since early spring, when an odd disengagement had been effected at Khesanh and when a multidivision operation into the A Shau Valley had ended abruptly after two weeks, like a speech cut at mid-sentence. The A Shau held the North's great supply depot, they had tanks and trucks and heavy antiaircraft guns dug in there, and while the American Mission had made its reflexive claims of success for the operation, they were made for once without much enthusiasm, indicating that even the Command had to acknowledge the inviolability of that place. It was admitted at the time that a lot of our helicopters had been shot down, but this was spoken of as an

expensive equipment loss, as though our choppers were crewless entities that held to the sky by themselves, spilling nothing more precious than fuel when they crashed.

Between then and now, nothing larger than company-size sweeps
had worked the western Z, generally without contact. Like all of the
war's quieter passages, the spring–summer lull had left everyone
badly strung out, and a lot of spooky stories began going around, like
the ones about NVA helicopters (a Marine patrol supposedly saw
one touch down on the abandoned Marine base at Khesanh and
wait while a dozen men got out and walked around the perimeter,
"like they was just checking things out"), or the one (true) about
the "Caucasian," certainly American, who was killed while leading
an NVA patrol against Marines. It had been a mild season for Vietnam correspondents too (the lull aside, home offices were beginning
to make it clear to their Saigon bureaus that the story was losing the
old bite, what with Johnson's abdication, the spring assassinations
and the coming elections), and we were either talking about how the
Vietnam thing was really finished or bitching about getting shot at
only to wind up on page nine. It was a good time to cruise the country, a day here and a week there, just hanging out with troops; a good
time to make leisurely investigations into the smaller, darker pockets
of the war. Now, word had come down that a large mass of NVA
was moving across the DMZ, possibly building for a new offensive
against Hué, and battalions of the Fifth Marines were deploying
in rough conjunction with battalions of the Ninth to find and kill
them. It had the feel of what we always called a "good operation,"
and the six of us had gone up for it.

But there was nothing here now, no dreaded Cong, no shelling,
no pictures for the wires, no stories for the files, no sign that anyone
had been on this scalding ridge for at least six months. (A few miles
north and a little east, a company of the Ninth was in the middle
of an evil fire fight that would last until nightfall, leaving eleven
of them dead and nearly thirty wounded, but we knew nothing
about that now. If we had, we might possibly have made an effort
at getting to it, some of us at least, explaining it later in cold professional terms and leaving all the other reasons unspoken, understood
between us. If a Marine had ever expressed a similar impulse, we
would probably have called him psychotic.) The only violence on
Mutter's Ridge was in the heat and whatever associations with that
terrible winter you could take from the view; from Cam Lo, Route
Nine into the Khesanh, the Rockpile. A few more Marines had joined

the group around us, but they were being cool, pausing to read the tags sewn on our fatigue shirts as though to themselves, but out loud, just to show us that they knew we were here.

"Associated Press, yeah, and You Pee Eye, uh-huh, and Esquire, wow, *they* got a guy over here, what the f - - - for, you tell 'em what we're wearing? And—hey man, what's *that* supposed to be?" (Sean Flynn had only the words Bao Chi on his tags, Vietnamese for "journalist.") "That's pretty far out, what's that, in case you're captured or something?"

Actually, Bao Chi was all the affiliation that Flynn needed or wanted in Vietnam, but he didn't go into that. Instead, he explained that when he had first begun taking pictures here in 1965, most operations had been conducted by the South Vietnamese, and reporters would identify themselves this way so that they would not be mistaken for American advisers and shot by the ARVN during the routine hysteria of routine retreats.

"Boy, if that ain't just like the Slopes," one of the Marines said, walking away from us.

Flynn was cleaning his camera lens with a length of Australian sweat scarf that he always wore into the field, but the least movement sent up a fine-grained dust that seemed to hang there without resetting, giving the light a greasy quality and caking in the corners of your eyes. The Marines were looking hard at Flynn and you could see that he was blowing their minds, the way he blew minds all over Vietnam.

He was (indeed) the Son of Captain Blood, but that didn't mean much to the Grunts since most of them, the young ones, had barely even heard of Errol Flynn. It was just apparent to anyone who looked at him that he was what the Marines would call "A dude who definitely had his s - - - together." All four of us on the ridge looked more or less as though we belonged there; the A.P.'s John Lengel had covered every major Marine operation of the past eighteen months, Nik Wheeler of U.P.I. had been around for over a year, I'd had the better part of a year in now, we were all nearly young enough to be mistaken for Grunts ourselves, but Flynn was special. We all had our movie-fed war fantasies, the Marines too, and it could be totally disorienting to have this outrageously glamorous figure intrude on them, really unhinging, like looking up to see that you've been sharing a slit trench with John Wayne or William Bendix. But you got used to that part of Flynn quickly.

When he'd first arrived in Vietnam in the Summer of 1965, he had been considered news himself, and a lot of stories were written about his early trips into combat. Most of them managed to include all the clichés, all of them called him "swashbuckling." There were still a lot of easy things to say about him, and a lot of people around who were more than willing to say them, but after you knew him all of that talk just depressed you. There were a number of serious (heavy) journalists who could not afford to admit that anyone who looked as good as Flynn looked could possibly have anything more going for him. They chose not to take him as seriously as they took themselves (which was fine with Sean), and they accused him of coming to Vietnam to play, as though the war was like Africa had been for him, or the South of France, or one of the places he'd gone to make those movies that people were always judging him by. But there were a lot of people in Vietnam who were playing, more than the heavies cared to admit, and Flynn's playing was done only on the most earnest levels. He wasn't much different from the rest; he was deeply fascinated by war, by *this* war, but he admitted it, knew where he stood in it, and he behaved as though it was nothing to be ashamed of. It gave him a vision of Vietnam that was profound, black and definitive, a knowledge of its wildness that very few of his detractors would have understood. All of this was very obvious in his face, particularly the wildness, but those people only saw it as handsome, making you realize that, as a group, newspapermen were not necessarily any more observant or imaginative than accountants. Flynn moved on and found his friends among those who never asked him to explain himself, among the G.I.'s and the Apaches of the press corps, and he established his own celebrity there. (There would be occasional intrusions; embarrassingly deferential information officers, or a run-in with Colonel George Patton Jr., who put him through one of those my-father-knew-your-father trials.) The Grunts were always glad to see him. They'd call him "Seen," a lot of them, and tell him that they'd caught one of his flicks on R&R in Singapore or Taiwan, something that only a Grunt could bring up and get away with, since all of that was finished for Flynn, the dues-paying and the accommodations, and he didn't like to talk about it. Sometime during his years in Vietnam, he realized that there really were people whom he cared for and could trust; it must have been a gift he'd never expected to have, and it made him someone whom his father, on the best day he ever had, could have envied.

It was still a little too soon for the Marines to just sit down and start talking, they would have to probe a little more first, and we were getting bored. By the time they had finished cutting the lz there was no cover left from the sun, and we were all anxious for the scouting platoon to reach the top so that we could get together with Dana Stone, put a little pressure on for a helicopter, and get out. The trip back to the press center in Danang could take two hours or two days, depending on what was flying, but it was certain to go faster with Stone along because he had friends at every airfield and chopper pad in I Corps. Danang was Soul City for many of us, it had showers and drinks, flash-frozen airfreighted steaks, air-conditioned rooms and China Beach and, for Stone, a real home; a wife, a dog, a small house full of familiar possessions. Mutter's Ridge had sickening heat, a rapidly vanishing water supply and boredom, so there really wasn't any choice. Judging by the weathered, blackened bits of ammunition casing (theirs and ours) that were littered on the ground around us, the ridge also had a history, and Dana told us something about it.

Stone was a lapsed logger from Vermont (he always spoke about going back to that, especially after a bad day in the field, screw all this bulls - - -), twenty-five years old with sixty-year-old eyes set in deep behind wire-rimmed glasses, their shrewdness and experience almost lost in the lean anglings of his face. We knew for certain that he would be walking well ahead of the rest of the platoon on the trail, standard Dana and a break for the Marines, since he was easily the best-equipped man in the party for spotting booby traps or ambushes. But that had nothing to do with his being on point. Dana was the man in motion, he just couldn't slow himself down; he was the smallest man on the trail, but his engines would drive him up it as though the incline ran the other way. G.I.'s who had forgotten his name would describe him for you as, "that wiry little redheaded cat, *crazy* mother-f - - - er, funny as a bastard," and Stone *was* funny, making you pay for every laugh he gave you. Hard mischief was his specialty—a thumb stuck abruptly into your egg yolk at breakfast or your brandy at dinner, rocks lobbed onto the metal roof of your room at the press center, flaming trails of lighter fluid rampaging across the floor toward you, a can of ham and limas substituted for peaches in syrup when you were practically dying of thirst—all Dana's way of saying hello, doing you good by doing you in. He'd wake you at dawn, shaking you violently and saying, "Listen, I need your glasses for just a minute, it's really important," splitting with them for an hour. He also took beautiful pictures (he called them "snaps" in accordance with the wire-service ethic which said you must never reveal your pride in good work) and in almost three years as a combat photographer he'd spent more time on operations than anyone else I knew, getting his cameras literally blown off his back more than once, but keeping otherwise unhurt. By now, there was nothing that could happen around him in the field that he hadn't seen before, and, if his joking was belligerent and even ghastly, you knew at least where it came from, saw the health that it carried. And that morning, waiting by the base-camp airstrip for the assault to begin, he started to tell us about the other time he'd been up on Mutter's Ridge, in the days before it even had a name. It had been, in fact, two years ago *to the day,* he'd said, on that *exact same ridge.* He'd gone up there with the Ninth that time, and they'd *really stepped in deep s - - -.* (It was true, we all knew it was true, he was doing it to us again, and a smile showed for just an instant on his face.) They had been pinned down on the ridge all night long without support or resupply or medevac, and the *casualties* had been *unbelievable,* running somewhere around seventy percent. Flynn laughed and said, "Dana, you bastard," but Stone would have gone on like that in his flat Vermont voice, telling it to those of us about to go up there as though it were nothing more than the history of a racehorse, except that he looked up and saw that we weren't alone; a few of the guys from Kilo Company had come over to ask questions about our cameras or something, and they'd heard some of it. Stone turned a deep red, as he always did when he realized that he'd gone a little too far. "Aw, that was just a bunch of s - - -, I never even been *near* that ridge," he said, and he pointed to me. "I was just trying to get him uptight because this is his last operation, and he's already f - - - ed up about it." He laughed, but he was looking at the ground.

Now, while we waited for him, a Marine came up to Lengel and me and asked if we'd like to look at some pictures he'd taken. Marines felt comfortable around Lengel, who looked like a college basketball star, six-four and very young (actually, he was twenty-nine), a Nevadan who'd parlayed a nice-kid image into a valuable professional asset. The pictures were in a little imitation-leather folder, and you could tell by the way the Marine stood over us, grinning in anticipation as we flipped over each plastic page, that it was among his favorite things. (He'd also taken some "number-one souvenirs," he said, leaving the details to our imaginations.) There were hundreds of these albums in Vietnam, thousands, and they all seemed to contain the same pictures: The obligatory Zippo-lighter shot ("All right, let's burn these hootches and move out"); the severed-head shot, the head often resting on the chest of the dead man or being held up by a smiling Marine, or a lot of heads, arranged in a row, with a burning cigarette in each of the mouths, the eyes open ("Like they're *lookin'* at you, man, it's scary"); the VC suspect being dragged over the dust by a half-track or being hung by his heels in some jungle clearing; the very young dead with AK-47's still in their hands ("How old would you say that kid was?" the Grunts would ask, "Twelve, thirteen? You just can't tell with Gooks"); a picture of a Marine holding an ear or maybe two ears or, as in the case of a guy I knew near Pleiku, a whole necklace made of ears, "love beads" as its owner called them; and the one we were looking at now, the dead Vietcong girl with her pajamas stripped off and her legs raised stiffly in the air.

"No more boom-boom for that mammasan," the Marine said, that same, tired remark you heard every time the dead turned out to be women. It was so routine that I don't think he even realized that he'd said it.

"You posed that one," Lengel said.

"Not me," the Marine said, laughing.

"Now come on, you rascal. You mean you found her just like that?"

"Well, some other guy fixed her that way, and it was funny, 'cause that guy got zapped later on the same day. But look, look at that bitch there, cut right in half!"

"Oh, that's a honey," John said, "really terrific."

"I was thinkin' about sending some into the *Stars and Stripes.* You think the *Stripes* would run 'em?"

"Well. . . ." We were laughing now, what could you do? Half the combat troops in Vietnam had these things in their packs, snapshots were the least of what they took after a fight, at least pictures didn't rot. I'd talked to a Marine who'd taken a lot of pictures after an operation on the Cua Viet River, and later, when he was getting short and nervous about things, he'd brought them to the chaplain. But the chaplain had only told him that it was forgivable and put the pictures in his drawer and kept them.

A couple of Marines were talking to Flynn and Wheeler about their cameras, the best place to buy this lens, the right speed to use for that shot, I couldn't follow any of it. The Grunts were hip enough to the media to take photographers more seriously than reporters, and I'd met officers who refused to believe that I was really a correspondent because I never carried cameras. (During a recent operation, this had almost gotten me bumped from the command chopper because the colonel, for reasons of his own, was partial to photographers. On that one, a company of his battalion had made contact with a company of Vietcong and forced them out on a promontory, holding them there between their fire and the sea for the gun ships to kill. This particular colonel loved to order the chopper in very low so that he could fire his .45 into the Cong, and he'd always wanted pictures of it. He was doubly disappointed that day; I'd not only turned up without a camera, but by the time we got there all the VC were dead, about a hundred and fifty of them littered across the beach and bobbing in and out with the waves. But he fired off a few clips anyway, just to keep his piece working.)

Marines were all around us now, about fifteen of them, and one, a short, heavy kid with a flat, dark face and the bearing of an over-developed troll came up and looked hard at us.

"You guys're reporters, huh? Boy, you really get it all f - - - ed up," he said. "My old man sends me stuff from the papers, and he thinks you're all full of s - - -."

A couple of Marines booed him, most of them laughed. Lengel laughed too. "Well, podner, what can I tell you? I mean, we try, we really take a shot at it."

"Then why can't you guys just tell it right?"

"F - - - in' Krynski," someone said, hitting the kid hard on the back of the head. It was The Avenger himself, it said so on his helmet, and he'd come to work for us now, just in time. He looked like a freshman in divinity school; clear blue eyes, smooth snub nose, corn-silk hair and a look of such trust and innocence that you hoped there would always be someone around to take care of him. He seemed terribly embarrassed about what had just been said to us.

"Don't you listen to that asshole," he said. "God *damn*, Krynski, you don't know any f - - - in' thing about it. These guys are number-one dudes, and that's no s - - -."

"Thank you, friend," Lengel said.

"I didn't mean nothin'," Krynski said. "Don't go gettin' your balls in an uproar."

But The Avenger wasn't letting it go. "Man, these guys take plenty of chances, they eat C's just like us, and sleep in the mud, and all that good s - - -. They don't have to stand around here and listen to you bitch. They don't even have to be here at all!"

"Now what's *that* supposed to mean?" Krynski said, looking really puzzled. "You mean you guys *volunteer* to come over here?"

"Well, dumb s - - -, what'd you think?" The Avenger said. "You think they're just some dumb Grunt like you?"

"Oh man, you *got* to be kidding me. You guys *asked* to come here?"

"Sure."

"How long do you have to stay?" he asked.

"As long as we want."

"Wish *I* could stay as long as *I* want," the Marine called Love Child said. "*I'd* been home las' March."

"When did you get here?" I asked.

"Las' March."

The lieutenant who had been supervising the blasting looked down from the lz and yelled for someone named Collins.

"Yes sir?" The Avenger said.

"Collins, get your bod up here."

"Yes sir."

There was some movement on the lz now, the platoon had reached the clearing. Stone came out first, backing out very fast with his camera up, referring quickly to the ground just behind him between shots. Four Marines came out next, carrying a fifth on an improvised litter. They brought him to the center of the clearing and set him down carefully on the grass. We thought at first that he was dead, taken off by a booby trap on the trail, but his color was much too awful for that. Even the dead held some horrible light that seemed to recede, vanishing through one layer of skin at a time and taking a long time to go completely, but this kid had no color about him anywhere. It was incredible that anything so motionless and white could still be alive.

"Collins," the lieutenant said, "you go find the Old Man. Tell him we've got a real serious heat casualty here. Remember, tell him serious."

"Yes sir," The Avenger said, starting at a slow run along the ridge toward the C.P.

Dana took a few more pictures and then sat down to change film. His fatigues were completely darkened with sweat, but except for that he showed no signs of exertion. The rest of the column was coming off of the trail now, dropping in the clearing like sniper victims, the packs going first, staggering a few feet and falling. A few were smiling up at the sun like happy dreamers, more went face down and stopped moving except for some twitching in their legs, and the radioman made it all the way across the clearing to the commo section, where he eased the equipment from his back slowly, set his helmet very carefully on the ground for a pillow after picking his spot, and fell immediately asleep. Stone ran over and photographed him.

"You guys know something?" he said.

"What's that?"

"It's hotter than a bastard."

"Thanks."

We could see the colonel approaching, a short, balding man with flinty eyes and a brief black moustache. He was trussed up tightly in his flak jacket, and as he came toward us small groups of Marines broke and ran to get their flak jackets on too, before the colonel could have the chance to tell them about it. The colonel leaned over and looked hard at the unconscious Marine, who was lying now in the shade of a poncho being held over him by two corpsmen, while a third brushed his chest and face with water from a canteen.

Well hell, the colonel was saying, there's nothing the matter with that man, feed some salt into him, get him up, get him walking, this is the Marines, not the goddamned Girl Scouts, there won't be any damned chopper coming in *here* today. (The four of us must have looked a little stricken at this, and Dana took our pictures. We were really pulling for the kid; if he stayed, we stayed, and that meant all night.) The corpsmen were trying to tell the colonel that this was no ordinary case of heat exhaustion, excusing themselves but staying firm about it, refusing to let the colonel return to the C.P. (The four of us smiled and Dana took a picture. "Go away, Stone," Flynn said. "Hold it just like that," Stone said, running in for a closeup so that his lens was an inch away from Flynn's nose. "One more.") The Marine looked awful lying there, trying to work his lips a little, and the colonel glared down at the fragile, still form as though it was blackmailing him. When the Marine refused to move anything except his lips for fifteen minutes, the colonel began to relent. He asked the corpsmen if they'd ever heard of a man dying from something like this.

"Oh, yes sir. Oh, wow, I mean he really needs more attention than what we can give him here."

"Mmmmmm . . ." the colonel said. Then he authorized the chopper request and strode with what I'm sure he considered great determination back to his C.P.

"I think it would have made him feel better if he could have shot the kid," Flynn said.

"Or one of us," I said.

"You're just lucky he didn't get you last night," Flynn said. The evening before, when Flynn and I had arrived together at the base camp, the colonel had taken us into the command bunker to show us some maps and explain the operation, and a captain had given us some coffee in Styrofoam cups. I'd carried mine outside and finished it while we talked to the colonel, who was being very hale and friendly in a way I'd seen before and didn't really trust. I was looking around for someplace to toss the empty cup, and the colonel noticed it.

"Give it here," he offered.

"Oh, that's okay, Colonel, thanks."

"No, come on, I'll take it."

"No, really, I'll just find a. . . ."

"*Give it to me!*" he'd said, and I did, but Flynn and I were afraid to look at each other until he'd returned underground, and then we broke up, exchanging the worst colonel stories we knew. I told him about the colonel who had threatened to court-martial a Spec. 4 for refusing to cut the heart out of a dead Vietcong and feed it to a dog, and Flynn told me about a colonel in the American Division (which Flynn always said was sponsored by General Foods) who believed that every man under his command needed combat experience; he made the cooks and the clerks and the supply men and the drivers all take M-16's and go out on night patrol, and one time all of his cooks got wiped out in an ambush.

We could hear the sound of our Chinook coming in now, and we were checking to see if we had all of our gear, when I took a sudden, terrible flash, some total dread, and I looked at everyone and everything in sight to see if there was some real source. Stone had been telling the truth about this being my last operation, I was as strung out as anybody on a last operation, there was nothing between here and Saigon that didn't scare me now, but this was different, it was something else.

"F - - - in' heat . . ." someone said. "I . . . oh, man, I just . . . can't . . . f - - - in' . . . *make it!*"

It was a Marine, and as soon as I saw him I realized that I'd seen him before, a minute or so ago, standing on the edge of the clearing staring at us as we got ourselves ready to leave. He'd been with a lot of other Marines there, but I'd seen him much more distinctly than the others without realizing or admitting it. The others had been looking at us too, with amusement or curiosity or envy (we were splitting, casualties and correspondents this way out, we were going to Danang), they were all more or less friendly, but this one was different. I'd seen it, known it and passed it over, but not really. He was walking by us now, and I saw that he had a deep, running blister that seemed to have opened and eaten away much of his lower lip. That wasn't the thing that had made him stand out before, though. If I'd noticed it at all, it might have made him seem a little more wretched than the others, but nothing more. He stopped for a second and looked at us, and he smiled some terrifying, evil smile, his look turned now to the purest hatred.

"You f - - - ing guys," he said. "You guys are *crazy!*"

There was the most awful urgency to the way he said it. He was still glaring, I expected him to raise a finger and touch each of us with destruction and decay, and I realized that after all this time, the war still offered at least one thing that I had to turn my eyes from. I had seen it before and hoped never to see it again, I had mis-understood it and been hurt by it, I thought I had finally worked it out for good and I was looking at it now, knowing what it meant and feeling as helpless under it this last time as I had the first.

All right, yes, it had been a groove being a war correspondent, hang-ing out with the Grunts and getting close to the war, touching it, losing yourself in it and trying yourself against it. I had always wanted that, never mind why, it had just been a thing of mine, the way this movie is a thing of mine, and I'd done it; I was in many ways brother to these poor, tired Grunts, I knew what they knew now, I'd done it and it was really something. Everywhere I'd gone, there had always been Marines or soldiers who would tell me what The Avenger had told Krynski, *you're all right, man, you guys are cool, you got balls.* They didn't always know what to think about you or what to say to you, they'd sometimes call you "Sir" until you had to beg them to stop, they'd sense the insanity of your position as terrified volunteer-reporter and it would seize them with the giggles and even respect. If they dug you, they always saw that you knew that, and when you choppered out they'd say good-bye, wish you luck. They'd even thank you, some of them, and what could you say to that?

And always, they would ask you with an emotion whose intensity would shock you to please tell it, because they really did have the feeling that it wasn't being told for them, that they were going through all of this and that somehow no one back in the world knew about it. They may have been a bunch of dumb, brutal killer kids (a lot of correspondents privately felt that), but they were smart enough to know that much. There was a Marine in Hué who had come after me as I walked toward the truck that would take me to the airstrip, he'd been locked in that horror for nearly two weeks now while I'd shuttled in and out for two or three days at a time. We knew each other by now, and when he caught up with me he grabbed my sleeve so violently that I thought he was going to accuse me or, worse, try to stop me from going. His face was all but blank now with exhaustion, but he had enough feeling left to say, "Okay, man, you go on, you go on out of here you c - - - - - - er, but I mean it, you tell it! You tell it, man, if you don't tell it. . . ."

What a time they were having there, it had all broken down, one battalion had taken sixty percent casualties, all the original N.C.O.'s were gone, the Grunts were telling their officers to go die, to go f - - - themselves, to go find some other fools to run up those streets awhile, it was no place where I'd have to tell anyone not to call me "Sir."

They understood that, they understood a lot more than I did, but nobody hated me there, not even when I was leaving. Three days later I came back and the fighting had dropped off, the casualties were down to nothing, and the same Marine flashed me a victory sign that had nothing to do with the Marine Corps or the fading battle or the American flag that had gone up on the Citadel's south wall the day before; he slapped me on the back and poured me a drink from a bottle he'd found in one of the hootches somewhere. Even the ones who preferred not to be in your company, who despised what your work required or felt that you took your living from their deaths, who believed that all of us were traitors and liars and the creepiest kinds of parasites, even they would cut back at the last and make their one concession to what there was in us that we ourselves loved most; "I got to give it you, you guys got balls." Maybe they meant just that and nothing more, we had our resources and we made enough out of that to keep us going, turning the most grudging admissions into decorations for valor, making it all all right again.

But there was often that bad, bad moment to recall, the look that made you look away, and in its hateful way it was the purest single thing I'd ever known. There was no wonder left in it anywhere, no amusement, it came from nothing so messy as morality or prejudice, it had no motive, no conscious source. You would feel it coming out to you from under a poncho hood or see it in a wounded soldier staring up at you from a chopper floor, from men who were very scared or who had just lost a friend, from some suffering apparition of a Grunt whose lip had been torn open by the sun, who just couldn't make it in that heat.

At first, I got it all mixed up, I didn't understand and I felt sorry for myself, misjudged. "Well f--- you, too," I'd think. "It could have been me just as easily, I take chances too, can't you see that?" And then I realized that that was exactly what it was all about, it explained itself as easily as that, another of the war's dark revelations. They weren't judging me, they weren't reproaching me, they didn't even mind me, not in any personal way. They only hated me, hated me the way you'd hate any hopeless fool who would put himself through this thing when he had choices, any fool who had no more need of his life than to play with it in this way.

"You guys are *crazy!*" that Marine had said, and I know that when we flew off of Mutter's Ridge that afternoon he stood there for a long time and watched us out of sight with the same native loathing he'd shown us before, turning finally to whoever was around, saying it maybe to himself, getting out what I'd actually heard said once when a jeep load of correspondents had just driven away, leaving me there alone, one rifleman turning to another and giving us all his hard, cold wish:

"Those f - - - ing guys," he'd said, "I hope they die."

II

Name me someone that's not a parasite,
And I'll go out and say a prayer for him.
                    —Bob Dylan, *Visions of Johanna*

I keep thinking about all the kids who got wiped out by seventeen years of war movies before coming to Vietnam to get wiped out for good. You don't know what a media freak is until you've seen the way a few of those Grunts would run around during a fight when they knew that there was a television crew nearby; they were actually making war movies in their heads, doing little Guts and Glory Leatherneck tap dances under fire, getting their pimples shot off for the networks. They were insane, but the war hadn't done that to them. Most combat troops stopped thinking of the war as an adventure after their first few fire fights, but there were always the ones who couldn't let that go, those few who were up there doing numbers for the cameras. A lot of correspondents weren't much better. We'd all seen too many movies, stayed too long in Television City, years of media glut had made certain connections difficult. The first few times that I got fired at or saw combat deaths, nothing really happened, all the responses got locked in my head. It was the same familiar violence, only moved over to another medium; some kind of jungle play with giant helicopters and fantastic special effects, actors lying out there in rubber body bags waiting for the scene to end so they could get up again and walk it off. But that was some scene, you found out, there was no cutting it.

A lot of things had to be unlearned before you could learn anything at all, and even after you knew better you couldn't avoid the ways in which things got mixed, the war itself with those parts of the war that were just like the movies, just like *The Quiet American* or *Catch 22* (a Nam standard because it said that in a war, everybody thinks that everybody else is crazy), just like all that combat footage from television ("We're taking fire from the tree line!" "Where?" "There!" "*Where?*" "Over *there!*" "Over WHERE?" "Over THERE!!" Flynn heard that go on for fifteen minutes once; we made it an epiphany), your vision blurring, images jumping and falling as though they were being received by a dropped camera, hearing a hundred horrible sounds at once; screams, sobs, hysterical shouting, a throbbing inside your head that threatened to take over, quavering voices trying to get the orders out, the dulls and sharps of weapons going off (Lore: When they're near they whistle, when they're really near they crack), the thud of helicopter rotors, the tinny, clouded voice coming over the radio, "Uh, that's a Rog, we mark your position, over." And out. Far out.

That feedback stalked you all over Vietnam, it often threatened you with derangement, but somehow it always left you a little saner than you had any right to expect. Sometimes its intrusions could be subtle and ferocious. One afternoon during the battle for Hué, I was with David Greenway, a correspondent for *Time* magazine, and we found it necessary to move from one Marine position to another. We were directly across from the south wall of the Citadel and air strikes had dropped much of it down into the street, bringing with it torn, stinking portions of some North Vietnamese who had been dug in there. We had to make a run of something like four hundred meters up that street, and we knew that the entire way was open to sniper fire, either from the standing sections of the wall on our right or from the rooftops on our left. When we'd run to our present position an hour earlier, David had gone first, and it was my turn now. We were crouching among some barren shrubbery with the Marines, and I turned to the guy next to me, a black Marine, and said, "Listen, we're going to cut out now. Will you cover us?" He gave me one of those amazed, penetrating looks, "You can go out there if you want to, baby, but shee-it," and he began putting out fire. David and I ran all doubled over, taking cover every forty meters or so behind boulder-sized chunks of smashed wall, and halfway through it I started to laugh, looking at David and shaking my head. David was the most urbane of correspondents, a Bostonian of good family and impeccable education, something of a patrician even though he didn't care anything about it. We were pretty good friends, and he was willing to take my word for it that there was actually something funny, and he laughed too.

"What is it?" he said.

"Oh man, do you realize that I just asked that guy back there to *cover us?*"

He looked at me with one eyebrow faintly cocked. "Yes," he said. "Yes, you did. Oh, isn't that *marvelous!*"

And we would have laughed all the way up the street, except that toward the end of it we had to pass a terrible thing, a house that had been collapsed by the bombing, bringing with it a young girl who lay stretched out dead on top of some broken wood. The whole thing was burning, and the flames were moving closer and closer to her bare feet. In a few minutes they were going to reach her, and from our concealment we were going to have to watch it. We agreed that anything was better than that and we finished the run, but only after David spun around, dropped to one knee and took a picture of it.

A few days after that, David's file from Hué appeared in *Time*, worked over into that uni-prose which all newsmagazines and newspapers maintained, placed somewhere among five or six other Vietnam stories that had come in that week from the five or six other reporters which *Time* kept in Vietnam. About six months after that, a piece I'd written about the battle appeared in this magazine, turning up like some lost dispatch from the Crimea. I saw it in print for the first time on the day that we returned from Mutter's Ridge, while the issue of *Time* which carried David's story was on sale in Saigon and Danang within a week of the events described. (I remember that issue in particular because General Giap was on the cover and the South Vietnamese would not allow it to be sold until a black X was scrawled over each copy, disfiguring but hardly concealing Giap's face. People were doing weird things that Tet.) What all of this means is that, no matter how much I love the sound of it, there's no way I can think of myself as a war correspondent without stopping to acknowledge the degree to which it's pure affectation. I never had to run back to any bureau office to file (or, worse, call it in from Danang over the knotted clot of military wires, "Working, operator, I said working, hello, working. . . . Oh, you moron, *working!*"). I never had to race out to the Danang airfield to get my film on the eight o'clock scatback to Saigon; there wasn't any bureau, there wasn't any film, my ties to New York were as slight as my assignment was vague. I wasn't really an oddity in the press corps, but I was a peculiarity, an extremely privileged one. (An oddity was someone like the photographer John Schneider who took a white flag and walked from the top of Hill 881 North over to Hill 881 South during a terrible battle, in what came to be known as Schneider's March; or the Korean cameraman who had spent four years in Spain as a matador, who spoke exquisite, limpid Castilian and whom we called El Taikwando; or the Portuguese novelist who arrived at Khesanh in sports clothes, carrying a plaid suitcase, under the impression that field gear could be bought there.)

I'd run into Bernie Weinraub in Saigon, on his way to The New York Times Bureau carrying a bunch of papers in his hand. He'd be coming back from a meeting with some of "the beautiful people" of the Joint U.S. Public Affairs Office, and he'd say, "I'm having a low-grade nervous breakdown right now. You can't really see it, but it's there. After you've been here awhile, you'll start having them too," laughing at the little bit of it that was true as much as at the part of it that had become our running joke. Between the heat and the ugliness and the pressures of filing, the war out there and the J.U.S.P.A.O. flacks right here, Saigon could be overwhelmingly depressing, and Bernie often looked possessed by it, so gaunt and tired and underfed that he could have brought out the Jewish mother in a Palestinian guerrilla. ("That's because I'm so sensitive," he'd say, a smile filling a little of the hollow in his cheeks. "I'm *much* more sensitive than you are." "Just because I act tough, don't let it fool you," I'd remind him. "Oh no, I don't," he'd say, "I couldn't. I'm much too sensitive for that." To say that Bernie looked sensitive was like remarking that the Pope dresses up.)

"Let's have a drink," I'd say.

"No, no, I can't. You know how it is, we on The *Times*. . . ." He'd start to laugh. "I mean, *we* have to file every day. It's a terrible responsibility, there's so little time. . . . I hope you'll understand."

"Of course. I'm sorry, I just wasn't thinking."

"Thank you, thank you."

But it was fine for me to laugh; he was going back to work, to write a story that would be published in New York hours later, and I was going across the street to the terrace bar of the Continental Hotel for a drink, possibly to write a few leisurely notes, probably not. I was spared a great deal, and except for a small handful of men who took their professional responsibilities very solemnly, no one ever held that against me. Whatever they came to know about the war was one thing; I know how they tried to get it into their stories, how generous they were as teachers, and how embittering it all could become.

Because they worked in the news media, for organizations that were ultimately reverential toward the institutions involved: the Office of the President, the Military, America-at-War, and, most of all, the empty technology that characterized Vietnam. There is no way of remembering good friends without remembering the incredible demands put on them from offices thousands of miles away. (Whenever the news chiefs and network vice-presidents and foreign editors would dress up in their Abercrombie & Fitch combat gear and come by for a firsthand look, a real story would develop, *Snow In The Tropics*, and, after three days of high-level briefings and helicopter rides, they'd go home convinced that the war was over, that their men in the field were damned good men but a little too close to the story.) Some-

where on the periphery of that total Vietnam Issue whose daily reports made the morning papers too heavy to bear, lost in the surreal
contexts of television, there was a story that was as simple as it had
always been, men hunting men, a hideous war and all kinds of victims. But there was also a Command that didn't feel this, that rode
us into attrition traps on the back of fictional kill ratios, and an Administration which believed the Command, a cross-fertilization of
ignorance; and a press whose tradition of objectivity and fairness (not
to mention self-interest) saw that all of it got space. It was inevitable
that once the media took the diversions seriously enough to report
them, they also legitimatized them. The spokesmen spoke in words
that had no currency left as words, sentences with no hope of meaning in the sane world, and if much of it was sharply queried by the
press, all of it got quoted. The press got all the facts (more or less),
they got too many of them. But they never found a way to report
meaningfully about death, which of course was really what it was all
about. The most repulsive, transparent gropes for sanctity in the midst
of the killing received serious treatment in the papers and on the air.
The jargon of Progress got blown into your head like bullets, and by
the time you waded through all the Washington stories and all the
Saigon stories, all the Other War stories and the corruption stories
and the stories about brisk new gains in ARVN effectiveness, the suffering was somehow unimpressive. And after enough years of that,
so many that it seemed to have been going on forever, you got to a
point where you could sit there in the evening and listen to the man
say that American casualties for the week had reached a six-week low,
only eighty G.I.'s had died in combat, and you'd feel like you'd just
gotten a bargain.

If you ever saw stories written by Peter Kann, William Tuohy,
Tom Buckley, Bernie Weinraub, Peter Arnett, Lee Lescaze, Peter
Braestrup, Charles Mohr, Ward Just or a few others, you'd know
that most of what the Mission wanted to say to the American public
was a psychotic vaudeville; that Pacification, for example, was hardly
anything more than a swollen, computerized tit being forced upon
an already violated population, a costly, valueless program that
worked only in press conferences. Yet in the year leading up to the
Tet Offensive ("1967—Year of Progress" was the name of an official
year-end report), there were more stories about Pacification than there
were about combat; front page, prime time, just as though it were
really happening.

This was all part of a process which everyone I knew came grudg-
ingly to think of as routine, and I was free of it. What an incredible

hassle it would have been, having to run out to the airport to watch the mayor of Los Angeles embrace Mayor Cua of Saigon. (L. A. had declared Saigon its Sister City, dig it, and Yorty was in town to collect. If there had been no newspapers or television, Cua and Yorty never would have met.) I never had to cover luncheons given for members of the Philippine Civic Action Group or laugh woodenly while the Polish delegate to the International Control Commission lobbed a joke on me. I never had to follow the Command to the field for those interminable get-togethers with the troops. ("Where are you from, son?" "Macon, Georgia, sir." "Real fine. Are you getting your mail okay, plenty of hot meals?" "Yes sir." "That's fine, where are you from, son?" "Oh I don't know, God, I don't know, I don't *know!*" "That's fine, real fine, where you from, son?") I never had to become familiar with that maze of Government agencies and sub-agencies, I never had to deal with the Spooks. (They were from the real Agency, the C.I.A. There was an endless Vietnam game played between the Grunts and the Spooks, and the Grunts always lost.) Except to pick up my mail and get my accreditation renewed, I never had to frequent J.U.S.P.A.O. unless I wanted to. (That office had been created to handle press relations and psychological warfare, and I never met anyone there who seemed to realize that there was a difference.) I could skip the daily briefings, I never had to cultivate Sources. In fact, my concerns were so rarefied that I had to ask other correspondents what they ever found to ask Westmoreland, Bunker, Komer and Zorthian. (Barry Zorthian was the head of J.U.S.P.A.O.; for more than four years he *was* Information.) What did anybody ever expect those people to *say*? No matter how highly placed they were, they were still officials, their views were well-established and well-known, famous. It could have rained frogs over Tan Son Nhut and they wouldn't have been upset. Cam Ranh Bay could have dropped into the South China Sea and they would have found some way to make it sound good for you, the Bo Loi (Ho's Own) could have marched by the American Embassy and they would have characterized it as "desperate"—what did even the reporters closest to the Mission Council ever find to write about when they'd finished their interviews? (My own interview with General Westmoreland had been hopelessly awkward. He'd noticed that I was accredited to *Esquire* magazine, and asked me if I planned to be doing "humoristical" pieces [ha ha, General], and beyond that very little was really said. I came away feeling as though I'd just had a conversation with a man who touches a chair and says, "This is a chair," points to a desk and says, "This is a desk." He was supernaturally good-looking and I think extremely good-hearted, but I couldn't think of anything to ask him, and the interview ended.) I honestly wanted to know what the form was for those interviews, but some of the reporters I'd ask would get very officious, saying something about "Command postures," and look at me as though I were insane. It was probably the kind of look that I gave one of them when he asked me once what I found to talk about with the Grunts all the time, expecting me to confide (I think) that I found them as boring as he did.

And just-like-in-the-movies, there were a lot of correspondents who did their work, met their deadlines, filled the most preposterous assignments the best they could, and withdrew, viewing the war and all its hideous secrets, earning their cynicism the hard way and turning their self-contempt back out again in laughter. If New York wanted to know how the troops felt about the assassination of Robert Kennedy, they'd go out and get it. ("Would you have voted for him?" "Yeah, he was a real good man, a real good man. He was, uh, young." "Who will you vote for now?" "Wallace, I guess.") They'd even gather troop reflections on the choice of Paris as the site of the peace talks ("Paris? I dunno, sure, why not? I mean, they ain't gonna hold 'em in Hanoi, now are they?"), but they'd know how funny that was, how wasteful, how profane. They knew that no matter how honestly they worked, their best work would somehow be lost in the wash of news, all the facts, all of the Vietnam stories. Conventional journalism could no more reveal this war than conventional firepower could win it, all it could do was view the most profound event of the American decade and turn it into a communications pudding, taking its most obvious, undeniable history and making it into a secret history. And the very best correspondents knew even more than that.

There was a song by The Mothers of Invention called *Trouble Every Day* that became a kind of anthem among a group of around twenty young correspondents. We'd play it often during those long night gatherings in Saigon, the ashtrays heaped over, ice buckets full of warm water, bottles empty, the grass all gone, the words running,

> *You know I watch that rotten box until my head begin*
> *to hurt*
> *From checkin' out the way the newsmen say they get the*
> *dirt*

[bitter, funny looks passing around the room]

> *And if another woman driver gets machine-gunned from her*
> *seat*

*They'll send some joker with a Brownie and you'll see it all
complete*

[lip biting, flinching, nervous laughter].

*They say that if the place blows up, we'll be the first to tell
'Cause the boys they got downtown are workin' hard and
doin' swell. . . .*

That wasn't really about *us*, no, we were so hip, and we'd laugh and
wince every time we heard it, all of us, wire-service photographers and
senior correspondents from the networks and special-assignment types
like myself, all grinning together because of what we knew together,
that in back of every column of print you read about Vietnam there
was a dripping, laughing death-face; it hid there in the newspapers
and magazines and held to your television screens for hours after
the set was turned off for the night, an afterimage that simply wanted
to tell you at last what somehow had not been told yet.

On an afternoon shortly before the New Year, a few weeks before
Tet, there was a special briefing held in Saigon to announce the latest
revisions in the hamlet-rating system of the Pacification program, the
A-B-C-D profiling of the country's security and, by heavy inference,
of the Government's popular support "in the countryside," which
meant anyplace outside of Saigon, the boonies. A lot of correspondents went, many because they had to, and I spent the time with a
couple of photographers in one of the bars on Tu Do, talking to
some soldiers from the 1st Infantry Division who had come down
from their headquarters at Lai Khe for the day. One of them was
saying that Americans treated the Vietnamese like animals.

"How's that?" someone asked.

"Well, you know what we do to animals . . . kill 'em and hurt 'em
and beat on 'em so's we can train 'em. S - - - , we don't treat the Dinks
no different than that."

And we knew that he was telling the truth. You only had to look
at his face to see that he really knew what he was talking about. He
wasn't judging it, I don't think that he was even particularly upset
about it, it was just something he'd observed. We mentioned it later
to some people who'd been at the Pacification briefing, someone from
The *Times* and someone from the A.P., and they both agreed that
the kid from the Big Red One had said more about the Hearts and
Minds program than they'd heard in over an hour of statistics, but
their bureaus couldn't use his story, they wanted Ambassador Komer's.
And they got it and you got it.

I could let you go on thinking that we were all brave, witty, attractive and vaguely tragic, that we were like some incomparable commando team, some hot-s--- squadron, the Dreaded Chi, danger loving, tender and wise. I could use it myself, it would certainly make for a prettier movie, but all of this talk about "we" and "us" has got to get straightened out.

At the height of the Tet Offensive alone, there were between six and seven hundred correspondents accredited to the Military Assistance Command, Vietnam. Who all of them were and where all of them went was as much a mystery to me and to most of the correspondents I knew as it was to the gentle-tempered bull-faced Marine gunnery sergeant assigned to the department of J.U.S.P.A.O. which issued those little plastic-coated M.A.C.V. accreditation cards. He'd hand them out and add their number to a small blackboard on the wall and then stare at the total in amused wonder, telling you that he thought it was all a f---ing circus. (He's the same man who told a television star, "Hold on to your ass awhile. You people from the electronic media don't scare me anymore.") There was nothing exclusive about that card or its operational match, the Bao Chi credential of the Republic of South Vietnam; thousands of them must have been issued over the years. All they did was admit you to the Vietnam press corps and tell you that you could go out and cover the war if you really wanted to. All kinds of people have held them at one time or another; feature writers for religious organs and gun magazines, summer vacationers from college newspapers (one paper sent two, a Hawk and a Dove, and we put it down because they hadn't sent a Moderate over as well), second-string literary figures who wrote about how they hated the war more than you or I ever could, syndicated eminences who houseguested with Westmoreland or Bunker and covered operations in the presence of Staff, privileges which permitted them to chronicle fully our great victory at Tet (Right on, Joseph Alsop!), and to publish evidence year after year after year that the back of the Cong had been broken, Hanoi's will dissolved. There was no nation too impoverished, no hometown paper so humble that they didn't get their man in for a quick feel at least once. The latter tended to be the sort of old reporters that most young reporters I knew were afraid of becoming someday. You'd run into them once in awhile at the bar of the Danang press center, men in their late forties who hadn't had the chance to slip into uniforms since V-J Day, exhausted and bewildered after all of those briefings and lightning visits, punchy from the sheer volume of facts that had been thrown on them, their tape recorders broken, their pens stolen by street kids, their time almost up. They'd been to see Cam Ranh Bay and quite a bit of the countryside (Mission diction, which meant that they'd been taken out to look at model or "New Life" hamlets), a crack ARVN division (where?), even some of our boys right there at the front (where?), and a lot of military Information Office people. They seemed too awed by the importance of the whole thing to be very clear, they were too shy to make friends, they were all alone and speechless, except to say, "Well, when I came over here, I thought it was pretty hopeless, but I have to admit it looks like we've gotten things pretty much under control. I must say, I've been awfully impressed. . . ." There were a lot of hacks who wrote down every word that the generals and officials told them to write, and a lot for whom Vietnam was nothing more than an important career station. There were some who couldn't make it and left after a few days, some who couldn't make it the other way, staying year after year, trying to piece together their very real hatred of the war with their great love for it, that rough reconciliation that many of us had to look at. A few came through with the grisliest hang-ups, letting it all go every chance they got, like the one who told me that he couldn't see what all the fuss had been about, *his* M-16 never jammed. There were Frenchmen who'd parachuted into Dienbienphu during what they loved to call "the First Indochina War," Englishmen sprung alive from *Scoop* (a press-corps standard because it said that if the papers didn't get it, it didn't happen), Italians whose only previous experience had been shooting fashion, Koreans who were running PX privileges into small fortunes, Japanese who trailed so many wires that transistor jokes were inevitable, Vietnamese who took up combat photography to avoid the draft, Americans who spent all their days in Saigon drinking at the bar of L'Amiral restaurant with Air America pilots. Some filed nothing but hometowners, some took the social notes of the American community, some went in the field only because they couldn't afford hotels, some never left their hotels. Taken all together, they accounted for most of the total on Gunny's blackboard, which left a number of people, as many as fifty, who were gifted or honest or especially kind and who gave journalism a better name than it deserved, particularly in Vietnam. Finally the press corps was as diffuse and faceless as any regiment in the war, the main difference being that many of us remained on our own orders.

It was characteristic of a lot of Americans in Vietnam to have no idea of when they were being obscene, and some correspondents fell into that, writing their stories from the daily releases and battlegrams, tracking them through with the cheer-crazed language of the

M.A.C.V. Information Office, things like "discreet burst" (one of those tore an old grandfather and two children to bits as they ran along a paddy wall one day, at least according to the report made later by the gun-ship pilot), "friendly casualties" (not warm, not fun), "meeting engagement" (ambush), concluding usually with 17 or 117 or 317 enemy dead and American losses "described as light." There were correspondents who had the same sensibility concerning the dead as the Command had: Well, in a war you've got to expect a little mud to get tracked over the carpet, we took a real black eye but we sure gave Charlie a s - - - storm, we consider this a real fine kill ratio, real fine. . . . There was a well-known correspondent of three wars who used to walk around the Danang press center with a green accountant's ledger. He'd sit down to talk and begin writing everything you'd say, entering it in, so to speak. The Marines arranged for a special helicopter (or "fragged a chopper," as we used to call it) to take him in and out of Khesanh one afternoon, weeks after it had become peaceful again. He came back very cheerful about our great victory there. I was sitting with Lengel, and we recalled that, at the very least, two hundred Grunts had been blown away there and around a thousand more wounded. He looked up from his ledger and said, "Oh, two hundred isn't anything. We lost more than that in an hour on Guadalcanal." We weren't going to deal with that, so we sort of left the table, but you heard that kind of talk all the time, as though it could invalidate the deaths at Khesanh, render them somehow less dead than the dead from Guadalcanal, as though light losses didn't lie as still as moderate losses or heavy losses. And these were American dead they were talking about; you should have heard them when the dead were Vietnamese. Those people were really on the edge, only words away from the kind of thinking which said, "The Tet Offensive has provided the Government of South Vietnam with a golden opportunity to show the people what it can do for them," or, "We had to destroy Ben Tre in order to save it."

So there we all were, no real villains and only a few heroes, a lot of adventurers and a lot of drudges, a lot of beautiful lunatics and a lot of Normals come to report what was ultimately the Normals' war; and somehow, out of all that, a great number of us managed to find and recognize each other. You could be hard about it and deny that there was a brotherhood working there, but then what else could you call it? It wasn't just some wartime clique of buddies, it was too large in number for that, including members of at least a dozen cliques, some of them overlapping until they became indistinguishable, others standing in contemptuous opposition to one another; and it was far too small to incorporate the whole bloated, amorphous body of the Vietnam press corps. Its requirements were unstated, because other than sensibility and style, it had none. Elsewhere, it would have been just another scene, another crowd, but the war gave it urgency and made it a deep thing, so deep that we didn't even have to like one another to belong. There were a lot of things that went unsaid at the time, but just because it was seldom spoken didn't mean that we weren't very much aware of it or that, in that terrible, shelterless place, we weren't grateful.

It made room for correspondents who were themselves members of Saigon's American Establishment, it included young marrieds, all kinds of girl reporters, a lot of Europeans, the Ivy League-in-Asia crowd, the Danang bunch, the Straights and the Heads, formals and funkies, old hands (many of whom were very young), and even some tourists, people who wanted to go somewhere to screw around for awhile and happened to choose the war. There was no way of thinking about "who we were" because we were all so different, but where we were alike we were really alike. It helped if you went out on operations a lot or if you were good at your work, but neither was very necessary as long as you knew something of what the war was (as opposed to what the Mission and M.A.C.V. told you it was), and as long as you weren't a snob about it. We were all doing terribly upsetting work, it could often be very dangerous, and we were the only ones who could tell, among ourselves, whether that work was any good. Applause from home meant nothing next to a nice word from a colleague. (One reporter loved to call his New York superiors "those leg motherf - - - ers," taking it from the Airborne term for anyone who was not jump-qualified; if you can appreciate the 4th Division Lurp [long-range recon patrol] who called himself The Baptist even though he was an Episcopalian, you get the idea.) We were all studying the same thing, and if you got killed you couldn't graduate.

We were serious enough about what we were doing over there, but we were also enchanted by it (not even the most uncomplicated farmboy P.F.C. can go through a war without finding some use for it), and even when you got tired, felt you'd had too much, grown old in an afternoon, there were ways to take that and work it back into the style that we all tried to maintain. Things had to get really bad before you saw the war as clearly as most troops came to see it, but those times were rare enough and we were incorrigible. Most of us had times when we swore that we'd never go near any of it again if we could only be allowed out this once, everybody made those deals, but a few days in Danang or Saigon or even Hong Kong, Singa-

pore or Bangkok would get you over that, and the choice to go back
was still there, still yours, priceless option, property of the press corps.

Friendships were made directly, with none of the clutter that had
once seemed so necessary, and once they were made they outvalued
all but your oldest, most special friendships. Your scene before Vietnam was unimportant, nobody wanted to hear about it, and we often
seemed a little like those Green Berets out in their remote, harassed
outposts, groups of eight or twelve Americans commanding hundreds
of local mercenaries who could be as hostile as the Cong, who often
were Cong; living together this way for months at a time without
ever learning each other's first names or hometowns. ("Listen," I
told someone once, trying to give them an idea of it, "I knew Bernie
Weinraub for nearly seven months before I learned that he was Jewish." "But how is that *possible?*" "I don't know. It just never came
up.") You could make friends elsewhere, a Special Forces captain in
the Delta, a Grunt up in Phu Bai, some decent, witty (and usually
suffering) member of the Embassy Political Section. But whether
you hung out with them or with other correspondents, all you ever
talked about anyway was the war, and they could come to seem like
two very different wars after awhile. Because who but another correspondent could talk the kind of mythical war that you wanted to
hear described? (Just hearing the way Flynn pronounced the word
"Vietnam," the tenderness and respect that he put in it, taught you
more about the beauty and horror of the place than anything the
apologists or explainers could ever teach you.) Who could you discuss politics with, except a colleague? (We all had roughly the same
position on the war; we were in it, and that was a position.) Where
else could you go for a real sense of the war's past? There were all
kinds of people who knew the background, the facts, the most
minute details, but only a correspondent could give you the exact
mood that attended each of the major epochs; the animal terror of
the Ia Drang or the ghastly breakdown of the first major Marine
operation, code-named Starlight, where the Marines were dying so
incredibly fast, so far beyond the Command's allowance, that one
of them got zipped into a body bag and tossed to the top of a pile of
K.I.A.'s while he was still alive. (Karsten Prager of *Time* told me
this.) He regained consciousness up there and writhed and heaved
until his bag rolled to ground, where some corpsmen found him and
saved him. The Triangle and Bong Son were as remote as the Reservoir or Chickamauga, you had to hear the history from somebody you
could trust, and whom else could you trust? And if you saw some
piece of helmet graffiti that seemed to say everything, you weren't

going to pass it along to some colonel or tell it to a Psyops official. "Born to Kill," placed in all innocence next to the peace symbol or, "A sucking chest wound is Nature's way of telling you that you've been in a fire fight," were just too good to share with anyone but a real collector, and with very few exceptions those were all correspondents.

We shared a great many things; field gear, grass, whiskey, girls (that Men-Without-Women trip got old all the time), sources, information, hunches, tips, prestige (during my first days there, bureau chiefs from *Life* and CBS took me around to introduce everyone they could think of, and somebody did as much for other new arrivals), we even shared each other's luck when our own seemed gone. I was no more superstitious than anyone else in Vietnam, I was very superstitious, and there were always a few who seemed so irrefutably charmed that nothing could make me picture them lying dead there; having someone like that with you on an operation could become more important than any actual considerations about what might be waiting on the ground for you. I doubt whether anything else could be as parasitic as that, or as intimate.

And by some equation that was so wonderful that I've never stopped to work it out, the best and the bravest correspondents were also usually the most compassionate, the ones who were most in touch with what they were doing. Greenway was like that, and so were Jack Laurence and Keith Kay, a reporter–camera team for CBS who worked together for nearly two years. There were people like Peter Arnett and Horst Faas, with seven years in apiece, with their Pulitzers and their war-wise grace in helping new reporters, there was Stone and John Wheeler and Robert Shaplen (a good run of names, it's *my* movie), Dick Swanson, Co Rentmeester, Don Moser, Colin Leinster, Bill Tuohy, John Apple, very busy professionals who had room and time to show you around, get you started. And there was Larry Burrows, who had been photographing the war for *Life* since 1962, a tall, deliberate Englishman of around forty with one of the most admirable reputations of all the Vietnam correspondents. We were together on one of the lz's that had been built for the operation that was supposedly relieving Khesanh, and Burrows had run down to take pictures of a Chinook that was coming in to land. The wind was strong enough to send tarmac strips flying fifty feet across the lz and he ran through it to work, photographing the crew, getting the soldiers coming down the incline to board the chopper, getting the kids throwing off the mailbags and cartons of rations and ammunition, getting the three wounded being lifted carefully on board, turning again to get the six dead in their closed body bags, then the rise of the chopper (the wind now was strong enough to tear papers out of your hand), photographing the grass blown flat all around him and the flying debris, taking one picture each of the chopper rearing, settling and departing. When it was gone he looked at me, and he seemed to be in the most open distress. "Sometimes one feels like such a bastard," he said.

And that was one more thing we shared. We had no secrets about it or the ways it could make you feel. We all talked about it at times, some talked about it too much, a few never seemed to talk about anything else. That was a drag, but it was all in the house; you only minded it when it came from outside. All kinds of thieves and killers managed to feel sanctimonious around us; battalion commanders, civilian businessmen, even the Grunts, until they realized how few of us were making any real money in it. There's no way around it; if you photographed a dead Marine with a poncho over his face and got something for it, you were *some* kind of parasite. But what were you if you pulled the poncho back first to make a better shot, and did that in front of his friends? Some other kind of parasite, I suppose. Then what were you if you stood there watching it, making a note to remember it later in case you might want to use it? Those combinations were infinite, you worked them out, and they only involved a small part of what we were thought to be. We were called thrill freaks, death wishers, wound seekers, war lovers, hero worshipers, closet queens, dope addicts, low-grade alcoholics, ghouls, Communists, seditionists, more nasty things than I can remember. There were people in the military who never forgave General Westmoreland for not imposing restrictions against us when he'd had the chance in the early days. There were officers and a lot of seemingly naïve troops who believed that if it were not for us, there would be no war now, and I was never able to argue with any of them on that point. A lot of the Grunts had some of that sly, small-town suspicion of the press, but at least nobody under the rank of captain ever asked me whose side I was on, told me to get with the program, jump on the team, come in for the Big Win. Sometimes they were just stupid, sometimes it came about because they had such love for their men, but sooner or later all of us heard one version or another of, "My Marines are winning this war, and you people are losing it for us in your papers," often spoken in an almost friendly way, but with the teeth shut tight behind the smiles. It was creepy, being despised in such casual, off-handed ways. And there were plenty of people who believed, finally, that we were nothing more than glorified war profiteers. And perhaps we were, those of us who didn't get killed or wounded or otherwise fucked up.

Just in the regular course of things, a lot of correspondents took close calls. Getting scratched was one thing, it didn't mean that you'd come as close as you could have, it could have been closer without your even knowing it, like an early-morning walk I took once from the hilltop position of a Special Forces camp where I'd spent the night, down to the teamhouse at the foot of the hill, where I was going to have some coffee. I walked off the main trail onto a smaller trail and followed it until I saw the house and a group of eight giggling, wide-eyed Vietnamese mercenaries, Mikes, pointing at me and talking very excitedly. They all grabbed for me at once when I reached the bottom, for, as it was explained to me a moment later, I'd just come down a trail which the Special Forces had rigged out with more than twenty booby traps, any one of which could have taken me off. (Any One Of Which ran through my head for days afterward.) If you went out often, just as surely as you'd eventually find yourself in a position where survival etiquette insisted that you took a weapon ("You know how this thang works n' airthang?" a young sergeant had to ask me once, and I'd had to nod as he threw it to me and said, "Then git some!", the American banzai), it was unavoidable that you'd find yourself almost getting killed. You expected something like that to happen, but not exactly that, not until events made things obvious for you. A close call was like a loss of noncombatant status; you weren't especially proud of it, you merely reported it to a friend and then stopped talking about it, knowing in the first place that the story would go around from there, and that there wasn't really anything to be said about it anyway. But that didn't stop you from thinking about it a lot, doing a lot of hideous projecting from it, forming a system of pocket metaphysics around it, getting it down to where you found yourself thinking about which *kind* of thing was closer; that walk down the hill, the plane you missed by minutes which blew apart on the Khesanh airstrip an hour later and fifty miles away, or the sniper round that kissed the back of your flak jacket as you grunted and heaved yourself over a low garden wall in Hué. And then your *Dawn Patrol* fantasy would turn very ugly, events again and again not quite what you had expected, and you'd realize that nothing ever came closer to death than the death of a good friend.

In the first week of May, the Vietcong staged a brief, vicious offensive against Saigon, taking and holding small positions on the fringes of Cholon and defending parts of the outlying areas that could only be retaken from the Y Bridge, from the racetrack grounds, from Plantation Road and the large French graveyard that ran for several hundred yards into a grove and a complex of Vietcong bunkers. The offensive's value as pure revolutionary terror aside (those results were always incalculable, our good gear notwithstanding), it was more or less what M.A.C.V. said it was, costly to the VC and largely a failure. It cost the Friendlies too (between Saigon and the A Shau, it was the week that saw more Americans killed than any other in the war), a lot more damage was done to the city's outskirts, more homes were bombed out. The papers called it either the May Offensive, the Mini-Offensive (you know I'm not making that up), or the Second Wave; it was the long-awaited Battle of Algiers-in-Saigon that had been maniacally predicted by the Americans for practically every weekend since the Tet Offensive had ended. In its early hours, five correspondents took a jeep into Cholon, past the first files of refugees (many of whom warned them to turn back), and into a Vietcong ambush. One of them escaped (according to his own story) by playing dead and then running like an animal into the crowds of Cholon. He said that they had all yelled, "Bao Chi!" a number of times, but that they had been machine-gunned anyway.

It was more like death by misadventure than anything else, as if that mattered, and of the four dead correspondents, only one had been a stranger to me. Two of the others were good acquaintances, and the fourth was a friend. His name was John Cantwell, an Australian who worked for *Time*, and he had been one of the first friends I'd made in Vietnam. He was a kind, congenial mock-goat whose talk was usually about the most complex, unimaginable lecheries, architectural constructions of monumental erotic fantasies. He had a Chinese wife and three children in Hong Kong (he spoke fluent Chinese, he'd take it through the Cholon bars for us sometimes), and he was one of the few I knew who really hated Vietnam and the war, every bit of it. He was staying only long enough to earn the money to settle some debts, and then he was going to leave for good. He was a good, gentle, hilarious man, and to this day I can't help thinking that he wasn't *supposed* to get killed in Vietnam, getting killed in a war was not John's scene, he'd made no room for that the way some others had. A lot of people I had liked a lot, G.I.'s and even some correspondents, had already died, but when Cantwell got murdered it did more than sadden and shock me. Because he was a friend, his death changed all the odds.

In that one brief period of less than two weeks, it became a war of our convenience, a horrible convenience, but ours. We could jump into jeeps and mini-mokes at nine or ten and drive a few kilometers to where the fighting was, run around in it for a few hours, and come back early. We'd sit on the Continental terrace and wave each other in, get stoned early and stay up late, since there was no question of five-thirty wake-ups. We'd been scattered all over Vietnam for months now, friends running into friends now and again, and this put everyone together. There was no other time when that was needed so badly. A day after John and the others died, a strange, death-charged kid named Charlie Eggleston, a U.P.I. photographer, got killed at the Cemetery, reportedly while returning fire at a Vietcong position in revenge for the four murdered reporters. (He willed everything he had to Vietnamese charities.) A Japanese photographer was killed later that same day, a Brazilian lost a leg the day after that, and somewhere in there another correspondent was killed; by then everyone had stopped counting and worked at keeping it away. Again in the Cemetery, a bullet tore through Co Rentmeester's hand and lodged under the eye of another photographer, Art Greenspon. A Frenchman named Christian Simonpietrie (known as "Frenchy" to his movie-warped friends), was hit above the eye by some shrapnel from the same round which crippled General Loan; not a serious wound, but one more out of too many, more than correspondents had ever received at one time. By the fifth day, eight had died and more than a dozen others had been wounded. We were driving toward the racetrack when an M.P. stepped in front of our car to ask for identification.

"Listen," he said, "I saw those four other guys and I never want to see any more like that. You know those guys? Then what the f - - - do you want to go in there for? Don't you people ever learn? I mean, I *saw* those guys. Believe me, it ain't worth it."

He was firm about not letting us through, but we insisted and he finally gave up.

"Well, I can't really stop you. You *know* I can't stop you. But if I could, I would. You wouldn't be driving up to no s - - - like those four guys."

In the early evenings we'd do exactly what correspondents did in those terrible stories that would circulate in 1964 and 1965, we'd stand on the roof of the Caravelle Hotel having drinks and watch the air strikes across the river, so close that a good telephoto lens would pick up the markings on the planes. There were dozens of us up there, like aristocrats viewing Borodino from the heights, at least as detached about it as that, even though many of us had been caught under those things from time to time. There'd be a lot of women up there, a few of them correspondents (like Cathy Leroy, the French photographer, and Jurate Kazickas, a correspondent of great, fashion-model beauty), but most of them wives and girls of reporters. Some people had tried hard to believe that Saigon was just another city they'd come to live in; they'd formed civilized social routines, tested restaurants, made and kept appointments, given parties, had love affairs. Many had even brought their wives with them, and more often than not it worked out badly. Very few of the women really liked Saigon, and the rest became like most Western women in Asia; bored, distracted, frightened, unhappy and, if left there too long, fiercely frantic. And now, for the second time in three months, Saigon had become unsafe. Rockets were dropping a block from the best hotels, the White Mice (the Saigon police) were having brief, hysterical fire fights with shadows, you could hear it going on as you dropped off to sleep; it was no longer simply a stinking, corrupt, exhausting foreign city.

At night, the rooms of the Continental would fill with correspondents drifting in and out for a drink or a smoke before bed, some talk and some music, The Rolling Stones singing "It's so very lonely,/ You're two thousand light-years from home," or, "Please come see me in the Citadel," that word putting a chill in the room. Whenever one of us came back from an R&R we'd bring records. Sounds were as precious as water; Hendrix, The Airplane, Frank Zappa and The Mothers, all the things that hadn't even started when we'd left the States, Wilson Pickett, Junior Walker, *John Wesley Harding* (one copy worn thin and replaced within a month), the Grateful Dead (the name was enough), The Doors, with their distant, icy sound. It seemed like such wintry music; you could rest your forehead against the window where the air conditioner had cooled the glass, close your eyes and feel the heat pressing against you from outside. Flares dropped over possible targets three blocks away, and all night long armed jeeps and massive convoys moved down Tu Do Street toward the river.

When we were down to a hard core of six or seven, we'd talk tired, stoned talk about the war, doing commanders who were always saying things like, "Well, Charlie's dug in there pretty good, but when we can get him out where we can see him we find we're getting some real decent kills, we got Charlie outgunned for sure, only thing is we can't kill him if we can't see him 'cause Charlie's always running. Come on, we'll take you up and get you shot at." We talked about a discothèque we were going to open in Saigon, The Third Wave, with a stainless-steel dance floor, blowups of the best war photographs on the walls, a rock group called Westy and the K.I.A.'s. (Our talk had about as much taste as the war did.) And we'd talk about LZ Loon, the mythical place where it got dark so fast that by the time you realized that there wouldn't be another chopper in until morning, you'd already picked a place to sleep for the night. Loon was the ultimate Vietnam movie location, where all of the mad colonels and death-spaced Grunts we'd ever known showed up all at once, saying all the terrible, heartbreaking things they always said, so nonchalant about the horror and fear that you knew you'd never really be one of them no matter how long you stayed. You honestly didn't know whether to laugh or cry. Few people ever cried more than once there, and if you'd used that up, you laughed; the young ones were so innocent and violent, so sweet and so brutal, beautiful killers.

One morning, about twenty-five correspondents were out by the Y Bridge working when a dying ARVN was driven by on the back of a half-ton pickup. The truck stopped at some barbed wire, and we all gathered around to look at him. He was nineteen or twenty and he'd been shot three times in the chest. All of the photographers leaned in for pictures, there was a television camera above him, we looked at him and then at each other and then at the wounded Vietnamese again. He opened his eyes briefly a few times and looked back at us. The first time, he tried to smile (the Vietnamese did that when they were embarrassed by the nearness of foreigners), then it left him. I'm sure that he didn't even see us the last time he looked, but we all knew what it was that he'd seen just before that.

That was also the week that Page came back to Vietnam; A *Scrambler to the Front* by Tim Page, *Tim Page* by Charles Dickens. He came a few days before it started, and people who knew about his luck were making jokes blaming the whole thing on his return. There were more young, apolitically radical, wigged-out crazies running around Vietnam than anybody ever realized. Between all of the Grunts turning on and tripping out on the war and the substantial number of correspondents who were doing the same thing, it was an authentic subculture. There were more than enough within the press corps to withstand a little pressure from the upright, and if Flynn was the most sophisticated example of this, Page was the most extravagant. I'd heard about him even before I came to Vietnam ("Look him up. If he's still alive."), and between the time I got there and the time he came back in May, I'd heard so much about him that I might have felt that I knew him, if so many people hadn't warned me, "There's just no way to describe him for you. Really, no way."

"Page? That's easy. Page is a child."

"No, man, Page is just crazy."

"Page is a crazy child."

They'd tell all kinds of stories about him, sometimes working up a passing anger over things he'd done years before, times when he'd freaked a little and become violent, but it always got softened, they'd pull back and say his name with great affection. "Page. F - - - ing Page."

He was an orphan boy from London, married at seventeen and divorced a year later. He worked his way across Europe as a cook in the hotels, drifting East through India, through Laos (where he claims to have dealt with the Spooks, a little teen-age espionage), into Vietnam at the age of twenty. One of the things that everybody said about him was that he had not been much of a photographer then (he'd picked up a camera the way you or I would pick up a ticket), but that he would go places for pictures that very few other photographers were going. People made him sound crazy and ambitious, like the Sixties Kid, a stone-cold freak in a country where the madness raced up the hills and into the jungles, where everything essential to learning Asia, war, drugs, the whole adventure, was close at hand.

The first time he got hit it was shrapnel in the legs and the hip. That was at Chu Lai, in '65. The next time was during the Buddhist riots of the 1966 Struggle Movement in Danang; head, chest, arms, more shrapnel. (A *Paris-Match* photograph showed Flynn and a French photographer carrying him on a door, his face half covered by bandages, "Tim Page, blessé à la tête.") His friends began trying to talk him into leaving Vietnam, saying, "Hey, Page, there's an air strike looking for you." And there was; it caught him drifting around in a Coast Guard cutter in the South China Sea, blowing it out of the water under the mistaken impression that it was a Vietcong vessel. Three of the crew were killed and eight critically wounded. Page took over two hundred individual wounds, and he floated in the water for hours before he was finally rescued.

They were getting worse each time, and Page gave into it. He left Vietnam, allegedly for good, and joined Flynn in Paris for awhile. He went to the States from there, took some pictures for *Time-Life*, got busted with Jim Morrison in New Haven, traveled across the country on his own (he still had some money left), doing a picture

story which he planned to call "Winter in America." Shortly after
the Tet Offensive, Flynn returned to Vietnam, and once Page heard
that, it was only a matter of time. When he got back in May, his
entrance requirements weren't in order, and the Vietnamese kept
him at Tan Son Nhut for a couple of days, where his friends visited
him and brought him things. The first time I met him he was giggling
and doing an insane imitation of two Vietnamese immigration authorities fighting over the amount of money they were going to hold
him up for, "Minh phung, auk nyong bgnyang gluke poo fhooc phuc
fart, I mean you should have *heard* those beastly people. Where am
I going to sleep, who's got a rack for Page? The Dinks have been
mucking about with Page, Page is a *very* tired boy."

He was twenty-three when I first met him, and I can remember
wishing that I'd known him when he was still young. He was bent,
beaten, scarred, he was everything by way of being crazy that everyone had said he was, except that you could tell that he'd never get
really nasty again when he flipped. He was broke, so friends got him
a place to sleep, gave him piasters, cigarettes, liquor, grass. Then he
made a couple of thousand dollars on some fine pictures of the offensive, and all of those things came back on us, twice over. That was
the way the world was for Page; when he was broke you took care of
him, when he was not he took care of you. It was above economics.

"How would Elsworth Bunker like The Mothers of Invention?"
he'd say. (He wanted to rig loudspeakers around the Lower House
and along the park facing it and play the freakiest music he could find
as loud as the equipment would permit.)

"On your head, Page," Flynn would say.

"No. I ask you, would William C. Westmoreland dig The Mothers
or wouldn't he?"

His talk was endlessly referential, he mixed in images from the war,
history, rock, Eastern religion, his travels, literature (he was very
widely read and proud of it), but you came to see that he was really
only talking about one thing, Page. He spoke of himself in the third
person more than anyone I ever knew, but it was so totally ingenuous
that it was never offensive. He could get very waspish and silly, he
could be an outrageous snob (he was a great believer in the New
Aristocracy), he could talk about people and things in ways that
were nearly monstrous, stopping short of that and turning funny and
often deeply tender. He carried all kinds of clippings around with
him, pictures of himself, newspaper stories about the times he'd been
wounded, a copy of a short story that Tom Mayer had written about
him in which he got killed on an operation with the Korean Marines.

He was especially vain about that story, very proud and completely spooked by it. That first week back, he'd had things brought around to where he could remember them again, remembering that you could get killed here, the way he almost had those other times, the way he had in the story.

"*Look* at you," he'd say, coming into the room at night. "Every one of you is *stoned*. Look at you, what are you doing there if it isn't rolling a joint? Grinning, Flynn, grinning is sinning. Dope is hope. Help! Give us a bit of that, will you? I ain't doin' no Evil, give us just a toke. Ahhhhh, yesh! It *can't* be my turn to change the record because I've only just come in. Are any birds coming by? Where are Mimsy and Poopsy? [His names for two Australian girls who dropped over some evenings.] Women is good, women is necessary, women is definitely good for business. Yesh."

"Don't smoke that, Page. Your brain is already about the consistency of a soggy quiche lorraine."

"Nonsense, utter nonsense. Why don't you roll a five-handed joint while I prepare a steamboat for this ugly, filthy roach?" He'd jab his misshapen left index finger at you to underline key words, taking the conversation wherever his old child's whimsy took his thoughts, planning projects which ranged from full-scale guerrilla ops in New York City to painting the front of our hotel in Day-Glo colors in the belief that the Vietnamese would love it. "They're all stoned all the time anyway," he'd say. If any girls showed up, he'd tell them lurid stories about the war, about the Middle East (both he and Flynn had caught a couple of days of the June war, flying down from Paris for it), about venereal diseases he'd had, talking to them the way he'd talk to anybody. He only had one way of speaking, it could have been to me or the Queen, it didn't matter. ("What do you mean, of *course* I love the Queen. The Queen's a very lovable bird.") If he was too absorbed to talk, he'd stand in front of a full-length mirror and dance to The Doors for an hour at a time, completely lost in it.

When Saigon became quiet again during the third week of May, it seemed as though the war had ended. Nothing was happening anywhere, and I realized that after seven months straight of this, I needed some time out. Saigon was the place where you always noticed how tired your friends looked anyway; a place needs a lot of character for that, and in Saigon you could look perfectly marvelous one day and then perfectly terrible the next, and friends were telling me about it. So while Flynn went up for a month with the 4th Division Lurps, walking point on unearthly four-man night patrols through the Highlands (he came back from that one with three rolls of exposed film), I left for a month in Hong Kong, followed by practically everyone I knew. It was like moving my scene intact to more pleasant surroundings, a recess session. Page came over to buy expensive toys; more cameras, a fisheye lens, a Halliburton. He stayed for a week and talked of nothing but how awful Hong Kong was, how Singapore was much, much groovier. When I got back to Vietnam in early July, he and I spent ten days in the Delta with the Special Forces, and then we went to Danang to meet Flynn. (Page called Danang "Dangers," with a hard G. In a war where people quite seriously referred to Hong Kong as "Hongers" and spoke of running over to Pnompers to interview Snookie, a British correspondent named Don Wise had made up a Vietnam itinerary: Canters, Saigers, Nharters, Quinners, Pleikers, Quangers, Dangers and Hyoo-beside-the-Sea.)

Page's helmet decor now consisted of the words "HELP I'M A ROCK!" (taken from another Zappa song), and a small Mao button, but he didn't have much chance to wear it. Things were still quiet everywhere, fini la guerre, I wanted to leave in September and it was already August. We went out on operations, but all of them were without contact. That was fine with me, I didn't want contact (what the hell for?), that month in Hong Kong had been good in a lot of ways, one of them being the leisure it offered me to recall with some precision just how awful Vietnam could be. Away from it, it was a very different place. We spent most of August on China Beach sailing and goofing, talking to Marines who'd come down for in-country R&R, coming back in the late afternoons to the press center by the Danang River. It was perfectly peaceful, better than any vacation could be, but I knew that I was going home, I was short, and a kind of retrospective fear followed me everywhere.

In the bar of the press center, Marines and members of the Naval Support Activity, all information specialists, would gather after a long day in the I.O. Shop to juice a little until it got dark enough for the movie to start outside. They were mostly officers (no one under E-6 was allowed in the bar, including a lot of combat Grunts whom many of us had tried to bring in for drinks over the past year), and there was a constant state of mistrust between us. The Marines from the Combat Information Bureau seemed to like most civilian reporters about as well as they liked the Vietcong, maybe a little less, and we grew sick of their constant attempts to impose Marine order on our lives there. That winter, you'd return to the press center from places too terrible to believe, and a lot of our tact would become impaired in transit, causing stupid quarrels over things like T-shirts and shower clogs in the dining room and helmets worn in the bar. We'd walk in now from China Beach and they'd all look at us, wave, laugh harshly and ask us how it was going.

"We're winning," Flynn would say cryptically, smiling pleasantly, and they'd smile back uncertainly.

"Look how nervous Page makes them," Flynn said. "He really makes the Marines nervous."

"Freak," Page said.

"No, honest to God, I mean it. Look, the minute he walks in they sort of shy like ponies, they move just a little closer together. They don't like your hair, Page, and you're a foreigner, and you're insane, you really spook the s - - - out of them. They might not be sure of how they feel about this war, some of them may even think it's wrong, some of them may dig Ho a little bit, they're not sure about a lot of things, but they're sure about you, Page. You're the enemy. 'Kill Page!' You wait, man. Wait, Page."

Just before I went back to Saigon to begin arrangements for flying home, the three of us met at a place called Tam Ny, near the mouth of the Perfume River, where Page was trying out his fisheye lens on the airboats that had just come back to Vietnam after an earlier failure in the war. We rode around on those for a day and then took a boat downriver to Hué, where we met Perry Dean Young, a reporter for U.P.I. who came from North Carolina. (Flynn called him "the fullest flowering of Southern degeneracy," but the closest to degeneracy any of us ever came was in our jokes about it, about what bad, dope-smoking cats we all were. We were probably less stoned than the drinkers in our presence, and our livers were holding up.) Perry had a brother named Dave who ran the small Naval detachment that had been set up during the battle, directly across from the south wall of the Citadel. For months now, Flynn and I had been living vicariously off each other's war stories, his Ia Drang stories and my Hué stories, and Perry's brother got a Navy truck and drove us around the city while I gave a running commentary which would have been authoritative if only I'd been able to recognize any of it now. We were sitting on the back of the truck on folding chairs, bouncing around in the heat and dust. Along the park that fronted the river we passed dozens of lovely young girls riding their bicycles, and Page leaned over and leered at them, saying, "Good mornin', little school-girl, I'm a li'l schoolboy too."

When I'd been here before, you couldn't let yourself be seen on the riverbank without machine guns opening up on you from the opposite bank, you couldn't breathe anywhere in Hué without rushing somebody's death into your bloodstream, the main bridge across the river had been dropped in the middle, the days had been cold and wet, the city had been composed seemingly of destruction and debris. Now it was clear and very warm, you could stop by the Circle Sportif for a drink, the bridge was up and the wall was down, all the rubble had been carted away.

"It *couldn't* have been *that* bad," Page said, and Flynn and I laughed.

"You're just pissed because you missed it," Flynn said.

"That's you you're talking about, boy, not Page."

And I was realizing for the first time how insanely dangerous it had been, seeing it in a way I hadn't in February.

"No," Page said. "It got awfully exaggerated, Hué. I know it couldn't have been that bad, I mean look around. I've seen worse. Much, much worse."

I meant to ask him where, but I was already back in New York City when I thought of it.

III

Back in the world now, and a lot of us aren't making it. The story got old or we got old, a great deal more than the story had taken us there anyway, and many things had been satisfied. Or so it seemed when, after a year or two or five we realized that we were simply tired. We came to fear something more complicated than death, an annihilation less final but more complete, and we got out. Because (more lore) we all knew that if you stayed too long you became one of those poor bastards who had to have a war on all the time, and where was that? We got out and became like everyone else who has been through a war; changed, enlarged and (some things are expensive to say) incomplete. We came back or moved on, keeping in touch from New York or San Francisco, Paris or London, Africa or the Middle East; some fell into bureaus in Chicago or Hong Kong or Bangkok, coming to miss the life so acutely (some of us) that we understood what amputees went through when they sensed movement in the fingers or toes of limbs lost months before. A few extreme cases felt that the experience there had been a glorious one, while most of us felt that it had been merely wonderful. I think that Vietnam was what we had instead of happy childhoods.

During my first month back I woke up one night and knew that my living room was full of dead Marines. It actually happened three or four times, after a dream I was having those nights (the kind of dream one never had in Vietnam), but that first time it wasn't just some holding dread left by the dream, I knew they were there, so that after I'd turned on the light by my bed and smoked a cigarette I lay there for a moment thinking that I'd have to go out soon and cover them. I don't want to make anything out of this and I certainly don't want sympathy; going to that place was my idea to begin with, I could have left anytime, and as those things go I paid little enough, almost nothing. Some guys come back and see their nightmares break in the streets in daylight, some become inhabited and stay that way, all kinds of things can trail after you, and, besides, after awhile my thing went away almost completely, the dream, too. I know a guy who had been a combat medic in the Central Highlands, and two years later he was still sleeping with all the lights on. We were walking across Fifty-seventh Street one afternoon and passed a blind man carrying a sign that read, MY DAYS ARE DARKER THAN YOUR NIGHTS. "Don't bet on it, man," the ex-medic said.

Of course coming back was a down. After something like that, what could you find to thrill you, what compared, what did you do for a finish? Everything seemed a little dull, heaviness threatened everywhere, you left little relics lying around to keep you in touch, to keep it real, you played the music that had been with you through Hué and Khesanh and the May Offensive, tried to believe that the freedom and simplicity of those days could be maintained in what you laughingly referred to as "normal circumstances." You read the papers and watched television, but you knew what those stories were really all about beforehand, and they just got you angry. You missed the scene, missed the Grunts and the excitement, the feelings you'd had in a place where no drama had to be invented, ever. You tried to get the same highs here that you'd had there, but none of that really worked very well. You wondered whether, in time, it would all slip away and become like everything else distant, but you doubted it, and for good reason. The friendships lasted, some even deepened, but our gatherings were always stalked by longing and emptiness, more than a touch of Legion Post Night. Smoking dope, listening to The Mothers and Jimi Hendrix, remembering compulsively, telling war stories. But then, there's nothing wrong with that. War stories aren't really anything more than stories about people anyway.

In April I got a call telling me that Page had been hit again and was not expected to live. He had been up goofing somewhere around

Cu Chi, digging the big toys, and a helicopter he was riding in was ordered to land and pick up some wounded. Page and a sergeant ran out to help, the sergeant stepped on a mine which blew his legs off and sent a two-inch piece of shrapnel through Page's forehead above the right eye and deep into the base of his brain. He retained consciousness all the way to the hospital at Long Binh. Flynn and Perry Young were on R&R in Vientiane when they were notified, and they flew immediately to Saigon. For nearly two weeks, friends at *Time-Life* kept me informed by telephone from their daily cables; Page was transferred to a hospital in Japan and they said that he would probably live. He was moved to Walter Reed Army Hospital (a civilian and a British subject, it took some doing), and they said that he would live, but that he'd always be paralyzed on his left side. I called him there, and he sounded all right, telling me that his roommate was this very religious colonel who kept apologizing to Page because he was only in for a checkup, he hadn't been wounded or anything fantastic like that. Page was afraid that he was freaking the colonel out a little bit. Then they moved him to the Institute of Rehabilitation Medicine in New York, and while none of them could really explain it medically, it seemed that he was regaining the use of his left arm and leg. The first time I went to see him I walked right past his bed without recognizing him out of the four patients in the room, even though he'd been the first one I'd seen, even though the other three were men in their forties and fifties. He lay there grinning his deranged, uneven grin, his eyes were wet, and he raised his right hand for a second to jab at me with his finger. His head was shaved and sort of lidded now across the forehead where they'd opened it up ("What did they find in there, Page?" I asked him. "Did they find that quiche lorraine?"), and caved in on the right side where they'd removed some bone. He was emaciated and he looked really old, but he was still grinning very proudly as I approached the bed as if to say, "Well, didn't Page step into it this time?" as though two inches of shrapnel in your brain was the wiggiest goof of them all, that wonderful moment of The Tim Page Story where our boy comes leering, lurching back from death, twin brother to his own ghost.

That was that, he said, fini Vietnam, there could be no more odds left, he'd been warned. Sure he was crazy, but he wasn't *that* crazy. He had a bird now, a wonderful English girl named Linda Webb whom he'd met in Saigon. She'd stayed with him in the Long Binh hospital even though the shock and fear of seeing him like that had made her pass out fifteen times on the first evening. "I'd really be a fool, now, to just give that one up, now wouldn't I?" he said, and we all said, Yes, man, you would be.

On his twenty-fifth birthday there was a big party in the apartment that he and Linda had found near the hospital. Page wanted all of the people to be there who, he said, had bet him years ago in Saigon that he'd never make it past twenty-three. He wore a blue sweat suit with a Mike patch, black skull and bones, on his sleeve. You could have gotten stoned just by walking into the room that day, and Tim was so happy to be here and alive and among friends that even the strangers who turned up then were touched by it. "There's Evil afoot," he kept saying, laughing and chasing after people in his wheelchair. "Do no Evil, think ye no Evil, smoke no Evil. . . . Yesh."

A month went by and he made fantastic progress, giving up the chair for a cane and wearing a brace to support his left arm.

"I've a splendid new trick for the doctors," he said one day, flinging his left arm out of the brace and up over his head with great effort, waving his hand a little. Sometimes he'd stand in front of a full-length mirror in the apartment and survey the wreckage, laughing until tears came, shaking his head and saying, "Ohhhhh, f - - -! I mean, just *look* at that, will you? Page is a f - - - ing hemiplegic," raising his cane and stumbling back to his chair, collapsing in laughter again.

He fixed up an altar with all of his Buddhas, arranging prayer candles in a belt of empty 50-caliber cartridges, flanked by seasoned Vietnamese opium pipes. He put in a stereo, played at organizing his slides into trays, spoke of setting out Claymores at night to keep "undesirables" away, built model airplanes ("Very good therapy, that."), hung toy choppers from the ceiling, put up posters of Frank Zappa and the Cream and some Day-Glo posters which Linda had made from slides of his photographs of monks and tanks and solid soul brothers smoking joints in the fields of Vietnam. He began talking more and more about the war, often coming close to tears when he remembered how happy all of us had been there.

One day a letter came from a British publisher, asking him to do a book whose working title would be "Through With War," and whose purpose would be to once and for all "take the glamour out of war." Page couldn't get over it.

"Take the glamour out of war! I mean, how the bloody hell can you do *that*? Go take the glamour out of a Huey, take the glamour out of a Sheridan . . . can you take the glamour out of a Cobra or getting stoned at China Beach? It's like taking the glamour out of an M-79, taking the glamour out of Flynn." He pointed to a picture he'd taken. Flynn laughing maniacally, secretly ("We're winning," he'd said.), triumphantly, "Nothing the matter with *that* boy, is there? Would you let your daughter marry that man? Ohhhh, war is *good*

for you, you can't take the glamour out of that. It's like trying to
take the glamour out of sex, trying to take the glamour out of The
Rolling Stones." He was really speechless, working his hands up and
down to emphasize the sheer insanity of it.

"I mean, you *know* that, it just *can't be done!*" We both shrugged
and laughed, and Page looked very thoughtful for a moment. "The
very *idea!*" he said. "Ohhh, what a laugh! Take the bloody *glamour*
out of bloody *war!*"

STUDY QUESTIONS

1. What effect have the media had on the war in Vietnam?
2. Does it seem that the real story gets told by the journalists?
3. Are the journalists generally honest, thorough, and well-meaning
   in their efforts to get the news?
4. How reliable is the official information that gets handed out to
   journalists by authorities such as J.U.S.P.A.O.?
5. How is Herr's assignment different from that of most other
   journalists?
6. What kind of attitude do the Marines have toward the correspondents?
7. Do the correspondents take any more or any less of a chance of
   being killed than the Marines do?
8. What seems to be the normal Marine response to brutality and
   massacres?
9. When the Vietnamese are mentioned, how are they treated? Is
   there a prevailing attitude toward them?
10. Is there much of a concern among the correspondents for end-
    ing the war?

SUGGESTIONS FOR WRITING

1. Herr pretends to be writing a movie during most of this essay.
   Why? What is the implication? How effectively does this framework convey the aura of things as they are in Vietnam?
2. In a brief essay, describe what you think are the standard attitudes
   toward U. S. Army and Marine personnel on the part of the correspondents. How does Herr's own attitude differ from the
   "norm"? Use as many details as possible from the essay and its
   portraits of other correspondents.

3. Does this picture of Vietnam differ dramatically from the picture we get from standard news reports? What helps create such differences? Describe the differences, characterize them, and suggest how Herr's writing helps him make effective use of them.
4. Construct an argument that defends or attacks the entire concept of having journalists accompany military expeditions in time of war. Is it likely, for example, that journalists crossed the Alps with Hannibal?
5. Herr says that Mayor Yorty and the Mayor of Saigon had a meeting in Saigon to celebrate their being mayors of sister cities. He suggests that this meeting would never have taken place if there had been no newspapers or TV. Do you think he may also be subtly suggesting that there would have been no war if there had been no mass media? Use information from the essay to back up your view.
6. How do you react to the story about Tim Page? What do you think Herr means to convey by highlighting it so fully? Is there a sense in which Page is more typical of correspondents than he at first seems?
7. Write a brief description of what you imagine a day in the life of a correspondent's wife is like in Vietnam. Use as many details from the article as you can.
8. From the information provided in this article, prepare a brief essay that would be helpful in orienting new correspondents in Vietnam. What do they need to know in order to stay alive and to do their jobs well?

BLACK POWER/WHITE POWER

James A. Linen

James A. Linen, the president of the National Urban League, delivered this speech before a group in Washington. It was at a time when student demonstrations and minority-group protests were widespread in America. But Linen does not focus on those developments. He speaks instead about the forces of Middle America, the America that is silent.

Before we can rebuild or reshape our society—or even make a meaningful contribution to that process—we must arrest the malevolent forces that are tearing it apart.

The dominant trend in our country today is not the youth revolution, or the black revolution, or the revolution of rising expectations. It is the counter-revolution of a political majority in this country that has *also* become afraid, unhappy and frustrated.

In recent years, this group has seen its authority and stability challenged. It has reacted by exercising the balance of political power it holds. Tom Bradley has gone down to defeat in Los Angeles; so has a sensible high school reform plan in Denver; so even a brand-new open-housing law in a little, all-white town on Long Island. And, inevitably, those who brought about these events will have a substantial impact on the future.

The so-called backlash tends to express itself through existing institutions. An equally somber threat lurks outside those institutions. There is a vast difference between power justly acquired and used with reason, and the crude, jackboot power that is being ·flaunted throughout our country today. Some—but surely not all—of what is going on in our university administration buildings—in our churches

BLACK POWER/WHITE POWER   Reprinted from the October 1969 issue of *Journal of the American Association of University Women* by permission of *Journal of the American Association of University Women*.

—in the heart of the cities and their suburbs as well—holds very grave danger for our cherished freedoms.

As these destructive forces rage around us, black people have redefined their goals. The gains won by black people during the early civil rights revolution were never enough. Black Americans now insist not only on a seat at the lunch counter, not only on equal *opportunity*. They insist on equal results—fair distribution of successes and failures between majority and minority. If this sort of justice is achieved, it will compel the majority to share the power it wields. I'd like to speak about these sorts of black *and* white power.

The ghetto is a special culture whose values and beliefs have been severely distorted by oppression. It is also an enormous reservoir of talent. Today's challenge is to help liberate the ghetto—to harness its vast energies to constructive ends. It is to enable the highly creative millions of black people to use their wits not on anti-social purposes —not even as social workers treating individual cases—but as dynamic builders of a new institutional order. As a nation, we have no more urgent need.

However, the times compel us to make very careful distinctions about what *kind* of black power we are talking about. It takes deep courage to stand up forthrightly against those whose goal, in the name of a popular cause, is to destroy. But the difficulty of the task makes it no less imperative. It has never been more important to build the power of the black communities. And it has never been more important to challenge those who usurp that power and use it recklessly.

In the present climate of violence, polarization, and separatism, the great weight of this crucial task falls on those who are black. Black people no longer want—or need—white people looking over their shoulders every step of the way. And generally, it is no more desirable than it is easy for whites to try to crash their way into the black world where black people are usually able to do the job far better themselves.

If those of us who are white really want to help—if we really want things to change—then the best place for us to make our personal stands is in the heart of the *white* community.

A small part of the backlash has been brought about by those who are genuine racists. A greater part has been a result of fear or selfishness. But the greatest contributor of all has been the *lack* of positive action on the part of millions of white *moderates*.

These are the middle of the road Americans who harbor in their souls a deep sense of justice. Potentially, they have the influence to move the nation. But they have not yet spoken.

Our job in the white community is to bring the masses of these moderates to the fore—to create conditions in which they will re-articulate—and act upon—what they basically believe.

"The middle of the road American is like a preoccupied king," wrote John Gardner. "He doesn't react readily, but once aroused he rules the nation."

Moderate white Americans must be convinced that the problems we are struggling to overcome today are *national* problems with an urgent priority and a reasonable price tag—and that they, too, will immeasurably benefit from solutions.

Social reform is not achieved by legislative or legal decree. It comes from within the minds of men, and only then from within the minds of men who can find a reason for that reform in terms of God, country, family, and personal well-being.

One way to help uncommitted white citizens find those reasons is to design strategies that have broad appeal—to structure reform programs so that they can gather support from the widest possible constituency.

As we work to replace our repressive and burdensome welfare system with a more enlightened program, for instance, we are wise to advocate measures that provide for *all* families with special needs. It would be far easier to get a general family allowance measure through Congress than to urge enactment of a bill providing help *only* for poor households headed by females.

Aid to education programs can equally benefit black children and white children.

When it comes to open housing, we could bring forward programs that make it highly attractive for suburban communities to include significant members of minority residents. Incentives in health, education and housing itself could prove powerful.

If publicly-supported housing is designated to fit the needs of the middle class, it can then be made available to poor people by means of rent supplements or other subsidies.

If ways can be found to make police function more efficiently and less repressively in the black community, then the police can also render better service in the white community.

As we bring forward these sorts of programs, we must also correct the basic misunderstanding and downright untruths that flaw the thinking of many of those who influence the decisions.

We must sharply remind them that a major number of poor people are *white* people; that 77 percent of all poor family heads are making honest efforts to *earn* a living by working full or part time; that black and white crimes are no different, that, by any objective standard, our "war" on black *and* white poverty has so far only been a little skirmish.

We must advance the cause of Black America, and at the same time defuse the race issue and all of its tense overtones. *Time*'s Senior Correspondent John Steele points out that "Surely the problems of poverty and ghetto living are susceptible to solutions outside of purely racial terms, with all those terms imply in racism, anxieties, frustrations, separatism and violence. Our problems, though they keenly involve issues of race, transcend even race itself. A hungry baby is a hungry baby—black or white. A slum dweller is just that. An unemployed man is a man barren of hope—be he black or white. This is the somber truth which we must tell to all our people."

This is the truth that we whites can best bring home to our own community. If there is to be progress there must be black pressure and black militancy, community organization and community action. Only that sort of pressure forces us to *begin* questioning our old hypocrisies. But, just as whites can no longer fully function within the black community, black efforts to *persuade* whites are often misconstrued as threats. Unless those of us who are committed *and* white are willing to organize the white community *ourselves* and help change its values, then the necessary agitation of black people will largely remain politically ineffective.

Let us not underestimate the difficulty of this job. To be coldly realistic about where we stand, it is not only to advocate a major shift in national priorities, not only to apply pressures designed to bring about the shift. It is to make such a shift feasible. There is no hope for that shift unless it is preceded by continuing changes in the beliefs and emotions of our voters and politicians.

I have said much that is depressing. I have tried not to minimize the obstacles that we must overcome. But fortunately, around the country, amidst the backsliding and procrastination that have become all too familiar, I see the faint outlines of a new and constructive power; I see groups that once shunned their responsibilities now beginning to shoulder them.

We have the power to draft and execute a new social contract for this country—a charter whereby black people will resolve to "build, baby, build," and white people will resolve to make some real sacrifices—sacrifices beyond the point where it begins to hurt—for the sake of a stronger and reunified America.

The forces trying to pull us apart are strong. But if we can marshal the resources at our disposal—and we must—I have no doubt that we can win.

STUDY QUESTIONS

1. What are the "malevolent forces" Linen feels are tearing apart our society?
2. What does Linen mean when he says it is not the revolution of the minorities, but the counter-revolution of the majority that is the dominant trend of our times?
3. How does backlash express itself?
4. What does it mean to insist not just on equal opportunity, but on equal results?
5. What role could white moderates play in changing our social order?
6. Where does social reform really come from, according to Linen?
7. How can middle-income housing be made available to the poor?
8. What is the racial issue in American poverty? Does Linen emphasize it?
9. Why is Linen optimistic at his closing?

SUGGESTIONS FOR WRITING

1. What kind of an audience do you think first heard this speech? Being as detailed as possible, and relying on clues in the speech itself, describe the people in Linen's audience. Try to determine their social status, age group, and sense of commitment to the movement to achieve racial equality.
2. Are there indications that a racial backlash actually exists in America today? Is it evident in your own community or state? Using your experience and your reading, cite instances of backlash which might help us gain a better understanding of the way it really works.
3. Assume that you are an editor of an "underground" newspaper and write a critical review of Linen's speech. Take a clear stand

on the contents of the speech and its effects. Is it adequate for the situation? Is it helpful in pinpointing what needs to be done? Would it satisfy a black militant? Be sure to be specific in relating the details of the speech to your judgments.
4. Describe what you think are Linen's real feelings toward Middle Americans, those who are in the vast majority in the country. Who does he say they are? What are they like? What are their views?
5. Why does Linen title the speech in the manner that he does? What is the significance of talking about both black and white power instead of talking only about one or the other? Is the significance warranted, do you think, by the circumstances?

BLACK PANTHER KILLINGS IN CHICAGO

Christopher Chandler

For many black people, the killing of Fred Hampton was
an act of war. Even some whites who do not sympathize
with Black Panther politics question the official account
of Hampton's death. Was it a police action, or was it
simply murder?

It was 4:44 A.M. on the morning of December 4. The block
on Chicago's West Side was cordoned off. Police stood guard on rooftops. State's Attorney's police were stationed at the front and rear of
the first floor apartment, armed with a submachine gun and shotguns.

There was a knock on the front door, and then the sound of more
than 200 shots echoed through the early morning hour. When it was
over, Fred Hampton, chairman of the Illinois Black Panther Party,
was dead in bed. Mark Clark, a Panther member from Peoria, Ill.,
was dead behind the front door. Four others were critically wounded,
and three were arrested unharmed. One policeman was slightly
wounded.

State's Attorney Edward V. Hanrahan held a press conference later
that day, displaying what he said was the arms cache recovered from
the apartment (each bullet carefully placed on its end) and pronounced to the television cameras: "We wholeheartedly commend
the police officers for their bravery, their remarkable restraint and
their discipline in the face of this Black Panther attack—as should
every decent citizen in our community." He stressed the word "decent."

Under normal circumstances, that would have been the end of it.
Hanrahan, the key figure in Mayor Daley's 1968 election strategy, the
man named to run the city's "war on gangs" last June, would ordinar-

BLACK PANTHER KILLINGS IN CHICAGO   From the January 10, 1970 issue of
The New Republic. Reprinted by permission of *The New Republic*, © 1970
Harrison-Blaine of New Jersey, Inc.

ily have enhanced his reputation as a tough crime fighter and as the most popular Democratic vote-getter.

But these are not normal times. The story did not end with that press conference, but grew into an international scandal. The glare of publicity that focused on every aspect of that eight-minute raid illuminated the workings of Chicago's law enforcement machinery and we glimpsed momentarily, as by a flash of lightning, the face of repression.

The story would not die, in part because of the stark imagery of the early morning raid by heavily armed police. "For those of us alive in the late '30s," said Professor Hans Mittick of the University of Chicago, "this brought back one of those nightmare images—the knock on the door at night, the Jews intimidated and dragged away."

It would not die because the Black Panther Party opened up the apartment at 2337 W. Monroe Street for the world to see, and the evidence was inescapable: police had massed a heavy concentration of machine-gun and shotgun fire at one living room wall and into two bedrooms. There was little if any sign of return fire.

It would not die because Hanrahan, distressed by what he said were the "outrageous" and "slanderous" statements made to the press, decided to try his case in the *Chicago Tribune*. But evidence provided to substantiate his account of the raid turned out to be fraudulent, and the competing newspapers jumped at the chance to recover some honor by exposing the fraud. A picture purporting to show bullet holes where the Panthers shot at police in the kitchen turned out to be a picture of nail holes, and the bullet-ridden "bathroom" door turned out to be the inside of the bedroom door.

It would not die because the coroner's office misrepresented Hampton's fatal wounds, because Hanrahan would not permit the FBI to interrogate his men in private. It developed that the FBI was involved, having been wiretapping and tailing the Panthers, and that the Justice Department itself had set up a special task force on the Black Panthers last August, a task force aimed at countering the threat to national security.

Events had shaken the country's trust in the social order. Calls for a thorough and impartial investigation intensified to the point that there are now some eight bodies planning such a probe. But there is little prospect that findings of the investigations will convince any large spectrum of the population.

The Panther Party would not have it otherwise. They are not interested in the findings of a "blue ribbon committee" or a "grand jury investigation" designed, in the words of one newspaper editorial, to "restore confidence" in government, or, in the words of Attorney General John Mitchell, to "put an end to rumors and speculation that surrounded this incident." The Panthers' belief is that to restore confidence and end speculation is to mask the exposed face of a growing fascism. Last month's Chicago raid has given the party widespread new support for its viewpoint.

Fred Hampton said last June: "I just went to a wake where a young man had been shot in the head by a pig. And you know this is bad. But it heightens the contradictions in the community. These things a lot of times organize the people better than we can organize ourselves."

All of the investigations of the raid will be forced to sift through a mass of conflicting testimony. The police version, reenacted for CBS television in a special 28-minute program directed by the State's Attorney's office, must be rejected on the basis of the available evidence. One policeman in the reenactment, for example, describes three shots being fired at him as he enters the kitchen door, the film having been taped before those three bullet holes had been shown to be nail holes.

The Panther version may never come to light in its entirety. Defense attorneys for the seven surviving Panthers (charged with attempted murder) plan to retain their best evidence until the trial, and they may be in a powerful bargaining position to have the charges dropped. Panther officers have generally confined themselves to characterizing the raid as a "political assassination" and denying that any Panthers fired at police.

The hard physical evidence is sparse, but heavily weighted toward the worst possible construction of the raid.

There are two bullet holes in the front door leading from a small anteroom into the living room. One is about heart high, and was fired through the door from the outside while the door was slightly ajar. This shot probably killed Mark Clark, whose body was found in a pool of blood behind the door. A second hole in the door, about a foot and a half below the first, may have been made by a shotgun blast from the inside of the apartment into a far corner of the anteroom near the ceiling. The crazy angle of the blast suggests that Clark's gun may have gone off as he fell.

The right-hand side of the living room wall is covered with 42 closely stitched bullet holes, mainly from a machine gun. The shots were fired from the doorway and from the center of the living room, the shots from the center of the room penetrating the walls of two adjacent bedrooms.

The back door was forced from the outside. Two rear windows, in the kitchen and in Hampton's rear bedroom, were broken in from the outside. There is no sign of gunfire in the rear of the house except for the bedrooms, which are punctured with bullet holes. Standing in the entranceway between the kitchen and the dining room, you can see that four shotgun blasts were fired from that area, three into Hampton's bedroom and one, penetrating two closets, lodging in the far wall of the middle bedroom.

Hampton was shot from above while lying in bed. According to an independent autopsy conducted by the former chief pathologist for the County Coroner's office and witnessed by three physicians, two bullets entered Hampton's head from the right and from above, at a 45 degree angle.

Whatever happened in that apartment on the morning of December 4, it could not possibly have been the 20-minute "gun battle" that the police and the State's Attorney's office have described again and again. Clearly the State's Attorney's police went to the apartment heavily armed to do more than serve a search warrant for unauthorized and unregistered guns (a minor offense). But why now? Why the Panthers?

The answer furnished by many columnists and commentators— that the Panthers were an unpopular, probably dangerous group, and therefore the authorities may have overstepped the bounds of propriety in curbing their activities—does not hold up.

The Panthers were and are a popular, successful group, and it is precisely because of that success that they have become the targets of a nationwide governmental campaign of control. This fact presents us with a far more serious issue of national policy. Theoretically we believe that any organization (and particularly any political organization) is entitled to win as much popular support as its platform and leadership permit. Surely this is the democratic way. But we make exceptions to that rule, particularly during periodic "red scares." Then, any group associated with an "international Communist conspiracy" or, in the words of the *Chicago Tribune*, a "criminal conspiracy" are denied that basic right.

So, with the rapid spread of Black Panther Party chapters across the country in the past two years, and with the intellectual leadership that has made the Panther Party the ideological leader of most of the white radical left, and with the surprising organizational strength in cities from Hartford, Connecticut, to Peoria, Illinois, came increased governmental attention.

When Mitchell took office last January, *The New York Times* relates, he officially labeled the Black Panther Party a subversive threat to the national security—thereby authorizing the FBI to tap Panther phones and bug Panther offices. In July, J. Edgar Hoover gave the Panther Party the distinction of being "the greatest threat to the internal security of the country" among black militant groups. In August, the Justice Department took the extraordinary step of setting up a special task force on the Panthers, made up of representatives from its civil rights, internal security and criminal divisions.

The situation was similar at the local level. The Illinois chapter of the Black Panther Party was founded in November of 1968 by Hampton and by Bobby Rush, the current chairman. Six months later, the Panthers had become the strongest organization in Chicago's black community. Its influence extended beyond the ghetto to alliances with a variety of groups including the national office of the Students for a Democratic Society, an Appalachian white youth gang called the Young Patriots and a Puerto Rican gang called the Young Lords.

The Panthers were respected because they spoke of carrying arms for self-defense (although they never publicly bore arms in the city), because they had a coherent socialist ideology and because they had a genius for organizing and administration. In the March special aldermanic election they aided an independent candidate by stationing members outside of precincts where there were complaints of vote fraud. The candidate almost forced a runoff in one of the Democratic Party strongholds. In April, a party spokesman lambasted 5000 peace marchers for not checking with the Panthers before conducting the march, and the march's leadership admitted its error. In May, they concluded an agreement with the Black P Stone Nation, Chicago's most powerful teen gang, after having converted its traditional rivals, the East Side Disciples, to full Panther membership.

Days later, Mayor Daley announced that the city was launching a "war on gangs," which would be headed by State's Attorney Hanrahan. Hanrahan listed the Panthers as prime targets in his campaign, and talked about soaring gang violence (although a study conducted by the *Chicago Journalism Review* revealed that gang-related youth crime had actually declined during the year).

Fred Hampton soon had 25 criminal charges filed against him, but only one conviction—the somewhat strange case of assault in connection with the robbery of $71 worth of ice cream. (Hampton commented: "I may be a big dude, but I can't eat no $71 worth of ice cream.")

Despite the constant arrests and the repeated raids on their headquarters the Black Panther Party continued to grow in strength. Favorable articles about the party's free breakfast program for schoolchildren were carried in three of the city's five daily newspapers, embarrassing city officials into launching their own, hopelessly bureaucratic free breakfast program. Plans were announced, funds raised and equipment procured for a free medical clinic, to be opened on the West Side. By October, Chicago newspapers did not find it unusual to quote Hampton's reaction to the "Weatherman" demonstration scheduled for downtown Chicago: he denounced them as "anarchistic" and "Custeristic."

On November 4, the Black Panther Party, somewhat weakened by arrests and raids, was still the most powerful single independent organization in the city. Its program of putting socialism into practice had attracted wide support. Its policy of analyzing problems by reference to economic class, not race, was working to depolarize whites and blacks during demonstrations, and erroneous descriptions of the members as "racists" or "black power militants" in the local press were beginning to be corrected.

The Black Panthers made the federal subversive list, they became a prime target for Chicago officialdom because of their success. I don't suggest that Mayor Daley cynically set out to destroy the party because it might bring success to his enemies at the polls—or that the Justice Department set out to crush the party nationally because it wanted to protect the country's big businesses against socialism.

Mitchell and Hoover see the Panthers as an arm of an International Communist conspiracy (has not Panther information minister Eldridge Cleaver visited Cuba and Algeria while in exile—even lavishing his highest praise on the North Korean government?).

Mayor Daley views the Panthers as much of the rest of the population views them—as "Communists"; and worse still, young black Communists who carry arms. (The Panthers are not reticent to express their views: they will explain patiently at a press conference that their political ideology is based on Marx and Lenin, and that they look to other revolutionary leaders, including Mao Tse-tung, for examples of how to translate ideology into political power.)

Policemen all over the country see the Panthers as their explicit enemies. The Panthers called the police "pigs," and even talk of killing pigs. (To the Panthers, "pig" means most importantly the "pig power structure," and secondarily the "pig police" who enforce the will of that power structure on the country's black colonies.)

There is a "conspiracy" to get the Panthers, and it is a conspiracy tied together by the mutual convictions of policemen, local government and federal government. It is a conspiracy that puts the country's professed ideals to a hard test. Are we prepared to allow revolutionary Marxists-Leninists to campaign for public support and public office? Theoretically we are. Theoretically (at least according to a June 9 Supreme Court decision) we also cannot convict someone for merely advocating the moral propriety or necessity of using violence to overthrow the government.

But in practice we are not prepared to view the Black Panthers as a political party. One might argue that the Panthers should disarm if they are serious about politics and about only using their weapons for self-defense. The bearing of arms may be a fetish carried over from the formation of the party in Oakland in 1966, when it was called the "Black Panther Party for Self Defense," and when its primary goal was to defend blacks from police harassment. Undoubtedly, the very existence of arms does much to provoke the police. But there are problems with this argument: there is nothing illegal about carrying arms; that right is protected by the US Constitution. Twenty Panthers have died in gun battles with police around the country (although police have died also—two in Chicago just two weeks before the raid). The Hampton killing itself raises the grim possibility that the Panthers, even today in Chicago, *do* need guns for self-defense.

The State's Attorney's raid suggested another disturbing view— that this country is moving steadily toward the extreme political right. The proposed investigations of the raid provide an example of the extent of that shift. The FBI investigating? But the FBI has been involved in nationwide raids against the Panthers. The Justice Department? Attorney General Mitchell's approach to law enforcement is not reassuring.

The main investigation is to be conducted by a special US District Court grand jury in Chicago. A seven-man racially integrated team of federal investigators, headed by Assistant Attorney General Jerris Leonard, will present the evidence to the jury. Leonard, head of the civil rights division, last May explained to Jay Miller, the executive director of Illinois American Civil Liberties Union, why Bobby Seale had been included among the Chicago Conspiracy trial defendants. "The Panthers are a bunch of hoodlums," he said. "We've got to get them."

STUDY QUESTIONS

1. What kind of "attack" did the Panthers conduct?
2. Who is Edward Hanrahan, and what is his political significance?
3. An allusion is made here to the Jews in Germany in the 1930s. Why is it made? Is it warranted?
4. Why did the Panthers open the apartment to public investigation?
5. What weakened Hanrahan's argument in the press?
6. What purposes do the many investigation teams serve?
7. Why has the federal government taken an interest in the Panther Party?
8. What kind of political influence have the Panthers been in Chicago?
9. Does their open affiliation with Communism seem to be the most important factor in the government's distaste for the Panthers?
10. What arguments do the Panthers have for carrying firearms?

SUGGESTIONS FOR WRITING

1. Is this article clearly biased or slanted in its presentation of this case? Decide yes or no, then firmly establish your own argument based on your analysis of Chandler's interpretation of the details. Be sure to quote relevant phrases as part of your argument.
2. What kind of attitude should the government, and particularly the police, take toward the Panthers? If the Panthers continue to carry weapons and to assume a posture of self-defense, what should municipal governments do? What are the rights of the Panthers? What are the rights of the government?
3. After reading this article, what do you think happened in Chicago that night? Describe the events and the motives that might have determined the events. Do you think Chandler forces you to accept one view rather than another? How well do you feel you understand the situation?
4. One of the strongest arguments for attacking the Panthers relates to the fact that they are avowedly responsive to Communist ideas. Should the government tolerate the actions of organizations that are receptive to Communism, or should it crack down on them and stop their activity? Take a stand on this issue and be detailed in your arguments.

5. If the general suggestion of this article—which is that the government is cracking down heavily on unpopular organizations—were proven to be true, would you feel comfortable or uncomfortable in America? Discuss your own circumstances in relation to this article. What does the killing of Fred Hampton have to do with your rights as a citizen and with the living of your life?

6. The Democratic party has now "disowned" Hanrahan, formerly its biggest vote-getter in Chicago. Do you think it was right in doing so? If you were an official of the Democratic party, what kind of statement would you release to the press?

A BLACK VALUE SYSTEM

Imamu Amiri Baraka (LeRoi Jones)

One of the most distinguished American playwrights has dedicated himself to working for the unification of the black race in America. In Newark, his home town, he has begun to promote the teachings of an organization called US. Its principles form a value system that may have meaning both for blacks and for whites.

Umoja (Unity)——To strive for and maintain unity in the family, community, nation and race.

Kujichagulia (Self-Determination)——To define ourselves, name ourselves, and speak for ourselves, instead of being defined, and spoken for by others.

Ujima (Collective Work and Responsibility)——To build and maintain our community together and to make our brothers' and sisters' problems our problems and to solve them together.

Ujamaa (Co-operative Economics)——To build and maintain our own stores, shops and other businesses and to profit together from them.

Nia (Purpose)——To make as our collective vocation the building and developing of our community in order to restore our people to their traditional greatness.

Kuumba (Creativity)——To do always as much as we can, in the way we can in order to leave our community more beautiful and beneficial than when we inherited it.

Imani (Faith)——To believe with all our heart in our parents, our teachers, our leaders, our people and the righteousness and victory of our struggle.

The 7 principles are 7 because the number is a meaning-symbol for this world. As a throw of dice it speaks of spiritual concepts and scien-

A BLACK VALUE SYSTEM   Reprinted from the November 1969 issue of *The Black Scholar* by permission of *The Black Scholar*.

tific principles. It is because of this that the seventh day was the cul-
mination, as a period of devotion and meditation, for the 6 days of
divine work, Sun-Day. So Maulana speaks of spiritual concepts and
scientific principles embodied as a morality system—complete in itself, as a contemporary black philosophy old as the sun.

The 7 principles are the spine and total philosophy of the US organization. They are simple in what they say, but total in that they
evoke all the levels of meaning associated with philosophical systems.
The 7 principles are "10 commandments" yet more profound to
us—US because they are pre and post 10 commandments at the same
time. If there is *Umoja*, for instance, thou cannot kill, steal, bear false
witness, commit adultery, or any of the things the western world
thrives on. The commandments are fulfilled by the initial need of
blackness for unity—oneness.

But unity is political too. The meaning vibrates as a totality.
Spiritual unity is the needed completion of physical and mental unity.
(The doctrine is made up of the 3 sides of the ancient pyramid—
physical, mental and spiritual—in each of its statements. The three
pyramids of the US symbol meaning "our traditional greatness," and
by this, our traditional understanding.) The 7 principles are solutions
to the political dilemma of Black people. I would say solutions to
the political dilemma of all men, but I recognize we are different by
virtue of our concerns and the context of our lives.

We, the different peoples, are as different rays of light, each bent
to particular articulation of the initial life force, and at different
stages of evolution (self-consciousness). All men would benefit by
the 7 principles. But the black man has created them out of his *specific* need. The balancer of East and West, completer of this cycle.

Umoja (definition: To strive for and maintain unity in the family,
community, nation and race). We are a *body* of people, the large
Being of Blackness. The many of us are parts of the body. The whole
cannot function *as it will* (*Kujichagulia*—Self-Determination) if it
is scattered, the head one place, the heart another. Physical unity.
Mental unity. We must think one way of total movement to liberate
ourselves. Each has a function but as complementary parts of a whole.
All organizations, *organs* really, they must function as of the whole
body.

Ujima—Collective Work and Responsibility. All of the organs
must function by the same will. We must have a head with control
over all the organs. The I's must be our many eyes and be a basis for
seeing in all the places.

One being in harmony with itself, this is the first need to be satis-

fied before we can deal with an outside world. But it is internal unity
that makes a single will, which is self determination. What we will
be what we will do, are questions only we ourselves have the proper
answers to.

The concept of *oneness* is old and black and spiritual. The One
God. And the 7 principles are a religious creed, in its most practical
application, a code of common morality.

We need a value system to be predictable in our behavior, Maulana
has said. Predictable, meaning stable, pointed toward a single goal.
The liberation of our soul, mind and body. A value system is the spine
of all cultures. What is good or bad aside from specific interpretation
in specific context? Through unity, we arrive at self-determination and
can then proceed to collective work and responsibility (in the organs,
or as each one teach one, or painting a wall), *Ujima*. The value system selects the goal we apply ourselves to it, live by it, the rest follows.
Why Moses gave the commandments for the same result, as a best
way to live. And they will *raise* us.

So that Maulana Karenga's doctrine is first a value system. It sets
forth a value system, to be followed, called Kawaida, literally ("that
which is customary, or traditionally adhered to, by black people"). A
nation is only as great as that set of values it *actually* practices . . .
no matter what it says, e.g., witness America (white and negro). The
value system is how you live, to what end. And Kawaida is, as the doctrine teaches, "a weapon, a shield, and a pillow of peace."

One cannot have a slave's mentality and hope to be free, or one
can hope, but that will not make anything really happen. The freeing
of the mind, before anything else can happen. The people *must
actually want* to be free. Want it bad enough to be it.

A value system that is itself the way of life of a free man of high
morality, is what the Kawaida teaches. A morality (more) is *the
meaning* of what people do. Culture is how they live, morality is
what it means. What it means as cause and effect, past what you or
anyone else might *think*. What happens as a result of . . . is what
morality directs. And there is a finality to this path-making that is
part of the heaviest truth. To live better, you must live better. It is
simple and complex.

Kawaida, or the doctrine of Maulana Karenga, is the measure of
that "better" life. It is African, because we are African, no matter
that we have been trapped in the West these few hundred years. But
by the quality of what our lives *meant* we have transformed the West,
even transformed the white man. The value system, especially as the
Nguzo Saba begins to focus it, can give us the identity, purpose and

direction to move to that better life. At each level it is a contrast to Euro-American *morality*, because first it is based on teachings that are superior to the practiced morality of Euro-American civilization. It is also a value system beneficial to black people. And there is no reason for the practiced value system of Euro-America to be beneficial to black people, quite the contrary, it has always been absolutely detrimental to black people. For instance the fourth principle of the Nguzo Saba is Ujamaa, collective or cooperative economics.

But Ujamaa is not, as it has been called, "African Socialism," it is Ujamaa. If anything you could say European Ujamaa, but never the reverse. The reason? Ujamaa is the traditional way of distributing wealth for the black man. It is an economic attitude older than Europe, and certainly older than the term Socialism. Which finally is another thing, coming from the European definition, since the European definition is a state that will exist "after the decay of capitalism." Ujamaa has always been the African *attitude* towards the distribution of wealth (until they decay that made our kingdoms fall). It has never been a European attitude, but rather a *theory*. Can you dig it? (See Julius Nyerere's paper *Ujamaa* in *Uhuru na Umoja*.)

The "decay of capitalism" theory is also another aspect of the European attitude of "world revolution," and do not mistake my meaning, I am talking about the life style of violence. Vita (violence or war) in Swahili equals *life* in Latin. When we say "revolution" we mean the restoration of our national sovereignty as a people, a people, at this point, equipped to set new paths for the development of man. We mean the freeing of ourselves from the bondage of another, alien, people. We are not warring upon our own society among ourselves. These pigs are no kin to us. We are trying to destroy a *foreign oppressor*. It is not "revolution" but *National Liberation*.

When you speak of capitalism you speak of the European mind. We do not want to be Europeans. No, not of any persuasion. Just as the, as he calls them, "economic radicals" of the twenties tried to stop J. A. Rogers, whom they called "a black capitalist," from doing his research and rewriting our destroyed archives saying Rogers was "chauvinistic" and suffered an "inferiority complex"; they said he should be studying people like "Marx, Engels, and Lafargue and be preparing for the worker's utopia which was just around the corner . . ." (See Introduction to Rogers' "World's Great Men of Color, Vol. 1.") But are not Marx, Engels, and Lafargue just another list of "great" men . . . but great white men, or at least white men thought great by one particular group of white men? Another group of white men might give you another list . . . like say Washington, Jefferson, Lincoln, Kennedy, etc. But it is, either way, still a commitment to Euro-American values, to whiteness.

In order to free ourselves, and this may come as a shock to many "hip negroes," we are going to have to do it ourselves! For ourselves. Yes, the world will benefit, but they are not going to do it, any more than you helped free the Chinese! If you cannot have faith in blackness, in the black mind and the black man to find a way out of this slavery, you are full of despair, or else emotionally committed to whi e people. Which is the terrible truth for many of us, even our so-called "revolutionaries." They are so committed to whiteness that they must find a way to make white relevant some way. The Right will not save us so the Left will. This group of white people will not do it, but this other group of white people will. (Do not misunderstand, we will take aid from a scorpion, but we must not confuse our identity. Or try to crawl under rocks, with scorpions.)

Another fallacy of many "revolutionaries" is the "right around the cornerism" that Rogers cites and Maulana Karenga always emphasizes as dangerous. There is no such thing. The work of National Liberation is hard and its resolution is to be sought but not fantasized as the result of unprepared spontaneous outbursts of emotionalism. It is work. It will only be achieved by disciplined, dedicated people, with a value system that allows them to persevere and remain healthy and rational and committed for as long as it takes no matter what happens to anybody or everybody else.

Too often so called revolutionaries without a black value system, like Kawaida, do exactly the same things as the oppressor-people, and as I said, they are always emotionally committed to the oppressor people. They speak the same language, think the same things valuable, have the same "taste." In fact they are so much the same they can make alliances that are unnatural as far as the natural life styles of the new peoples are concerned. The bush-smoking, wine drinking, homo-superhetero sexual bellbottomed life of the hippy (a truly interracial though white committed phenomenon) is just a phase of death rattle for a culture and a people. The magnetism of the final death will compel to death all those with the jingling matching magnets around their brains.

An epoch passes because it is played out. To imitate the played out is to simulate, and then not to be able to stop, death.

So *Nia*, purpose. What is your purpose, for anything? For being alive? If you are black your purpose should be the building of Black. The Nguzo Saba says our purpose must be the rebuilding of our people to their traditional greatness. One reason for the stress on history, if you do not even know of your traditional greatness, then you will not aspire to anything but dry rock white "radicalism" (like some 1930's vampire rerisen again from the grave to suck black peoples' blood) as some kind of alternative to the maggoty pork that exists. But neither is our shot, brother. Initially our purpose is *National building*. To raise black people to "our traditional greatness." National Liberation as Malcolm called it.

Karenga stresses cultural nation for the same reasons that Mao continues his cultural revolution on a continuous basis in China even after his political revolution has been realized. It is a constant process. The minds of the people are the most important factor of any movement, without them you can have nothing else. And we do not have to settle for maggoty pork or renewed draculaism (a white "radical"). We can have and be ourselves.

But you must have the cultural revolution, i.e., you must get the mind before you move another fuhtha. There is no violent revolution except as a result of the black mind expanding, trying to take control of its own space. Our armies are not yet formed, as armies. We cannot fight a war, an actual physical war with the forces of evil just because we are angry. We can begin to build. We must build black institutions. In all the different aspects of culture. Political, Religious, Social, Economic, Ethical, Creative, Historical, institutions, all based on a value system that is beneficial to black people.

All these institutions will be alternatives to the Euro-American or Negro institutions that exist, but will exist in their own right as expressions of the black sensibility, and not merely as reactions to an alien sensibility. If Mao does not control the minds of the Chinese, his political victories are lost, his military is hostile, Maoism is another name for what was. Ghana should have had a continuous cultural revolution. To maintain the consciousness of the people. So that they could not be taken off by the criminal sickness of the white led Negro mentality that re-invaded Ghana. If the chief of state of Biafra names as his country's national anthem "Finlandia," then we know where his politics are right off. The internalization of a white value system, will always militate for white decisions about the way things should be. Whether it is a national anthem or an economic system.

Black creativity, *Kuumba*, is the sixth principle. Which tells us how we must devise a way out of our predicament. How we must build, with what methodology. In what emotionalism, the fire of blackness. So that even Ujamaa is Kuumba in regards to the distribution of wealth among men. For the European, Ujamaa, like jazz, is a saying, a pretending illusion, rather than a being. And we are not racists, when we say this, we are merely recognizing the traits of different peoples.

When we call white people evil it is based on empiricism, not theory. Do you remember how you Africans got here to the Western Hemisphere in the first place? (I mean as slaves, not as Egyptians and Moorish explorers and settlers.) The recital of the horrors black people have suffered at the hands of the white makes us racists? Only to the white, or the *white committed*. Herodotus came up with the Teutonic Origins theory of why white was best and how the rest were not, on a descending xenophobic scale all the way down to us. A theory, not a fact. The lynching and oppression and enslavement of black people by European, and the capacity for such cruelty by the European mind is fact, not theory. It is empirical, we have witnessed, and lived through it, are still living through it. And just because some dude wants to sleep with a white woman, let him not call those of us who do not racists. There are facts, to which any honest man had better bear witness.

When we said, Black Art, we meant Kuumba. The spiritual characteristic of revelation through the creative. The artist is respected in Bantu philosophy because he could capture some of the divinity. Because it flowed through his fingers or out of his mouth, and because he would lend this divinity to the whole people to raise them in its image, building great nations reared in the image of righteousness. What is soul (like the one sun the sole solar force, in this system) our connection, our relation with the infinite. And it is feeling, like inner revelation, that is the connection, the force of the uncreated, which we constantly make reference to, bringing into creation. Yehh! we scream, bearing witness to the power of Kuumba.

But black creativity is what will save us—not just "artists" but all of us—after all is said and done—nothing else. An antidote to birth or mind control! The Nguzo Saba itself is one of the strongest examples of Kuumba. And each idea or act that animates our lives must be measured against the Nguzo Saba in each of its components. You must ask of each new idea or dissociation that comes to mind, what does this have to do with bringing about unity for black people, what does it contribute to black people's self-determination—does it have anything to do with Ujima, collective work and responsibility, and so on. So, for instance, a "black TV program" with a straight haired sister dancing a Martha Graham–Merce Cunningham–esque tribute to the ghetto (?) is not Kuumba—neither the dance nor the program.

A nation coming into being is a new creation. It must be willed into existence by itself. It is new—it is literally something other than what exists.

Imani is faith—Faith in your leaders, teachers, parents—but first faith in *blackness*—that it will win. Faith in Nationalism, that *we* can build *ourselves* into a conscious nation once again—that we can free ourselves, from the chain of white commitment—this is all that binds us to slavery—*the fact that we are emotionally committed to it*—to being slaves.

Imani is the supra rational aspect of Nationalism, but the aspect that we cannot survive without. We must believe past 2 + 2 or 180 vs 40 that the number we want is the one we can achieve.

Simple faith, like church people say and that's what we want— hardrock emotional faith in what we're doing. The same way your grandmamma used to weep and wring her hands believing in Jeez-us, that deep deep connection with the purest energy, this is what the Nationalist must have. Can you understand this? That we must believe past any bullshit "rationale" that we may or may not achieve based on 7 million subjective-objective variables. We must believe in Nationalism. We must believe in the justness of our struggle and the certainty of our victory. *No matter how long this might take.* There is no time. Only change.

Nationalism must be the basis for our entire lives. It must be the content and initiator of anything we do. Always, as the formulator of any act must be the need to see that act contribute to the building of a Nation. That is our purpose, Nationalism our direction. Black is our identity. The totality of these as a life focus is simple faith, even before it exists as spirituality. But that is what faith is, if it is directed toward grace—spirituality.

We say spirituality because the spiritual is the blessing of life. It is what all life points toward. Complete consciousness and Nationalism, at this point, is the definer and director of our people toward that goal of absolute, yes, absolute consciousness.

So the 7th principle, Faith, is actually at one with the 1st—to create the whole, the one (it's what Umoja means).

There is nothing anyone can do about the fact of the Nguzo Saba. It does—they do—exist. Now it is only for the studying or aspiring Nationalist to accept these principles as the clearest statement of the badly needed new value system.

It is spiritual without being religious. That is, it moves to the higher levels of human aspiration but describes no ritual dogma. The Nguzo Saba would organize the morality of the would-be Nationalist, give him a new and more relevant morality, to begin to build Blackness anew.

As long as we are committed to old ways and ideas, to paraphrase Touré, we will never move from where we are. A value system is a describer of your life on the planet, how you lived, in what manner and for what reasons, i.e., to what purpose. If you do not consciously create a new value system, one that is quite different from the rest of crazy America's—you will be exactly what crazy America is and die the way she dies.

But we want to survive. We want life. We want to build and create. We do not want a modified version of what exists, we want the totally new—newly claimed but as the eastern, the tradition, the African, the black—i.e., we want a whole different version of men's life on earth. We do not want what Marx wanted or what Abbie Hoffman wants. We want our new black selves as absolute masters of our own space. Can you dig it *space*, and I repeat it for all these simple "black" cryptohippies who believe in Malcolm solely *because he is dead—Space* is what we are fighting for. And it manifests itself as anything or everything. Institutional space, living, i.e. human space, thinking space or the actual planet-room una fahamu? Like they say, land. It is all space. CAN YOU UNDERSTAND??

But the point man is Malcolm never had a *doctrine*—we learned from him because he was straight and true but he made no doctrines, no real *organization*, and we must face this. This is *our* work now, today, to organize better than Malcolm did. Can you understand? Malcolm's teachings must now be analyzed, formalized, and a structure and program issued out of them.

Elijah had a formal teaching, something close to a doctrine and Malcolm sprung from it, but made some other decisions. But he, Malcolm, made no doctrine. But now a doctrine has been made, formalized around a black value system, and this is what we need. How you live is how you project and how you will project. Your progeny, your creations are products of life, manifestations of your way, scenes from your path. The Nguzo Saba is the key to the new Nationalism. It is the key to the new learning. And that learning is the complete doctrine of Maulana Karenga.

The Nguzo Saba is the first, the basic, primary teaching. The rest of the doctrine, covering the completeness of modern experience is a black ideology in toto. A path itself to blackness and Nationhood.

The doctrine now is in the head and hands mostly of organization people, and a few key organizers and student leaders around the country. (*The Quotable Karenga* is a light sampling of some of the doctrine's content.) But soon it will be published and available to most of us. It is the central ingredient of the new nationalist organization. It will transform black people and by doing this, transform yes, America.

You better get ready for it.

STUDY QUESTIONS

1. Are these seven principles religious in nature? How do they relate to religious values?
2. In what ways do these principles differ from the basic values of most Americans?
3. Would these principles be offensive to white Americans? Would white Americans be able to live by them?
4. In what sense are the seven principles like the Ten Commandments?
5. Why is a value system essential?
6. What is the relationship of morality to freedom?
7. Is there an economic morality implied in this value system?
8. What does Baraka mean when he says he will take aid from a scorpion? Does that conflict with his pronouncement that the black man must free himself by himself?
9. What does Baraka think of "hip-ness"?
10. What kind of faith does Baraka demand of his readers?

SUGGESTIONS FOR WRITING

1. Do you agree with Baraka that a black value system, as distinct from a white value system, is necessary for the freedom of blacks? Use information and details from the essay, but feel free to include information and experiences from your own life.
2. What would be the implications for America if Baraka insisted that these seven principles be applied to all Americans instead of only to blacks? How would the country be changed? Would whites benefit as much as blacks? Cite as much evidence as you can.
3. Baraka constantly insists he is talking about nationalism; he considers it the basis of his thinking. In a brief essay, show how nationalism is treated in his argument. How is it expressed? How is it to be realized? How important is it to his views?

4. In a brief essay suggest how Baraka's views would be received by the mass of white Americans and by black Americans. Would there be widespread disagreement between the groups? Would there be disagreement among various social classes? What are the chances that this value system will be accepted by anyone?

5. What are your reactions to this proposal? Can you accept Baraka's views, and could you actually go out and persuade others to accept them? What sort of response would you expect?

THE GENTLE REVOLUTIONARIES: BROWN POWER

Ralph Guzman

Racial problems in America are not simply a matter between blacks and whites. Many other ethnic groups are also struggling for a measure of freedom and independence. In this article the author describes the ways in which Mexican-Americans have begun to assert their rights.

Last October a group of Mexican-Americans invaded and occupied the august chambers of the Los Angeles City Board of Education. Those six days and nights of sit-in and sleep-in were a shock for the board, and even more shocking for citizens of the city of Los Angeles. Something mysterious had bitten the complacent Mexicans of the city's East Side.

On the face of it, this invasion of the highest level of Los Angeles educational bureaucracy was an angry protest. The protesters hoped to force the board to hear substantive complaints about the quality of Mexican education. There was also the matter of the reinstatement of Sal Castro, a Lincoln High School social science teacher accused of leading school walk-outs the previous spring. But the real event, the significance of which was not lost on the board, the city, or the Mexican-American community, was the first public appearance of something called Brown Power.

Who were the protesters? What is Brown Power? What is the meaning of this sudden uproar among the presumably passive 650,000 Mexicans living in Los Angeles County?

The protesters at the Board of Education were, to say the least, a very mixed company. There were at least one Catholic priest, one Episcopalian priest and several Protestant ministers. There were Mexican-American college students from UCLA and from California

THE GENTLE REVOLUTIONARIES: BROWN POWER   Reprinted from the July 1969 issue of *The Black Politician* by permission of *The Black Politician*.

State College, Los Angeles. Most were, indeed, Mexican-Americans and very few were more than 30 years of age.

The trouble at the moment—and the most important single fact about Brown Power—is that none of the October protesters can agree on exactly what Brown Power is, or on what it ought to be. Paradoxically, Brown Power is almost sure to become whatever the larger American community decides it *ought* to be.

For some of the young militants, Brown Power is a sort of life-condition shared by all Mexican-Americans. It is a feeling, a mystical sort of thing created by being Mexican in a sea of Anglos. It is being a member of *la raza* (meaning "the race" or "our people"). It is also the accumlated history of the Mexicans in the United States—of anger and clotted rage at poor education, poor jobs, and the grinding misery of thousands of Southwestern *barrios* (ghettos).

But the most important part of Brown Power is a kind of cocky aggressiveness—an angry mustache and an insolent *guerrillero* beard that carries a special message for the "racist" white Anglo-Saxon Protestant. The Brown Power Mexican is telling the Anglo that things have changed.

All of these young militants know very well what they're doing when they are compared to Black Power. They admire the aggressiveness and the sophistication of the Black Power militants.

The Brown Power equivalent of a youthful Stokely Carmichael does not yet exist. Reies Tijerina, the fiery champion of land reform in northern New Mexico, and Cesar Chavez, the Ghandian supporter of peaceful social change, are both well over 30. But there are many appeals to a spirit of brotherhood with the blacks.

La Raza Unida, an informal organization of Brown Power militants in large southwestern cities, claims that it holds no important meetings without the presence of sympathetic Negroes. But Brown Power lacks the real toughness of the Black Power men. In part this is its newness, in part the fact that while Negroes are trapped inside their skin as firmly and irrevocably "black," the Mexican-American has many more options available to him in American society.

What do the Brown Power militants want? They really don't know. Yet they do know, vaguely, that they want full equality everywhere and possibly some rectification of past wrongs.

But Mexican-American wrongs and troubles are somewhat different in different parts of the Southwest. Young militants from different cities thus have different aims for Brown Power. Some are upset about the treaties that gave Mexican land to the United States. Others are preoccupied with Mexican economic troubles, particularly the almost endless farm labor warfare in Delano (California). Others see Brown Power as an instrument of politics. Some Mexican young people, born in the city and wise to its ways, are concerned with the half-hearted efforts of the educational Establishment in keeping Mexican boys and girls in high school. They deeply resent the "custodial" manner that emphasizes attendance and discipline at the expense of learning. "They don't know how to teach and they don't believe we want to learn," an East Side student said. Some see themselves as eventually learning techniques of guerrilla warfare. Others, with no sense of incongruity, study ways of remedying troubles with policemen, antipoverty workers, school counselors and so on. This rather confusing mixture of goals merely reflects the rather confusing situation of the modern Mexican-American. Very few Mexicans dare to refuse the burdens of *la raza*. But the Brown Power techniques are still quite limited. Few people in the community are likely to join *any* Mexican protest.

This inexperience has been used against Mexican activists in the past. Anglos believed always that any Mexican civic leader, whatever his professed dedication, could be bought off. In the past, hundreds of indigenous leaders and potential revolutionaries accepted Establishment jobs and the social prestige that goes with the jobs. When militant students take administrative jobs with salaries and titles— well, to the Mexican community it sounds like another Mexican general accepting another ranch.

The goals of Brown Power may yet be confused but the Brown Power groups are not confused about their desire for action—direct action. They want confrontation and meaningful results. Nothing is more strongly rejected than the famed passivity of the Mexican-American. Nothing is more hated than the "quiet fighting" strategies of the past. Older leaders, older symbols and all the assimilationist yearnings of the past are scrapped ruthlessly. Jail is a mark of social acceptability. Brown Power will not wait for the compromises and the study committees of the past. Leaders of Brown Power are not elected. They demonstrate themselves by "performance in action." A temperate leader is almost by definition no longer fit to be a leader. The "battlefield commission" is won by direct courage against the Anglo establishment.

The meaning of Brown Power to the Mexican-American community can yet hardly be guessed. There is a new pride among many. The school walk-outs of last March merely dramatized a fact of life in East Los Angeles: The poor quality of these schools is an open scandal, even among those who teach and administer them. Thus the success of the protest pleased many people even if they will not say so publicly.

The second important consequence is almost unbearable pressure on the current generation of Mexican-American leaders. Consider, for example, the position of an administrator on a college campus who has been hired specifically to look after the special needs of Mexican-American students. As a member of the Establishment he is naturally an object of suspicion to the young militants. Yet he is supposed to represent both the militants and the larger community. Between the apostles of Brown Power and an Anglo community still deaf to protest and slow to change, there is hardly any place to hide. And yet an honest and responsible leader must remember that the demands and ultimatums of Brown Power may or may not interest the whole minority community.

Nowhere is this more true than in Los Angeles. The very accomplishments of Mexican-Americans in this city make it truer. Thousands of Mexicans have worked themselves into small homes and middle-class status. This was a stunning accomplishment for a group of immigrants hardly a generation removed from the railroads and fields of the Southwest. Middle-class Mexicans in the modest homes of Montebello and Monterey Park have no intention whatever of proclaiming themselves beautiful Indian brown and persuading their sons and daughters to walk out of school. There are surely no more than 75 active Brown Berets in all Los Angeles. Some Brown Power advocates are not even Mexican, but Latin-Americans with backgrounds quite different from Los Angeles. For the moment their youth, their idealism, and the ideals of *la raza* confer a sort of immunity. This may end rather suddenly if Brown Power is ever successful in speaking for all Mexican-Americans to all Los Angeles.

Most of the future of the Brown Power militants depends, oddly, on just how the white community reacts to them. To date, in Los Angeles the Board of Education, the law enforcement agencies, and particularly the District Attorney receive an "F." One suspects a condition of profound ignorance. A revolutionary experience isn't possible unless the Establishment agrees there is going to be one. Thus mass arrests, jury indictments and almost hysterical television coverage simply accommodate the militants. One is tempted to suggest that to refuse to arrest any member of a militant group might even destroy them. In the case of the walk-outs, Los Angeles *saw* a revolution and, almost by magic, there was one.

By contrast, the Stockton Unified Schools in northern California took a less panicky view. When a militant Negro schoolteacher led a walk-out, it seemed to Stockton school administrators that she had demonstrated rather remarkable qualities of leadership. She was promoted to an administrative position and the "revolution" ended. The demonstrating students returned to their classrooms, the school system gained a talented administrator, and Black Power there turned to other goals. The technical word for dealing with radical militancy in this fashion is "co-option." Black militants have learned to watch for it and to guard against it. Co-option shoots revolutions right in the heart. It also supplies valuable new leaders to the Establishment and demonstrates that American society is open to talent. So far Los Angeles has shown that only the California State Penal Institutions are open to talent.

The reaction in Los Angeles was very close to nuclear "overkill." The resulting complications will take years of expensive litigation at taxpayer expense, produce a fine new crop of martyrs to Brown Power and offer the militants a fertile field for almost any kind of direct action. It confirms the most paranoid view of American society as a creaky, one-hoss, mule-cart that ought to be demolished anyway. And it diminishes the chances that Brown Power might show its brightest possibilities. Brown Americans might some day develop into a truly important Third Race between white Americans and black Americans. Mexican intellectuals in the late 19th century predicted that some day Mexicans might be *una raza de bronce* (a bronze race).

There are some traces of this already in Brown Power. It is clear to blacks that Mexican-Americans are not quite white. Brown Power militants understand black aspirations and share the black distrust of the good intentions of the Anglo community. Young Mexican-American militants show real compassion of a kind lacking now even among most white liberals. Yet they are committed to American society in a way that Negroes have never been. If they are defined as "bad," as "dangerous," as a "revolution" they will probably oblige Los Angeles and do their best to live up to this rather pleasing image. Perhaps, to steal a line from the educators, the Los Angeles Establishment should take courses in remedial reading and make sure that America was created in a rage at injustice. Who can scold the young, whatever their color, for a rage at injustice?

STUDY QUESTIONS

1. Why was the sit-in and sleep-in of the Mexican-Americans a surprise for the Los Angeles Board of Education?
2. Why were the Mexican-Americans protesting?
3. What is Brown Power?
4. What is the meaning of *la raza* for Mexican-Americans?
5. Is there a meaningful relationship between Black Power and Brown Power? Are there differences?
6. What are some of the goals of the Mexican-American?
7. Why have many past efforts at Mexican progress failed?
8. What are the qualities needed by a leader of Brown Power?
9. Is there a class-consciousness developing among Mexican-Americans?
10. What is the meaning of "co-option"? Is Guzman in favor of it?

SUGGESTIONS FOR WRITING

1. Where does Guzman stand on the issue of Brown Power? Is he in favor of it, or does he wish to see it diminished? Use whatever evidence you can spot in the essay—tone, details, or sentiments—to bolster your view.
2. Do you think Guzman is right when he says that all that's needed for a revolution is repressive action on the part of the Establishment? Is there a causal relationship between harsh reaction on the part of authority and the "revolutionary" zeal of younger people?
3. Describe the way you think a society ought to react to those who stage walk-outs, sit-ins, or other nonviolent demonstrations against situations they dislike. What reaction would be the most beneficial to all concerned?
4. Do you feel that the situation of Mexican-Americans is as serious as that of Afro-Americans? Is the situation more or less hopeful? more or less emotional? more or less important? Be as thorough and specific as you can.
5. Why are the exponents of Brown Power described as the "gentle

revolutionaries"? Is this description consistent with the reputation afforded to most Mexican-Americans? What are the prejudices Anglos usually have against Mexican-Americans? Do they in any way support the concepts of compassion and gentleness that Guzman develops here?

GROWING UP ON MECHANIC STREET

Peter Schrag

Most American youngsters will never attend college nor even seriously consider it. They have had their fill of education long before they reach college age. High school smothers their last interest in classroom instruction, and leaves them feeling defeated, inferior, and resentful.

It is impossible to think of those adolescents without a strange mixture of affection, apprehension, and fear. To imagine them at all, it becomes necessary to shoulder aside the black/white clichés of youth-talk—about middle-class revolt and ghetto rebellion—and to perceive a grayer reality. I am not writing here of affluent suburbs or what others have called blacktown, but about the children of those whom Americans once celebrated as workingmen. Again sociology fails us; there are no definitions or statistics. If there were, the matter would be better understood.

Phrases like "the forgotten man" and "the silent majority" are too political to serve as normative descriptions, but there is no doubt that there are forgotten kids who are, indeed, genuine victims: children of factory workers and truck drivers, of shop foremen and salesclerks, kids who live in row houses above steel mills and in ticky-tacky developments at the edge of town, children who will not go to college, who will not become affluent, who will not march the streets, who will do no more, no less, than relive the lives of their parents.

We have all seen them: the kids on the corner with their duck-tail haircuts; the canvas-bag-toting types, lonely and lost, lining up at induction centers; kids in knocked down cars that seem to have no springs in back, whose wedding announcements appear daily in the newspapers of small towns (Mr. Jones works for the New York Central Railroad—no particular job worth mention—Miss Smith is a senior at Washington High) and whose deaths are recorded in the weekly reports from Saigon—name, rank, home town. On the south side of Bethlehem, Pennsylvania, just above the mills, there is an alley called Mechanic Street; once it was the heart of the old immigrant district—the first residence of thousands of Hungarians, Russians, Poles, Mexicans, Germans, Czechs, and Croats. Most of them have now moved on to materially better things, but they regard this as their ancestral home. Think of the children of Mechanic Street; think of places called Liberty High and South Boston High, of Central High and Charlestown High, and of hundreds of others where defeat does not enjoy the ironic distinction of the acknowledged injustice of racial oppression.

They exist everywhere, but convention has almost wiped them from sight. They are not supposed to be there, are perhaps not really supposed to believe even in their own existence. Thus they function not for themselves but to define and affirm the position of others: those who are very poor, or those who are affluent, those who go to college. In visiting the schools that they attend, one must constantly define them not by what they are, but by what they are not, and sometimes, in talking to teachers and administrators, one begins to doubt whether they exist at all.

The fact that defeat is not universal makes the matter all the more ugly. The record of college placement and vocational success, which schools so love to celebrate, and the occasional moments of triumphant self-realization, which they do not, obscure—seem, in fact, to legitimate—the unexpressed vacancy, the accepted defeat, and the unspoken frustration around and beyond the fringe. When we see a growing number of students from blue-collar families going to college we begin to assume that they all go, and that they will all be happy and successful when they get there. Yet it is still a fact—as it always was—that the lower ranks of the economic order have the smallest chance of sending their children on, and that those who fall below the academic middle in high school tend to represent a disproportionate percentage of poor and working-class families. It seems somehow redundant to say all this again; but if it isn't said there will be no stopping the stories of blissful academic success.

The social order of most white high schools—the attitudes that teachers and students have about other students—is based (in proper democratic fashion) on what people do in school, on their interests, their clubs, their personalities, their accomplishments. (Students from blue-collar families with serious college ambitions associate with the children of white-collar professionals, and share their attitudes, styles, and beliefs, which tend to be more liberal—politically and personally—than those of their parents. A few participated in the Vietnam moratorium last fall, and a handful, unknown to their fathers, have gone to the local draft counselors. But they represent a minority.) It is possible to leave Mechanic Street through school achievement—to community and state colleges, to technical schools, to better jobs—yet it is hardly universal. Fewer than half actually go. What kids do in school tends, as always, to be predetermined. The honors class is filled with the children of professionals, kids whose parents have gone to college. The general course (meaning the dead end) and the vocational track are composed of the sons and daughters of blue-collar workers. The more "opportunity," the more justified the destiny of those who are tagged for failure. The world accepts the legitimacy of their position. And so do they. Their tragedy and the accompanying threat lie precisely in their acceptance of the low esteem in which school, society, and often their parents regard them, and in their inability to learn a language to express what they feel but dare not trust.

Imagine, says a school counselor, that you could become an animal, any animal. What species would you choose? The secret heart would choose freedom: Eagles soaring over mountains, mustangs racing across the plain, greyhounds loping through fields. Freedom.

Dreams are to be denied. The imagined future is like the present without parents. Jobs, domesticity, children, with little joy, seen in shades of gray. Coming out of school in the afternoon, the boys already resemble their fathers when the shifts change, rows of dark, tufted mail order house jackets, rows of winter hats with the ear flaps laced above the head, crossing the road from the plant to the parking lot, from the high school to the waiting buses and the bare-wheeled Chevies. The girls, not yet stretched by pregnancy, often trim in short skirts and bright sweaters, will catch up with their mothers, will be married at eighteen or twenty, will often be engaged before the tedium of school is at an end. "Unwanted kids," says a school administrator,

> kids of guys who got girls in trouble, kids of Korean War veterans and veterans of World War II who didn't want the first child, and before they knew it they had two or three. All their lives their kids have been told to get out of the way, to go watch television. They don't have anybody to talk to. There was a recent survey that indicated that 72 per cent of the first children of this generation were unwanted. These are the kids.

They sit in rows of five, five by five in the classroom, existing from bell to bell, regurgitating answers, waiting for the next relief. The mindless lessons, the memory and boredom, and the stultifying order of cafeterias and study halls—no talking, sit straight, get a pass—these things need not be described again. From bell to bell: English, mathematics, history, science—and, for some, release to the more purposeful and engaging activities of the shop: auto mechanics, data processing, welding, wiring, carpentry, and all the rest—some relevant, some obsolete, but all direct. There is an integrity, even joy, in material behavior—a sharp tool, an engine repaired, a solid joint—that the artificial world of the conventional academic course rarely allows. Material things respond; theory is applicable and comprehensible—either the thing works or it doesn't; it never prevaricates or qualifies, while words and social behavior, metaphors and politics remain cloudy, elusive, and distant. You see them wiring an electric motor or turning a machine part on a lathe, or fixing a car: pleasure, engagement, or, better, a moment of truth. The Big Lie, if there is one, will be revealed later. ("No," says the director of a vocational school in an industrial city,

> we don't tell the students that the construction unions are hard to join; it would discourage them in their work. They'll find out soon enough that it helps to know someone, to have a father or an uncle in the union. . . . But after a kid manages to break in, he's proud of what he learned in the school of hard knocks, and he'll do the same thing to the new guys.)

From class to class, from school to home and back, there is a sort of passing-through. What is learned is to defer—to time, to authority, to events. One keeps asking, "What do they want, what do they do, what do they dream about?" and the answer is almost always institutional, as if the questions no longer applied: They go to school; they have jobs—in the candy factory, at the gas station, in a little repair shop, in a diner—and they ride and repair their cars. Many of them live in a moonlight culture, a world where people have second jobs, where mothers work, where one comes home and watches whatever is on television, and no longer bothers to flip channels in search of something better.

Some distinctions are easy and obvious. Schooling certifies place; it selects people, not only for social class, but also for geographic mobility. The college-bound students speak about moving somewhere else—to the larger cities, to the West Coast, wherever events still permit the fantasy of a better future, or at least of change; the more national the college, the more likely they are to move. Among those who don't go to college there is little talk (except in depressed towns) of moving on. Academic losers stay put. "I know this is a dreary place," said a high school senior in Bethlehem. "But I like dreary places." It wasn't meant to be a joke. Big cities, they tell you again and again, are dangerous. (And in the cities they talk about protecting the neighborhood, or about how they still live in a good neighborhood.) Some places, they say, you can't walk the streets without getting knifed—by you know who. You hear it from sixteen-year-olds.

The instrument of oppression is the book. It is still the embodiment of the Great Mystery; learn to understand its secrets and great things will follow. Submit to your instinctive and natural boredom (lacking either the skills to play the game or the security to revolt), and we will use it to persuade you of your benighted incompetence: "I didn't want to write a term paper, but the teacher said it would be good if I did; when I handed it in she made fun of it; so I quit school." The family knows that you should stay in school, that you should go to college and "get an education," but it does not know that often the school doesn't work, or that it works principally at the expense of its own kids. One of the tragedies of the black revolt is that it frequently confused the general incompetence of schools with racism, thus helping to persuade much of the blue-collar community that its children were in fine shape, that the educational system was basically sound, and that complaints came either from effete intellectuals or ungrateful, shiftless blacks. Teachers who purported to represent genuine intellectual achievement (The Book) were thus allowed to continue to conceal their contempt for both kids and brains behind their passion for conformity and order, and to reaffirm the idea—already favored among working-class parents—that schooling was tough, boring, vicious, and mindless.

The school is an extension of home: In the suburbs it is rated on college admissions, on National Merit winners, and similar distinctions; in the working-class neighborhood of the city it tends to be judged on order and discipline. Either way, the more talk there was nationally about the need for technologically trained people, the more the school was able to resist challenges to its own authority. "Technological complexity" replaced naked authority as the club of conformity in the school.

What the school did (and is doing) was to sell its clients, young and old, on the legitimacy of the system that abused them. Of course there were exceptions—students, teachers, schools—and even the drearier institutions are sufficiently equipped with the paraphernalia of *fun*—sports, bands, clubs—to mitigate the severity and enlist community support. It is hard to find schools that do not arrogate to themselves some sort of distinction: the state championship marching band, league leadership in football or track, a squad of belles who twirl, hop, bounce, or step better than anyone else in the county. A girl makes her way from junior pom-pom girl to cheerleader or majorette; a boy comes from the obscurity of an ethnic neighborhood to be chosen an all-state tackle. There is vitality and engagement and, for the moment, the welding of new common-interest groups, new friendships, new forms of integration. It is the only community adolescents have, and even the dropouts sometimes sneak back to see their friends. And yet, many of these things come to a swift and brutal end: a note in the yearbook, some clippings, a temporary sense of value and distinction convertible into an early marriage, a secretarial job, an occasional scholarship. The most prestigious activities of high school have no lasting value; next year, or the year after that, there will be no band, no football, no pep club. Too often life reaches its highest point at seventeen.

It may well be that even white working-class parents are becoming more suspicious of the mediocrity of their schools, more aware of their crimes, and less taken by the joys they offer. The imperious contempt of large-city administrators is not limited to the complaints of the black community, and the increase in number of defeated school bond issues and tax overrides is hardly a sign of growing confidence in the school people who propose them. And yet, the things that have been preached by the best people for a hundred years (and which many of them no longer believe)—order, hard work, self-denial, and the general legitimacy of schooling—these things die hard, or die not at all.

It is too easy to forget the faces, too hard to forget the crowd. American youth, Edgar Friedenberg wrote, are "already deeply implicated in the deeds and values of their culture . . . . They go along with it and sincerely believe that in doing so they are putting down trouble-makers and serving the best interests of their community." That was, of course, before Berkeley and Columbia, before revolt had reached sufficient mass to be called a "counterculture." For the children of Mechanic Street, however, nothing changed, except that it added yet another demon to the many others that could not be faced. The kids of the lower middle in the order of the school had always known that they don't have much to say about anything; they have been put down most of their lives by parents, contemptuous teachers, and by fellow students. (The blue collar is still stigmatized; in the school the vocational students are fender-benders, and occasionally a particularly nasty remark is answered with sudden, explosive violence: "He called us grease monkeys, so we pushed him right through that glass door. We stick up for our rights.") What they do have to say is often directed against the most threatening invitations to independence and the most obvious examples of freedom, which constitutes the secret dream. They would—most of them—not permit demonstrations against the Vietnam War, would prefer that their teachers maintain the very order that puts them down, are resentful of anyone that can be called a hippie. ("It's not the parents that cause that," said a student radical, "it's the school. It teaches people to be uptight.") If the war continues at the present rate, several in each of their high school classes will be dead before they ever have a chance to live; of course, they would rather not have the war—and a few have joined peace marches and demonstrations—but, they tell you (in tones of a text they wish they could remember with more confidence), we have to Resist Communism, have to stand up for our rights. What about Mylai, what about the massacre of women and children in Vietnam? Most of them aren't much disturbed, haven't thought about it, or been asked about it, and haven't discussed it. You hear about someone's cousin or brother, over in "Nam," who talked about how those crazy people even had kids throwing grenades at our convoys. It's war, and you never know who's going to try and kill you. But the agony of the reply, the painful speech, in class after class, makes it impossible to press too many questions; the Hard Line plays back no better than a Shakespearean sonnet or a Euclidean theorem never worth learning. You do what you're told. Propaganda and schooling are the same thing. You ought not, you tell yourself, to pick on kids.

There is no place to go. No place now, no place ever. For the lower half of the school population—the general course, the voc-ed course, the yet to be certified losers with their low-C grades, the high school is like a refugee camp, a camp for displaced persons waiting for something to happen. The central fact of existence is not school or home of the great institutions of American rhetoric, but the automobile, the one place where life can proceed apart from those institutions, the one place where the stunted remains of the dream of freedom can grow. We have heard all this many times before—the drag racers, the hot rods—sometimes in amusement, sometimes in indignation, but we haven't come close to understanding how much it means. The car, quite simply, is everything. It is the only place where adult experimentation is tolerated: experiments with sex, with self-realization, with independence, with courage, with change, with death. The car shuttles within the city limits, sometimes to McDonald's or the Burger King, sometimes to the drive-in movie (Clint Eastwood, John Wayne, *Easy Rider*), but rarely beyond, rarely even to the next town.

There is no place to go, except to the car itself. The radio—and the heater—thus become essential accessories, and parking becomes an all-purpose word for sex. It is the thing you do on a date. For the affluent, who have large houses and some privacy—and parental tolerance—to entertain, it may also be an invitation to turn on; sex at home, pot in the car. For those who are not rich, the car represents almost every level of reality. It is something you work on, something useful (or superpowered) that you maintain, it is a place to live, it is escape, it is privacy. It is hard to get through high school without at least one accident, perhaps even harder to become a man without being able to claim one close call—out on the spur route, or in the empty parking lot of a shopping center late on a Saturday night. Someone pulls alongside, you give the engine everything, and for a few brief moments you feel speed and power and triumph. People don't grow up with cars; they grow up in them.

There is much talk, in town after town, about having places for "young people to go," about teen centers and recreation halls (the chaperoned dances having been abandoned by all but junior high students), but that concern seems to reflect a deeper despair about the community, about *place*, and about the future itself. As the old ethnic and regional culture breaks up, the culture of aspiration—what we used to call the mainsteam—should grow in its power to attract and hold. But often, needless to say, it does not. In the smaller towns and in the hyphenated neighborhoods of cities, traditional patterns and institutions—food, family, the church, the Ukrainian Hall, the Polish-American Club—become increasingly tenuous; church membership grows older, the neighborhood more bland, the swimming hole more distant, the culture more thin. The local mill, the mine, the plant, once ferocious and mythic in its demands on men, in its economic unpredictability, in its brutality, is tamed by unions, by government, and by corporate management itself. The kids don't remember the last strike, the last layoffs, let alone the last fight with the Pinkertons, the National Guard, and the company dicks. Every year a few more landmarks disappear, another memory dies, another set of roots is destroyed.

For most parents, there is still the hope of a better place, and almost every one of them does his best to get his kid to go. But the ebullient romance, the Alger myths, the dream of adventure and enterprise—all those things have been inundated by size and technology, and abandoned by the very people who invented them in the first place. The fact that things are less manageable, that the country and the world no longer respond the way we once imagined they should (or that they have become unmanageable altogether) may not be as traumatic for the ethnic and social underclass that had never controlled much of anything anyway—but it does reduce the interest and the fun of trying to join. One of the striking things is that many kids are not ambitious for power or possessions. "My parents," said one, "never had what they wanted; they couldn't get along on what they had. But we can." And yet the life that he and many others imagine is almost identical to the life of the present. As today opens up a little—a better home, a car, a television set, and a steady job—tomorrow seems to close down. Modesty in achievement and ambition is matched by an inability to visualize anything richer—in experience or possessions, or in the world at large. The generation gap—for rich, for poor, for all—is precisely this: that many kids, for the first time, are growing up without a sense of the future. And that, for America, is new.

They are people who have lost one country and haven't yet found another. Some of them are at least marginal participants in the counterculture; the hair on the boys grows longer, the hard rock is universal, and drugs (pot and pills), now prevalent among the swingers —college prep, affluent, or black—are beginning to infiltrate the middle, often with the tacit acquiescence of the cops who know that they have lost some of their troublesome adolescent clients to the euphoria of pot, and who are, in any case, powerless to stop it. There may still be high schools in America where drugs aren't traded, but they are probably scarcer than dry towns. At the same time, the potential for revolt, for repression, for violence, random and directed, remains. In one high school, a senior—long hair, mustache, articulate —speaks about his plans: When he graduates he will join the Marine Corps, go to Vietnam "where the action is," then return home and become a state cop. "I'll cut my hair before *they* get to it," trading one form of expression for another. Perhaps there are few alternatives left. Perhaps Vietnam remains one of the viable ways to become a man, or to become anything at all.

"Maybe," said a sophisticated high school teacher, "we better leave everything alone. If these kids ever become politically conscious, who knows whether they'll join the SDS or the brown shirts." There are

signs that they could do either, just like anyone else. Some of them
have harassed peace demonstrators, heckled civil rights marchers, and
have beaten up black kids in integrated schools or on the periphery
of changing neighborhoods, and have been beaten up in return. And
while middle-class, college-oriented students—and blacks—have made
the papers with their activism, there also have been, in some of the
inner cities, self-styled protofascist gangs hunting blacks, hippies, and
other signs of vulnerable liberalism. In the 1968 election, the major
support for George Wallace within the labor movement came from
younger members—the older brothers of the kids now finishing
school.

Who is to say how things are learned? For the children of Mechanic Street—as for all others—the classroom has rarely been more
than a marginal place. Except for minimal literacy and a few tricks
picked up in a home-ec course, the girl who marries at eighteen was
educated at home, though she may well have used the school to find
her husband. Except for the certification that schools bestow on good
behavior and acceptable habits, the boy who takes a job immediately
after graduation (or who, with a fifth of his peers, never graduates
at all) takes little from his school, except perhaps a vaguely unex-
pressible sense of defeat.

And yet, something is learned—perhaps from television, perhaps
from the school community itself. The well-publicized tension between generations seems to have given language and content to the
specific tensions between parents and children. Which is to say that
"student revolt" or "youth revolt" seems to be applicable even where
there are no students and no "youths" who identify with larger causes.
Even politically conservative and/or apathetic kids now seem able to
articulate differences with their parents. Many of them revolve around
nothing newer than the company they keep, the people they date,
and the time they have to be home at night. Nonetheless, the atmosphere of revolt provides new strategies for all (long hair, for
example), opens new possibilities, and offers new ways of rationaliz-
ing old ones.

Marshall McLuhan's notion of the global village may still be more
vanity than reality; yet it is accurate in one major respect: The media
—television, radio, and records—are creating communities where
none existed before. Media are creating bonds of style, age, and interest that transcend the particularities of locality and background. The
surface manifestations of a style may themselves satisfy the longing
for place and identity, providing alternatives for neighborhoods,
rituals, and traditions that no longer exist. In this sense "revolt" is

the opiate of the masses. High school reform and protest may never go beyond the abandonment of the dress code. But the media may also be creating the possibilities both for the development of new forms of consciousness and culture and (for the same reason) centralized political management and control. Unless Americans are prepared to revolutionize their educational system—providing far more intellectual and cultural freedom and diversity than they are currently willing to allow—the high school will, in fact, be no more than a huge amplifier for the signals that the media are willing (or permitted) to transmit. Considering the unbelievable boredom of the slow track in the average high school, and the treatment accorded its students, no "educator" can berate TV without being laughed off the stage. If there is any escape from that boredom, it is in the car and in television itself. The children are moving away from Mechanic Street. But where will they go?

STUDY QUESTIONS

1. What does Schrag mean by a "grayer reality"?
2. Who are the children Schrag calls the children of workingmen? Are they realistically described here?
3. What is the sociological "problem" that confronts Mechanic Street and those who live on all the Mechanic Streets?
4. If it is possible to leave Mechanic Street by doing well in school, why is Schrag not more optimistic?
5. What does it mean to say that what people do in school tends to be predetermined?
6. Why does Schrag describe the kids of Mechanic Street as unwanted? If this is true, what effect has it had on them?
7. What is the curriculum of the high school described here? What aspects of it are most meaningful to the sons of blue-collar workers?
8. What is the relationship between talk of "moving away" or "moving on" and the kind of school one attends?
9. Schrag talks at length about conformity in the schools. Does it have any specific applicability to Mechanic Street kids?
10. What kinds of political and social ideas do the kids on Mechanic Street have? What have these ideas to do with the schools? How does the school system contribute to the development of such ideas?

SUGGESTIONS FOR WRITING

1. Schrag says propaganda and schooling are the same thing. In a brief essay, describe what you think he means by this comment. He does not mean that schooling is actually propaganda, but he does feel that there is a real connection between the two forces. Decide, as you describe it, whether or not the connection is valid.
2. The automobile is represented as "everything" in the life of the student who is left behind in the general course in high school, as the only reality in his life. Is this true? Can you, from your own experience, qualify this judgment? Either amplify Schrag's view by backing it up with what you know, or attack the view by presenting new evidence and new interpretations.
3. Do you know a place like Mechanic Street? A community that is dominated by a one-industry mill, or a community that is becoming more and more homogenized and colorless? If so, describe what you feel is a fair picture of life there for a person your age. What are his hopes, his feelings about school, the nation, his parents and friends? What can he expect from life?
4. Is there a chance that the high schools of the Mechanic Streets of America help to reinforce the dreariness and the dullness of life at the level Schrag describes? What are the characteristics and the qualities of high school as you remember it that would tend to produce this effect? How did you react to these qualities? Were you as aware of them then as you are now?
5. If you were asked to reorganize a high school so that it used its resources to excite people and get them "turned on" about life, culture, art, politics, society, and anything else worthwhile, how would you start? What important aspect of high school would have to be reformed before other reforms could follow? Be specific and detailed.

WHAT EDUCATION
FOR A MORE VIOLENT WORLD?

Douglas Heath

> It is altogether possible that our present educational sys-
> tem is preparing students for a world they will never
> experience. Their world will be characterized by vio-
> lence—yet we continue to educate them for order and
> stability. Can we do otherwise? Is it possible to educate
> for disorder and rapid change?

To educate for peace is too abstract and remote a goal for an
educator to reach. The practicing teacher in the classroom, as John
Dewey long ago insisted, must deal with specific concrete ends-in-
view that are obtainable for the individual children he teaches. Such
a goal is also inappropriate because peace defined as order, harmony
and quiet is too static and simplistic a goal for the restlessly changing
and complex world in which we live. To educate for order and quiet-
ness is to educate for boredom, stasis, the perpetuation of the status
quo and, given our increasing failure to adapt to our changing technology, our eventual self-destruction. Educators need a dynamic definition of their purposes that encompasses the process of becoming,
growing and changing—that recognizes frustration and conflict to
be necessary psychological conditions for healthy growth to occur.

Then what educational goal should we educators have to prepare
our students for what may well be a more violent world in the future?
Certainly not just academic excellence which has been *the* exclusive
and too narrow goal of most educators this past decade. It may even
be dangerous to our society, for the means by which academic excel-

WHAT EDUCATION FOR A MORE VIOLENT WORLD?   From the May 1970 issue of
Journal of American Association of University Women. Reprinted by permission
of the author and *Journal of American Association of University Women*. The
suggestions in this article appear in expanded form in the author's *Humanizing
Schools: New Directions, New Decisions*, Hayden Book Company, 1971.

lence is being implemented may actually accentuate the predisposition of many youth to use violence when they become frustrated.

Now I must be very clear. How a youth becomes predisposed to use violent means or to want to hurt, kill, and destroy others is obviously a consequence of many complex familial, peer culture, societal, and mass media influences. The models of violence and mayhem pictured on television, whether of Vietnam, the Democratic National Convention in Chicago or Mannix on CBS may more powerfully predispose a youth to violence than do our schools. Yet, within the too visible context of such a violent way of life, our national obsession with scholastic achievement has handicapped, if not set back, our pursuit of those goals most appropriate for bringing peace to an increasingly strife-torn world.

How could this be possible? Although the post-Sputnikian educational changes have produced better educated students, I believe they also have been making less educable ones. The supplantation of human excellence by academic excellence as the goal of educators has contributed to the impersonalization of a student's relationships, the suppression of his affective life and the isolation of his knowledge from any stable integrative values. We have built large schools to provide more specialized academic courses, but in the process, according to all available research evidence, have reduced a youth's opportunity to form close personal relationships with other students or his teachers, diminished the amount of his responsible participation in his school activities and alienated him from his school—and possibly his society as well. Our excessive academic expectations, accentuated by the SAT and college marathon, have aggravated competitiveness, inhibited spontaneity, induced poignant feelings of failure in large numbers of our youth and stretched others so out of shape as human beings that only by drugs which blow their minds do they find some illusion of emotional integration. Finally, our failure to be aware of and then integrate the value implications of the knowledge we teach has compounded for many of our more sensitive youth the absurdity and meaninglessness that they now perceive in their larger society.

In an increasingly conflictual and violent world, the only practical and realistic goal for educators is to educate for human excellence of which intellectual development is a central but only partial feature. Human excellence is a gloriously vacuous phrase. To be more specific, I must (1) define it or the word "maturity," the term I prefer, (2) sketch a model of how a youth matures that provides clues about how he could meet frustration and conflict adaptively and (3) suggest some specific educational changes that might further his ability to master conflict more maturely.

By maturity I mean the development of those skills, attitudes and values that help a person create a way of life that optimizes the fulfillment of his own needs *and* his adjustment to the demands of others. The goal of an educator is not just to actualize a student's potentials. Self-fulfillment is a deceptively appealing but simplistic educational goal, the realization of which can lead to immaturity, narcissism and self-aggrandizement. We must live with others not just because of the interdependence of our society but because personal growth occurs primarily as a consequence of the quality of our relations with others. Self-actualization is a practical goal only if one assumes a youth is *innately* (and predominantly) altruistic, social, considerate and responsive to the welfare of other persons. I know of no evidence that validates such an assumption. Just as a youth has the capability of being aggressive and hostile, so does he have the capability of caring and loving. Both types of potentialities are nurtured, strengthened and educed as a result of our relationships with others. So we need to learn how to actualize certain potentialities and socialize, inhibit and leave others well enough alone.

On the other hand, the goal of an educator certainly is not to conform or blindly adjust his students to the types of potentials that the society of today insists be developed. If he is to prepare his students for their world of tomorrow, he must anticipate as best he can the demands of 1984. Furthermore, the demands of today's society may be quite unhealthy and induce severe frustration, out of which pathology and violence may arise. For example, studies suggest the more feminine a girl is the less intellectually capable she is likely to be, probably due to the suppression of her assertiveness which is associated with intellectual capability but not femininity in our culture. How many girls have suffered truncated lives as a consequence of our value on femininity? Or how many males have become aggressive, even violent, to protect themselves against emerging tender and affectionate needs they dare not express for fear they will be called sissy in this society?

The dramatic changes predicted for the decades of the seventies and eighties compel us to educate our youth to remain continuously open to new growth, for they may well encounter more intense frustration and severe conflicts in their life time than we ever did in ours. For the practicing educator, the problem of how to educate for peace is the problem of how to help his students learn to respond maturely rather than immaturely to frustration and conflict—the conditions that most frequently trigger violence and strife.

Perhaps a concrete example of how a group of students in one school responded immaturely to a threat will illustrate the magnitude of the task we educators face in educating for a more peaceful world. A faculty committee dropped a student from this school because of his poor academic work. The faculty had not known at the time the student was close to the center of much of the school's drug activity, but the students assumed this was the cause of the suspension. Within hours of the decision, a near riot was sparked by the dismissed student. Hundreds of students signed petitions and held angry meetings. Accusatory protests erupted and quickly shifted to other issues as well, and abrasive and cruel comments about some members of the faculty committee were published in the student paper. The inflamed conflict alienated students and faculty from each other for months. At no time during the fracas did the students who signed the petition, including the leaders of the student body, search out the facts about the dismissal. None talked with the faculty directly involved. Few suggested constructive alternative procedures by which to clarify and resolve the issue. Few persisted in seeking to resolve the conflict without resorting to irrational paranoid accusations and fewer yet were able to maintain a judicious objective attitude in spite of their own apprehensions and anger. That intense fears and irrational hostility were so readily evoked and persisted so openly so long in seemingly highly intelligent and civilized youths suggests the school had failed to teach many of its students, even some of its most academically talented, how to meet threat and conflict with some degree of maturity.

So what criteria define how a youth grows healthily and how could they help educators educate their students to master frustration and conflict more maturely?

As a youth becomes more mature he becomes more able to symbolize his experience. He becomes more aware of his motives and values. He becomes more able to learn retrospectively from his past as well as imagine, plan and anticipate the consequences of his intentions. Frustration and conflict spur the development of reflection. We need to teach our students not only to *value* becoming aware of the causes that lie behind every conflict but also to master the reflective skills to be able to do so.

A second way that a maturing youth develops is to become more able to view a conflict from the point of view of others. He can accurately understand how others view him and his beliefs. The ability to entertain a multiplicity of viewpoints is essential for solving interpersonal conflicts in ways that do not destroy or violate the integrity of others. Furthermore, when one has empathy and can project himself into the life of another, he becomes more open to different value alternatives.

Students frequently say they began to care for another only after they had learned how similar they both felt despite how different they first appeared to each other. The process of development is from a belief in one's idiosyncratic uniqueness to a deeper appreciation of and identification with other human beings as human beings. With increasing maturity, a person feels a kinship with a wider circle of people, irrespective of ethnic, national or religious differences.

A third way a youth matures is that he becomes a more integrated person who strives to make his values and actions consistent with each other but who also remains open and flexible to their modification when faced with new challenges. He does not react to frustration in partial encapsulated or emotionally impulsive ways. He seeks to make his life more of one piece, seamed together by several guiding principles or values. When confronted by conflict, he actively seeks out the full range of information and viewpoints and tries to form more embracing alternative solutions. It is not that he just seeks compromise; rather, he seeks to discover or create a new pattern that synthesizes that which is most appropriate or true in the different conflicting viewpoints. To explain a complex problem by calling it the result of the "system," "imperialism," "establishment" or of a "racist conspiracy" or to take a morally absolute position by making non-negotiable demands, attributing evil motives and hypocrisy to one's adversaries or seeking to polarize rather than reconcile differences in opinions may be effective confrontation politics for this crisis, but what is being learned about how to meet the many conflicts to be faced later?

The fourth way in which a person becomes more mature is that he becomes progressively more stable. He develops a sounder concept of who he is and what his values are. One mark of such a mature person is the persistence with which he seeks to resolve conflict. In the process of testing out different alternatives, he can endure considerable tension and anxiety without resorting to defensive maneuvers like narrowing his awareness, ignoring the complexity of most human conflicts or impatiently responding by attacks of violence. To help a youth learn how to meet conflict more maturely, an educator should design programs that teach a youth how to tolerate frustration while he persists in testing his ideas. Our impatient students of today need to learn there are few quick, simple solutions to most personal, national or international conflicts. Only from tests of his own values and ideas in actual conflictual settings will he come to appreciate this fact.

The last emerging characteristic of a maturing person is that he becomes more autonomous and has an inner buffer against both capricious impulsive responses as well as the clamorous demands others make of him. His autonomy is not to be confused with social aloofness or a narcissistic individuality, for he is deeply allocentric. Though he understands conflicting viewpoints, he can reserve decisions to himself. A person does not maturely deal with frustration if he develops a hyperawareness about the sources of a conflict but does not seek to resolve the conflict. Thus, an educator must provide experiences in which the student learns how to endure persistent frustration without it overwhelming or distorting his judgment, how to select critically between the claims of others, and then how to assert what he believes to be right.

What specific programs might be introduced to assist our students to cope more maturely with frustration and conflict?

1. To expand the *awareness* of our students about their own predispositions to violence, we should introduce into our curriculum a course on violence and aggression. Such a course would include an analysis of the causes of violence, including biological, psychological and socio-political determinants of the nature of frustration, types of conflicts and adaptive and maladaptive ways of responding to them. To make such a course more experiential for each student, he should keep a log of his own violent and aggressive experiences during the semester, the cues that initiated his anger and his responses to it. He might share typical experiences with the others in order to help them expand their own understanding of how other people also respond to frustration.

A subsequent but more applied type of course on conflict-resolution should be offered which relies heavily on detailed case studies and field work that force a student to become personally involved in many different ways of resolving conflict at the personal, school, local, state, national and international levels. In generating their case studies and analyzing them, students might work on an issue confronting their city council, follow a case in a local court, examine in detail a current legislative fight or become involved in a local labor dispute. Finally, each student should describe in detail a personal conflict he faces, analyze its sources, propose alternative modes for its resolution and test his proposed solutions.

2. To provide more systematic programs to develop more *allocentric* students is an increasingly imperative task for our schools. We need to teach students much more self-consciously how to take another person's viewpoint, listen and be selectively open to persuasion, cooperate with and care for others. We will have to train our teachers to be more expert in human dynamics and group leadership skills. Psycho-drama, role reversal techniques and sensitivity types of activities could be usefully brought into many social studies and humanities courses in order to provide *experienced* knowledge, not just knowledge itself. We need to balance our overly competitive classrooms by providing more cooperative learning experience. We also need to develop programs that teach children how to care for others. For example, we could assign sixth graders to help individual second graders as a regular part of their curricular program.

At the college level, at least one semester of academic work should be devoted to academic and field work that brings a student into meaningful personal contact with the life and values of persons of a different social class, ethnic or national background. With respect to understanding and appreciating persons of other cultures, I am not persuaded that traditional foreign language training is a preferred way to attain that goal. For all but a few students, learning a foreign language in this culture requires more resources, energy and time than seem to be merited by the results. Few students ever encounter the language outside of the classroom or gain sufficient proficiency to use it in their other work. We need to make language learning more functional. I propose we eliminate all language requirements below the college level and provide language courses only for those who are talented linguistically. At the college level, students should take a preparatory course in the language they finally discover they will need and this course should be followed by living and studying in the culture of that language for at least a semester.

3. To help students learn how to form and test more *integrative* ways to deal with conflicts and develop more stable values as well, it is essential they encounter meaningful problems in which the probability that a conflict in values will occur is very high. We educators should convert our schools into genuine educational communities in which it is the frustrating operation of and potential conflicts in the school itself that become the principal growth experience for the student. Too many schools I visit are authoritarian and suppressive

of student initiative and activity. They induce frustration, negativism
and passivity. We must find ways to break up our large schools into
more functional, responsive and powerful educational communities.
They should be small enough so the entire community can plan and
organize its own activities. Students need to learn why groups need
structure, rules and leaders. They need to learn how a group estab-
lishes its own rules and ethical expectations and to participate in
those decisions that may engender conflict. We teachers also need
to change our attitudes about our role in our classes so that our
students can learn how to organize, direct and evaluate the educational growth of the class as well as of themselves.

4. A youth does not develop a *stable identity* and sense of independence and *autonomy* until he has been tested in a wide range of
frustrating and conflicting situations. I propose we abandon our traditional senior year in high school and develop apprenticeships in the
surrounding community. A student should have some responsible
work—whether in a social service agency, hospital, business, laboratory or municipal agency—in which he will test how he functions
as a more whole human being. Such work should be coordinated with
a reflective weekly seminar run by his teachers, in which the conflicts
and problems he has encountered and his responses are studied. For
me, an ideal field work experience for our suburban middle class
affluent youth would be working as a teaching assistant in a city
school in which each senior would share responsibility with the classroom teacher for the education of at least two disadvantaged elementary and junior high school students.

For our more mature college students, I would like to see political
internships made available at all levels of governmental activity. One
of the critical problems our country faces is how to train and select
young leaders who will help change our social and political institutions
to be more appropriate to the problems of tomorrow. I believe our
more talented youth should be represented now on various national
commissions and should work in our courts, governmental and congressional agencies and combine such field work with reflective semi-
nars in their field work settings.

If our society and world are to survive the storms ahead without
being torn apart by violence and anarchy, then we must prepare our
future leaders now about how to respond maturely to severe frustration and conflict. They need to learn more than just academic information and intellectual skill. I hope we educators will encourage our
youth to become healthily maladjusted to this society and educe
those skills, attitudes and values necessary to create a healthier society

tomorrow. If we fail to do so, civilization as we know it may be reclaimed by our more primitive biological inheritance, leaving death and destruction behind as our species' legacy to this earth.

STUDY QUESTIONS

1. Why is to educate for peace to educate for self-destruction? Do you think the logic of that concept is sound?
2. What has been the exclusive and "too narrow" goal of educators these last several decades? Why is it inadequate?
3. How have academic standards helped alienate students from their social order? Does it seem reasonable that this should be so?
4. What have been the worst effects of the SATs and other competitive exams on students and their society?
5. What does it mean to educate for human excellence?
6. Is it true that "personal growth occurs primarily as a consequence of the quality of our relations with others"?
7. What has personal maturity got to do with education?
8. What is the difference between the allocentric and the egocentric (or narcissistic) person?
9. Do you think a course on violence would be as effective as Heath suggests?
10. How do you react to the idea of small units within colleges that would function independently with a sense of self-direction?

SUGGESTIONS FOR WRITING

1. In what senses is it true that strong competitiveness, which does indeed characterize most of our schools, contributes toward producing an immature human being—even if he is an educated human being? If you think the opposite of this is true, develop a brief statement which will be convincing to someone who disagrees with you.
2. Is there any evidence that schools may be more and more concerned with producing a mature human being instead of simply an individual with an academic degree? Argue this case from your own experience and the experiences of your friends.
3. Imagine that you were anxious to begin some of the reforms that Heath describes here. Suppose your own college or school was

receptive to these ideas. Where would you begin? Who would you expect to give the most help? How would the students you know respond? If possible, write a brief scenario (a fictional or hypothetical description) of the first few days of change.

4. What are Heath's attitudes toward drugs? Are his perceptions accurate? Scour the essay for any clues you can find, and put together a statement that presents Heath's views and analyzes them in terms of their validity.

5. The essay ends with four basic proposals for educational change. What is your reaction to these proposals? How would you modify them, and what others would you add? Make your suggestions concrete and workable for your own situation, your school, and your friends.

SEX IN THE SCHOOLS:
EDUCATION OR TITILLATION?

Barbara Goodheart

One of the most emotional controversies in the academic world centers on the problem of sex education. In many school systems, the debate boils down not to deciding whose responsibility it is to teach sex education, but whether it ever gets taught at all.

It's been called "anti-Christian," "un-American," and "part of a giant Communist conspiracy."

Yet it's endorsed by the Interfaith Commission on Marriage and Family Life (Synagogue Council of America, U.S. Catholic Conference, National Council of Churches), The National Congress of Parents and Teachers, the YMCA and YWCA, and the U.S. Department of Health, Education, and Welfare.

And the Communist newspaper *Pravda* has called it part of "the western imperialistic, capitalistic plot"!

Suddenly sex education has become one of the most controversial issues facing our public schools. In many areas, opponents of sex education are disrupting school-board meetings and threatening to take their children out of school. In over a dozen states, bills have been introduced in attempts to ban sex education below the ninth grade (although, at this point, only Tennessee actually has a law on the books).

Yet sex-education programs are neither new nor unusual. Some were established a generation ago. Today over half of our schools offer sex education; some beginning in kindergarten, others in high school.

A recent Gallup poll shows that despite the current controversy,

SEX IN THE SCHOOLS: EDUCATION OR TITILLATION?   From the February 1970 issue of *Today's Health*, published by the American Medical Association. Reprinted by permission of the author and *Today's Health*.

seven out of 10 parents favor sex education in schools. Most physicians, psychologists, and educators do also. The American Medical Association has endorsed proper sex-education programs and has urged physicians to help in the development of such programs.

At a panel discussion during AMA's 1969 annual convention, Harold I. Lief, M.D., director of the Division of Family Study at the University of Pennsylvania, stated: "The most effective tool a physician can offer as aid to his fellow men in combating promiscuity, illegitimacy, venereal disease, perinatal mortality, marital disharmony, and divorce is sex education."

Calling a sound sex-education program a necessity for proper mental health, James L. McCary, Ph.D., University of Houston psychologist, relates the vast majority of sexual problems in our society to the disturbed attitudes toward sex that result from misinformation and lack of sex education. Since sex education "has not been and apparently cannot be properly given in the home or in the church," he adds, "it has to be given in the schools."

Yet many parents and professionals have strong reservations about sex-education programs. Some wonder if such programs belong in the schools at all—particularly in the elementary schools. Others, such as Rhoda L. Lorand, Ph.D., clinical psychologist and author, believe that some sex-education materials are inappropriate and may overstimulate and confuse children. Many parents feel that few teachers are qualified—professionally and psychologically—to teach about sex; others are worried about morality: "Do the schools teach that intercourse before marriage is wrong?" asks one parent. "If they don't, I don't think they should bring up the subject."

Recently, many persons with sincere concerns such as these have had little chance to express their views. In approximately two-thirds of the states, school officials are currently trying to cope with the organized, vocal opposition to sex education—groups of individuals who refuse to discuss the issues, disrupt school-board meetings, claim that sex education is a Communist plot, and want all sex-education programs removed from the schools. (Some of the movement's followers, however, are not right-wingers and see nothing Communistic in sex education. They have joined the organized opposition to fight sex education more effectively.)

In the *American School Board Journal*, Mrs. Evelyn Whitcomb, a Wichita, Kansas, school-board member, describes four types of persons who seem to be involved in the antisex-education campaign:

> (1) Members of far-right groups such as the Christian Crusade and the John Birch Society . . . (2) Religious fundamentalists

who consider school sex education not only antireligious and
anti-God but sometimes a means to destroy religion as well
. . . (3) Parents who are shocked at even the most factual biological instruction in the human reproduction process and who
make easy prey for organized critics . . . (4) Well-meaning
parents, stable families, who always had faith in their school
board until they were inundated . . . with materials distributed by sex education arch-opponents. They are frustrated,
confused, disturbed, and have begun to believe there must be
something valid in the criticism . . .

Luther G. Baker, Ph.D., professor of family life at Central Washington State College, analyzes the vociferous opposition as follows:

In nearly every community there are a few self-styled "defenders of the faith." They are against everything which seems
to violate their particular concept of the traditional "American
Way": taxes, welfare, do-gooders, hippies, and sex education.
They find support from certain organizations with national dimensions which obtain financial resources by playing upon
people's fears and prejudices, and which claim to find some
dark, lurking danger in any new idea or program. Over the
years one finds these same organizations attacking first this,
then that bogey, moving from mental health, to vaccination, to
fluoridation, to sex education, professing to see in all of them
a sinister design to weaken the will of the people, subvert the
truth, and destroy the nation.

The national antisex-education campaign began in September,
1968, when evangelist Bill James Hargis of Tulsa, Oklahoma, head of
the Christian Crusade, launched a direct-mail promotion of a Christian Crusade booklet, "Is the School House the Proper Place to Teach
Raw Sex?"

In the promotional letter, Hargis calls sex education in schools "All
a part of a giant Communist conspiracy!"—a "scheme to demoralize
youth, repudiate the so-called 'antiquated morals' of Christianity,
drive a cleavage between student and parents, and introduce to curious youth the abnormal in sex . . ." Hargis then asks for "gifts of
$1000 . . . $500 . . . $250 . . ." on down to $5, "or whatever you
can do in the name of our Lord Jesus Christ" to help publish the
booklet. (In 1966 the Christian Crusade lost its tax exemption as a
religious institution because, said the Internal Revenue Service, a
substantial part of its operation "is directed at the accomplishment of
political objectives.")

The John Birch Society joined the battle in January 1969, when the
Society's *Bulletin* called for the formation of local committees for the
Movement to Restore Decency (MOTOREDE) to oppose "this

filthy Communist plot"—sex education in the schools. MOTOREDE is now well established in many areas of the country. Among its creeds:

(1)   We believe that there can be no such thing as a good school course on sex education.

.   .   .

(2)   We do not believe that the current drive for sex education is even intended by its originators and promoters to provide a needed and beneficial service in the schools. It is their sinister objective instead, to create an unceasing and dangerous obsession with sex in the minds of our children.

Many local antisex-education groups have sprung up during the past two years. Among them: SOS (Sanity on Sex), PAUSE (People Against Unconstitutional Sex Education), MOMS (Mothers Organized for Moral Stability), POPE (Parents for Orthodoxy in Parochial Education), TACT (Truth About Civil Turmoil), and CHIDE (Committee to Halt Indoctrination and Demoralization in Education). Many of the groups use films, speakers, and pamphlets supplied by MOTOREDE and Christian Crusade.

Some opposition groups have met with counter-opposition. In Kansas, CASE (Concerned Americans for Social Education) encountered an organization of high-school seniors called SPAAM (Students for the Prevention of Asinine Adult Movements). CASE, said the students, felt that sex education should be "taken out of the schools and put back in the street, where it belongs." The students disagreed with this idea, and convinced most of the community; CASE gave up the struggle and disbanded.

In general, however, the opposition movement is gaining strength—and its attack is not limited to sex education. When 150 delegates from opposition groups in 21 states and Canada held a convention last August, other issues, such as sensitivity training and school busing, received almost as much attention as sex education. Several delegates displayed a bedsheet that proclaimed, in big black letters: "Teach the 3Rs. Not the 3Ss: Sin, Sex, Sensitivity." An official of the American Education Lobby (AEL)—a far-right antisex-education organization formed in 1968—passed out copies of an August 1969 AEL Newsletter in which school integration is equated with "jungle conditions" and which warns that the "arrogant dictators who forced prayers out of the schools now seek to replace them with filth and pornography, under the guise of sex education."

Also under fire at the convention were "godlessness," the philosophy of humanism, the National Education Association, the United Nations, the PTA, and the Department of Health, Education, and Welfare.

In their attack, the organized opposition has concentrated on "two tried and true tactics," says Central Washington State's Doctor Baker: "The first is name-calling. Sex education is un-American and it is anti-Christian. Those supporting it are 'dupes,' 'degenerates,' 'atheists,' 'filthy perverts.' The second is guilt by association."

Rumors and half-truths are used effectively. One currently being circulated is the following (from the AEL tabloid on sex education): "In Flint, Michigan, a teacher, intending to illustrate a point under discussion, removes all her clothing in front of her class. The local school board president, declaring that the teacher's intentions were 'in the best interests of her students,' dismissed the case against her."

According to Doctor Baker, this rumor was investigated: the teacher in question—a physical-education teacher—had simply demonstrated to her all-girl class how different types of clothing change a person's appearance. At no time had the teacher "stripped" before her class.

Another opposition tactic, according to school officials, is to alter local sex-education material and distribute it in the neighborhood, claiming it is genuine. Still another is to distribute material taken from sex manuals and claim—falsely—that it will be used in the local schools.

Major targets of the sex-education opponents are SIECUS (Sex Information and Education Council of the United States), its director, Mary Calderone, M.D., and the SIECUS Board, many of whom are prominent physicians, educators, or clergymen. SIECUS is a non-profit, voluntary health organization. Its stated goals are the establishment and exchange of information and education about human sexuality. SIECUS publishes a series of Study Guides and a newsletter, and, upon request, provides guidance and information about sex education to communities, school boards, and churches. It also reviews materials, helps train teachers, and suggests outlines. It has no program of its own, but helps interested communities develop programs tailored to local needs.

Opponents charge that SIECUS Study Guides on masturbation, premarital sex, and homosexuality are used in classrooms (the implication is that they are "how-to" pamphlets). SIECUS replies that these are not for classroom use, and not for children; that they are written by professionals with doctorate degrees and are actually background material for parents and teachers.

Another charge: Some of the SIECUS Board write for *Sexology*—

"a pornographic magazine." *Sexology* is a newsstand magazine written to provide poorly educated adults with accurate sex information. When *Sexology* was brought to trial, Justice Stanley J. Polack of New Jersey dismissed charges, stating the magazine "deals with sex, but not in an obscene manner. . . ." Justice Polack found the articles to be "literary, scientific and educational." The book review service of the Baptist Sunday School Board, in reviewing *Sexology* material published in book form, commented: "This is a 'must' for every parent, pastor, and leader of youth."

Finally, the opposition forces have called members of the SIECUS staff and board "leftists" or "Communists"—the same charges that were directed years ago at the late President Eisenhower.

Despite the antisex-education campaign, many surveys indicate that most parents continue to favor sex-education programs in schools. A recent Gallup survey shows 71 percent of all adults interviewed in favor of courses in sex education in school. And a poll by *Good Housekeeping* endorsed sex education in the elementary grades with 56.2 percent for and 39.7 percent against—with higher percentages supporting sex education in later grades. In general, parents seem to feel that although school programs are not a perfect answer to the dilemma of sex education, they are the best available.

A number of studies show most children are not getting adequate information about sex. At a youth health conference sponsored jointly by the Detroit Commission on Children and Youth, the Michigan School Health Association, and Wayne State University, most high-school juniors and seniors present complained that parents were "not able to or did not do an adequate job," according to Gertrude B. Couch, Ph.D., chairman of the conference. Many teens felt their parents were uninformed, suspicious, ashamed, shy and embarrassed, evasive or uncomfortable, and apparently "unable to cope with the reality that their children were really growing up," says Doctor Couch.

Similarly, the University of Houston's Doctor McCary points out that in a recent survey, "high school honor students criticized their parents most for having failed to discuss with them the subject of human sexuality." Two-thirds "had never been told anything about sex by their parents. The others had received only cursory information, and that was faulty and garbled."

Nor do most students get adequate information from other sources. In a four-year study of high-school boys, Daniel Offer, M.D., psychiatrist and author, found that none felt they had profited from anything they had been told by teachers or parents: "In their struggle with one of the most important aspects of their growing up, the students received very little help from the adult world."

Most parents realize their children need help in getting accurate information about sex, but have trouble providing the information themselves, according to Laurence Lang, Ed.D., of the department of child development and family relations of the University of Connecticut. In helping many communities develop sex-education programs, Doctor Lang has found that when a school offers a soundly prepared program, run by qualified professionals, the parents' reaction is one of "overwhelming relief."

What type of sex-education program do most parents want? Apparently a fairly comprehensive one. Sociologist Roger Libby of Washington State University asked parents if they would approve of a high-school program that would include "information and discussion about sexual attitudes, standards and behavior; sex roles and reproduction—especially as these affect personality development, the ways in which people relate to each other, and the decisions they make concerning sexual behavior." To this, 82 percent of the parents fully approved, 15 percent partially approved, and only three percent disapproved.

Some parents are concerned that school sex-education programs will encourage premarital intercourse and challenge the value of virginity and monogamy. . . . Doctor McCary points out, however, that there are several other approaches to sex education: "At one extreme is the ostrich-like position that there should not be any sex education; a problem not faced squarely, it is hoped, will quietly disappear. Sexual conflicts, unhappy marriages, premarital pregnancies, abortions, and a general anxiety in sexual matters" show that this approach does not work, he adds.

Another extreme point of view is the "thou shalt not" approach; sexuality is "a gift from God that is to be used solely for the purpose of procreation . . . sexuality used for any other reason becomes immoral, animalistic, and defiling." Doctor McCary believes that this approach probably produces more conflict than total ignorance.

Still another approach is the strictly factual one; sex is presented without any emotional or psychological considerations. This theory ignores the importance of love and affection.

Doctor McCary thinks there is a compromise solution: "Sexual needs should be permitted expression; unadorned information about the physiological and psychological aspects of sex should be presented to all; and the Judeo-Christian traditions within which we live must be understood and dealt with sensibly in the framework of present-day society."

No matter what approach a school district uses, conscientious parents in the community will raise questions about a number of controversial topics. Educators have found that if a district is to develop a good program, such issues must be brought into the open and discussed. Among them:

Morality. The question of morality is a particularly hot issue in the sex-education debate and a good deal of the anxiety surrounding it appears to stem from confusion about the meaning of "morality." There are many interpretations. For some it means strict adherence to a particular set of rules of conduct established by theological dogma. To others it simply means behaving responsibly in relationships with others.

Among the former is William Marra, Ph.D., assistant professor of philosophy at Fordham University and a conservative Catholic who believes that in order to be good we need controls and "thou shalt nots." Speaking at a Central Lake County (Illinois) MOTOREDE meeting, he stated: "When we enter this world we already are attracted more to evil than to good. It's very hard to be good; it's the easiest thing in the world to be bad."

In Doctor Marra's view, "Sex-education courses multiply the occasions of sin." Referring to the Rochester, New York, sex-education program, he stated: "Although Bishop (Fulton) Sheen approved of the Rochester Plan, I think it is a disastrous mistake." (Although many conservative Catholic laymen are strongly opposed to sex education, the Catholic Church has officially endorsed school sex-education programs. A survey of the Family Life Division of the U.S. Catholic Conference shows that one-third of all U.S. Catholic dioceses already have sex-education programs.)

Most sex educators feel that morality should not be approached with a "thou shalt not" attitude, that all viewpoints should be discussed, and that honesty and individual responsibility should be stressed. It has been observed that sexual moralities are exactly the same as the moralities that apply in any other human relationship, that there is absolutely no need to bring in theological considerations. Reverend Warren Schumacher, professor of moral theology and canon law, Seminary of Immaculate Conception, Huntington, Long Island, New York, agrees: "The sex educator in a school setting (as opposed to a religious setting) must have a deep respect for diversity in value systems and be able to help people reach their own decisions." Reverend Schumacher, who helps educate sex-education teachers, emphasizes that the sex educator must be honest; he must be able to say, "This is what some people think; this is what others think."

Sociologist Libby found that two-thirds of the parents in his study would not insist that chastity be stressed in sex-education classes, and two-thirds would approve of the objective discussion of a variety of attitudes, moral standards, and behavior—not just the ones most parents sanction. In any event, experts point out, parents are the major influence in shaping a child's attitudes; the vast majority of children have the same value systems as their parents.

Often parents say to teachers: "Tell them about the dangers of sex—venereal disease and pregnancy." John Gagnon, Ph.D., sociologist at the State University of New York, Stony Brook, finds this request legitimate and realistic. He notes that the pregnant teen is to a large degree rejected by adult society.

Not so realistic, most sex educators feel, are the attitudes of many parents toward masturbation.

When this topic was discussed at a national convention on sex education sponsored by the Comprehensive Medical Society, panelists brought up the fact that most girls and almost all boys masturbate, and that many have strong feelings of guilt because of it. Such guilt, they agreed, is not warranted. Said Reverend Ronald Mazur, minister of the First Church in Salem, Massachusetts: "Sex education should provide information to prevent or mitigate irrational guilt associated with masturbation." Reverend Schumacher commented: "The whole issue of the seriousness of masturbatory behavior is being seriously questioned by the Catholic Church."

William Simon, Ph.D., sociologist at the Institute for Juvenile Research, Chicago, Illinois, pointed out: "Boys say to themselves, 'If I'm really normal, why am I doing all these dirty things?' " If nothing else, said Doctor Simon, sex educators should get across the message that this behavior is within normal limits. Says a spokesman for the American Academy of Pediatrics: "Some authorities estimate the prevalence of masturbation as high as 100 percent among males and 90 percent among females. I would say, however, that over a period of time, above 90 percent for males and above 60 percent for females is, perhaps, more realistic."

Schools have approached the question of masturbation in various ways. Many avoid the topic. Some teachers correctly answer inquiries: "Doctors say that masturbation is not physically harmful and does not lead to mental illness." Others plan for open discussion considering all facts and feelings. Many teachers suggest that students also discuss the question of masturbation—or any topic related to morality —with their parents or clergymen.

Latency. Some psychiatrists and psychologists believe that children go through a latency period between ages of six and 12, during which time they tend to pay little attention to sex. These experts contend that to direct children's attention to sex during this period might be emotionally harmful.

Most psychologists and psychiatrists have discounted the latency theory, a Freudian concept. In any case, they point out, prepubertal children in our society are exposed to sex through the mass media. Many argue that basic factual material should be presented to children before they are old enough to react emotionally. In particular, they feel that before entering puberty, children should understand the changes that will be taking place.

The family. Some parents feel that sex education is the responsibility of the family rather than the school. Professionals in the behavioral fields emphasize that the family has the primary responsibility for sex education, particularly early in the child's life, when he is developing attitudes and moral values. They also are aware that some youngsters do not have a family to assume this responsibility.

Many feel, however, that most parents need help. Says David R. Hawkins, M.D., chairman of the psychiatry department at the University of Virginia Medical School: "The average family is made up of average human beings, and they aren't very enlightened about sexuality." Further, he feels that, because of the complex early relationships between parent and child, it probably is not appropriate, comfortable, or even feasible for them to discuss sexuality in the depths in which it should be discussed in the later years.

Many parents recognize that even if they have done a good job during the child's early years, most older children get their information from other children—and much of what they learn is inaccurate, distorted, or even frightening. It should, they feel, be contravened by accurate information.

Vann Spruiell, M.D., psychoanalyst on the staff of the Louisiana State University Department of Psychiatry, feels that some things cannot be taught by parents; that they must be learned alone or with others of the same generation.

In any case, proponents of sex education argue that polls and studies show that most parents do want the schools to provide some sort of sex education.

Will knowledge lead to experimentation? Some parents fear that if children learn about sex, the result will be venereal disease and premarital pregnancy. Says Herbert Ratner, M.D., health officer of Oak Park, Illinois: "If you give a high-school girl sex education, the only good it will do is to show her how and why she got pregnant."

Most experts disagree. Says Doctor McCary:

> The World Health Organization states that ignorance, not knowledge, of sexual matters is the cause of "sexual misadventure." The clinical experience of most psychotherapists and marriage counselors certainly lends support to this viewpoint . . .

He adds:

> A recent study of unmarried pregnant girls showed that they had received little or no sex education from home or school, and that their mothers either lacked proper sex knowledge themselves or were unable or unwilling to give proper instruction to their daughters.

Will knowledge about sex result in a decline in premarital pregnancy? Limited studies point in this direction, but most experts feel that not enough figures are available to justify a conclusion.

In emphasizing the dangers of ignorance, sex educators point out that worry about normal sexuality can lead to premarital intercourse. They state, for example, that many persons believe—incorrectly—that their sex organs will "dry up" and cease to function if they are not used.

Lack of understanding about emotions can also lead to premarital intercourse. Quoting a study that shows that one in six brides in America is pregnant when she marries, Doctor McCary states: "Curiously, many of these unwanted pregnancies occur among the religiously devout, who, despite their determination to 'refrain from sin,' somehow lose control of their emotions and get swept into the act of sexual intercourse."

Ignorance can, in some cases, cause emotional damage. Evalyn S. Gendel, M.D., of the Kansas State Department of Health, has found that often a normal boy who is approached homosexually by an adult becomes emotionally disturbed because he believes he is a latent homosexual and has sent out a "radar signal" to the other person.

Other examples are offered by Warren R. Johnson, Ed.D., professor of health education at the University of Maryland. In his book, *Human Sexual Behavior and Sex Education*, Doctor Johnson says, "Many men consider their first 'wet dreams' among the most terrifying experiences of their lives, brought on, they may conclude, by their masturbating . . ."

Guilt about masturbation causes many problems, says Doctor Johnson:

> I recall one time having to deal with a situation in which a seventh-grade boy changed overnight from being an eager, happy, well-organized "good student" to the reverse of these things. It finally came out that a classmate had informed him that the new dark hairs on the backs of his fingers and wrists proved that he masturbated. The other boy got this information from his father, who felt it his duty to terrorize his sons concerning this behavior.

Qualified teachers. Opponents of sex education have a valid point here, says Doctor Hawkins. He points out that many teachers are inhibited and have personality conflicts: "This means that we must be skillful in picking the educators to do the job and providing the graded curriculum that is age-appropriate and psychologically sound."

Professional training is another major problem. Only a few dozen colleges offer sex-education courses for future teachers. "Pre-service and in-service instruction should be stepped up," emphasizes Doctor John H. Cooper of the National Education Association. He points out that there is a severe shortage of teachers equipped to give basic sex education at any age level.

Until the situation improves, most teachers will need intensive advance instruction and preparation—including study groups, resource materials, and workshops—to do an adequate job.

Should a sex-education program be compulsory or voluntary? Should classes be mixed? Should the program start at high-school level, in junior high, or in kindergarten? Should it be part of an overall health program, or a separate course?

These are but a few of the questions a community must consider when planning a sex-education program. The American Medical Association believes that a great deal of controversy can be eliminated if school districts follow certain guidelines. The AMA has endorsed local, voluntary family life education programs, to supplement the role of the family, when: (1) the programs are part of an overall health education program, and are presented at appropriate grade levels; (2) the teachers and professionals involved have received special training and have an aptitude for working with young people; (3) the programs follow a professionally developed curriculum, foreviewed by representative parents; (4) parents and other concerned members of the community are involved with the programs on a continuing basis; (5) the programs are developed around a system of values defined with the aid of physicians, educators, and clergymen.

To succeed, a program must be developed slowly and carefully, and must have strong community support. The school board, administration, and staff must be thoroughly familiar with all aspects of the program. Contact with parents must be continuous—even after the program is established.

Sincere and well-informed persons in the community who are opposed to various aspects of sex education must be encouraged to express their point of view; such persons often hold the key to the development of a suitable local program. Sprague H. Gardiner, M.D., chairman of the AMA Committee on Maternal and Child Care, has pointed out that educators should listen carefully to such persons. He maintains that by working with the schools, these persons can help "evaluate and define the material and methods of instruction best suited for each grade . . . so that we can be sure our children are receiving sound and accurate information, in an appropriate sequence, regarding family life and human sexuality."

Trouble often occurs despite careful planning. This was the case in Renton, Washington, where the school district embarked on a comprehensive sex-education program at the request of a citizens' committee and the district parents.

Months before the program was to begin, the district began its preparation. Officials called on local clergymen to help coordinate the program, then set up a committee of teachers, school personnel, parents, and professional people to preview the proposed materials. Teachers were given special preparation, including a series of workshops conducted by physicians, psychologists, and educators. Finally, the district conducted a series of nine grade-level workshops to give parents an opportunity to see the materials their children would be using, and to discuss questions the children might bring up at home.

Nevertheless, the program encountered active opposition. From a small but well-organized minority came a variety of charges—including "Communist plot" and "pornographic literature." In response, the Renton School District prepared a three-page guide listing 11 common charges of the organized opposition and answers for each. One example: Referring to Sweden's sex-education program, the opposition commented, ". . . look at the premarital sex . . . illegitimate births, VD and divorce." The Renton School District's response:

> Sweden's sex education program prepares them for Sweden's society and its moral code which includes premarital sex. Renton's sex-education program prepares youth for adulthood, courtship, and marriage according to the expectation of our

society—of parents in Renton. Premarital or extramarital sex is
not the expectation of society in our time and place.

While the controversy continued, the school district did not waver
from its policy of openness and community involvement. School officials listened to residents who offered well thought out criticism, and
incorporated some of their suggestions. As a result, the Renton program thrived. Says the May 1969 *Newsletter* of the Division of Family
Planning and Education of the University of Washington:

> When a school's activity is under such close scrutiny by the
> community, teachers and administrators put their best foot for-
> ward and become even more dedicated to perfecting a cur-
> riculum . . . In Renton, for example, where tenacious protest
> has continued for many months, the developing curriculum
> may be one of the best in the United States.

Your local program. Does your school offer a sex-education program? If so, is it a good one? Doctor Simon points out that it is easy
for parents and educators to sit back and say, "Good, something is
being done." He warns, however, that sex-education programs must
be judged by extremely critical criteria. "Vague feelings of good intention don't fill the bill," he says.

What can you do? Experts advise:

Keep informed. Attend parents' meetings or workshops. Examine
materials used in the program, and discuss them with your neighbors,
clergymen, and physician. Find out what nearby schools are offering.
Is your program markedly different?

If opposition groups are circulating pamphlets or other materials,
check them out with your citizens' committee, PTA, or school board.
Remember, according to a number of school officials, altered materials
and materials intended for parents and teachers have, in some districts, been passed as classroom materials; tape recordings of school-
board meetings have been altered, spliced, and passed as genuine.

If parts of the program concern you, discuss your feelings with your
citizens' committee and with school officials.

If, after a thorough investigation, you feel that your program is a
good one, support your school officials. During periods of controversy
and extremist opposition, a school district and its officials urgently
need the backing of the community.

Continue to evaluate the program as it progresses. Changes will
almost certainly be necessary.

While emphasizing that mistakes have been made and will be
made, students, parents, and educators feel that the possible benefits of sex-education programs far outweigh the risks.

They stress that in addition to providing factual information, sex-education programs should help guide young people toward a better understanding of themselves and others, including the opposite sex. They should help young people develop a personal moral standard based, not on inhibition through guilt, but on self-control and concern for others. Finally, they should help prepare young people to use their sexuality in mature and responsible ways, and to be happier, healthier adults.

STUDY QUESTIONS

1. How widespread is the opposition to sex education? How much sex education actually exists in the schools now?
2. Is there any relationship between sex education and mental health?
3. What are some of the moral problems related to sex education?
4. What kinds of people oppose sex education? Are they all alike politically? Religiously?
5. How did the Communists get "involved" in sex education?
6. What are the "three Rs"? The "three Ss"?
7. How broad is the attack of groups that oppose sex education? What else do they oppose?
8. What are the principal techniques used by opponents of the move toward sex education in the schools? Are they always aboveboard and honest?
9. Why do some parents have trouble explaining the fundamentals of sex to their children?
10. What are some of the principal approaches to sex education? What do they sometimes lack?

SUGGESTIONS FOR WRITING

1. Assume you are an opponent of sex education in the schools. Write a brief but convincing essay that avoids the weaknesses of the antisex-education arguments described in this article. Be factual, logical, and avoid hysterical name-calling. In other words, present what you feel is an intelligent and reasonable argument against the position that sex education must be taught in public schools.

2. How would you want the moral aspects of sex education to be handled in the best program you could devise? Is there any reasonable argument that can be presented, insisting that there is no morality involved in sex education? What are the arguments that would oppose such a view?

3. How serious are the fears of well-meaning parents and religious leaders about the harm sex education can do our society, especially young people? Basing your argument on your own experiences with sex education in your school, present a clear and definitive statement of your views.

4. How do you react to the view that sex education is acceptable in the schools, but not before the student reached high school? Is this a legitimate and desirable position? If not, why not? If so, what responses have you to the arguments presented at the end of the article?

5. Why, in your opinion, do organizations opposed to sex education argue in terms of a Communist plot or an anti-Christian plot? Can sex or sex education legitimately be linked to these political and religious views? How do the opposition groups make the link seem convincing? Why do they make it at all?

6. Was the sex-education program in your school of some value? If not, why? Even if it was fairly good, suggest what could have been done to improve it. Be as detailed, as fair, and as clear as possible.

A CHARADE OF POWER:
BLACK STUDENTS AT WHITE COLLEGES

Kenneth B. Clark

The introduction of significant numbers of black students to the major private universities is a fairly recent phenomenon. The author of the article, one of America's most distinguished educators, talks about the racial problems that have developed on many of these campuses and the dilemma that confronts the black college student.

The dilemma of the Negro, especially of the black college student, in these turbulent days is full of irony and paradox. His dilemma is compounded by the appearance of change in American institutions, particularly education, and his need to respond appropriately in terms of the degree of reality of this change. He often finds that change is an illusion, that he is presented with, and seems sometimes to invite, merely new forms of racism, in new guises but, in the end, made of the same stuff.

His dilemma is rooted in one dominant fact: however noisy his rhetoric, however flamboyant the manifestations of his protest, he is still the minority. Even his "victories" are guided and permitted by the majority. The armed black students at Cornell had no real power —not they, but the white majority were in control. The fact that the white administration and faculty chose not to act violently in response, but rather to acquiesce—or appear to acquiesce—to demands, did not obscure the evidence of real power. The guns at the ready were a charade; they were permitted only because the majority understood they could be put down whenever it wished to do so. To the extent that whites encourage in blacks acceptance of this pretense of

A CHARADE OF POWER: BLACK STUDENTS AT WHITE COLLEGES   Reprinted from the Summer 1969 issue of the *Antioch Review* by permission of the *Antioch Review*.

power, they are participating in but one more manifestation of an old racism.

Negroes have had centuries of experience of benevolent racism that permits bizarre behavior on the grounds that the Negro is going through a phase that will be outgrown. Whites believe this now—and often state it candidly. Black separatism, particularly among the young, is seen as racially adolescent behavior, to be understood, tolerated, and even condoned as long as it does not threaten the real sources of authority. That many black students do not grasp the pervasive and subtle forms of white racism is clear in their exultant reaction after "non-negotiable" demands lead to apparent concessions. They believe that Black Studies Institutes, separate from the governance of the university, free from the regulations of faculty or degree requirements, or black dormitories from which whites are "excluded," are evidence of surrender of majority power. But whites have not given up, thereby, anything other than the requirement of persistent confrontation with blacks on a basis of black equality. Negro students miss the fact that voluntary surrender of "power" by those who hold it is seldom loss of actual power. Symbolic power may be tendered, however, particularly when those in authority perceive that negotiators will be satisfied with the mere appearance of power, indeed, that in some complex way, they may prefer not to take the risk of competing for the responsibility of genuine power. Those in power seldom give up more than is necessary to restore stability—for stability is essential to their orderly exercise of authority.

If a mayor can buy peace by strategic patronage (no less patronage when black militants rather than old-fashioned wardheelers demand it), he will do so. He need not transform the ghetto into a viable community if this is not the non-negotiable demand. If a white-dominated Board of Education can appease militants, and simultaneously strengthen top quality white-segregated schools, it need not insist on basic reorganization of the system. If a national political leader can ease the pressure by offers of subsidies to a few black capitalists, he need not move to abolish poverty, among both Negroes and whites. If a university administration can restore harmony and the image of innovation by a no-strings-attached financial grant to a separate black studies program that may cover a few salaries or subsidize a gas station, it need not move to transform itself into a genuinely nonracial institution dedicated to developing human beings and to helping them develop effective strategies for fundamental social change. No more power is granted than it is necessary to yield.

It is probably true that many black students understand this and, in cynicism born from despair at the tenacious hold of white racism, take what can be easily won, settling for the charade. It is, in many ways, a tempting choice. Many probably know, though the admission is too painful to endure, that a university could not surrender to student control a Black Studies Institute with exclusionary characteristics and without even minimal academic standards if it truly valued the humanity of blacks. If the university does not insist that Negroes be as rigorously trained as whites to compete in the arena of real power, or that studies of racism be as thoroughly and systematically pursued as studies of nuclear physics, one must question whether it is really serious.

It is clear that whites desperately need to know the history, the psychology, the economics of their own racism, yet a university that agrees promptly and without struggle to exclude whites from such studies, except in isolation from militant blacks, has in fact protected whites from ruthless encounter with that knowledge. Painful though such confrontation would be, whites need to face with a terrible honesty the consequences of their own inheritance, and they need to do it in the presence of blacks. One can surely understand their reluctance to do so, for, although Negroes cannot escape the daily encounter with themselves as Negroes, whites can and usually do seem to escape the necessity of facing themselves as whites. They are not consciously aware of race every moment of every day, as Negroes are. They are able to train themselves as economists, as lawyers, without such concerns; they are able to live as human beings without conscious modification. Why—if they are rational, non-masochist individuals—should they present themselves to be flagellated or, even more painful, commit themselves to a genuine struggle for equality if it is not required? Why, particularly, if blacks collaborate in helping them by rewarding such evasion of reality with accolades of radical relevance? If the white applauds black separatism and at the same time enhances his liberal image, he has the best of both worlds—he need not challenge white domination of all institutions in America, and he is absolved from guilt all at once.

One must understand and respond to the reluctance of blacks to further the education of whites, especially at deep emotional cost. However, it is more difficult to accept the collusion of many of the most creative and brilliant of young black leaders in programs that are separate and unequal. Must the struggle against racism be given up so easily? Has a realistic despair been rationalized by a decision that competition for genuine power to achieve positive social change is itself undesirable—not only that it is unachievable, but also that it is undesirable, corrupt evidence of a corrupt society? It may indeed be true that it is hopeless to try to change the deeply rooted racism in American society. Certainly, those confined to Nazi concentration camps would have been right in an appraisal of their own situation as hopeless. But is it required of blacks that they, as some concentration camp inmates did—according to Viktor Frankl and Bruno Bettelheim—identify with the oppressor, collaborate in the efficient implementation of his goals, and rationalize this surrender of spirit and integrity as a realistic adaptation?

It may well be that stubborn commitment to an integrated—an equal—society is unrealistic, and that an unremitting search for strategies to achieve it, therefore, is irrational, given the forces arrayed against it. Those who predicted "the wave of the future" in the face of the apparently irresistible Nazi onrush certainly would have agreed. But history is littered with the ruins of unconquerable empires and irresistible crusades. And, even if the predictions of defeat are correct, would a retreat into the new black monasteries with their secret rituals and their new theologies be the rational (or even the most comforting) solution? How long can one accept exclusion as a self-desideratum? When one leaves college to enter the outside world one can either create new enclaves, a ghetto within the ghetto, or can struggle to free the ghetto's inhabitants.

And if one enters the hard struggle for freedom, one must bring resources and skills to the inevitable encounter with the majority, who have built and guarded the ghetto's walls and fostered and profited from its ruin. Even if one could retreat oneself, can young blacks face the desperate need of their brothers—without response? The ghetto resident has not chosen his exclusion; it is forced upon him. There are no rats in the black dormitories. They are an unreal haven. Life within them, while warm, and deeply comforting, and intensely exhilarating—like the womb, cannot sustain life long. White segregationists could devise no better strategy than to persuade white liberals that they could absolve themselves from corrosive guilt by supporting black exclusion (under less rigorous standards than those required for white exclusion) in the heart of that institution most likely to provide black leaders for the future—the university—and at the same time, to persuade many of the best young black students that this is a radical victory.

But no such strategy needs to be devised, for the symbiotic needs of each group help to sustain it: the need of the guilty white to feel innocent again, the need of the angry young black to nurse his pain in private. Together they serve the cause of inequality. The ultimate victory of white racism would be to encourage black suicide—whether the suicide of physical self-destruction or the suicide of self-imposed withdrawal from the conditions of life.

This is the contemporary dilemma of the Negro in American universities. Whether the dilemma will be resolved in time to save the nation from the consequences of its history is still unclear. But even if despair is the only realism, there remain fundamental values and ideals by which one must live, even in despair. One cannot make the lie of racism palatable.

STUDY QUESTIONS

1. What kinds of racism is Clark alluding to in the early paragraphs of his essay?
2. What kinds of racism are implied in permitting black students to have guns at Cornell? How seriously does Clark take these students' power?
3. How does the control of power affect the racial situation in any community? In any university or college?
4. Clark talks about a "nonracial institution." What does he mean? Is such a thing possible? Is it desirable?
5. Why does Clark insist that black students must be as rigorously trained in studies of physics as in studies of racism?
6. Why is it that whites can live day by day without confronting themselves as whites?
7. How do black separatists collaborate with white efforts to keep the real power in the hands of the whites? Would the separatists agree with Clark?
8. What are the "new black monasteries"?
9. In what ways are all black dormitories *not* like black ghettos?
10. What kind of a nonracial society does Clark envisage?

SUGGESTIONS FOR WRITING

1. If you were a black separatist and an advocate of Black Studies Institutes in universities, how would you respond to Clark's argument? Analyze his position closely and try to find its weaknesses. It is not enough to rail against him; you must argue as coolly and as carefully as he does.

2. Clark uses the phrase, "A charade of power." What does he mean
   by it? Is he right? Why might others fail to observe that it is a
   charade instead of the real thing? Be specific and detailed.
3. What, for Clark, is the "real arena of power"? Is he right? Be as
   cautious and careful as possible in trying to establish the reality
   of that power—remember that Clark uses the term "illusion" frequently. Be sure you are talking about the real thing, not a "real"
   illusion.
4. Analyze the following statement and decide whether or not it is
   true and relevant to Clark's final position: "The ultimate victory
   of white racism would be to encourage black suicide—whether
   the suicide of physical self-destruction or the suicide of self-
   imposed withdrawal from the conditions of life."
5. If you are black, describe what you feel would be a predictable response to this essay by a white reader of your own age and general situation. If you are white, describe what you feel would be
   a predictable response from a black reader in your situation.

GRADES MUST GO

Sidney Simon

Among the perennial questions in education at all levels is whether giving grades on assignments or in courses is good or bad. This article is a highly charged and by no means impartial discussion of the question.

In Shirley Jackson's eerie short story, "The Lottery," a village holds a drawing each year to decide whom it will stone to death. In our colleges and universities—and our high schools, as well—we do it twice a year.

One character in Miss Jackson's story raises a question about why the villagers continue to perform this inhuman ritual, but an elder quiets him with, "We have always had a lottery."

So it is with grades, and midterms, and true-and-false questions, and multiple choices, and essay questions (choose three out of four), and bell-shaped curves, and dean's lists, and No-Doz, and blue books, and crib sheets, and proctors, and the rest. We have always had them —or something akin to them.

We have indeed always had them, although there is literally not a shred of research evidence which supports the present grading system. It is about as accurate as the gas mileage statements out of Detroit. That we have tolerated grades for so long makes me seriously question whether we have even fewer brains than we do intellectuals on our campuses.

Grades must go. Their only genuine function is to serve certain administrative conveniences. They do allow the registrar and members of the deanery to decide who is on probation, and who can take an honors course, and who sits on the dais at Phi Bet banquets, etc., but they are too destructive to be allowed to continue to debase what a university could be.

GRADES MUST GO   Reprinted from *Changing Education* (Spring 1970), official publication of the American Federation of Teachers, AFL–CIO.

Five reasons why grades must go:

Grades separate students and professors into two warring camps, both armed with dangerous weapons, none of which have anything to do with a notion of a community of scholars. The grades keep student from teacher and teacher from student as effectively as if each wore the sweaty jerseys of two archrivals fighting for a bid to a bowl game.

A student cannot praise a professor's teaching within earshot of other students, or he would be slashed to ribbons for "brown-nosing." However, in the comfortable privacy of a professor's office, the slippery students keep their appointments, and get in the brownie points which, they have well learned, are one of the practical ways to up their grade-point averages. Sadly, this same information keeps many students with integrity away from the professor's office.

If praise can't be given, open criticism of a professor to his face is even rarer. It simply would not be politic. Even if you had some hint about how to make his course better, the implied disapproval would surely earn retaliation. So it passes that students and faculty—the two groups on a campus which most need to find each other—are separated by a wall as impenetrable as barbed wire, and it is called a transcript.

Grades over-reward the wrong people and often punish students who need to be punished the least. There is something basically immoral about a system which passes out its highest institutional appreciation to a meritocracy based on memorization, clever use of mnemonic devices, test-wisdom, and various symptoms of anal compulsiveness.

The dean's list is made of just too many such people—gradegrubbers who seem to lack a certain spark of creativity, sensitivity, and humanity. The finely sifted ones who make the honorary societies are often not necessarily dishonorable, but their unmitigated self-advancement tends to make you wonder why the university makes so much fuss over such people at graduation. The world is dying from selfishness and yet the academic world gives asterisks for it on commencement programs.

At the other end of the continuum, grades have been used systematically to screen out black students, to decide who to ship out to Vietnam, and to firmly remind those who will not conform that they are failures. It becomes increasingly clear that those who knuckle under to the grading system and learn what reality is all about ("Look, the guy likes Buber, so I give him Buberisms all semester,") are the ones who reap the rewards. Those who question the system or resist it often get flunked out, neatly and sometimes finally.

Grades tend to destroy what learning should be all about. Students sign up for snap-and-crap courses they neither need nor want, but which give a sure "B" without requiring many papers, or much reading, etc. Students avoid courses which they might be curious about but cannot afford a low grade in because it would mess up their "cum."

Craftier students soon learn to balance their 15–18 semester hours with a mixture of hard markers and easy markers, and, like good consumers, they budget their time each night and study a little of this and a little of that. Passionately wanting to go and learn something in real depth is somehow looked upon as slightly uncouth. After all, those "meaty" courses with a mid-term, a term paper or two, a final, and three snap quizzes scattered here and there (so we can divide by 5 and get a good, objective average in order to give you a good, objective grade) have to be spread out carefully if one is to "keep up."

Only the wastrel reads novels or plays which are not assigned, and no one except a fool spends more time in the library than he needs to pad out, with the right number of footnotes, a paper which the student guesses the professor will like (whether the student cares deeply about it doesn't matter). Grades make it almost unthinkable to consider writing a paper which might later be sent as an article to a magazine.

Pragmatism, then, requires students to begin approaching the selection of courses like the directors of a conservative mutual fund picking out a portfolio of safe investments—everything in moderation. It is little wonder that so many graduates later join the Book-of-the-Month Club to be told what to read and allow the Theatre Guild to pick their drama for them.

Grades reinforce an archaic notion of "competition" which may well turn out to be deadly in the 1970s. Sure, life is competitive, at least if you are in the business of selling storm windows or aluminum siding. Yes, Ford, Chevy, and Plymouth would like to slice each other's throats for a bigger chunk of the market, and all three of them would like to rub Volkswagen off the map. Nevertheless, the skills of cooperation actually dominate a sane man's life much more than do the skills of competition.

God save the marriage where the man is in constant competition with his wife. Pray for the family where the siblings are turned against each other's jugular veins. Most of our efforts to make our neighborhoods and communities healthier and happier depend on some complex forms of cooperation. And almost everything the college graduate does today to make a living demands cooperation. Almost everything gets done through committees, and the really valuable co-worker knows the intricate skills of group process, and has the humanity necessary to control his ego and his competitive instincts. The point is, we don't have to teach competition; the beast in us is instinctively competitive. But we had better do more thinking about how to help ourselves become more civil so that we develop some range of responses beyond "What's in it for me?"

Competition for grades has made today's campuses lonely places. There are entirely too many students working for their own slightly sullied advancement into the above-$20,000 brackets. Altruism and a sense of community just don't exist at most colleges and universities. Too many pages are slit from library books, making it impossible for the next person to get the assignment, and in one of those classes where the prof proudly tells you he will give as many F's as A's, just don't be absent, because you won't find many people who will give you their notes.

Four years and more of this kind of a competitive treadmill might prepare a college graduate for ruthless dashes down the expressway at rush hour, but I surely would not want to be the first black to move into his block.

Of all the destructive things grades do, probably the ugliest is that they contribute to debasing a student's estimation of his own worth. The emphasis and extreme focus upon grades, term after term, seems to squeeze a student's identity and self-image within the narrow confines of his transcript.

Students everywhere are in a quandary. They have too little else upon which to test themselves. They are saddled with an extended adolescence. They have no real opportunities to be either independent or courageous or to test under duress their love of their fellow man. As a consequence, students often stake their identity, almost their total sense of self, upon that grade-point average.

We do not know how many of them, in the lonely hours of the night, sit and divide their grade-point averages out to the 10th decimal point. However, we do know that a large percentage of the suicides at our universities stem, in part, from those decimals—at least, from misguided interpretations of their significance.

How could we have allowed those numbers to spew widespread feelings of inadequacy, inferiority, and lack of power among perfectly useful and decent people? Have you heard of students who have given up careers because they thought they just didn't "have it" when they received a low grade in a basic course in their major? The worshipping at the shrine of numbers is a kind of madness which we accept almost without reflection, and which has about as much validity as treating a cancer with a spray deodorant.

The pursuit of grades has dried up the average student's sense that he can shape and change the world around him. With his eye on the carrot at the end of the semester, he does not really believe that he can make a course better. He doesn't really believe that students can and should have some stake in evaluating their education. It is almost heresy for him to believe that he has some valid insights in the hiring and firing of professors. Not wanting to antagonize the grade-givers, he does not complain about large classes, irrelevant lectures, inappropriate assignments, unnecessary prerequisites, or unreadable textbooks.

How many of our students simply do not know who they are because for so many years they have been jumping hurdles put up by other people? Finally on their own, they do not seem to have the resources for making meaningful choices or building values to live by. Otherwise, would so many of them end up like the characters in John Cheever's Shady Hill suburb? Those urbane, handsome, ivy-league types going off to high-paying jobs that they hate (made tolerable by martinis at lunch), raising children who greet them with, "What did you buy me?" and tolerating terrible abuse from their bosses so as not to get fired and thereby jeopardize the country-club membership, the $40,000 development house, the vinyl hardtop, and their credit with the orthodontist: Is that what an education is supposed to produce?

Over and over, I hear the phrase, "Well, that's reality." I think we are long overdue in examining a greater reality behind the grading system. It may be called "reality" to say, "All colleges have grades," but all colleges do not have them. It may be reality to say, "Grades are the only thing that graduate schools are concerned about," but the best of the grad schools are not all that concerned about them. When people say, "Well, that's the system," I want to shout, "Systems have been changed."

I believe we ignore at great peril the greater reality of a learning environment in which students and professors become increasingly alienated from each other, where cheating and the con-man are daily operative, and where what a student gets out of a course can be boiled down to a single, crude letter of the alphabet.

I am convinced that a real onslaught upon the grading system could have dramatic and immediate positive impact upon our universities. If nothing else, many of the most flagrant academic abuses might be flushed into the open.

Professors who can't teach will be forced to face that truth if ve take away the protection of their dangling As and Fs. Professors w 10 can teach but who get more of the institutional rewards from doing research or playing grantsmanship, may get back to teaching. Busy-work assignments will be challenged and so will those fraudulent read-ing assignments (2,000 pages a weekend?). Students will shape and change many assignments they now merely accept. Assignments will be more individualized and the curriculum will take on a new rele-vancy. It is no wonder that the old guard, including those Uncle Tom students who say, "Why, I don't see what's wrong with the grading system. Mister Charlie, he treats me real good, especially at transcript time," will resist doing away with the present grading system.

Change is coming, however. The danger is that we may be satisfied merely with a little tinkering here and a bit of adjusting there. A limited pass-fail system will not be sufficient to remove that inane cry from our colleges, "Wadjaget?"

What we really need is a sweeping awareness among students that they are being short-changed at that supermarket they call alma mater. They need to realize that they are the customers and, as such, they have every right to demand that they get a real education. They must learn to see through our ruses. They must not allow themselves to be bought off with green stamps which they glue into their tran-scripts and turn in at the redemption center at graduation time for credentials. Grades must go.

STUDY QUESTIONS

1. What, according to Simon, is the first and most usual response to the question of why we have grades in schools?
2. How much research exists to support the theory that grades are important?
3. What is "the only genuine function of grades"?

4. How do grades cause a gulf between teacher and student?
5. Who are the people grades benefit most? What kinds of intelligence or learning do grades encourage?
6. How is selfishness related to grades?
7. How do "snap-and-crap" courses benefit from a grading system?
8. What is the relationship between grades and competition? Is competition good or bad?
9. How does the "competitive treadmill" affect the general life style of the student after college?
10. Would a gradeless college improve or otherwise alter the quality of teaching?

SUGGESTIONS FOR WRITING

1. Memorize one or two of the arguments Simon presents here and offer them to a teacher of yours who is interested in defending the grading system. Note his arguments carefully, and when you have finished talking with him write a brief description of your experience, trying to discern as clearly as possible which side of the argument is more persuasive.
2. If you agree with Simon, describe what your academic day would be like if you had no grades to worry about. Which of your courses would you emphasize in your study time and how different would your study habits be? Do you think you could really adapt to a gradeless college?
3. Based on your own feelings, your own experience, and what you know about your friends, construct an argument that takes the opposite point of view from Simon's. Be sure to take into account each of Simon's arguments so that you do not side-step any important features of the issue.
4. Suppose you did indeed agree with Simon. Suppose your professors did, too. What would be the reaction on your campus to an active concerted move on your part to get rid of grades? Take into account not only the administration or other faculty people but consider the average student's response as well.
5. Are there any arguments in favor of getting rid of grades that Simon did not mention? Using arguments of your own design, try to push even further than Simon does in pointing up the need for eliminating grades.

THE QUESTION OF BLACK STUDIES

Charles V. Hamilton

The debate rages, even now, on the advisability of having black studies courses on college campuses; on who
should enroll in such courses if they exist; and on
whether or not they should have the same academic
standing as other programs given at the university.
Charles Hamilton thinks that the question has many
serious implications for higher education.

Several years from now, when historians studying race and politics in the United States look back on the 1960s, they will see a decade
of innumerable phrases and labels. They will see such terms as *integration, busing, nonviolence, violence, freedom now, law and order,
black power, community control, white racism, institutional racism,
separatism, black nationalism, revolution, black studies.* Hopefully,
those historians will realize the intense political environment out of
which these terms came. These terms were abbreviated ways—and
therefore dangerous because of the great possibility of oversimplifica-
tion—of explaining or projecting complicated phenomena. Arising
out of an emotional, intense political struggle, these terms became
less the subject for penetrating, in-depth analyses and more the basis
on which a polemical, momentarily dramatic debate was engaged.

The black studies issue is one example of this sort of treatment.
The term rose out of the protest demands of black students on college campuses in the late 1960s. The demands generally were summed
up in another phrase: "a relevant education." The black students
wanted their exposure to higher education to be "relevant" to them
as black people. They were dissatisfied with the nature of the college
curriculum as it existed in most places around the country—and they
were specific in their criticisms, with particular emphasis on the hu-

THE QUESTION OF BLACK STUDIES   Reprinted from the March 1970 issue of
The Kappan by permission of the author and *The Kappan.*

manities, history, and the social sciences. They pointed out major substantive gaps in American academia, and many of them concluded that these gaps were as much a function of a value system that deliberately chose the kinds of subjects to include in the curriculum as they were simply the result of scholarship yet to be done. In other words, the failure to depict the true role of black people in American history, or the exclusion of black writers from the reading lists of courses in American literature, for example, was a clear reflection of the values of American academia. Law schools and other professional schools were vehemently criticized for offering a course of study which did not "relate" to the developmental needs of a depressed black community.[1]

Thus the students began to demand black studies as an academic mechanism to overcome these normative and substantive problems. One has to understand that these demands were *political* precisely because they reflected—explicitly and implicitly—a feeling among the students that the colleges and universities were not "legitimate." That is, the students were demanding that the institutions change in many ways: in how they recruited black students, in what they did with the black students once they were on campus, in how the schools related to black communities, in the recruitment of black professors, in the kinds of courses offered. Therefore, as *political* demands for *academic* innovation, the demands were subject to negotiation and compromise. At all times, the demands were focal points of a political struggle. The struggle was political in the sense that the right of the college and university to rule unchallenged in the traditional ways was being questioned. *This was the central question: the question of legitimacy.*

Most schools readily admitted that changes (in curriculum, recruitment, community relations) had to be made. But then ensued an unfortunate period when many of the specific alternatives—which had to be understood as products of a political struggle—were taken as absolute academic ends. And before there was time to examine perceptively the kinds of *academic* changes that could be made, many people began to join the polemical debate. Black studies were called "soul courses"; they were seen as places where a cadre of revolutionaries would be trained; respected scholars admonished that black students needed "higher education" in order to compete, not something called black studies.

If one examined closely some of the black studies proposals, there

---

[1] See mimeographed newsletter issued by Harvard Black Law Students Association, Spring, 1968.

is no question that he would find many of them being concerned with issues of ideology and what might be called subjective matters. This is so precisely because the proposals were trying to—and in many instances did—articulate a new system of legitimacy. The proposals were rejecting, for example, traditional and widely accepted political science literature that argued in favor of the virtual inviolability of a two-party system. The proposals in that field called for courses that attempted to explore new ways to approach socio-political change in modern America—at least from the vantage point of black Americans. Perhaps those courses were aimed at "getting ourselves together" and at developing political power among black people. Why are these "soul courses"—in the catharsis-serving and demeaning sense of that phrase? Have not some political science courses traditionally been dealing with how groups operated "effectively" in the society? Have not many of the economics courses not only dealt with mere descriptions of the existing economic order but also with ways to strengthen and make that order more viable? Are we unaware of the mass of research carried on on the college campuses by scholars under contract with the government in the natural, physical, and policy sciences? Indeed, virtually all of American education (and surely this would apply to any educational system) has served as a socializing process.

The black students—perceiving blatant weaknesses in that process vis-à-vis their own lives and experiences—were calling for a substantive alternative. They no longer believed in the myth that higher education was value-free, objective, above the social turmoil. Traditional American scholarship has been geared to maintenance of the status quo. The black studies proposals were out to alter that orientation. Professors Seymour Martin Lipset and Philip G. Altbach—who cannot be accused of being generally and unequivocally sympathetic to the black student demands—made an interesting observation on the nature of the university:

> In the developing countries, there is an intrinsic conflict between the university and the society, thereby creating a fertile ground for student political awareness and participation. The university, as one of the primary modernizing elements in largely traditional societies, necessarily finds itself opposed to other elements in its society, and must often fight to protect its values and orientation. Students are often involved in these conflicts and are key protectors of the modern orientation of the university. . . . In the developed nations, on the other hand, no such conflict exists. The university is a carrier of the traditions of the society, as well as a training agency for neces-

sary technical skills. It is a participant in a continuing moderniz-
ing development, rather than in the vanguard of such development. University students are not called upon to protect the
values of their institutions against societal encroachments. In
most cases, they are merely asked to gain the qualifications
necessary for a useful role in a technological society.[2]

This is an interesting observation because the black students *are*
asking their universities to be in the vanguard of development.
The black students and the black studies demands have a valid
political point. If this is generally accepted, as very many thoughtful
people have conceded, it would appear that the next step would be
to begin to work out the kinds of *academic* changes those demands
call for. Clearly, the students who have served as the catalyst for this
should not be expected to come up with the final answers. Those
people who style themselves scholars have the burden of proceeding
to try to develop new knowledge consistent with a new orientation.

Much of the empirical work has yet to be done, because the questions have never been asked. What is the feasibility of massive economic cooperative ventures in rural and urban black communities?
What is the nature of and significance of the black culture vis-à-vis
new forms and styles of political action in the black community?
Is it possible to talk about a peculiar "black experience" that has
relevance to the way black Americans organize themselves and conduct their lives? What is the impact of the oral tradition on social,
economic, and political phenomena? Black Americans have a heritage, a black experience of abrupt cultural transformation to trau-
matized conditions of slavery in a distant, alien land with a different
language and different life styles; to legal freedom from legal slavery
in the same place and economic position; to an urban, atomized,
technological environment from a rural, intimate, agrarian environment. What is the meaning of this heritage and experience in terms
of new adaptive cultural characteristics, characteristics that can sustain black Americans as a viable people? What are the implications
of all this for enlightened public policy? What does it mean for the
kinds of effort made to bridge tradition and modernity in the black
community? What is meant by the "crisis-oriented" nature of the
black political experience? What is meant by "political traumatiza-
tion" (as opposed to "political apathy") that makes this distinction
relevant to one trying to understand and deal with the problems of
black community development?

[2] Seymour Martin Lipset and Philip G. Altbach, "Student Politics and Higher
Education in the United States," in *Student Politics,* Seymour Martin Lipset, ed.
(New York: Basic Books, Inc., 1967), p. 242.

These are some of the kinds of questions that their proponents want black studies to deal with. Are these "soul courses"? Are they "separatist," "violent advocacy of revolution," "catharsis-serving" courses? Do they take one *out* of "higher education"?

I believe that, *if these courses are carefully thought out, they will be the epitome of higher education.* They will prepare the student to engage the total society, not to withdraw from it. One is not going to know much about how to proceed with black economic development or with black educational development or with black political development without knowing a great deal about the total economic, educational, and political systems. And if one listens carefully to the major thrust of the student arguments—rather than focusing on particular polemical sentences here and there—this point will come through clearly.

One must understand that the demands made in a particular environment—political, suspicious, hostile—have many functions: They serve to wrench an entrenched, closed system into a new awareness; they serve to state specifically a rejection of old values and to state generally a framework for new values. The new directions *cannot* be very specific; they are new programs for experimental times. All answers are not known. There is a tendency on the part of some people to require certainty of results and consequences before they are willing to innovate. In social dynamics, this is hardly reasonable. Of course, there is the possibility of unanticipated consequences. But if those who led the fight in the American colonies to break with England in the 1770s had waited until they knew the precise consequences, they probably would not have moved. Or, to take a less "ruptured" case, those who began to implement New Deal measures in the crises of the 1930s could not wait until they had definitive answers about results. They were faced with crises, and, hopefully bringing the best judgment to bear, they had to act.

American higher education faces a serious series of crises. The demands for black studies simply point up one area of intense concern. It is unfortunate, but understandable (if one agrees with Lipset and Altbach) that some *so-called* culturally disadvantaged black students had to take the lead in pointing out serious educational weaknesses. And precisely because *they* had to assume the role of innovator in an area traditionally felt to be in the province of "experts," it is quite possible that many people in power positions have forfeited their claim to authenticity. Many of them have been lax and unimaginative and listless for so long that many black students now view them as anachronisms.

If all the colleges and universities now rushing to set up some sort of black studies department are sincere in agreeing to the validity of their moves, then why—the black students ask—did they not recognize the need before now? Why did they have to be prodded and poked and seized? (If they are acting now simply to avoid another sit-in or disruption, then they should be exposed as spineless hypocrites!) The point is that the credibility of many of the schools in the eyes of many black students is so low—the students, indeed, in some instances, question their integrity—that the students do not trust the traditional administrators and faculty to set up and implement a viable program. And this is the crux of the control problem. *The students do not want control because they want to insure easy grades, but because they want to insure a quality program.* They ask: How can the people who have been so negligent and value-oriented in harmful ways now be *trusted* to administer this exciting, vibrant new educational innovation? These are important questions.

In a sense, it is the *pride* of established academia that is hurt. And frequently their vanity requires its representatives to call for assurances that "high standards" be maintained—in evaluation of class work, recruitment of professors, etc. It is rather strange to hear such calls issue from a group that has admitted its own failure and ineptness. How could a scholar in American intellectual history, for example, not recognize the genius of W.E.B. DuBois? What sort of standards must have prevailed that permitted such a scholar to assume a position of authority?

Let us consider proposals for black studies submitted by black students. Do the black students have the answers? Obviously not; they are still in the early stages of their formal education. But they have enough insights gleaned from their black experience (a term which some people have come to see as delightfully mystic or just quaint) to know that much of what has been taught is inconsistent with—indeed, irrelevant to—the lives they lead as black Americans. *And it is this recognition that accounts for a great part of the thrust for black studies.* Many of the proposals may sound, and in fact are, extreme and farcical. But one should not be too quick to dismiss the entire "movement." [3]

A Harvard University faculty committee on African and Afro-

---

[3] One writer made the following observation: "To recruit thousands of young blacks into hitherto restricted American universities and to fill their heads full of something called black studies is to prepare them for nothing." Arnold Beichman, "As the Campus Civil War Goes on, Will Teacher Be the New Dropout?" *The New York Times Magazine*, December 7, 1969, p. 48.

American studies made the following statement: "We are dealing with 25 million of our own people with a special history, culture, and range of problems. It can hardly be doubted that the study of black men in America is a legitimate and urgent academic endeavor." [4]

Is American academia seriously prepared to embark on such an important intellectual pursuit? Or will there continue to be nit-picking and polemics and energy-wasting efforts over momentarily glamorous and dramatic issues (kicking white students out of black studies classes, separatism, etc.)? The black students have performed an invaluable educational service by raising in a political context the hard academic questions—a political context, incidentally, which many students perceived to be absolutely necessary, given the arrogance, smugness, and entrenched nature of many sources of power. The question now becomes whether higher education can be perceptive and intelligent enough to deliver the empirical goods.

American professors and deans are not unfamiliar with political struggles on their campuses. Campus politics has a long history in this country: interdepartmental rivalries; personality clashes; competition for promotion and tenure; faculty-wife gossip and clashes; at times, in some places, vindictive vetoing of each others' Ph.D. candidates; bitter maneuvering for fewer and smaller classes (and larger office space) at choice (i.e., not 8 A.M.) hours of the day and week.

But the demands and the criticism leveled by many black students today will make those perennial squabbles seem like tea parties—or perhaps one should say panty raids. The demands of the black students are not nearly so frivolous. The black students are raising serious politico-academic questions that cut to the core, to the very nature of the university and college systems. The black students are political modernizers vis-à-vis higher education in a way never before experienced on American campuses. And traditional American academia may well flunk the test (a metaphor not entirely unintended) if it does not do its homework (hard, empirical, relevant research and teaching).

STUDY QUESTIONS

1. In what senses can the black studies movement be considered a political movement?

[4] Report of the Faculty Committee on African and Afro-American Studies, Harvard University, January 20, 1969, p. 14.

2. How is "relevance in education" a part of this issue?
3. What does Hamilton mean by saying the debate eventually became "polemical"? How does such a debate differ from an ordinary debate?
4. Why is it relevant to Hamilton's argument to say that traditional American scholarship has been geared to maintaining the status quo?
5. How have black students demanded that the university become part of the vanguard of change, according to Hamilton?
6. How is black community development related to the black studies issue?
7. How could black studies courses become the "epitome of education"? Is this what Hamilton is hoping for?
8. Hamilton sees the crisis of black studies as only one of the crises higher education faces. What does he mean by this?
9. In Hamilton's view, why do students want control over the black studies programs?
10. Why is the political context of black studies essential to the entire issue?

SUGGESTIONS FOR WRITING

1. Apart from the political aspects—or at least from the immediate political qualities that Hamilton praises—what do you feel are the chief virtues of having black studies programs on college campuses? If such a program was available at your school, would you take courses in it?
2. Who should take black studies courses? Hamilton's view is predicated on the innovations forced on colleges by black students, but does he suggest that only black students should take courses in black studies? How relevant are such courses to all students?
3. Assume that you favor a strong black studies program. How would you counter the arguments of someone who then proposed an equally vigorous white studies program? Or would you counter it? Establish your position as carefully as you can, being as thorough as Hamilton is in establishing his position.
4. Hamilton accuses the universities of being essentially so conservative that they institute fundamental change only when they are forced to do so. Is this true? Using your own and others'

experiences, examine this statement and decide whether it is completely true, partly or sometimes true, or basically untrue.

5. Analyze Hamilton's style of writing in this essay. He argues against polemical styles in the early and middle parts of his essay, but toward the end seems to lapse into that very polemicism he deplores. What effect does this have on his entire argument?

POLITICAL TERRORISM: HYSTERIA ON THE LEFT

Irving Howe

Until the recent rash of bombings in major cities across the United States, we were accustomed to thinking of political terrorism as a tool of the Far Right: the Nazis, the Ku Klux Klan, the political assassins of our times. That distinction between the Left and the Right may no longer be valid.

The life of the political terrorist is overwhelmed by loneliness, not merely because he can no longer trust completely friend or comrade, but because he cuts himself off from all movements and communities in which choices can be weighed. Staking everything on the act, he blocks off all that comes before it and all that comes after. Deciding whom to smite, he replaces God. Choosing whom to punish, he replaces the justice (be it good or bad) of society. And since the conflicts of social classes must be bent to his will, he replaces history, too. The terrorist carries a moral burden only saints or fanatics would undertake—worst of all, fanatics mistaking themselves for saints.

Greater still is his political loneliness. The terrorist surrenders the possibility of sharing the experiences of a mass political movement, be that movement democratic or authoritarian. He discards responsibility to his people, his class, his generation. For you cannot hold an open discussion on where to throw the next bomb, and, while you may keep mumbling "power to the people," you deny in effect whatever power the people may have over your behavior. In a hallucinatory transaction you "become" the people.

We have had plenty of terrorism in the United States, mostly by far-right lunatics and racists; lynching is an American contribution to the repertoire of death. But the far right, shrewder than its sym-

POLITICAL TERRORISM: HYSTERIA ON THE LEFT   From *The New York Times* of April 12, 1970. © 1970 by The New York Times Company. Reprinted by permission.

biotic opposite on the far left, has never articulated an ideology of the rope and the bomb: it has done its dirty business and kept its mouth shut.

A few years ago it would have seemed—it would have *been*—a gross slander for anyone to ask whether terrorism might become a weapon of the dissident young, so hopeful did many of them seem in their idealism and fraternity. Today, that question must be asked about a fringe of the New Left. Serge Nechayev, heroic and ruthless terrorist of 19th-century Russia, would until recently have seemed a creature alien to our national experience; now it is possible that his spirit has migrated to our shores.

I say this not because I accept the scatter-shot malevolence that men in authority direct against students, but because I have witnessed the conduct and read the journals of the New Left grouplets. The great majority of the young, dissident or not, still seem to believe in democratic norms and nonviolent methods, though they are sadly unable to reach coherent articulation. But fragments of the New Left, by now fractured to the point of jungle warfare, are inflamed with the rhetoric of violence. Some flirt with sabotage and terror; others inflict minor physical brutalities on intra-left opponents. Perhaps there have also been a few ventures in actual bombings. We don't yet know.

About the recent incidents I have no revelations. All I propose to do here is to look into the rationales developed by the far-out wings of the New Left, the responses these get from half-sympathetic students and the likely repercussions of terrorism. I confess at the outset that I have no comprehensive theory to account for everything.

There is a standard liberal explanation for the growth of terrorist moods in or near the New Left, and like all standard liberal explanations it is neither entirely right nor wrong. The young rebels, we are told, tried every method of peaceful persuasion; they protested and picketed; they marched and electioneered. But the country, choosing Nixon and Agnew, turned its back on their outcry. As a result, they have become desperate, and see no solution but guerrilla warfare. At this point, usually over a drink or in a faculty lunchroom, the more chuckleheaded kind of liberal will add, "Of course I don't approve of such methods, *but still* . . ."

Though it contains a good portion of the truth, perhaps even a decisive portion, this analysis strikes me as too simple, and the "*but still*" as a proviso that could lead us to disaster.

There is plenty of reason for dismay and disgust at the state of American society. Every sensible person knows the list of our troubles. The thought of three, or seven, or more years of an Administration that regards Judge G. Harrold Carswell as a fit candidate for the Supreme Court and the barbaric regime in Athens as an appropriate ally fills many of us with bitterness. But—and I want to underscore this point—there is no necessary political, logical or moral connection between this response to our present condition and the methods the *kamikaze* segments of the New Left are turning to.

It does not follow that if you feel the country to be in a desperate condition you should necessarily start throwing bombs. First, you ought to do some thinking. You must take into account the sentiments of millions of middle- and working-class Americans; you must reckon the power of the state; you must ask whether the consequences of terrorism, whether "successful" or not, would be worse than the problems we already have. All this is on the prudential level; I will come to the moral issues later. If you do consider such matters, the only rational conclusion is, I believe, to continue political activity— the creation of movements and alliances—so that, through elections, public programs and militant protest we can turn this country onto the path of social reconstruction.

To say that all means of peaceful action have been exhausted is nonsense: they have barely begun to be employed. To say that nothing has been achieved by opponents of the war is a masochistic delusion: the results of protest have been notable. True, some of the New Left young have by now devoted as much as five or six years to politics and appear shocked that the centuries-long struggle for social justice did not come to instant triumph in 1969. It is not callous, it is merely humane, to suggest that this struggle seems likely to continue a while longer, and that among the requirements for it are the maturity needed for speaking with patience and decency to the unconverted. No one has ever been convinced by a bomb.

I am impatient with the maudlin claim that the young "have tried everything." For those who wish to change society there is no shortage of tasks: help Sam Brown organize the Moratorium against the war; join Cesar Chavez in unionizing grape pickers and Leon Davis in unionizing hospital workers; campaign for Allard K. Lowenstein's re-election to Congress; work with Ralph Nader for consumer rights and Philip Stern for tax reforms; and a thousand and one other things crying to be done and far more useful, *far more radical*, than the posture of bomb-throwing. What's more, if you don't like my list, make up your own.

Now, I do not mean to say that the despair felt by thousands of young Americans has nothing to do with the turn a few of them seem to have taken toward terrorism. Obviously, there is a strong connection, but mainly as an encompassing condition rather than as a direct and immediate cause. For since the despair is widespread and the terrorism very limited, there must also be other sentiments and convictions behind the throwing of bombs.

The despair felt by the extremist segments of the New Left is given an explosive or, if you prefer, hysterical quality by their having yielded to ideologies such as Maoism and Castroism, which has cut them off from both American realities and democratic norms. And the severe internal disintegration of the New Left seems also to have driven some of its adherents to the thought of desperado tactics.

The two main wings of Students for a Democratic Society—the Maoists chained to a totalitarian ideology and the anarcho-authoritarians running wild in search of another ideology—analyze precisely the dilemmas of one another. The Maoist cadres, hair cut and contemptuous of drugs, make devastating criticisms of the dilettantism and political "Custerism" (last-ditch bravado) of their factional opponents, especially the Weathermen. But it is precisely the unreality of Maoist dogma, with its faith in a proletarian revolution in the United States, that leads many young radicals to the scatter of opposing groups. In turn, the increasingly suicidal and pathological character of groups like the Weathermen, to say nothing of their political incoherence, creates a strong revulsion among the more rational young leftists. All are trapped. To be profoundly caught up in the fevers of ideology, to be unable to settle upon one that has a touch of realism, to drive oneself through rituals of "discussion" and then to exhaust one's body and imperil one's skin in hopeless street battles—all this must lead to desperation.

Though its sympathizers may have increased in number, the New Left meanwhile is incapable of reaching organizational or political stability. Its inner life is befouled by dreary factionalism and, sometimes, plain hoodlumism. It remains a sect, even if a large one, that cannot gain acceptance from any major segment of the population beyond the campus. To have grown and then to fracture, to know wild hopes and yet to be unable to suppress intimations of futility— this, too, must lead to despair.

Such, I wish to suggest, is the immediate or triggering factor in the outbreak of desperado moods. There are others. American radicalism, alas, has almost always looked abroad for its models. Today, none of the traditional wings of the European left, neither Social Democracy nor Bolshevism, command much authority among the young, since, for all their differences, they are both too rational and disciplined to satisfy the moods of youth. Brezhnev—who but a bureaucrat could identify with him? Mao—a warlord of the left. The style that captures romantic imaginations is that of Guevara: personally heroic, dashing, free-lance, though a mediocre thinker and a scandalously inept revolutionist (he did not even know the language of the Bolivian peasants he meant to "liberate," any more than his local admirers know the language of the American workers). Guevara signifies to the radical young a vision of instant revolution, personal risk, guerrilla exposure: the old Hemingway notion of discovering one's manhood through physical risk, but now in the context of political exaltation.

Let us also remember that a large percentage of the New Left young are the children of the middle class and the rich. (It is curious that a movement calling itself Marxist does not perform a class analysis on itself. Why does New Leftism appeal mostly to upper-class youth and not to young proletarians?) The affluent young leftists have little experience in doing significant work, either work that is socially useful or that could give them a sense of personal independence. They are riddled with guilt, they have no clear awareness of their place in the world, they have been raised to expect instant gratification. And, therefore, they often debase the admirable impulse to social involvement and sympathy with which they begin.

In the past I have avoided the view that the desperado wings of the New Left show symptoms of being the "spoiled children" of affluence, but it becomes hard to resist precisely that impression. A significant proportion of the young desperadoes—we have no statistics—comes from the upper *bourgeoisie*. Untrained at persisting in behalf of personal or public ends, unwilling to dig in at the job of persuading the American people to accept their ideas—and perhaps afraid that even making that effort would create the risk of being influenced by the very "masses" they have yet to meet—at least a few of these children of the rich, at once idealistic, disturbed and very bright, abandon themselves to the delirium of terrorist fantasy.

In utterly American style, it is a delirium with a large portion of innocence. They talk about and may even take a crack at violence, but deep down they seem still to expect that the society will treat them with the indulgence they have come to expect from at least some of their liberal teachers. They are innocent of history and innocent of social reality. A Columbia student is quoted in justification of terrorism: "If we don't take an active part in the revolution, the workers won't listen to us." Poor deluded boy. Does he have any idea what the American workers think of him, his politics and his methods?

Tragedy in comedy, comedy in tragedy. Identities shuffled, costumes tried on, the revolution as theater. Nobody knows who he is, everyone plays parts. Abbie Hoffman, accredited clown of the moment, chants praise to the bombs—"Boom!"—and his educated admirers chant back, "Boom, boom!" Jewish boys and girls, children of the generation that saw Auschwitz, hate democratic Israel and celebrate as "revolutionary" the Egyptian dictatorship. Some of them pretend to be indifferent to the anti-Jewish insinuations of the Black Panthers; a few go so far as to collect money for Al Fatah, which pledges to take Tel Aviv. About this I cannot say more; it is simply too painful.

Meanwhile, the ideology of the New Left itself creates strong inducements to political desperation. That ideology runs along these lines: There is a worldwide class war between imperialism, led by the United States, and the third world of revolutionary nations. In this international class war it is "our" job to weaken, disrupt and help destroy the main enemy, which is the American Government. In this view, which might be called the politics of Dean Rusk stood on its head, there is a tiny plausibility and a mountain of errors.

The third world does not exist as any sort of unified, let alone revolutionary, force; the underdeveloped countries have enormous differences in political character, social progress and economic need. Some, like India and Venezuela, are democratic and to propose "revolution" in these countries is to favor imposing élitist dictatorships. Others require modest beginnings in both industrialization and democracy. The "revolutionists" celebrated by our New Left are often tiny bands of deracinated intellectuals and students who have no contact with the people of their countries. And, finally, the relation between the United States and the third-world nations, while requiring radical correction, is far more complicated than the New Left picture allows. Yet, even if one does accept the Guevarist analysis, Weathermen tactics don't necessarily follow—unless, perhaps, a "final conflict" is expected within the next year or two.

To all of which I would add two factors, not as direct causes but as aggravating conditions: the mass media and the intellectuals.

That the mass media, especially TV, have been irresponsible in their coverage of "youth rebellion" and black upsurge seems to me beyond question. (Living in California last year, I sometimes felt the S.D.S. was a creation of TV, providing it with an unfailing flow of usable items; on reflection, I concluded it was a phantom dreamed up by Ronald Reagan to insure his re-election.) The irresponsibility of the mass media takes the form of a raging thirst for sensation, and this, I am inclined to think, is built into the very nature of modern communications. If the medium is the message, then the message is bad news: gross simplification and exploitation. There is no time for qualifying nuances, no appetite for complex reflection; the idiot box processes the life of man into polarities of mindlessness. If a Roy Wilkins spends a lifetime fighting Jim Crow and a Bayard Rustin comes up with a program for training ghetto kids for jobs, that hardly constitutes news by the standards that allow fly-by-night loudmouths to scream "Burn, baby, burn!" at audiences of wide-eyed or dull-eyed suburbanites. Television seems inherently melodramatic and thereby made to order for farceurs like Abbie Hoffman; it encourages New Leftists, born to the corruptions of publicity, to act out an endless serial: *Which building will be liberated today?*

More serious is the role of the intellectuals, too many of whom have proved susceptible to the delights of being 90-day campus heroes. I think of the distinguished movie critic, yesterday an absolute pacifist, who helped raise money for S.D.S. after the Columbia events; the brilliant novelist who told his admirers they must prove their courage by feats of bravado and speculated on the moral propriety of beating up 50-year-old candy-store keepers; the erudite Hegelian philosopher who taught the young that tolerance is bourgeois deception and liberal values are a mask for repression; the fierce sociologist who kept reminding us that "violence is as American as apple pie," without troubling to ask whether that pie might give one a bad case of food poisoning; the bright young journalist who announced that "morality comes out of the barrel of a gun"; the stylish literary paper that ran a diagram on its cover, perhaps as part of an adult-education program, describing how to make a Molotov cocktail.

Of course, none of these people favor terrorism; their only violence is of the phrase. But at some point sorcerers must take a bit of responsibility for their strayed apprentices. For it's not as if everything leading up to the present debacle on the New Left—the élitism, the authoritarianism, the contempt for democracy, the worship of charismatic dictators, the mystique of violence—hadn't already been visible two or three years ago, when such intellectuals began offering the New Left an aura of intellectual responsibility. What the young radicals needed from the intellectuals was sober criticism; what they got too often was a surrender of critical faculties. And it did no one any good.

As for the sympathetic young, unhappy with the idea of terrorism yet inclined to murmur *"but still . . ."* let me print a little dialogue, all too true to life, between one of them, whom I'll call *He*, and an

interlocutor, whom I'll call *I*. No illusions need be entertained that *I*
persuades *He*:

He: "If this country can drop endless numbers of bombs on defenseless Vietnamese, why get so outraged when these fellows, whoever they are, drop some here?"

I: "If I thought that dropping them here could speed up the end
of dropping them there, I'd still be against doing it, but at least I'd
admit there's something to argue about. But you know as well as I
do that dropping bombs here isn't going to help end the Vietnam
War; if anything, quite the contrary. Besides, why can't we be indig-
nant toward both?"

He: "Well, I don't like terrorism any more than you, but nothing
else has worked."

I: "Does that mean that if bombing emptied buildings doesn't
'work,' they'll take the next step?"

He: "And bomb buildings with people in them? I don't know. So
far they've only bombed buildings, but not hurt people."

I: "Sorry, that won't do—for three reasons:

"First, I don't trust their aim.

"Second, I don't share your faith in the efficiency of the police.
Suppose the cops hadn't proved fast enough in responding to one of
those phone calls that give them 20 minutes to empty out a building.
Or suppose they'd been distracted from a 'revolutionary' phone call
about a real bomb by a nut's phone call about an imaginary bomb.

"Third, they already have, it seems, killed some people: themselves."

About the political consequences of continued terrorism there can
be no doubt. The first and mildest consequence would be Reaganism.
("The one indispensable element in Reagan's political survival," says
Jesse Unruh, who ought to know, "is campus unrest.") The Reagan
backlash, suave in manner and graced with a Hollywood smile, depends more on police than street mobs, and it rests upon the assurance of winning elections. Ultimately, Reaganism might be the least
of it, for this country can produce far worse. It has.

For most New Leftists, the argument concerning backlash in particular and consequences in general has little persuasive power. They
affect to see little or no difference between Reagan and a liberal
Democrat, and some even prefer a victory for Reagan out of the
suicidal expectation that after apocalypse their turn will come. A
good portion of the S.D.S. campus guerrillas can retreat, if necessary,
to their parents' town and country houses, or quickly find the money
to flee the country. But no such luxury of choice is open to the resi-

dents of Watts, the patients in California's hospitals, the teachers and students in its colleges; they must suffer the consequences of Reagan's policies.

Now, in a country with an atomized population, weak military forces, widespread illiteracy, feeble structure of government and no tradition of national unity, terrorist methods might prove effective. But it is really a sign of political dementia to suppose that a few hundred people could terrorize a country with unprecedented wealth and power, enormously vigorous agencies of government and a population with a large conservative segment. All terrorism might do in the United States is to frighten or enrage authority that now acts with a measure of restraint but could brutally smash its opponents.

Some New Leftists, however, are enchanted by their "clever" tactics: they don't have a centralized organization that can be infiltrated on top, so they reason, they are not as vulnerable as were past radical groups. Another delusion! For while it's true that "confrontationist" tactics have been shrewd and at first have caught authorities unprepared, radicals ought to recognize that there are intelligent and determined people on the other side too. Each time "confrontation" has brought into play student ingenuity, it has resulted in an escalation of retaliatory measures. Nevertheless, it speaks rather well for the people of this country that, despite what they consider to be provocations and outrages, they have thus far refrained from letting themselves be stampeded into hysterical and repressive moods.

Terrorism by small groups is admittedly hard to detect, but one consequence of this could be that if limited responses don't cope with bank-burners and bomb-throwers, men in authority will be driven to employ total measures, e.g., large-scale "preventive detention." Those of us who believe in civil liberties would fight as hard as we could against such proposals, just as Norman Thomas fought for the rights of Communists who had steadily abused him. But who is prepared to say that in the kind of social atmosphere created by terrorism we would have much chance of success? Every state, whether good or bad, must react against terrorism; otherwise, it ceases to exist.

What for the Government might be an intermittent nuisance could, for American radicals, be a complete disaster. It is hard enough for the American left to gain a hearing, hard enough to convince our fellow citizens that we wish an extension of democracy into all areas of social and political life and share their loathing for all varieties of dictatorship.

But now, if that amorphous entity called "the left" is in the slightest to be identified with terrorist methods, we will be thrown back 100 years—literally 100 years—to the point where, in both Europe and America, the left movements had to spend decades disassociating themselves from a handful of anarchist bomb-throwers. How one despairs of the indifference to history shown by the radical young! If only they would read, say, the second volume of G. D. H. Cole's authoritative "History of Socialist Thought," in which he shows with crushing detail the way the terrorists hurt the Socialist movements of Europe and America, exposing them to provocation and smear. Cole goes still further by remarking of the bomb-throwers: "In the 20th century they would have become Fascists or Nazis; and some of them got as near to this as they could by joining the special anti-Anarchist police after a spell of Anarchist activity."

For civil-libertarians, the consequences of terrorism will be equally disastrous. In the past, people of the liberal-left community could usually assume that charges of "plotting to overthrow the Government," when brought by prosecuting attorneys against radicals, were politically motivated and false in substance. When Communist leaders were so charged in the nineteen-fifties, those of us on the left who had long been anti-Stalinist could nevertheless react immediately in opposition to such prosecution. We knew that people like Eugene Dennis and Gus Hall weren't manufacturing dynamite or planning a coup. They *were* trying to strengthen their position in the unions and other institutions. But whatever else, they were not fools.

In the future, however, how will we know? By its reckless talk and mindless acts, the far-out fringe of the New Left lays itself open—but also lays open all other sections of the left, old or New—to endless legal harassment and, to be blunt, to a maze of provocations and frameups. Yet, such provocations and frameups will be greatly helped if there is at least a smidgin of reality behind them, if there are in fact sticks of dynamite as well as the rhetoric of dynamite. Given that possibility, civil-libertarians will be hard pressed to distinguish between victims of persecution and candidates for prosecution.

Lest anyone think I am exaggerating, here is a statement put out by a committee in defense of three persons charged in New York City with bombings:

> Either the accused did strike a magnificent blow against those who make profit through the destruction of our lives and our world and they are our most courageous and beloved comrades; or they are being framed by a government bent on destroying our movement. . . . In both cases, they deserve our total support.

In short, hurrah if they threw bombs and hurrah if they did not. But what about those people who choose to be more discriminating with their hurrahs?

It would be a grave error to argue against terrorism mainly on grounds of expediency. To throw bombs is wrong. It is wrong because it is inhumane, because it creates an atmosphere in which brute force settles all disputes, because even if the bomb-throwers could win power through such methods they would no longer be (if they ever had been) the kind of people who could build a good society. Above all, it is wrong because minorities in a democratic society, as long as their right to dissent and protest is largely protected, do not have the right to impose their will upon the majority through violence or terror. This has always been a central argument of democratic socialism, an argument classical liberalism also accepts.

I would extend this argument to property. In a democratic society minorities have no right to inflict damage on property simply because they oppose the arrangements of capitalism. The aim of Socialists is to socialize the control of property, not to vandalize or destroy it. Toward this end we must first achieve a certain little detail: persuading millions of our countrymen that our goal is a desirable one. Until and unless we do that, we must abide, no matter with what pain, by the judgments of the majority, so long as our rights of criticism and dissent are protected. There is a still more essential matter: that, as the history of our century shows, any effort to establish "socialism" through terror ends and must end as a ghastly caricature of our hope.

There remains one issue concerning the consequences of terror, and I wish to stress it more strongly than all the others. *What kind of people are you going to become if you turn to such methods?* "Those who set out to kill monsters should take care not to turn into monsters themselves." These words were spoken by Nietzsche before the experience of totalitarianism, and all the blood and pain of our century confirms their wisdom. Ironically, some seven or eight years ago, when the then-young radicals were turning away from Leninism, it was precisely such perceptions that struck them as central.

The moral consequences for the lives of the young terrorists are already clear. Bernadine Dohrn, a Weatherman leader, is quoted by a New Left paper, *The Guardian*, as saying that the Weathermen "dig" Charlie Manson, accused leader of the gang that allegedly murdered several people in Beverly Hills. "Dig it, first they killed the pigs, then they ate dinner in the same room with them, then they even shoved a fork into a victim's stomach! Wild!" is how *The*

Guardian quotes Miss Dohrn. Other New Leftists have expressed their admiration for Sirhan Sirhan, killer of Robert Kennedy. Some have even toyed with the notion that fascism is a necessary prelude to the introduction of utopia: first arsenic and then strawberries and cream. Are these the kind of people who are going to create a bright new world and to whom we are to entrust the future of our children?

But a youthful voice answers me: "Our moral integrity will be protected by our revolutionary commitment, by our fight against injustice, by our sacrifice and ideology."

Alas, too slender a reed! Do you suppose that some of the G.P.U. men who tortured innocent victims in Stalin's prisons had not once told themselves the same thing? Do you suppose that some of them might not have imagined that their maiming and murdering was in behalf of "the revolution," and that in the end "history" would vindicate them? No, what matters is the quality and discipline of the life one leads at a given moment, and what one sees at the outer edges of the New Left—I do not speak of it as a whole—is at least as discouraging as what one sees in American society at large.

The bomb-thrower and the jailer are brothers under the skin. Is it not possible to revitalize in America the politics of democratic norm and radical change? Our traditions, our best impulses, our most humane energies, our needs all speak for it. Do that, and terror will die.

STUDY QUESTIONS

1. What are the peculiar circumstances of the life of the political terrorist?
2. How does morality affect the terrorist's life?
3. What kinds of ideologies have lynchers accepted? Are these important for understanding their acts?
4. What are some of the consequences of terrorism?
5. How do terrorists expect to improve the country?
6. Why does Howe resent the claim that the young have tried everything?
7. What are some of the Maoist ideologies? How do they support terrorism?
8. Who are the children of the New Left? What is their socio-economic class?
9. What role do the American workers have in the plans of the terrorist organizations of the Left?

10. How much of a role have the mass media played in creating the leftist organizations and their appeal?

SUGGESTIONS FOR WRITING

1. Identify what you feel are Howe's politics. Is he a rightist who reviles the leftist orientation of the Weathermen, or is he a leftist who feels left out of the new movement? Is it possible that he is a neutral observer or a moderate in political affairs? By reading closely for clues, see if you can tell where he stands on major issues of the day.

2. How would a New Left member react to this essay? What aspects of it would he be most likely to attack? How would he develop his rebuttal? In other words, in what ways is Howe's argument vulnerable?

3. Do you think Howe is correct when he reluctantly concludes that those young people of the New Left who consider throwing bombs are spoiled children? Is there anything that argues against this position? Howe offers a few reasons for his conclusions; do you know of others?

4. What most irritates you about this article? Describe what it is that bothers you most and explain why it bothers you. Do you think it would bother the average student? The average teacher? The average American worker? Describe and explain their probable reactions.

5. If terrorism were practiced on a wide scale in America, do you think you could predict how the citizens and the government would react? Describe what you believe would be the character of life in America. Do you think the results would be good or bad? What would be the implications for American foreign policy?

CAMPAIGNS AND THE NEW TECHNOLOGY

James Moriarity

It is usually conceded that one of the most important factors in the Kennedy defeat of Nixon in 1960 was Kennedy's superior use of television. Nixon's concern for his television image during the 1968 Presidential campaign would seem to support that view. Technology is now a major part of election campaigns at all levels of government and it is beginning to reshape our political process.

McCluskey too picked up the pace, chiefly by increasing the number of his television appearances. . . . Skeffington, before all else, favored the direct and personal contact with the voter; this approach had left McCluskey cold. He wanted television, and—more significant—so did his principal supporters.

—The Last Hurrah

Because he ignored the power of television in politics, Frank Skeffington, mayor of Boston in Edwin O'Connor's 1956 novel, went down in defeat.

This fictional account had its basis in fact. Ever since Dwight Eisenhower used television to overwhelm the 1952 Republican Convention, nullifying the political party power held by his rival for the nomination, Robert Taft, politicians and political scientists alike have observed that the medium brings a new dimension to politics. Instead of operating through the buffer of the party structure, the candidate on TV appeals directly to the voter. As a result, the traditional two-step process of communication, in which voters were largely influenced by local opinion leaders, has been short-circuited.

But the role of television has altered since it first proved so effec-

CAMPAIGNS AND THE NEW TECHNOLOGY   Reprinted, with permission, from the September 12, 1970 issue of *Science News*, the weekly news magazine of science and the applications of science, copyright 1970 by Science Service, Inc.

tive. Once merely a tool that could be used with skill, it is now part of an election technology that includes not only communications, but the increasingly precise techniques of polling, the sophisticated conclusions of research on persuasion and influence, and the versatility of computer analysis of voter patterns to pinpoint issues to emphasize and those to stay away from.

The campaign is generally packaged and presented by advertising specialists—"The campaigns can best be followed in the media trade press, where political campaigns are treated alongside beer accounts," says Dr. Harold Mendelsohn of the University of Denver. But the entire process has called into being a new group of technocrats that Dr. Dan Nimmo of the University of Missouri at Columbia has termed the management-pollster-communicator complex.

This new group, in effect, has replaced the party structure as a buffer between the voter and the candidate. The professionals organize a candidate's campaign, collect data on the electorate, determine the issues and image that the candidate should put forth, and then develop strategies that the candidate should pursue if he is to be elected.

As a result, far from bringing the candidate more directly in contact with the electorate, TV, in combination with the other techniques in the system, has interposed a new buffer that is even less responsive to voter pressure than the political party.

The first step in developing a campaign according to the new technology is to profile the electorate. A potent tool in this process is census data, which yields information on social rank, based on educational and occupational levels, ethnic ratings and housing. Another source of information is the growing body of social science research on attitudes and values of voters, stimulated by the growing enthusiasm for computer-based research that is sweeping behavioral science. Correlating the census data with the research on attitudes allows the campaign director to develop his strategy on issues and communications.

Once the electorate is profiled, the optimum means of communication is chosen to reach the audience. Here several decades of communications research come into play.

Starting back in World War II, for instance, Dr. Carl Hovland and a communications study group at Yale University found that an audience with a relatively low I.Q. responds best to material in which the conclusions of an argument are stated explicitly, rather than implied.

Other studies by the Yale group indicate the importance of the order of presentation in persuasion. When conflicting views are discussed, other factors being equal, the last argument presented is the most effective. This law of primacy is a technique that President Nixon has used, probably instinctively as a good campaigner, in his public presentations. He will state a number of opposing points of view on an issue and then close with his own view: "But now I wish to make my position clear."

More recent studies have attempted to probe the relative effectiveness of television and other media. Research by Dr. Bruce Westley of the University of Kentucky, for example, indicates that women of low education and income, and with working-class status and a minimal interest in politics are particularly trusting of television. If the electorate profile showed a substantial number of such voters, then heavy TV exposure, employing the techniques developed by Hovland and others, would be an indicated strategy.

The whole process of campaigning, from traditional rallies and street meetings to the packaging of brief spot appearances on TV and radio, are thus judged on the basis of their effectiveness in the whole campaign.

Computers are useful not only for electorate profiles but also for a variety of data storage functions. Mayor John Lindsay of New York in the 1968 primary campaign catalogued the reactions of 100,000 registered Republicans to phone calls asking them to rate him and his opponent on a scale of one to five; the printout was later used in the election campaign when Lindsay was running as an independent against both a Republican and a Democrat.

Mailing lists are another tool. Sometimes they are compiled by the campaign organization, but more often they are simply bought from consultants who specialize in direct mail techniques. The lists are used not only to spread campaign literature but to solicit contributions—an increasingly important campaign function.

Funding in the new political technology is critical, and is one of the major points of controversy about modern political campaigning. Computer analysis and campaign packaging are a highly skilled, expensive business, and TV is inordinately expensive and equally important. Studies at the University of Michigan Survey Research Center show that in 1960 and 1964 television accounted for 60 percent of voters' information about Presidential elections; and Dr. Mendelsohn reports that in 1968, of the more than $50 million spent on the Presidential election, $20 million to $25 million went directly to purchase broadcast time. A new peak was reached this spring as Richard Ottinger spent $830,000 on a New York Senate primary campaign for television advertising. His total expenditure of $1.92 million was about nine times what three rivals spent.

The implications of extensive communications technology in politics are still being assessed. But some of the developments are clear.

"This means the movement into politics of high-powered media and public relations personnel," says Dr. Mendelsohn.

> Because candidates can utilize their services they are displacing the political party; candidates can bypass the party with a management team and money. And of course private money in political coffers is not entirely altruistic.

Joseph Napolitan, president of a successful political consultant firm, agrees with Dr. Mendelsohn's assessment of the effect of the new technology on the political party. But he does not think the effect is bad.

"Political parties are obsolete," he says. "Technology has surpassed political parties as they function in their present status. Now instant electronic communication is the chief vehicle of comment between the voter and the candidate."

Napolitan feels that the more business-like approach of management teams eliminates the waste of traditional political organizations. "In the past, campaigns were sloppy, poorly managed and often not staffed with professionals," says Napolitan. But more important, he feels that the new technology and use of professional management allows men who were successful in other fields to enter politics.

"Some of the best men in the Senate came in from business and the academy. Otherwise people would be deprived of their leadership," he contends.

"This development is probably more dangerous than not," says Dr. Mendelsohn. "Traditionally the party develops candidates and acts as a buffer between the public and the office. It disrupts party discipline and means that a candidate with money can be elected without being responsible to anybody, including the electorate."

"Personally I don't feel comfortable that a man could be elected without a record of public service," says Dr. Angus Campbell of the University of Michigan, an analyst of American voting behavior for the past 20 years. "It has a disruptive effect on the party and means service to the party has nothing to do with ability to get elected."

Dr. Nimmo points out in his book, "The Political Persuaders," that the increased cost of campaigning brought about by expensive communications usage will eliminate a number of candidates. He also suggests that in a period of increasing disillusionment with the political process, candidates who might appeal to disenchanted voters may be hindered from entering the arena of expensive campaigning.

But Dr. Nimmo believes that the majority of middle-class Americans are not particularly disturbed by this development. "The large number of small donations in recent campaigns," he says,

> suggests that many citizens intuitively see campaign costs as a way of keeping the riffraff out of American elections; perhaps the financial contributors, large and small, prefer unregulated spending so long as it assures their interests a minimal control over elections.

As is happening in so many other fields, political behavior is being altered by technology and the technocrats who are adept in its uses. Dr. Nimmo maintains that the new technology is surpassing the importance of the political party that was the base of the old politics. But it is also in conflict with a growing movement calling for a new politics based on principle rather than party loyalty.

"Elections are approached neither as conflicts between parties nor as confrontations of principle," he states. "They are viewed instead as contests of personalities and, even more basically, they offer a choice between the sophisticated engineers working on behalf of those personalities."

STUDY QUESTIONS

1. How did Eisenhower use TV in his 1952 Presidential campaign?
2. What technological tools will candidates use in the next election besides television?
3. How do you feel about the role of public opinion polls during election periods?
4. What is the "management-pollster-communicator complex"?
5. Does the new technology make the candidate any more directly responsible to his constituency than he used to be?
6. What is the value of the research at Yale examining the attitudes of people with low I.Q.s?
7. Given the high cost of using the new technology, do you think candidates are going to be able to "buy" elections?
8. Do you think technology has actually begun to supplant political parties?
9. How does the new technology promise to keep the "riffraff" out of the political running?

SUGGESTIONS FOR WRITING

1. Do you feel that the new technology is basically unfair? Do you think it destroys the old American ideal that any boy can grow up to be President? If so, how do you justify your feelings? How would you convince someone who felt differently that this new approach to politics is not fair to the average citizen?
2. What specific aspect of this new technology do you feel is potentially the most dangerous? Why? Do you feel it threatens the nature of our ideals as Americans? Why should we fear it more than any other instrument in the arsenal of the new politician?
3. If you wanted to have politics make use of all the available tools of modern technology, what would you suggest Americans do to make sure the technology is not abused, and to avoid becoming a nation enslaved by our sciences?
4. Construct an argument that suggests the entire hullaballoo over the new technology is unwarranted and silly. What reasons have you for a feeling of confidence in regard to these issues? Try to be specific and discuss all the forms of technology that are mentioned in the article.

THE FUTURE OF AMERICAN VIOLENCE

Richard Hofstadter

Every modern society is involved with violence to some degree. During the last decade this country seemed to become preoccupied with it. One of the nation's most distinguished historians examines the role of violence in American life and its growing acceptance as a means of social change.

On the cover of the June 30, 1969, issue of *New Left Notes*, the organ of the Progressive Labor faction of Students for a Democratic Society, there is a large woodcut illustration which must surely be one of the minor signs of the times. Two young men, one white, one black, are seen crouching on a rooftop above a city in flames. Both are armed with automatic rifles, and both wear, Mexican-fashion, the crisscrossed bandoliers of the rural insurrectionary or *bandito*. They are revolutionaries, urban guerrillas. Alongside them is the legend: "We are advocates of the abolition of war, we do not want war: but war can only be abolished through war, and in order to get rid of the gun it is necessary to take up the gun." One must, I think, pass by the resemblance of this promise of a war-to-end-war to other such promises in the past; one must pass by also its hauntingly perverse echo of the words of the American officer in Vietnam that "In order to liberate the village we had to destroy it," to consider its larger meaning for American political culture.

There is in America today a rising mystique of violence on the Left. Those who lived through the rise of European fascism, or who have watched the development of right-wing groups in this country over the last generation, or have fully recognized the amount of violence leveled at civil-rights workers in the South, are never surprised at violence cults on the Right. They still see them in action in such crank groups as the Minutemen, and hear their accents in some of the uninhibited passages in George Wallace's speeches. What has been more arresting is the decline of the commitment to nonviolence on the Left, and the growth of a disposition to indulge or to exalt acts of force or violence. What was once the Student Nonviolent Coordinating Committee has taken the "Nonviolent" out of its title. Frantz Fanon's full-throated defense of the therapeutic and liberating effects of violence has been one of the most widely read books of our time. During a summer of exacerbated rioting, *The New York Review of Books*, one of the most influential and fashionable periodicals on the American campus today, elected to feature on its cover a set of instructions, complete with diagram, for making a Molotov cocktail. In its columns, a widely read left-wing journalist, Andrew Kopkind, has told us that morality comes out of the muzzle of a gun. The Weatherman faction of SDS has made a primary tactic of violent encounters with the police. A young leader of the Black Panthers rises at the 1969 summer convention of the SDS to taunt the white delegates with the boast that the Panthers have "shed more blood than anyone" and that white Leftists have not even shot rubber bands. Dotson Rader, a young veteran of Columbia's wars, informs the readers of *The New York Times* in its correspondence columns that the justice the New Left seeks will be won by "fighting in the streets." Some, no doubt, are reminded of the Paris Commune. Others will be reminded of the promises of Mussolini.

Certain ironies in the new cult of violence are inescapable. The sidewalk Sorels who preach violence know very little about it, and sometimes prove pitifully ineffectual in trying to use it. Those who practice it with the greatest effect—the police and the military—find preaching superfluous. The new prophets of violence are almost certain to become its chief victims, if it becomes general and uncontrolled, especially when their own romanticism carries them from the word to the deed. Historically, violence has not been an effective weapon of the Left, except in that rarest of rare circumstances, the truly revolutionary situation. Under normal circumstances, violence has more characteristically served domineering capitalists or trigger-happy police, peremptory sergeants or fascist hoodlums. And even in our day, I think it should be emphasized, the growing acceptance of violence has been unwittingly fostered from the top of society. The model for violence, which has rapidly eroded the effectiveness of appeals to nonviolent procedures, has been the hideous and gratuitous official violence in Vietnam. And after having created and made heroes of such a special tactical force as the Green Berets, we should not be altogether surprised to find the Black Panthers wearing *their* berets and practicing close-order drill. It may be childishly irrelevant to cite the example of Vietnam as an answer to every reproach for domestic acts of force or violence, but there is in that answer a point of psychological importance that we should not overlook: now, as always, the primary precedent and the primary rationale for violence comes from the established order itself. Violence is, so to speak, an official reality. No society exists without using force or violence and without devising sanctions for violence which are used to uphold just wars and necessary police actions. But the frequency and the manner in which official violence is used is of signal importance to the legitimation of the civic order. Any liberal democratic state is in danger of wearing away its legitimacy if it repeatedly uses violence at home or abroad when a substantial number of its people are wholly unpersuaded that violence is necessary.

Neither establishments nor revolutionary movements can do without sanctions for violence. What any man sees as a just war or a necessary police action will, of course, depend upon his situation and his politics; but only a few pacifists quarrel with the idea that just wars are conceivable, and only a few utopian anarchists are likely to deny that under some circumstances authorities have to use force or violence to keep order. The right of revolution is itself an established and sanctified rationale for violence. It can hardly be banished from the established sanctions in a country like America that was born in a revolution. One of our most sacred texts lays down the circumstances under which revolutionary resistance becomes legitimate. "Prudence," it also remarks (there *were* revolutionaries for whom prudence was a consideration),

> will dictate that governments long established should not be changed for light and transient causes. . . . But when a long train of abuses and usurpations, pursuing invariably the same object, evinces a design to reduce them under absolute despotism, it is their right, it is their duty, to throw off such a government, and to provide new guards for their future security.

In our own time we have no difficulty in thinking of some tyrants against whom the right of revolution was or could have been justifiably invoked, and responsibly so when the circumstances warranted hope of success. Unfortunately, in this age of verbal overkill, the epithet of tyranny can be hurled at any regime that is intensely disliked by a morally self-confident minority, and the prospects of revolutionary success may seem astonishingly good to those who gull themselves with their own miscalculations and fantasies. The classic rationale for revolution is now widely used to sanction piecemeal violence against democratic regimes in which no shadow of a revolutionary situation exists. The word "revolution" has been distended to apply to any situation in which there is rapid change or widespread discontent. Hence acts of forcible or violent adventurism can be given a superficial legitimacy by defining any situation one pleases as a "revolutionary situation." One radical thinker, Barrington Moore, Jr., who cannot be accused of lack of concern for the oppressed or of hostility to revolutions, has deplored the current disposition "to cast some vague universal cloak of legitimacy upon violence—even upon violent resistance to oppression," and has warned against occasions when "revolutionary rhetoric outruns the real possibilities inherent in a given historical situation." Today, in America, "talk about revolution is . . . pure talk with potentially dangerous and tragic consequences."

One of the essential difficulties in justifying violence is that its success is an ingredient in its justification, and such success is usually a matter of chance. There *are* some blunders that are worse than crimes, and among these are the blunders of those who, even in a good cause, precipitate violence without reasonable grounds for believing that violence will serve its purpose or that it can be contained within bounds that will be proportionate to the ends in view. No doubt it is tempting to think of putting a final end to some grave and massive social evil by a quick, surgical, limited act of violence. But the difficulty lies in being reasonably sure, before the event, that the evil will indeed be ended and not exacerbated or succeeded by some equal or greater evil; that the violence can really be limited both in time and in the casualties it inflicts, and that the reaction will not be more harmful than the surgery. For this reason all politicians, revolutionary no less than establishment politicians, must work with a terrible calculus in human misfortune.

In order to justify the use of violence as a means toward the accomplishment of some humane and "progressive" end, one must first believe that he knows, roughly at least, two things: first, that so-and-so much violence is in fact necessary to achieve the end; and second, what the countervailing human cost of the violence will be—that is, where its repercussions will stop. There are, of course, many people who imagine that they have this kind of command of the future; but some of us are not so sure, since we are not even sure that we can judge the necessity or usefulness of *past* violence in many cases where all the returns seem to be in hand.

But let us not deceive ourselves. Current credulity about the benefits of violence is rarely based upon a careful concern about when and how violence can be justified, or upon sober estimates of its past role or its prospects of future success. We are not living in a period of moral casuistry or measured calculation but in one of robust political romanticism. The protest politics of the 1960s threatened at times to break with the historic politics of liberal American reformers—who aimed to persuade a wide public, had scruples about methods, were willing to compromise, to move patiently from one limited end to another. For a decisive but now perhaps waning segment of the Far Left, politics has become all too much a matter of self-expression and of style, and such efforts as its more extreme exponents make at calculation and casuistry seem feeble as compared with the full-blown bravado of their actionist creed. There are moments when the aim of the political act seems to have become little more than the venting of a sense of outrage, and there have been activists more concerned with their freedom to carry the Vietcong flag in a peace parade or to use four-letter words than with their ability to persuade. There is less hope that any particular foray will yield visible results or affect public policy, more desire to get a sense of emotional satisfaction out of a mass happening. The demand for programmatic achievement has become less fixed, that of self-assertion central. The distinction between politics and theater has been systematically blurred by activists in politics and activists in the theater.

In the new politics, force or violence has a new place: for some it is satisfying merely to use it, but others have devised strategies to provoke counter-violence to show up the Establishment, as they put it, for what it is. In any case, violence has come to have the promise of redemption. "Violence alone," writes Frantz Fanon in *The Wretched of the Earth*, one of the canonical works of the new politics, "violence committed by the people, violence organized and educated by its leaders, makes it possible for the masses to understand social truths and gives the key to them." Fanon, writes Sartre in presenting him, "shows clearly that this irrepressible violence is neither sound and fury, nor the resurrection of savage instincts, nor even the effect of resentment: it is man recreating himself. . . . No gentleness can efface the marks of violence, only violence itself can destroy them."

Violence, then, is not only useful but therapeutic, which is to say indispensable. It seems natural enough for those who have been victims of a great deal of violence, or simply of the constant threat of overwhelming force, to conclude that they can restore their dignity only when they use violence themselves. But the restorative power of violence, if indeed violence can have that power, must surely depend upon its being used successfully. The unsuccessful use of violence, ending in defeat and fresh humiliations, may in fact intensify the original malaise. It is hard, for example, to imagine that the survivors of the grim massacre of the Indonesian Communist party in 1965–66 would have the same enthusiasm for the restorative power of violence as the victorious Algerian rebels. And this is why the existential mystique of violence, which tries to circumvent the rational calculus of tactical probabilities, will not do: its claims for therapy or sanctification through violence rest upon an arbitrary assumption of success. There is no satisfactory refuge from political calculation in psychology or metaphysics.

But of course there *are* examples of success in our time—examples set by Mao, Castro, the Algerian rebels, Ho Chi Minh and the Vietcong. The circumstances in all these cases have a special quality: the successes have been among "backward" peoples with a firm territorial base and a history of colonial exploitation. It is now suggested that violence can be equally successful in modern industrial countries, that guerrilla action suitable to the Sierra Maestre or the terror and sabotage that won in Algiers can be adapted to New York, Chicago, Oakland, or even, it appears, Scarsdale. A good deal of tactical ingenuity has in fact been stimulated, but the chief intellectual consequences have been pathetic: many young blacks have begun to think of themselves as being a colonial people, and of their problems of liberation as having exactly the same characteristics.[1] The psychological similarities are, of course, there—and a book like Fanon's *The Wretched of the Earth*, the work of a psychiatrist, argues its case largely in psychological rather than in social structural terms. American blacks may have the psyches of other victims of colonialism but they lack all the essential features of the true colonial situation: a terrain suitable to guerrilla action, the prospect of becoming a majority, territoriality, and the promise of integral control of the economy after the colonial power has been expelled. Except for these indispensable elements, the comparison is excellent, and therefore we may indulge ourselves in the fantasy that Watts is just like Algiers.

But in the end one must give the prophets of violence their due:

---

[1] Since so much has been accomplished by strategic minorities, it may not matter for the future of violence in America that the black militants have not yet converted a majority of Negroes. In *Newsweek*'s 1969 poll, 63 per cent (as against 21 per cent) thought that Negroes could win their rights without violence. Overwhelming majorities also repudiated separatism in response to questions about integrated schools and integrated neighborhoods. (*Newsweek*, June 30, 1969.) The appeal of militant ideas, however, is much higher among the young.

violence *is* pervasive in human experience and has been pervasive in American history, and however it repels us, we must see it as an instrument of common use. The creed its proponents put before us is simple but forceful: Violence has been all but universal in the past. Violence changes things and nothing else does. Violence is therefore necessary. "Violence," said Rap Brown in what must surely remain one of the memorable utterances of our time, "is necessary and it's as American as cherry pie." Presumably he did not expect his listeners to be so uncritically patriotic as to think that violence must be good because Americans have so often used it. No doubt his hope was that if a decent respect for the normality and inevitability of violence could be instilled in the minds of his contemporaries, they would be less censorious about the violence supposedly necessary to black liberation. And one should grant all that is sound here: certainly violence that would in fact lead to a full realization of the rights of blacks would have a great deal to be said for it, and would stand in quite a different moral position from the violence, say, that many lynchers used for their own entertainment and for the edification of their children. Here, as always, however, one encounters the latent, the unexamined assumption: violence *will* deliver that which is expected of it. It is an assumption shared more and more among the very young, black or white: justice will be won by "fighting in the streets." Fighting in the streets as a revolutionary technique—it is one of the few old-fashioned ideas still alive.

Certainly world history yields plenty of cases in which some historical logjam seems to have been broken up by an eruption of violence, which is then followed by a period of peaceful, gradualist improvement. It is always possible in such cases to argue (though difficult to prove) that the violence was a necessary precondition of the peaceful change that followed. The trouble is that there are so many other cases in which violence has decided issues in ways we are less likely to applaud. American experience with the large-scale violent resolution of fundamental crises is mixed. The Revolution and the Civil War pose an interesting antithesis. The question of American independence was settled by violence, and, as historical issues go, settled with considerable success. But one of the keys to that success may be found in the minimum of gratuitous violence with which the Revolution was carried out. There could be no regicide and there was no terror. There were frequent incidents, but there was no wholesale mobbing of dissidents. Few Loyalists outside the ranks of the British army were killed, though many were terrorized, many went into exile, and many lost large properties. Even the military action did not characteristically go beyond what we would call guerrilla warfare. Most important, the revolutionaries did not turn upon each other with violence or terror. The Thermidor, if the adoption of the Constitution can be correctly called that, was equally mild, and in part simply nationalized and embodied in institutional form some of the principles set forth in the Revolution itself. Not only was independence secured and the political life of the American states markedly democratized but some social reforms were given a strong impetus. In spite of the difficult questions of national organization that were not settled, and in spite of the tumultuous passions raised by the political issues of the Federal era, the episodes of domestic violence that followed the Revolution—and there were quite a number of them—were in a relatively low key and proved eminently controllable. The early rebellions mounted by Daniel Shays, the Whiskey rebels, and John Fries, though of much political consequence, were, as episodes of violence, kept at the level of skirmishes, and their leaders were afterwards treated with judicious consideration. The Revolution was followed by relative peace: on the whole, the era from 1790 to 1830, though far from violence-free, was one of the least violent periods in our domestic history.

The Civil War stands in marked contrast. Again, it did settle historical issues, the issues of union and of the legal status of slavery. But it was preceded by a decade of searing civil violence and climaxed by a war that cost 600,000 lives, and it left an extraordinary inheritance of bitterness and lethal passion that has not yet ended. The legal liberation of the slave was not followed by the actual liberation of the black man. The defeated states became less rather than more democratic. The violence of the war was followed by the resounding and horrifying episodic violence of Reconstruction, and the Thermidor in the South went on for a full generation after the guns were stilled. The war seems in retrospect to have been an intensely cruel and wasteful way of settling—if that is the right word—the issues that gave rise to it. I do not agree with the categorical form or exaggerated rhetoric of Barrington Moore's pessimistic world-historical estimates that "violence has settled all historical issues so far, and most of them in the wrong way," but in the considerable list of historical cases that could be drawn up to support his judgment, the Civil War would surely rank high.

If we look at the use of violence in social situations of less profound consequence than those which led to the Revolution and the Civil War, we can find instances when violence in the United States appears to have served its purpose. And it has been, on the whole, the violence of those who already had position and power. Many vigilante movements, for example, achieved their limited goal of suppressing outlaws. Lynching clearly added a note of terroristic enforcement to the South's caste system. For years employers used violence and the threat of violence against labor with success: in the main, the outstandingly violent episodes in industrial conflicts were tragic defeats for labor, although there were occasions when violence initiated on behalf of employers became too blatant for public acceptance and boomeranged. Labor has used violence less often than employers and with only rare success. There was, to be sure, one very effective series of extralegal actions by labor—the sit-downs of the 1930s. However, in these instances the workers, though using illegal *force*, were using a tactical device that tended to avert rather than precipitate acts of outright violence. This may explain why they won considerable sympathy from the public, which was at the same time becoming acutely aware of the violence, intimidation, and espionage used by employers in many industries. In any case, the sit-downs were a transient tactic which labor leaders abandoned as soon as collective bargaining was achieved, and it is difficult to imagine the sit-downs repeatedly successful as a standard device.

In sum, violence can succeed in a political environment like that of the United States under certain conditions. Those who use it must be able to localize it and limit its duration. They must use it under circumstances in which the public is either indifferent or uninformed, or in which the accessible and relevant public opinion (as in the case of vigilantes and, usually, of employers in the nineteenth century) is heavily biased in their favor. If violence is accompanied by exceptional brutality (lynching, employer actions like that at Ludlow), it must be kept a local matter, and one must hope that it can somehow be screened from the attention of the larger polity. The conditions for its success, in this respect, seem to have become more problematical in the age of mass communications, where the most vital tactical problem is to set the stage so that the onus for violent action can be made to seem to rest entirely upon one's adversaries.

If violence sometimes works, it does not follow that nothing but violence works. Most of the social reforms in American history have been brought about without violence, or with only a marginal and inessential use of it, by reformers who were prepared to carry on a long-term campaign of education and propaganda. The entire apparatus of the welfare state, from child labor laws, wage-hour regulation, industrial safety laws, and workmen's compensation to legally regulated collective bargaining, social security, and medical care for the aged, is the achievement of active minorities which, while sometimes militant and always persistent, were also patient and nonviolent. Ours, however, is an age that cannot wait, and it is doubtful that young militants, black or white, are taking much comfort from the example of such predecessors in the tradition of American reform. The activists, according to their temperaments, will argue either that earlier reforms, being props to the Establishment, were of little or no value, or that they were all a generation overdue when they came. The first response is simply inhumane, but the second has much truth in it: such reforms were indeed long overdue. However, it does not follow that the use of violence would have hastened their coming. Under some conditions the fear or threat of violence may hasten social reforms, yet if actual outbreaks of violence were the primary force in bringing reform, one might have expected social-welfare laws to come in the United States before they came to such countries as Great Britain and Germany where there was less industrial violence. The important element seems to have been not the resort to violence but the presence of powerful labor movements with a socialist commitment and the threat of sustained action through normal political channels.

But the confrontationist politicians of our time seem to have hit upon an approach to violence that surmounts one of the signal disadvantages under which social dissidents have labored in the past: they have learned the value not of committing violence but of *provoking* it. It remains true today, as it has always been, that most political violence is committed by the agents of authority. In the past, for example, labor often got the blame for violent outbursts that were primarily the work of police or other agents of employers. Hence one speaks of "labor violence" but not of "capital violence." Today, however, a technique has been found to put official violence to work in the apparent interests of dissent. A small cadre of determined activists, enveloped in a large crowd of demonstrators, can radicalize a substantial segment of public opinion by provoking the police into violent excesses—if necessary by hurling objects, but better still by hurling nothing more than verbal abuse. The activists have correctly gauged the temper of the police, who are often quite ready to oblige by lashing out indiscriminately against both those who have offended them and those who have not—orderly demonstrators, innocent bystanders, reporters, cameramen. Young radicals have thus found a way to put the police and the mass media to work for them, as the public sees a hideous spectacle of beating, kicking, and clubbing by officers of the law against unarmed demonstrators and witnesses. Outrage becomes the more blatant to those who are aware of and attracted by the milky innocence of the majority of young demonstrators.

Whether the larger public effect of such confrontations will actually work to the ultimate advantage of the activists is problematical. What they can see with their own eyes at the moment of conflict is that many persons, hitherto vaguely sympathetic, become, at least for a time, energized and activated out of indignation. What they choose to ignore is the other, less visible but usually larger public, which puts the full blame on demonstrators and backs the police and the authorities. (The behavior of the Chicago police during the Democratic Convention of 1968, one of the most flagrant police actions of this era, was approved by a substantial majority of the public.) Still, activist leaders are aware of *their* converts, and converts there usually are. Why not rejoice in the converts and dismiss the backlash? Hence the ubiquitous New Left agitator, Tom Hayden, has called for "two, three, many Chicagos," and the young activists interviewed by Jerome Skolnick's researchers for the National Commission on the Causes and Prevention of Violence show a shrewd if limited understanding of the implications of such tactics. The purpose of confrontations, they argue with striking candor, is to educate the public by staging spectacles of repression.

> Direct action is not intended to win particular reforms or to influence decision-makers, but rather to bring out a repressive response from authorities—a response rarely seen by most white Americans. When confrontation brings violent official response, uncommitted elements of the public can see for themselves the true nature of the "system."

The activists also believe that such experience lowers the "cultural fear of violence" natural among young middle-class radicals—a fear that is "psychologically damaging and may be politically inhibiting," and thus prepares them for a serious commitment to revolution. To some degree they have already been proved right: the "damaging" inhibitions against the use of guns, bombs, and arson have begun to break down.

Can this breakdown be extrapolated into an indefinite future? No doubt most Americans are more curious about where our penchant for violence is taking us than they are about a more precise explanation of its pattern in the past. But here prognosis is as hazardous as anywhere. In the past our violence has always been cyclical, and it is possible to believe that the 1960s will some day appear on the charts of the sociologists as another peak period rather more pronounced than many, which is followed by relative calm. As the young never tire of reminding us, we live in a situation that is new and in some decisive respects unprecedented. (I sometimes think that *all* American experience is a series of disjunctive situations whose chief connecting link is that each generation repeats the belief of its predecessor that there is nothing to be learned from the past.) In any case, our social violence is not a self-contained universe that holds within itself all the conditions of its future development. In fact almost everything depends upon external forces which no one dares to predict: the tempo at which we disengage from Vietnam, the national and international response to our undisguisable failure there, and our ability to avoid another such costly venture.

Who can really believe that he knows what to expect of the future of American violence? It is easy to draw up two plausible scenarios for the future, one apocalyptic, the other relatively benign though hardly exhilarating. Apocalyptic predictions are conventionally in order—indeed they have become so conventional that they constitute a kind of imperative intellectual fashion. But in them there is more of omniscience than of science, and their function seems more psychological than pragmatic. In a magical gesture one predicts evil in order to ward it off. Or worse, in moments of terrible frustration one threatens one's audience with some ultimate catastrophe by way of saying: This is what you will all get for not having followed the social policies I have prescribed for you. However, over the past generation the visions of the future that have prevailed among the most modishly apocalyptic intellectual circles in this country have been so largely wrong that they could almost be used like odd-lot buying in the stock market as a negative indicator of future realities. Perhaps the most cogent reason, aside from the perverse element of self-indulgence inherent in it, for not yielding too easily to the apocalyptic frame of mind is a pragmatic one: apocalyptic predictions, repeated too often and believed too automatically, could at best reduce men of good will to a useless passivity and at worst turn into self-fulfilling prophecies. Pragmatic wisdom argues for assuming that our difficulties are manageable, so that we may put our minds to thinking about how in fact they can be managed.

Still, it requires no remarkable ingenuity to see how some of the recent trends in American society, continued and magnified, could bring about the eclipse of liberal democratic politics. The danger is not that the alienated young and the militant blacks will wage a successful revolution. The United States is basically a conservative country, and its working class is one of the anchors of its conservatism. Its overwhelming majority is not poor, not black, and not in college. College activists, themselves only a fraction of the college population, command so much attention from the mass media that the actual state of mind of the American young has been obscured. Almost three-fourths of those in the 17–23 age bracket do not go to college, and their political direction is quite different from that of the college activists. Their responsiveness even to the cruder forms of backlash sentiment may be measured by their votes in the 1968 election, in which George Wallace had proportionately somewhat *more* support among white voters in the age groups 29 and under than in the age groups 30 and over.[2]

In a nation so constituted, the most serious danger comes not from the activities of young militants, black or white, but from the strength of the backlash that may arise out of an increasing polarization of the society. The apocalyptic scenario spells itself out rather easily: an indefinite prolongation of the war in Vietnam, or a re-escalation, or the launching of yet another such provocative and disastrous foreign undertaking; a continued unwillingness or inability to make adequate progress in accommodating the demand for racial justice; an intensification of confrontation politics in the colleges and on the streets; a heightened alienation of the intelligent young; violent scenes, vividly reported on TV, of provocative conduct by demonstrators and brutal responses by police; a continuing polarization of the political public into Right and Left which shuts off just such political and social efforts as might relieve the crisis; the formation of numerous armed groups of black and white citizens, highlighted perhaps by a few mass gunfights in the big cities; the breakdown of one or both of the major parties; the capture of the Presidency and Congress by a nationwide movement dedicated to political repression at home and a hard line in foreign policy.

Not altogether impossible, one must say, though to me it somehow fails to carry conviction. The particular forms of violence that flourished in the 1960s seem now to be on the decline: ghetto riots have been tapering off, and the crest of violence touched off by campus protest may have been reached in the years 1967 to 1969. Black militancy is certain to be with us for an indefinite future, and it is a sobering thought that the one major breakdown of the American political system came in association with an unresolved problem of race; but black agitation tends to grow more selective about methods and goals, and it is by no means clear that it must involve large-scale violence

[2] An American Institute for Public Opinion national sample showed that Wallace had the following support in four age brackets: 21–25, 13 per cent; 26–29, 18 per cent; 30–49, 13 per cent; 50 and over, 11 per cent.

or mass casualties. Student activism too seems likely to outlast the American withdrawal from Vietnam, since it rests on a profound cultural malaise that goes beyond any political issue, but it may work at a lower level of emotional intensity. An end to the war would bring about a political and economic climate in which the effort to relieve urban blight and poverty and to come to terms with the demand for racial justice can be resumed under far more favorable conditions than those of the past five or six years. It is a rare thing in our experience to be centrally preoccupied with the same problem for two successive decades, and it is quite conceivable that even a persisting and relatively high level of violence in the 1970s will come to be regarded as a marginal rather than a central problem. At some time in the near future the destruction of the environment, and the problems attendant upon pollution and overpopulation, are likely to take the center of the historical stage and to have such a commanding urgency that all other issues will be dwarfed. The styles of thought, the political mood that will be created by such problems, as well as the political alignments they will bring about, may be so startlingly different from those of the 1960s, that the mentality of the 1960s will seem even more strange by 1980 than the mentality of the 1950s has appeared during the past few years.

When one considers American history as a whole, it is hard to think of any very long period in which it could be said that the country has been consistently well governed. And yet its political system is, on the whole, a resilient and well seasoned one, and on the strength of its history one must assume that it can summon enough talent and good will to cope with its afflictions. To cope with them— but not, I think, to master them in any thoroughly decisive or admirable fashion. The nation seems to slouch onward into its uncertain future like some huge inarticulate beast, too much attainted by wounds and ailments to be robust, but too strong and resourceful to succumb.

STUDY QUESTIONS

1. What is ironic about the slogan "a war-to-end-war"?
2. What does pride in violence have to do with the politics of America?
3. When has violence been of genuine value to the Left?
4. Who has helped America most in its growing acceptance of violence?

5. From what quarter does the precedent for violence in American life come?
6. Is Hofstadter totally opposed to violence of all kinds at all times?
7. Why is it difficult to know exactly what the value of violence will be in any act aimed at revolutionary change?
8. How hopeful is Hofstadter that the actions of the Far Left will help persuade citizens to their cause?
9. In terms of violence, how does the Civil War contrast with the Revolutionary War? What is the importance of that contrast?
10. If violence sometimes works, does it not follow that violence should at least be tried?

SUGGESTIONS FOR WRITING

1. Hofstadter observes at one point that one unifying faith of the young during any period in American history is their belief that nothing can be learned from the past. Do you think Hofstadter is correct in ascribing this belief to the young? What are your own observations on this issue? Are your feelings toward the past shared by most of your peers?
2. Is it possible that the decade of the 1960s, or at least the last half of that decade, will be remembered as a "high spot" on the graph that measures violent times in American history? What about violence in the 1970s so far? Do the 1960s represent a trend or an incident in American history?
3. Is there any aspect of the question of violence in American politics that Hofstadter seems to be ignoring? If you were to write an accompanying statement with this essay, what would you add? What would you try to emphasize that Hofstadter plays down?
4. Why is it, do you think, that violence in the 1960s was centered in the inner city and on the college campuses—two very different environments? What is the significance of the fact that there was little or no violence in the American suburbs? Is this a sociological fact that ought to be more carefully analyzed?
5. Hofstadter discusses a number of different kinds of violence in American life and American politics. How do they help shape the distinctive political climate of America? How do they affect the quality of life throughout the nation?

THE NEW MYTHOLOGY OF HOUSING

Michael A. Stegman

America is in such a serious housing crisis that President Nixon actually proposed mobile homes as the most practical immediate solution. The Federal Government is undertaking some new long-range housing programs but the assumptions on which they are based may have already doomed them to failure.

Good housing can make good people, even out of poor people. Such, cruelly compressed, was the cherished belief of housing reformers as they campaigned 30 years ago for low-rent public housing for the urban poor. By now, needless to say, that belief has been exposed as a myth. It has been shown to rest on faulty assumptions not only with respect to why poor people are poor, but also about what can be done to make them "better." As one student of urban affairs put it:

> Once upon a time, we thought that if we could only get our problem families out of those dreadful slums, then papa would stop taking dope, mama would stop chasing around, and Junior would stop carrying a knife. Well, we've got them in a nice apartment with modern kitchens and a recreation center. And they're the same bunch of bastards they always were.

This is to state the disillusionment rather crudely, to be sure; but that is exactly the trouble with founding public policy on mythic grounds. The poor are held to be incurable. The reformers who helped spread the faulty gospel are crucified as false prophets or fade away as the public action they helped get going fails to solve the "problems." But, worse than this, their failures never seem to stimulate any attempts to correct the myths or modify the procedures. Rather, they serve only to weaken subsequent efforts to rally political support for further public action. In the case of low-rent public housing, the

THE NEW MYTHOLOGY OF HOUSING   Reprinted from the January 1970 issue of *Transaction* by permission of *Transaction*.

whole purpose of the program—the provision of decent shelter for the poor—was smeared along with the exposure of its guiding myth.

Today, the public housing program goes without its traditional liberal and intellectual support; it goes without union support; and it goes without any broad demand among the electorate. And as for the poor, they go without decent housing. As John P. Dean wrote 20 years ago in a review of our disappointing efforts in housing reform ". . . in the meantime, the patient has continued to sicken."

What I want to do here is take a hard look at what I believe are the *emerging* myths concerning community development and housing. It is only prudent to acknowledge that it would be much less risky to wait another decade or so to pass judgment. Yet by discussing the emerging myths before they become crystalized, I may be able to raise some fundamental questions about their utility as a basis for public action. Moreover, the time seems particularly ripe now that the federal government has passed a multibillion dollar housing bill.

The Model Cities program provides a sophisticated example of current thinking about the complexities of the slum housing nexus. Its pronouncements at least indicate a heightened awareness that housing and social service needs are closely interrelated and might best be met simultaneously with a global attack. This is a far cry from the "good housing = good people" theory of years past, but I still get the nagging feeling that the emerging housing reform myths are going to be equally counter-productive.

The old myths developed as justifications for direct federal intervention in an area previously dominated by the private sector. The new myths are rationalizations for particular federal responses to housing problems that have remained unsolved in spite of earlier governmental involvement. These myths, which are concerned more with notions of how the problems can be solved than with their basic causes, can be summarized as follows:

Myths surrounding the nature of the owners of substandard housing.

Mythical explanations of the potential role of nonprofit sponsors in solving the nation's housing problems.

Myths involving the potential value of adopting a systems approach to neighborhood renewal.

Myths surrounding emerging efforts to involve unemployed ghetto manpower in the rehabilitation of slum housing.

Myths explaining why low-income *ownership* programs should be expected to solve those same social problems that the previous low-income minimum *rental* programs could not solve.

Myth #1—Slumlords.

> *. . . the slumlord, that small body of landlords [who] are out to squeeze every last dollar out of the property as quickly as they can, regardless of the consequences in terms of human life, suffering and sickness. It is against this small minority that battle must be given—constant, unremitting and unrelenting battle.*
>
> —Former Mayor Robert Wagner of New York

Believers in this specimen myth frequently wind up their "argument" with the observation of David Hunter that all owners of substandard housing "look as though they had spent their childhoods drowning their playmates" and then grew up to play that same deadly game as an adult—only now in more subtle and painful ways.

This amateurish personality profile of the "typical slumlord" tends to confuse the real issues and has served to distort our national housing policy since the end of World War II. It has encouraged a myopic view of the housing problem, and it has demonstrably provided an outright faulty basis for public action. The stereotype of the slumlord strongly implies that the owners of substandard housing are largely responsible for our chronic housing problem, simply because they are evil men. This is not so for at least four reasons.

First, the stereotype doesn't stand up statistically. There are upwards of six million substandard housing units in our nation's cities and literally hundreds of thousands of individual landlords. Can *all* their owners match the above grotesque? Surely it is more reasonable to assume that their personal characteristics distribute in a pattern similar to that found in any large sample of population.

Second, slumlords and tenants enjoy, if that's the word, a perfectly symbiotic relationship; that is, they need each other. The owners need the poor and troubled because few others would consider living in depressed housing; and who but the poor and troubled must seek the cheapest possible shelter? Yet, this is no justification for blaming the owners for creating the shortages in decent low-rent housing that mark the inner cores of our cities. The notion that owners of substandard units cause the sickness and suffering that plague the unfortunate families who dwell there sounds suspiciously like an inversion of the "good housing = good people" theory.

Third, the charge that most owners of slum properties are making excess profits may be seriously questioned, both within the real estate industry and in comparison with other major industries. While financial information on slums is extremely scarce, such relatively recent works as Woody Klein's *Let in the Sun* include some economic data that will disconcert liberal believers in the bloated slumlord myth. For example, the 36-unit tenement Klein wrote about grossed nearly one-half million dollars over a 60-year period ending in 1966. The New York City Planning Commission has estimated that such structures generally return around 36 percent of gross revenues on a net basis. With respect to the building in question, then, aggregate net revenues for the 60 years would have amounted to approximately $180,000, or an annual average of $3,000. Since fixed expenses (taxes, water and sewer charges and insurance) of such substandard tenements average 25 percent of gross revenues, it's obvious that when you then add on fuel and minimal maintenance costs, there will be little left over for major repairs. In fact, Klein estimates that in order to bring the tenement up to the standard specified in New York City's housing code, annual operating expenses would have to increase by $4,000 per year, which means an annual loss of $3,278. Undermaintenance therefore may be not only a rational, but a necessary means of survival in an industry beset with increased unionization and its concomitant, rising costs, as well as tenant incomes that remain either the same or fall over the years and the same or lower levels of occupancy.

Fourth, it is an incontrovertible fact that almost half (47 percent) of our national housing inventory was built before 1929. Our cities are getting older. And in housing, as in humans, aging causes problems, but it seems naive to place the responsibility for such problems at the feet of the landlord. Old structures are found in old neighborhoods, and more and more of them are becoming slums. Data from the South Los Angeles area show that the proportion of substandard units in that community increased from 18 percent to 34 percent between 1960 and 1965. In New York City the number of slum housing units went from 475,000 in 1960 to an estimated 800,000 in late 1968. The Department of Labor estimates that 600,000 rural and semirural individuals are migrating into large urban areas each year. The housing crisis will surely increase as greater pressures are exerted upon an already aged and obsolete housing stock.

By adopting the myth of the slumlord, the public forecloses any consideration of an alliance with the owner of substandard housing in an attempt to find an enlightened approach to the problem. Also written off is much of the huge investment locked into the existing low-rent private housing stock.

Myth #2—Nonprofit Sponsors. Top housing officials have apparently accepted the myth of the slumlord. They have washed their hands of the individual low-rent property owner. A measure of their disenchantment is the increasing federal attention being paid to such nonprofit institutions as churches, foundations, fraternal organizations and labor unions in their low- and moderate-income housing efforts. In fact, a program was initiated in 1961 which could be interpreted as designed to stimulate such housing efforts. Known by the call letters 221(d)(3), it provides mortgage monies at low interest rates to nonprofit sponsors. Yet at this writing only 1,568 rental units have been rehabilitated under 221(d)(3), while only 46,565 new units have been built.

The meager contributions of 221(d)(3) can be readily explained. First, there has been an insufficient and uneven flow of federal funds to purchase below-market mortgages. Second, Congress cannot make up its mind whether the Federal Housing Authority should continue to broaden its social perspective, or model its role on that of a conservative Back Bay banker. Third and finally, the federal requirements for obtaining the financing are so complex and difficult to satisfy, that only the most energetic and well-staffed sponsors can succeed in getting any. The 221(d)(3) program requires filing forms for preapplication, application, precommitment processing, preinitial closing, initial closing and final closing stages—more than 40 forms in all. Urban America, Inc., recently published a guide to the program which is 359 pages long.

Simply put, the concept of nonprofit sponsors such as churches developing housing throughout the nation's urban areas on a scale large enough to have any measurable impact is basically ill conceived. When one considers the incredibly large number of steps involved in the residential development process, one has to conclude that the average church is just not prepared to carry the burden of solving even a fraction of our national housing problem. And as for the typical Negro church in the ghetto, the most appropriate potential sponsor for low-income housing, it unfortunately has even less resources and know-how.

It is true that some housing has been constructed under the 221(d)(3) program. The Kate Maramount Foundation in Chicago, the sponsor of nearly one-half of the 1,568 rental units rehabilitated under the program to date, has certainly mastered its technicalities. Yet, if Maramount were to concentrate all its future activities on Chicago's west side, and if it were able to rehabilitate 500 units a year under the program, which is highly unlikely, it would take 100 years to eliminate substandard housing in that community alone—assuming that no additional units became substandard in the interim.

Obviously, there are not enough Maramounts, nor is there sufficient time for them to act. The scale of the problem is simply too great to be handled in the manner implied in the program.

There are two additional difficulties with this approach that do not show on paper, but which we must anticipate lest they pop up when unsuspecting organizations attempt to duplicate the work of Maramount. First, the open market is a hostile environment for anyone—private developer, church, nonprofit institution or whoever—whose stated objective is to develop housing for black families outside the established ghettos. Frequently it becomes extremely difficult for indigenous institutions such as churches to secure appropriate project sites, sites that meet governmental specifications for mortgage insurance. Zoning, too, becomes a problem. It is most often necessary to secure changes in zoning laws before a project can be begun.

Second, the management of an efficient and financially sound housing development conflicts with the social goals of those institutions which might undertake such an enterprise. Management would have to screen potential tenants to avoid problem families, and it would have to evict families who could not pay their rent. If management begins to wink at rental arrears and is forced to downgrade its maintenance program, it would fall into a vicious cycle. Rental arrears lead to less maintenance. Less maintenance leads to infrequent occupancy. Infrequent occupancy leads to reduced revenue. Reduced revenue leads to still less maintenance. Q.E.D., the churches become the owners of tomorrow's slums.

The Maramount effort can never be sustained on more than a demonstration basis. The government will commit funds only to the most well-prepared groups to let them show the world what can be done. The irony of this lies in the assumption that this is supposed to highlight what others can do. In reality, when various organizations and institutions in low-income communities across the country hear about the program and become excited about its potential, they are forced to admit in time that they cannot possibly surround themselves with the personnel necessary to bring the needed housing into their communities. This is an illustrative example of the mythic quality of the nonprofit sponsor. On paper, anyone can do it; in reality, very few.

The role of the nonprofit institution in housing is still quite confused. The federal government has not loosened its purse strings, has not reduced the red tape, has not adjusted its mortgage insurance specifications, and has not helped the churches and other institutions prepare for a major role in the redevelopment it apparently wanted to stimulate.

What then is the true purpose of such a policy? Everyone would agree it is worthwhile to encourage such stable and committed institutions as churches to do their part in easing local housing problems—even though they are not yet well equipped for the job. But since the policy has not been enacted on any grand scale, the heart of the matter must lie elsewhere. It lies in the basic unwillingness of the federal government to give serious consideration to why private developers are not dealing in the low- and moderate-income sectors, and in its refusal to provide incentives to encourage such activity. The government has made a tradeoff—it has accepted the cleaner, less tainted nonprofit sponsor and has given up housing units.

Myth #3—Aerospace Systems Panaceas. There has been much recent speculation about how efficient community renewal might be if urbanologists and systems analysts jointly planned and implemented broad programs in our cities. Conceiving the neighborhood as a subsystem of interrelated physical, economic, social and political dimensions, which is related in turn to the larger urban system, the integrated approach obviously has value. Yet upon close examination, it reveals serious shortcomings and inaccuracies. The particular advantages of the aerospace systems approach to renewal are more managerial and administrative than they are substantive. Thus, the push for employing multidisciplinary teams and large-scale computers in rebuilding the cities cannot be but one of the most flagrant of the emerging myths of housing reform.

The problem of renewal is money. In the eight major cities recently surveyed by the U.S. Civil Rights Commission, "almost half of the families surveyed received incomes solely from sources such as welfare, AFDC, unemployment compensation or other nonemployment sources." What improvements could come from a sophisticated, fully programmed, multidisciplinary approach to community renewal in those cities? There are hundreds of communities in 42 states where welfare payments fail to meet the states' own standards of the minimum income required for families to live. It is ludicrous to assert that we need a systems approach to reveal that a mother with three children needs $237 a month to live and can be provided through welfare with a maximum of only $126. The basic problem here is lack of money. That is obvious; yet there is no reason to suppose that Congress will show any more willingness to deal with the fundamental problems of poverty than it has in the past.

Another problem is racism. A sophisticated analytical framework cannot be expected to eliminate racial conflict. What could a systems approach accomplish in the Bayside District of Oakland, for example, where the under- and unemployment rate is more than 30 percent? One cannot use a managerial tool and expect to redistribute income. Without basic economic and social reforms, the glamorous aerospace approach to renewal cannot possibly accomplish the ends for which it is intended. Yet Congress has demonstrated that it is far more prepared to sponsor the development of a city technology under the auspices of the aerospace industry than it is to deal with the fact that the poor lack money, that they are the victims of racial discrimination, or that their "assistance programs" are falling apart.

Like the more familiar task forces and blue ribbon commissions empaneled to identify the obvious, the systems approach to community renewal promises to be used as a politically valuable delaying tactic by those who refuse to commit themselves to the necessity of righting wrongs and reversing social or economic injustices.

Systems analysis has of course made many unique, highly visible contributions in the amply funded, high-priority realm of national defense. It is preposterous to expect that this expensive method will yield comparable results in a traditionally low-priority area where Congress is particularly tightfisted. The systems approach to the physical and human renewal of neighborhoods and communities promises to make much more efficient use of existing resources. It would avoid the piecemeal efforts of earlier renewal programs. Yet the Vietnam experience illustrates the system's failure to take into account the human and political variables. Racism and class conflict are the human and political variables of the cities; it can safely be predicted that systems analysis will be as little effective here as it has been in Vietnam.

Myth #4—Self-help Housing. The systems approach is being sold to Congress as the new urban panacea of the 1970s. It is an attractive panacea, suggesting the efficiency and reliability of moon shots and the like. But how well will it work in practice? While it is an obviously intelligent way to go about doing certain things, one may well wonder how well it will function on limited resources. Only time will tell.

As for public service and community facilities, the black ghettos have been the last to get the least. If one peruses a random sample of Model Cities program applications he will quickly learn that cities of all sizes are now quite willing to admit that their policies have been discriminatory. In response, the black community is now demanding direct and meaningful involvement in making policy and running programs designed to improve the quality of life in the ghettos. Most recently they have demanded the inclusion of low-income, low-skilled, unemployed ghetto men as workers in the construction and rehabilitation of low-income housing.

The myth is that housing programs can provide employment for the ghetto resident, and on paper it looks sound. Unemployed ghetto residents would be prepared for jobs in the building trades even as they are helping to alleviate the chronic housing problems in their neighborhoods. It would provide residents with a meaningful experience and a sense of contributing to neighborhood development. And maybe it would even reduce the vandalism in the houses being rehabilitated. All this is fine. Yet it is also, I think, naive to expect that a large share of the greater than six million substandard units in our metropolitan areas can be brought up to standard through such efforts.

Urban self-help housing has not yet assumed the stature of a major myth, but it is gaining increasing exposure and support as Model Cities monies become more available. I do not doubt that such efforts will result in rehabilitated housing; nor that unskilled labor can be trained in the building trades. However, as long as self-help housing is localized in the relatively few communities that have the talent and organizational base to push it, the number of units involved will remain small. And, as long as the rehabilitation efforts are headed by undercapitalized Negro contractors who do not pose overt threats to organized labor, it is a safe bet that direct involvement of black manpower in the rebuilding effort will fail to crack labor's stranglehold on the ghetto.

Localized self-help training programs seem too small a threat to the unions to warrant large mobilization against them. No better evidence need be sought than the fact that black workers themselves recognize the meagerness of these programs. Blacks are now demanding entry into the Chicago, Detroit and Pittsburgh construction unions. This marks the beginning of a much needed and long awaited national confrontation between the blacks and the buildings and trades unions. It also raises the conflict to a level beyond the point where training programs might have been an issue. Even were they to become an issue, the unions seem to have the procedural equipment to appear good guys. Consider the following scenario.

The unions select and deal with relatively small and isolated black contractors in scattered communities. They allow a certain number of trainees to work on the otherwise unionized rehabilitation jobs. If pressures for reform of the union arise, or if blacks make concerted efforts to penetrate the union ranks, the union local can then threaten to slow up or close down the rehabilitation job. As this would spell certain disaster to the usually undercapitalized black contractor, he would find ways to short-circuit the whole procedure. In the end, by permitting a scant few nonunion blacks to work on rehabilitation crews in a few ghetto communities, the unions appear progressive while still excluding blacks from where the main action is, in the unions themselves.

Yet, this issue seems to have the potential to escalate into a major conflict. A Negro contractor working in Cleveland's Hough district claims that "a union carpenter brought up in new construction is no better equipped for rehabilitation work than a raw man. . . . We can train a laborer to set up our prefab partitions in two hours. He can learn faster than a veteran carpenter because he isn't set in his ways and has no old work habits to overcome." If unskilled ghetto labor is capable of being trained to do rehabilitation work in significantly less time than the unions are willing to admit, and this appears to be the case, then massive training programs could be initiated. Such a new labor pool would be highly mobile and a threat to the unions. The unions would probably offer stiff resistance to such a development, so these self-help training programs may prove to be yet another false expectation.

With all these forces eddying around direct involvement in ghetto redevelopment, it is likely that a highly limited program will be enacted, which is tokenism at its worst. The myth is subtle. It plays upon the need and desires of the minority poor for a stake in the action. At the same time it guarantees that institutional changes in organized labor will be minimal or nonexistent, that the buildings and trades unions will not have to open their ranks to black labor on a large scale—because "they" will have their self-help training programs.

Myth #5—Home Ownership for the Poor. Congress recently considered more than 24 low income home-ownership bills; its action resulted in Section 235 of the Housing Act of 1968. The purpose of the program is to broaden the base of home ownership in an already predominantly home-owning nation through the provision of interest rate subsidies to low- and moderate-income families. The proponents of this program expect it to accomplish all the socially desirable ends that the welfare reformers of 30 years ago had hoped their public housing programs would achieve. Today public housing has come to represent a patronizing dole, they reason, while home ownership involves a stake in a piece of property, a sense of pride in one's home. Belief in this myth persists mainly because the public and the legislators see in home ownership a device to prevent more and greater rioting.

The myth of low-income home ownership is vulnerable on many counts. The most glaring error is that such programs are based on the projection of middle-class values onto a non middle-class culture. Moreover, it is perceived as a solution, a balm to salve the wounds caused by discrimination, cultural starvation and the structural problems of our national labor market. But there are several difficulties with this romanticized notion of what ownership can accomplish.

There was and is nothing about a publicly supported low-rent housing program that would necessarily rob a man of his pride or sap him of his self-respect. Nor is there anything about owning one's home that guarantees that pride and self-respect will spontaneously spring up in the owner's breast. As far as the actual low-income ownership programs are concerned they may amount to little more than saying that everyone should have a title to his slum.

Realistically speaking, one cannot expect much more than a limited low-income home-ownership program. The entrenched and anachronistic National Association of Real Estate Boards (NAREB) is making visible efforts to avoid opening up the market to Negroes. A recent NAREB circular was distributed to presidents of local real estate boards entitled, "Some Questions (and their answers) suggested by a reading of Title VIII of Public Law No. 90-284 related to forced housing." It was an exploration of means to circumvent the provisions of the federal open-housing bill. In spite of recent federal legislation in this area, and the Supreme Court's ruling that an almost forgotten law enacted in 1866 is effectively a sweeping fairhousing bill, a truly open housing market seems highly unlikely in the foreseeable future.

Moreover, to stimulate hopes for home ownership without moving toward reducing levels of unemployment and underemployment might be the cruelest hoax yet perpetrated on the low-income population. Let us assume that the program provides for monthly carrying costs equal to 20 percent of monthly income. I feel the average low-income family participating in the program would find it extremely difficult to pay for its housing-related needs (operation, maintenance, taxes, water and insurance) as well as its nonhousing needs from its limited budget. Consequently, such a program might provide the family a piece of middle-class America, but only a little piece—a piece obtained at the cost of accepting the increased pressures that go along with internalizing middle-class values, with only a fraction of the economic resources with which to play the game.

It is of paramount importance to remember that the *style* in which a program is administered has direct impact upon the quality of life of the participants. For example, if a project is administered in a paternalistic manner, that is, if the local authority sits in judgment of the moral suasion of tenant families, the project becomes the enemy. As David Hunter has observed: "The projects in Harlem are hated. They are hated almost as much as policemen and this is saying a great deal. And they are hated for the same reasons; both reveal, unbearably, the real attitude of the white world. . . ."

The way in which the program is administered could conceivably be as important as the housing it makes available to participating families. While the proponents of ownership for low-income families ceremonially chant incantations about the ideals that such an experience instills in one's soul, someone must begin to work out solutions to the many problems. How can the market be opened in the face of organized opposition? How can the low-income family be expected to absorb the hidden costs of ownership on a marginal budget? How can a home-ownership program improve the pride and self-respect of the participants? How can such a program be administered in a fashion that does not duplicate the inexcusably high-handed manner with which we have administered our low-rent housing programs throughout the country?

In the next generation we will have to build as many houses to accommodate population growth and normal replacement needs as we have built in our entire history as a nation. Yet we have seriously underestimated the extent and depth of our current housing crisis.

I cannot recommend a course that can eliminate existing inhuman housing conditions throughout the nation: I do not think that anyone can. The problem is too firmly rooted in our society. It is too much a part of our economic system. It is too closely related to such fundamental issues as the distribution of wealth and income to be dealt with in terms of housing alone. I would like to give serious consideration to several points that I believe are neither myths nor misconceptions, and that must be recognized in the development of any viable strategy to deal with the chronic shortage of decent housing.

First, uneven and underutilization of existing housing is a contributing factor to the perpetuation of the slum housing problem. Vacancy and abandonment rates are increasing in our small towns as well as in our large and congested cities. Therefore slum formation can no longer be equated solely with the unending crush of new arrivals forced to seek living space in already overcrowded and over-utilized housing.

Second, the slumlord of myth does not exist. In his place is a many-headed hydra, the hundreds of thousands of individuals who own the slums. These people all have varying economic resources, motives for entering the slum market, and knowledge of the dynamics of the market. But the owner of slum property is not as sophisticated and professional as many of us have been led to believe, nor is he as unin-telligent as many of us would like to think. In his study of slum properties in Newark, George Sternlieb found that "more than half the parcels are owned by people to whom real estate represents a trivial supplement to income . . . to a considerable degree this re-flects the comparatively amateur kind of holder who predominates in the market . . . many are . . . owners by default rather than by purchase; are owners by inheritance, or lack of purchasers to buy unwanted properties; or by a relatively trivial investment which is not too meaningful in terms of overall capital or income."

The owner of substandard housing is aware that the government frequently provides meaningful incentives to stimulate housing pro-grams. He is also aware that recent incentives have been largely limited to developing luxury housing or to aiding nonprofit sponsors. Until a meaningful program is developed for low-income housing, he will continue to shy away from government programs ostensibly de-signed to assist him to improve his housing but which will end up reducing the value of his investment, based upon existing market conditions.

Third, and in light of the above discussion, it is urgent that we devise a means for accumulating current and accurate information of the economics of slum ownership. Many owners of slum properties do not keep reliable financial records of their holdings. Without these, differences in the circumstances of various segments of the own-ership pool make it virtually impossible to devise meaningful pro-grams to help renew our inner cities. Therefore I suggest that the public perform an audit or accounting function in the low-income sector of the market. We could require, as a possible way to do this, that every renter-occupied dwelling unit found to be substandard in the course of routine inspection, be subjected to financial analysis by independent auditors employed or secured by local licensing and inspection departments.

This information would allow us to develop a multiplicity of plans for the various sectors of the substandard market. Matching each plan to its appropriate situation seems to be the only meaningful way to renew the existing housing inventory. Obviously the needs of an elderly widow without any capital except a five-unit substandard tenement are not the same as those of a real estate broker who owns 60 parcels and maintains a work crew to service them. Nor, of course, are their motives or knowledge of the market the same. Governmental policies and programs must reach both extremes; families living in units owned by the widow must not be penalized because the government has chosen to assist the broker.

Furthermore, if we can obtain the economic data to build a repertoire of programs, we will then be in a position to penalize those owners who fail to respond to the offer of aid. Outright public purchase would be justified, as would government assistance in the transfer of ownership from a recalcitrant owner to one who will cooperate.

In brief, I suggest we develop a data-gathering mechanism for an analysis of the economic patterns of slum ownership, that we develop a repertoire of solutions to the various problems, and that we stimulate property improvement by enforcing penalties upon those owners who fail to respond to the offer of aid. Should this plan fail, and the rate of deterioration of the existing stock continue unabated or increase in the future, some emergency measures should be adopted. I propose that we give serious consideration to the multifaceted implications involved in declaring this nation's existing inventory of low-rent housing a public utility. The basis for such a declaration would be the nation's compelling interest in maintaining the health, safety and social well-being of hundreds of thousands of American families living in substandard housing in the cities and the nation at large.

Such a proposal obviously includes, among other things, consideration of the regulation of profits, subsidies to those owners who cannot earn a reasonable return on their investment, the movement of structures into and out of the regulated sector, and the problem of defining the sector of the inventory to be covered. I offer this suggestion as an alternative approach to safeguarding the shrinking supply of privately owned low-rent units. It is indicative of the gravity with which I view the housing crisis.

STUDY QUESTIONS

1. Why does Stegman call the statement "Good housing can make good people" a myth?
2. Are the poor "incurable"?
3. Who once supported the public-housing programs? Why?
4. Is there a typical "slumlord"? How has he been stereotyped?
5. What has the aging of cities to do with the nature of the slums?
6. Why is the 221(d)(3) program beset with so many problems?
7. How fast are present housing units becoming substandard?
8. What is the systems-approach myth? Why is it a myth?
9. Why is home ownership a middle-class solution? What are the class implications of the entire idea?
10. What are the chances of a truly open housing market in the near future?

SUGGESTIONS FOR WRITING

1. What makes the myths Stegman talks about so attractive to large numbers of people? Do people want to believe in myths, or is there a reason or set of reasons that causes them to have faith in these particular myths?
2. If good housing is not going to make better people—if housing reform will not reform the "bad habits" of slum tenants—then why bother with it? What is the purpose of it?
3. Why should public funds be used in reforming slum housing? Isn't it the traditional American way of free enterprise and private development that makes America great? Argue this case from whichever viewpoint you wish.
4. If a government agent came to you and explained that your present housing was substandard and that there would be a new place made available for you in another neighborhood far across town, what would your reaction be? Would you be grateful? Should you be grateful? Describe your reactions carefully.
5. Which of these "myths" do you think is least likely to prove, in the end, to really be a myth? Stegman is careful to suggest that he is thinking about what is going to be the mythology of the future. He also cautions us that he may be wrong about one or all of them. Assuming he is right in that judgment, choose the one on which you think he is most likely to be proven wrong and explain your choice.

REVOLUTIONARY ACTION ON CAMPUS
AND COMMUNITY

Bobby Seale

When revolutionary politics is mentioned, it often summons up thoughts of paramilitary groups and random violence. Its less warlike aspects are usually lost in the rage. Bobby Seale, chairman of the Black Panther Party, suggests what black students can do if they wish to become "revolutionaries."

I am a political prisoner; in fact, I have been kidnapped and that's a crime committed against me.

For black students the significance of this lies in understanding the difference between a political prisoner and a criminal, and to understand this difference is to understand an important aspect of the history of black people in this country.

Generally the political prisoner's ideas relate to the need for freedom of the people at large and demand an end to their oppression and exploitation. A political prisoner's ideas then challenge the very premises of the state itself; in this case, the function and purposes of capitalist America. The state—all its institutions and structures—is the instrument whereby the ruling class maintains its economic power, which is its power to oppress the people, all people—blacks, Latinos, orientals, poor whites, Indians, what have you.

A political prisoner challenges these very foundations of the state itself. And that is why he is arrested. He is arrested because his ideas and actions challenge the state at its roots, challenge its power to repress, exploit and murder.

If you look over the history of America you find its political prisoners have been arrested and persecuted because they have supported

REVOLUTIONARY ACTION ON CAMPUS AND COMMUNITY   From the December 1969 issue of *The Black Scholar*. Reprinted by permission of Bobby Seale and *The Black Scholar*.

and led the people's struggle—Nat Turner, Toussaint L'Ouverture (who liberated Haiti and rotted in a French prison), Indian chiefs who were locked up on reservations and brothers like Huey P. Newton, David Hilliard, and Eldridge Cleaver.

America is a capitalist country, which is to say it is built on the idea of a handful of individuals exploiting the people for profit, owning the properties, the goods, the resources which belong to the people themselves and from whom they were stolen. To struggle against capitalist exploitation and its racism and class oppression is to be a revolutionary.

To be a revolutionary is to be an enemy of the state.

To be arrested for this struggle is to be a political prisoner.

A so-called "criminal" on the other hand is different from a political prisoner. A man becomes a so-called criminal because the state has not met his needs but oppressed, exploited and brutalized him from the very beginning: no jobs, no food, no clothing, no land, no housing, no freedom, no power to determine his own existence.

The difference is that the criminal does not understand that his enemy is the state itself, despite his lurking revolutionary consciousness. Instead, he attacks individual people in the state, and too often they're poor and oppressed people like himself. In other words, he attacks society, not the state.

A capitalist is just a grand scale criminal, a super gangster who robs countries, peoples, whole populations, instead of liquor stores.

But because the capitalists in America own, control and regulate the laws and machineries of the state, they can't be arrested, they can't be tried, they can't be brought to justice, even though they are the real criminals and their crimes against the people are enormous, their thefts and murders running into the millions each year.

So a political prisoner is a revolutionary who has been captured by the state because he challenges its crimes against his people—its wholesale robbery, rape, and murder and oppression of the people.

Capitalist America is not responsible to the people, it is the enemy of the people. Its theory and practice are criminal, its theory and practice are *lawless*, because all it's interested in is theft and oppression, and that's why it does not obey its own laws. That's why the fascist rulers in this country do not obey the Constitution or enforce it. Instead, they violate it.

My being kidnapped and held a political prisoner is a violation of the people's Constitutional rights. It shows most significantly the open oppression that the people suffer. When the state and government move to a position of open kidnap and political arrest, then this action is no different from the fascist operations in Germany or South Africa and the semi-fascist operations of the Ku Klux Klan, in lynching a man on a tree.

This Constitutional violation is really what is entailed by kidnapping, taking a prisoner illegally and against his will from one place to another, as I was and have been here. It was, in fact, actually illegal for the United States Federal Government to take me from California to the Chicago trial in order to railroad me.

So, I think the laws of this country and their history in relation to black people must be understood by black students. Black students must understand the Dred Scott Decision in 1857, one hundred and twelve years ago. They must know the reasons for black people being railroaded in courts—the Scottsboro case and just numerous brothers, Huey P. Newton, myself, Black Panther Party members who are being railroaded in court nowadays.

These so-called trials are nothing but a tantamount form of racism that has developed into an art of terror and murder and intimidation, of downright fascism here in America. So, I think the significance of this, as it relates to black students, is that black students must understand the need to move out and be more a part of the community, to educate the masses of people of the need to end the fascist, brutal war that has been going on against black people for hundreds of years. Students must understand what fascism is and must educate our community to the fact that this is a fascist state and the fact that our community is significantly related to the world people's struggle. Students must put these two facts together in the minds of the people so that they can move and rise like a mighty storm.

Let's get to a definition of fascism.

Fascism occurs when the capitalist state is in deep economic, political and racial trouble. In economic terms, fascism is the conversion of the economy to a warfare state, developing an enormous military machine to keep capitalism from collapsing. This war machine keeps the white proletarian masses employed. And its propaganda and practice keeps them agitated with racism. This constant racist agitation justifies the racist war machinery the fascist state uses abroad on non-white people and justifies the use of that same war machine for race wars on non-white people at home. Fascism is a racist, military machine that works both internally and abroad—at the same time.

Fascism brutalizes the masses, castrates the so-called "liberal" middle class and crushes people of color. Its plan is to brutalize the white masses and replace whatever class consciousness and sense of class struggle they might have had with racism, race hatred, and race war. Thus the white proletariat sees people of color as its enemy and identifies, supports and honors the police, the green berets, the FBI, all the fascists as they oppress black people.

The terrorized middle class of bourgeois liberal pretensions keeps its mouth shut and more shut. Because as we become more and more oppressed by the machinery of racist oppression, they become more and more intimidated by it.

So the fascist state's plan is to be at perpetual war—internally and around the world—to keep its capitalist economy going. To do that, it gets the white proletariat on its side with jobs provided by a racist war machine and makes the systematic elimination of non-white peoples an official policy of the state. To keep the masses and the petty bourgeoisie from developing revolutionary consciousness, fascism reduces the amount of education available—especially college education—in order to increase its supply of exploited, racist workers. Having this large surplus of workers, fascist capital moves to fascisize the labor force. Since many workers are employed making war machinery for race wars, they are easy prey to racist propaganda, and once persuaded that fascism is in their interests, they will support fascist capital. Once fascist capital has fascisized labor, the two move together for the systematic destruction of blacks, browns, orientals, Jews, etc. Fascist capital and fascist labor form the upper and lower jaws of a racist dog. That is fascism and that is what's happening here.

The duty on the part of the black students is to work to educate the masses, to be one-in-one with the masses and not to just isolate themselves on the campuses. Students must understand that when people are made political prisoners like Huey and myself and many others, that we have to move forward and not backward; we have to move positively and not be intimidated by the fascist system, but to move forward and amass the people to smash it.

What I have just finished saying is, in essence, the direction that Black Students' Unions and black studies programs on college campuses throughout the country should take. David Hilliard, Black Panther Chief of Staff, puts it in a very correct form:

> Black students, BSUs and Black Studies programs must understand that the only way to get a clear understanding of what the ideology of the revolutionary movement is today is to understand the history of the Black Panther Party, the history of the BSU, the history of black people, all historical experience;

all of this, the history of the party, the history of the struggle, the movement, presently in terms of the Black Panther Party, of the historical events of black people being translated by way of Marxist-Leninism.

Using this philosophy that the Chinese are using, using this same philosophy that the African Liberation Front in Mozambique and Angola and other places are using, is the direction that I see here for us.

This same philosophy must be used as a means to translate o ır overall historical experience here in the exploitative decadent system of America.

Black studies must be seen in this fashion, but not limited to non-participation and non-action. There has to be action, so that the philosophies and theories that are brought forth, the understanding of them and their ideas, are implemented. To understand the historical experience of black people translated by way of Marxist-Leninism is the direction that BSUs and black studies must take on college campuses.

BSUs and black studies programs on college campuses should understand that when we place revolutionary political programs in the community on a "for real" level, when there's breakfast for children, free clothing programs, free health clinic programs, community control of police—which is very primary—that when we place these programs in the community, that they are *real* programs, and these types of programs change the community, identify the historical experience of black people.

It's not enough for students to just sit down and be able to articulate an idea or a principle. The thing is to be able to implement it into a program and try to make it for real for the people, and in turn defend it, even when it is unjustly attacked, as many times it will be. We have to defend it. In this respect, I think it's high time a lot of BSU students stop playing with guns—some of them, not all of them. I think they must understand that the gun is for self-defense, which is a right and a human revolutionary necessity.

I think that cultural nationalism will never really give forth a precise understanding of the historical experience of black people. The historical experience of black people dictates that there must be revolutionary change. And cultural nationalism is not a changing operation. To try to customize some particular types of artifacts or symbols is to really stagnate a people's political and revolutionary development. That is why Huey P. Newton says that the only culture we are holding on to is the revolutionary culture—a culture that changes in direct relation to the revolutionary advance and progress that the people make against the exploiting, racist capitalist system.

It is necessary that the black studies departments and BSUs understand the need for revolutionary culture and relate as revolutionaries and place forth the revolutionary ideology by putting it into practice in the communities. For example, there are many writers needed for the Black Panther Party paper, but many of them just won't even send in a little article. We know a lot of black writers are scared of guns and things like that, but it's not necessary to run around in fear of the fact that to relate to the people in this manner means to defend the struggle and the people's struggle and one's self.

What you have to do is not let any fear overcome you, nor any intimidation of the pig power structure. Many of you students have demonstrated on campuses. But you must relate to the community more. The campus is not separable from the community. BSUs and black studies programs have to function both from an ideological level and from a very practical, practicing level. You are in the community and part and parcel of the community and never separate yourself from the community.

Power to the people!

STUDY QUESTIONS

1. Why does Seale consider himself a political prisoner?
2. Are all of Seale's concerns racial? What other kinds of concerns does he have?
3. How does Seale define capitalism? Does this square with your views?
4. What are the definitions of a revolutionary?
5. How does Seale distinguish between the society and the state? Is it an effective and reasonable distinction?
6. What are Seale's reasons for describing the United States as a fascist state? Are his reasons convincing to you?
7. What are the racial aspects of fascism?
8. How does Seale define "fascism"?
9. What does it mean to "fascisize labor"?
10. What is Seale's attitude toward guns for students?

SUGGESTIONS FOR WRITING

1. What, specifically, is Seale's recommendation to students? He urges them to move from campus to community, but what does that seem to mean? Explain in as much detail as you can what you think Seale's intentions are.
2. Offer your own analysis of Seale's interpretation of the governmental character of the United States. Do you think his appraisal of the United States as a fascist state is reasonable? Does it measure up to your own analysis of the nature and functioning of government?
3. If you wanted to counter Seale's argument, how would you go about it? What positive aspects of the government would you emphasize? Being as explicit as possible, construct an argument that you think effectively rebuts the points Seale raises.
4. Assuming Seale's analysis of society and government are accurate, how useful are his suggestions? If you agreed with Seale's premises, how would you feel about following his advice? Would you be able to do what Seale suggests?
5. What other paths could the revolutionary student follow if he were in agreement with Seale? Assuming that the student did not want to go into the community or was already in the community, what paths of action would you recommend to him as being most helpful for achieving Seale's ends?

THE GREENING OF THE PRESS

Tom Wicker

The recent attacks on the press by Vice President Agnew have centered on the fact that some newspapers lack objectivity. Tom Wicker, associate editor of **The New York Times,** maintains that they do not. On the contrary, he criticizes newspapers for often being **too** objective and suggests that what they really need is more self-reliance and independent thinking.

For more than a year Spiro T. Agnew has been traveling around the country making assertions about the news media, all of which in my judgment warrant considerable reflection by those who work in the field, and some of which have received that kind of reflection. I would sum up the reaction to this criticism in three categories. First, there have been rather nervous assertions of the virtue and professional integrity of the press, without much conviction. Then there have been strong restatements of First Amendment privileges and rights, without any real investigation into what the press has been doing to sustain the First Amendment. And finally, in a number of cases there have been strongly renewed efforts by editors and publishers to achieve a new sense of objectivity—which in effect means that they agree with the Vice President, because the basis of his criticism is that the news media have not been objective enough.

It seems to me that these reactions—particularly the last reaction —are exactly wrong, because the Vice President was making exactly the wrong criticism. Actually, what he has been expressing is a rather Marxist view of the news media, a view that the media really should serve the interests of the State. That is the element of the Agnew criticism that in too many cases we have failed to recognize.

THE GREENING OF THE PRESS *view*, May/June, 1971 ©.   Reprinted from the *Columbia Journalism Review*,

If I had been in Mr. Agnew's place and been trying to make an intelligent, useful criticism of the American press, I think I would have said that its biggest weakness is its reliance on and its acceptance of official sources—indeed, its "objectivity" in presenting the news. That is, that the fundamental reliance of the American news media in my experience has been, with rare and honorable exceptions, on the statement by the official source, be it government or business or academic or whatever. And much of what we mean by objectivity in American journalism concerns whether due credit is given to the official statement, the official explanation, the background explanation from the official source. This is certainly the Agnew measurement of objectivity and in most cases it has been the press's own measurement of objectivity.

Now why should this have been? I think, first, it is because of the pronounced lack of an intellectual tradition in the American press. I would be the last to assert that we don't have a muckraking tradition, that we don't have a rather notable record of catching the scoundrel with his hand in the till, or finding the official misdeed, the conflict of interest, and the like. We do have that. I refer to the lack of an intellectual tradition which will challenge official wisdom, challenge official statements, challenge institutional processes. We have never had that kind of an intellectual tradition in the American press and this has been a weakness.

Secondly, I think that we have had, historically, an orientation toward nationalism in politics and toward establishmentarianism in other areas of society, such as the economy or the academic world. Particularly in politics and diplomacy the orientation toward nationalism has been very pronounced in recent years. The obvious example, I think, is the failure of the American press, exemplified by the Washington Bureau of *The New York Times*, of which I was in charge at the time, adequately to question the assumptions, the intelligence, the whole idea of America in the world—indeed the whole idea of the world—which led this country into the Vietnam War in the 1960s. It is commonplace now, when the horse has already been stolen, to examine those assumptions. But where were we at the time we might have brought an enlightened public view to bear on that question? We were not, I think, very forward in challenging the rationale for that unhappy episode in American history.

Orientation toward nationalism on the one hand and toward establishmentarianism on the other also caused the American press almost to a man (again including me and again an unhappy lesson learned) in late 1967 to dismiss as at best a joke, and possibly even some form of conspiracy, the emergence of Senator Eugene McCarthy as a Presidential candidate. We can see in retrospect that that was a historical moment of great importance. But operating out of our orientation toward the conventional wisdom, in that case the conventional view of politics—what we could learn by going and asking the national chairman and the state chairman what we were supposed to think—we were told that the candidacy was a joke at best. Again this orientation toward the established view, the official source, led us astray.

It has carried all the way to the sports pages. As late as the time when the Jets, the football team from New York City in the American Football League, were getting ready to demolish the champion of the other league, every sports writer that I know of was writing that the American Football League was a "Mickey Mouse" league, a joke. Why were they doing that? They were doing that because, instead of using their own brains, they were told that by the official sources. Even reporters who had been out and seen those teams play should have known better. This is the sort of thing that is constantly happening in the American press.

Why were so many people, citizens as well as reporters, surprised last fall when it turned out that law-and-order in the demagogic sense was not the all-consuming, embracing political issue we had been told it was? We were surprised precisely because we had been told it was such an issue. We hadn't really looked into it. (Obviously, at this point I should say that you can't propound generalities such as these without making honorable exceptions. There certainly were honorable exceptions. I am referring to the general direction the American press has taken over the years.)

Why, as another example, has it been left mostly to people outside the press to raise the great issue of consumerism in America? Until Ralph Nader came along and began making challenges, until he began organizing teams to see whether the Federal Trade Commission was a moribund agency or was actually doing something, little of this was done. I am one of a long line of reporters hired in *The New York Times* Washington Bureau to look into and cover the regulatory agencies. I can name at least eight reporters who have been in our bureau who were hired precisely to do that, and the only one who has ever done it is the man who is there now, Christopher Lydon. In every other case, when the reporter would come into the Bureau, instead of really being turned loose to do this kind of job he always was given something of a more institutional nature to do. On my arrival, before I ever set foot in the FTC, I found that we needed one more man to cover Congress, and there I was covering Congress as many reporters before me had done.

If you think about objectivity in the American press—that is, the question of giving both sides of a picture, of trying to come to a rational balance of the facts in a case, trying to weigh pros and cons and see what is most important—you can see that the tradition of objectivity is bound to give a special kind of weight to the official source, the one who speaks from a powerful institutional position. If the chairman of the Democratic National Committee, for instance, tells you something about Democratic Party politics, the code of objectivity is bound to add a special weight to that, as against what you might be told by some relatively obscure professor of political science or some relatively obscure reporter in Omaha who says, "Well, that just doesn't seem to add up to what I think I hear, see, what I talk about." We tend to give weight to the official source, as if we believe that the man wouldn't be there if he didn't know what he was talking about; the institution wouldn't be functioning if it didn't have a certain relevance to whatever area it is functioning in.

Why, when the war in Vietnam first really became an American war with air attacks in February of 1965, was that accepted so universally and so uncritically as having been really the only thing that President Johnson could do? At that time there was a small American unit with airplanes stationed at Pleiku. But Americans, at least theoretically, were not in combat in Vietnam. They were there as advisers and helpers. The guard, the perimeter around the camp, was South Vietnamese. Then the perimeter was pierced by guerrillas and by mortar attacks from outside, a number of Americans were killed, and a number of American airplanes were destroyed. President Johnson, in retaliation, launched air attacks on the North.

Officials said it was the only thing he could do. But *Times* correspondent Charles Mohr, who had been in Vietnam for *Time* and then became our premier correspondent there, wrote what we call a "Q-Header," a news analysis which was conventional enough except that it raised one very interesting point in a fairly low paragraph. That paragraph said that it was difficult to see how air attacks on the North could deal with the situation that had been shown to exist at Pleiku, which was that South Vietnamese guards couldn't cope with the guerrillas. That was the essence: the South Vietnamese guards couldn't cope with the guerrillas. Yet no one in the daily press seized on that fact to say, "What are we doing, then, flying air attacks against the North?"

There are a number of reasons for that. I think the first is the orientation toward the official explanation, the feeling that the President said it so obviously it must be the case. Another, almost equally important reason was that there really wasn't an official spokesman on the other side. In the Senate there were only two outspoken critics of our whole involvement in Vietnam. One was Senator Morse of Oregon; the other, Senator Gruening of Alaska. Senator Fulbright told me, "You know, I'd like to be out there speaking with Morse and Gruening, except I can't allow myself to get associated with those fellows in that kind of Quixotic campaign against what the Administration is doing." So we had no official spokesman on the other side.

There was another example last October when Mr. Nixon came back from his European trip and plunged into the election campaign. Why did he campaign? There are statements in the *Times* and other papers that he was plunging in because "Republican prospects are so good" and he's going to go in there and "clinch the election victory" and he "really wants to be part of it" and "we're going to push it across the top" and "prospects are good everywhere, particularly for taking over the Senate." So election day came. Things didn't go so well. Official and background statements then came out declaring that the President had gone into the campaign in October because Republican prospects had been very bad and he had to get in and save the Republicans from a damaging defeat. Indeed, we were told, that is what he managed to do. Where they might have lost 15 seats in the House they only lost nine; where they would have lost a number of seats in the Senate they only lost two; and so forth. Both versions can't be true.

Since the election there has been a good deal of questioning on pragmatic grounds of the Nixon Administration's current rationale, but I don't think there has been a pronounced effort to go back and pin the President to the wall with the statements of October as against the statements of November; not just to say, "Mr. Nixon, you are a bad fellow, you misled us," but to say to ourselves, "What's going on here? What's happening when the President can say one thing in October and another thing in November and get equal coverage for both?" Instead of doing that we print today's official statement and then tomorrow's and then the next day's and then the next day's. And it often comes out a jumbled mess.

In science coverage, a first-class reporter like Walter Sullivan of *The New York Times* is allowed a good deal of leeway to use his own knowledge, to come to conclusions of his own, to say what he thinks is important and not important in that field. That is also true in the arts. When Clive Barnes was appointed drama critic of *The New York Times* he was a dance critic; he was not long-experienced in drama criticism although, as he quickly demonstrated, he knew a good deal about that field. But the day he was appointed he was allowed infinitely greater leeway to use his intelligence and come to esthetic and intellectual judgments on drama questions than any political reporter in the United States would be in a news column— no matter if that political reporter had been deeply involved for twenty years in politics and was a man of the highest academic background, the greatest integrity, and the deepest intellectual penetration. The political reporter would not be allowed the kind of leeway that any critic of the arts is allowed.

So there are certain areas in which journalists are allowed considerable leeway. But by and large we rely very heavily on the official source, and this really is what we talk about when we come down to the question of objectivity.

If that continues far into the future what will it mean? I think it will mean disaster. In the first place—and I have learned this lesson bitterly—institutions always serve their own interests. To the extent that you are reliant upon institutional sources for news you are reliant upon a self-serving source which in every case will attempt to put the best face on the news, to interpret information for you in the light of its own interests. That is obviously not something to be criticized; only the degree to which an institution would distort the news to serve its own interests is really to be criticized. You always attempt to put the best face on your behavior. It is only when you tell an outright, flat, provable, damaging lie that you really transgress moral bounds. So this is a truism—a fact of life—that reporters have to understand if they are relying upon institutions: they are relying upon a self-serving interest.

Secondly, institutions today, more than at any time in my lifetime, are under challenge precisely because they are irrelevant in many ways and are "out of touch." Life has changed, taken the ground out from under them. We see this in the universities, in the churches, in political institutions. These institutions have stood still while the world has moved out from under them. Therefore you are going not only to a self-serving source for news but to a source that simply may not know what it's talking about. Anybody who has been roaming the country as a reporter in the last few years can cite examples of having gone to a perfectly respectable institution, to a highly official source, and taken a statement that seems to have absolute surface validity, only to find that as events unfolded it meant nothing because it was out of touch with reality.

Another point, related to the second one, is that there are forces and currents at work in the world which are not institutional yet are profoundly important—which affect the way every person in the world lives, the way we will live, the way our children will live, the way we will organize ourselves. I question, for instance, whether three currents that are easily visible in this country are institutional in nature: the attempt among young people to find new ways of living; the dissatisfaction among black people; and the dissatisfaction of women. As is always the case, institutions are scrambling to get in touch and to take advantage of these movements. But if you restrict yourself to institutional sources you are going to miss a great deal of what is most important.

This can be seen in the debate in Washington over the protectionist trade measure known as the "Mills Bill." You may find the background in economic journals and in smaller magazines, but very little will be printed in the daily press about the fact that over a long period we have shifted from an industrial economy to a post-industrial economy. Production of services now is more important than the production of goods. By 1980 production of services will totally dominate our economy. You can export services through the international corporation, which is a proposition quite apart from trade restrictions; you can export services through foreign aid, which is government policy; but that is about the limit of it. What you export, by and large, are goods.

Now, if the American economy, out of a whole complex of forces that have nothing to do with institutional action, is shifting from production of goods to production of services, then at some point— perhaps already—exports become far less important than in the past. And if exports are less important then the question of foreign countries' retaliating against our exports is less important. It is this kind of movement that I think is a great force behind the trade bill. But it is this kind of thing on which we have too little reporting. If a reporter goes to cover the Mills Bill and all he knows is what Wilbur Mills or some trade association or a White House official tells him, then how can he help his readers understand what really is in the national interest?

The same thing is true on military policy. It is an article of faith among liberals that we are being taken over by the military, that military influences are running the Government. But that was really happening back in the Fifties when none of us realized it and nobody wrote anything about it. Today the trend is more nearly the other way, down, by almost any measure—by percent of Gross National Product, by absolute expenditures, by numbers of men in the military, by commitments abroad, by civilian opposition. By almost any measurement, militarism is on the defensive in America.

We not only missed the trend, and we're not only missing the trend nowadays, but we missed the turnaround point, in the sense of its being a turnaround point. The reason? We come back inevitably to reliance on official sources instead of reliance on our own brains, our own intelligence, our own ability to go out and find out and write about what is happening in the world.

The nature of the world we are coming into, I think, is clear. We are entering an age not of reform, because reform is when institutions themselves take the lead and change themselves and adapt to new conditions; and not an age of revolution because that is when revolutionaries replace one institution with another—usually worse than the one we had to begin with. Instead, we are entering an age of transformation. It is rather like the process that takes place within our own bodies; after so many years our bodies are totally changed, even though we don't realize it. The famous murderer Nathan Leopold, when trying to get a job in order to qualify for release from prison, made the point that there was not a single cell remaining in his body of the young man who killed a child in Chicago in the 1920s —that all the cells in his body were different. We change—from childhood into middle age to old age—and the process of regeneration continues with others who follow. I think it is this kind of age that we are coming into.

And it is proceeding at express-train speed. That is the thing we must grasp. It is happening in ways that aren't seen, aren't understood, aren't described to us, because it is not institutional. Institutionally, in Congress reform of the Electoral College has been blocked. But in fact for many years now our electoral processes have been changed in ways we still don't fully grasp, by television. Last year we thought that political spot commercials were going to have a tremendous impact, and they didn't. What does? We don't fully know. We just know that our electoral process is being changed, even though institutional reform of it has everywhere failed.

Another example: almost everywhere that state constitutional reforms go on the ballot they are ultimately defeated. Nonetheless state governments are being changed. Local governments are being changed. They are being changed by processes that we don't understand, by demands that people are making upon them that they didn't make before or by the absence of demands that once were made, by the rise and fall of sources of income, of problems, and so forth. What an impact on local and state government the automobile made! That was fifty years ago or more. It is that kind of thing, more than institutional acts, that describes the age.

In the mid-Fifties, particularly in the South, we thought that the Supreme Court decisions and the rise of the civil rights movement were going to be of enormous historical consequence. So indeed they were, but paling into insignificance by the historical consequences of something that many of us didn't even know was going on, which certainly had no institutional base—the enormous migration, one of the great migrations of history, of the black people out of the rural areas of the South into the cities. That was a historical movement of consequences that we yet can hardly begin to see, at a time when most authorities think the civil rights movement is, if not dead, at least merged into this other process of greater importance.

And isn't it true that the dehumanization of life by advancing technology, which we can all identify, is producing in our young people the profoundest demands for return to human principles and to human ways of living? The input is producing, in many ways, the opposite result.

How can the news media cope with this age of transformation? Certainly not by institutional coverage—by increasing the number of reporters in the Washington Bureau of *The New York Times* and spreading them more widely over governmental institutions, most of which, if not moribund, are at least by now centripetal in the sense that they serve mainly themselves. Nor can we cope with the age of transformation by formula writing and editing, by saying there are certain and only ways that you can communicate with people. The age can't be coped with by "brainstorming"—by selection of brilliant editors who confer with themselves twice a day and decide what ought to be in the newspaper and who ought to write it and where it can best be fitted. Nor can it be covered by the retarded child of brainstorming, group journalism—flooding an area with fifty reporters—or by the sort of comprehensive futility which has been the reliance of *The New York Times* so often in the past: the vacuum cleaner concept that everything that happens must be reported.

A lot of people say, "You know, Adolph Ochs was the great publisher of all time," which no doubt is true in the United States. "And his concept was comprehensiveness and objectivity." That was his concept for his time, but I believe his concept basically was to have a newspaper that served his time. And the newspaper that served his time is quite different from the newspaper that will serve our time.

I have no institutional formula for such a newspaper. Indeed, the essence of what I am saying is that there cannot be an institutional or a professional formula that will cope with it. "Let a hundred flowers bloom" is the only recommendation anyone can make. But there are at least two underlying things that we must do to serve the purpose. First, we must get the best people to work as journalists. We must seek out those with the highest intellectual standards, with the highest purpose, and above all the best writers we can get—good writers in the broadest literary sense, who have sensitivity to what happens around them, who understand how the specific can be translated into the general, who in the best sense are the novelists of their time. The novel, the good novel, has always been the best journalism.

The other thing we must do is, having got all those good writers, we must create the kind of conditions in which they can do their best work. We can't do that by imposing formula writing, by imposing group journalism. We are talking about artists. This is the only way that we can cope with an age of transformation, to really begin to serve our great purpose in life.

Just as dehumanizing produces—and will produce—ever growing demands for a humane life and for humane dealings with one another, it seems to me that as we are more and more bombarded with visual and auditory images, there will be an irresistible demand for the word and for the meaning the word can convey. For the long future of journalism, that is our challenge.

STUDY QUESTIONS

1. What is the basis of the Vice President's criticism of the news media? Does it seem to be reasonable criticism?
2. Why does Wicker call the "objectivity" of the press its biggest weakness?
3. What kind of intellectual tradition has the American press lacked?
4. Why does Wicker condemn the average newsman's orientation toward the "established source"?
5. Wicker mentions the incident at Pleiku that led to air raids on

North Vietnam. What does he want us to learn from his analysis of the reporting of that incident?

6. Are today's "official statements" ever measured up against yesterday's "official statements"?

7. How do art critics differ from news reporters in respect to the freedom they are given to say what they think? Should this difference be maintained?

8. Does Wicker suggest that institutions as such are irrelevant?

9. What is a "post-industrial" economy?

10. Why is ours an age of transformation?

SUGGESTIONS FOR WRITING

1. How do you think members of the present Administration would react to Wicker's suggestion that less objectivity and more personal analysis should characterize today's press? Try to be specific in pointing out the nature of the Administration's response. Would you generally defend its reaction?

2. The author criticizes the press for its objectivity and for its reliance on news releases from institutions that are obviously self-serving. In what other ways could the press go about reporting the news? Are any of the alternatives practical? Which could be put into action immediately?

3. What might be the dangers of disregarding Adolph Ochs's view of what a newspaper should be? Are these dangers serious enough to warrant our throwing out Wicker's proposals altogether? Whose kind of newspaper would you rather read, Ochs's or Wicker's? Which would your parents rather read?

4. Wicker suggests that a good newspaper should serve its own time. How would you change the newspapers in your community so that they met this requirement? Try to be specific and use as many illustrations as you can to show how the organization, advertising, and editorial policy of your papers are out of step with the times.

5. Write some sample articles on current affairs in the style that Wicker suggests. What difficulties does it pose? What do you learn by trying it? Do you feel that this is a valuable way to write news articles?

HUNTS POINT: RULED BY ADDICTS

Richard Severo and Barbara Campbell

Like Death and the Maiden, drug addiction and crime are inseparable. In some of our large cities, entire neighborhoods are terrorized by drug addicts who prey on anyone for a "fix."

In basic ways, portions of the Hunts Point section of the southeast Bronx have ceased to be a part of New York City.

Many city services, such as police protection, garbage collection, water supply—and citizen obligations, such as payment of taxes, decent maintenance of property, some semblance of civil order—do not occur with any degree of predictability in Hunts Point.

Repeated visits to Hunts Point uncover so much that is not supposed to be America in 1969 that the visitor wonders if he has suddenly entered a time machine and been transported back to frontier days. Nearly everything seems touched by lawlessness.

On three of the worst streets, residents have less than a 1-in-20 chance of dying a natural death.

Drug addiction is a major cause of what is wrong in Hunts Point. But the frequently heard argument that blight conditions may be creating the addicts, rather than the other way around, is both reasonable and meaningless at this point.

Although former addicts agree that the area's physical condition probably contributes significantly to the mental state of the people who resort to heroin, such reasonable explanations are small comfort to residents, who are literally living in a state of siege.

For Hunts Point, which conveys an overwhelming sense of despair, is a neighborhood whose life style is largely determined by the heroin addicts who live there, travel to buy drugs there, and, most important, steal there.

HUNTS POINT: RULED BY ADDICTS   From *The New York Times* of September 24, 1969. © 1969 by The New York Times Company. Reprinted by permission.

231

Heroin addicts are everywhere in Hunts Point—on street corners, in abandoned buildings, in occupied buildings, on rooftops, in hallways, in basements—buying and selling dope freely and openly at all hours of the day.

If any one word can describe their conduct, it is brazen—for at the intersection of Simpson Street and Westchester Avenue, junkie prostitutes sell themselves, pushers make deals and addicts purchase drugs. All just a half block from the 41st Precinct station.

And behind closed doors, wedged tight with iron bars bolted to the floor, sit the nonaddict residents of Hunts Point, most of them Puerto Rican, many of them with little knowledge of English or what it takes to survive in New York, wondering when they will be mugged, or when their flats will be burglarized, or when their children will come home with a bag of heroin purchased in the schoolyard.

Deputy Inspector Anthony J. McNally, commander of the 41st Precinct, says his men are doing a good job. He thinks that neighborhood critics misunderstand what the police can and cannot do to make arrests that do not violate the constitutional rights of addicts. Moreover, he does not think the heroin problem in Hunts Point is getting worse.

"We are emphasizing the problem more," he said.

The Catholic church that serves the Puerto Rican majority in Hunts Point, St. Athanasius, has no poor box. It was stolen too many times by junkies. There are grocers who drive to distant warehouses to pick up goods, because wholesalers will not deliver; junkies have been known to swarm over trucks, stealing them clean in broad daylight. Women are robbed of their purses at knifepoint at high noon, and passers-by scarcely notice it.

Residents telephone the police, explaining excitedly that they are watching junkies stealing a television set from a neighbor across the way. But the police do not come.

Two landlords report that they have to pay policemen as private bodyguards to protect them from marauding junkies on days when they deposit rent money in the bank. The police are paid $10 a trip.

Protection is a service hard to come by in Hunts Point. On Fox Street, a landlord has hired as his building superintendent a convicted murderer who patrols the halls around the clock, between cat-naps. He is armed with a machete, an ax and a 160-pound German shepherd.

"I treat people with respect," the superintendent says, "and that's why they respect me."

While junkies "respect" his building and avoid it, just outside one may wish he had the convicted murderer as his bodyguard. One warm afternoon this summer a visitor to Fox Street saw two men running down the street, the pursuer yelling profanities at the man ahead of him.

In the middle of the block—just two blocks from the police station —the men stopped, pulled out guns and began shooting at each other. As bullets ricocheted from the moldering bricks, junkies nodded in doorways, alcoholics slumped in the shadows of tenements, finger prints of wine, and small children waded through garbage-filled gutters gushing with water from a hydrant opened by an enterprising teen-ager.

Some of the children seemed mildly interested in the shooting that was taking place a few yards away.

At the tenement windows above, where people sat to catch a breeze, a few put their newspapers aside to watch the shoot-out. Laborers in a nearby building laughed at the scene but did not interrupt their work.

Then the shooting stopped as suddenly as it had started. The two men again ran down the street. Not a policeman was in sight.

Two days later the visitor was on Fox Street again, accompanied by a former drug addict. Near the corner of Fox and Westchester, two addicts, desperate for a fix but without money, had just attacked a pusher, stabbing him a few times and leaving him in the street. Ferreting through his pockets, they found enough heroin to provide "half a load"—not enough to make either junkie high, but enough to satisfy the gnawing desire, for a few hours.

The former addict spoke to the two men briefly. One of them had bloodstains on his shirt. As the pair left, the ex-addict shook his head. "Damn," he said, "if that man lives, he gonna be madder 'n hell at them two. Them two better watch themselves."

Such outbursts of violence illustrate what happens to a neighborhood overrun by junkies. Here are other facets of life in Hunts Point:

In late August, of the 42 buildings in the 900–1000 block of Simpson Street, at least eight owed $46,061 in back real-estate and water taxes. Landlords in the area claim junkies drive away good tenants, making their buildings unprofitable. Said one landlord: "If I paid taxes, I'd be in the poorhouse."

Two buildings on Simpson Street had neither drinking water nor working toilets (junkies had stolen water pipes, which they sell at a junkyard not far from the police station), an estimated 25 per cent of the families on the block paid no rent or paid it sporadically and drug addicts were living in at least six buildings declared uninhabitable by the city.

Ex-addicts from Odyssey House, an institution for the rehabilitation of heroin users, are at work in Simpson Street and estimate that 9 out of 10 teen-agers in the 900–1000 block are using drugs. "We don't care about marijuana here," said one Puerto Rican mother. "If our kids take marijuana only, we consider ourselves lucky."

Heroin flows so freely that a casual visitor to the neighborhood was able to buy a $3 bag in the street in broad daylight. Moreover, he saw at least 10 other sales in the same area over a three-week period.

If statistics compiled by Dr. Michael Baden, associate medical examiner, are taken as a guide, residents of three of the worst streets in Hunts Point—Simpson, Fox and Tiffany—have less than a 20-to-1 chance of dying a natural death. Of the 37 deaths the Medical Examiner's office investigated there between Jan. 1 and Aug. 10, only two were of natural causes. Only 7 per cent of all deaths in New York City are of other than natural causes.

The Medical Examiner's office investigates all deaths in the city in which a private doctor has not been in attendance a week or more before death. Since this sort of medical service is rare in Hunts Point, Dr. Baden believes his office has investigated virtually all the deaths there.

A breakdown of Dr. Baden's figures on the 35 people who died from other than natural causes showed:

There were five homicides, including a strangled 75-year-old widow, three fatal stabbings and one fatal shooting.

Seven persons died after injecting heroin into their veins. They ranged from a 16-year-old Negro to a 30-year-old Puerto Rican, both residents of Fox Street. Actual death was accompanied by a variety of ailments triggered by drug use, including hepatitis and acute vitamin deficiency.

Eleven persons died of alcoholism, almost all of them with severe liver damage. The youngest was a 30-year-old Puerto Rican; the oldest a 58-year-old Negro.

One man died of alcoholism complicated by drug use and another died of alcoholism and tuberculosis combined.

One man got drunk and died after he fell down a flight of stairs. Another man died of a brain hemorrhage. The medical examiner is not sure how the hemorrhage occurred, except that it was "traumatic" and caused by other than natural causes.

Four children fell out of windows, just on Fox, Simpson and Tiffany Streets. During the same period, only 16 children fell from windows in all of New York.

Three more children were battered to death, the Medical Examiner's office reported, all of them on two consecutive blocks in Fox Street.

A fourth child was classified as a "crib death." Dr. Baden is not sure whether the death was natural or deliberate but suffocation has not been ruled out.

Only one traffic fatality took place during the period studied in Simpson, Fox and Tiffany Streets. "Well, of course we don't get too much auto traffic," one addict explained. "Drivers know what can happen to their cars." An empty car can lose its tires in eight hours and be picked clean in 24.

Both deaths attributed to natural causes were heart failures. Nobody committed suicide.

Among the survivors in Hunts Point, a few have a tenacity that can only be compared to that of the pioneers who crossed the Great Plains.

One who has remained is Mrs. Margaret Hajos, a widow of 74 who looks 15 years younger. At one point during the summer she was the only resident of the five-story tenement at 1003 Simpson Street.

She was found in her $1-a-month basement apartment (the city had reduced her rent from $33.54 in recognition of the fact that the building had been declared unfit for human habitation). The place was quite neat and clean except for about 2 inches of water on the floor.

"The junkies," Mrs. Hajos explained. "They stole the pipes upstairs; all the water came down here."

Mrs. Hajos was upset that day. Junkies had stolen her year-old 18-inch Emerson television set, which had cost her $256—a major investment for a woman who receives $89.20 a month in Social Security and $44.90 from a union pension, earned for years of work in a handbag factory.

"Yes, they stole it," she said. "While I was on the front steps, and God only knows how they got in. They steal everything."

Asked how she managed without running water, she replied: "Oh, I get water from my neighbors. All I need."

Why didn't she move from the neighborhood? "No. My father always told me to work hard. He said, 'You gotta be tougher than they are.' I stay."

A few weeks later Mrs. Hajos moved next door to 1007 Simpson, which had running water of sorts; it took 20 minutes to fill a glass.

"I remember," she said, "40 years ago when there were cows in Hunts Point. It was beautiful. Trees everywhere. Nice people, too. Russians, Jews, Hungarians—all nice people. All hard workers. It could happen again."

Another resident who will not move is Mrs. Clara Spindler, 79, who lives at 957 Fox Street. Also a widow, she suffers from asthma, cancer and bad eyesight. She has been pushed and punched by her neighbors. A junkie recently threatened her with a knife. But she will not move in with her son in New Jersey ("I am independent") or apply for public housing.

"My husband and I lived in this block together," she said. "We lived just up the street and it was very nice."

Landlords as well as tenants are having trouble in Hunts Point. A landlord who owns two houses on Fox Street said he paid $600 a year just to replace broken glass.

"No, I don't pay any taxes," he said. "I figure the city is going to take this building for urban renewal some day. I'll get shafted when that happens, so I'm taking steps to protect myself now."

The residents complain that "dope is everywhere." Putting the statement to the test, a visitor, accompanied by a former addict, made a purchase at 2:30 p.m. on July 10, a couple of blocks from the 41st Precinct station.

The pusher, a fat man in a blue T-shirt, made the sale without hesitation. The visitor asked his companion if the pusher might suspect a stranger as a police undercover agent.

"Come on, man, you must be kidding," he replied.

Later, the contents of the package were analyzed. It contained 7.5 milligrams of heroin—about 10 per cent of the total contents, which was a normal dose. The rest was quinine and milk sugar.

In Hunts Point, as in other neighborhoods in the southeast Bronx—Mott Haven, Morrisania, South Bronx—pushers were hawking heroin. The words heard in front of the Bronx Casino on 149th Street were heard over and over again:

> *Hey, baby, you wanna deuce [a $2 bag of heroin] . . . you wanna a tres [$3 bag] I got cibas, man, cibas, cibas [Doriden, a sedative manufactured by the Ciba Corporation] . . . tengo, la tengo [I have it] . . . pito, pito [reefers] . . . you wanna bolsita [a little bag] . . . you wanna eye dropper . . . I know where you can get it . . . you lookin' for action . . . I got bams, baby [a kind of liquid stimulant, occasionally taken with heroin] . . . you wanna buy coke [cocaine] . . . watchoo lookin' for?*

Apathy and fear pervade Hunts Point in almost equal measure.

Morris Leschins, a pharmacist who owns the Farmacia Latina at 1429 Wilkens Avenue, keeps 30 brands of cough medicine, none of them with codeine. He will fill no narcotics prescriptions, even legitimate ones. He gets repeated requests for any medicine that comes with an eye dropper, since the dropper is used by addicts to pump liquified heroin through a hypodermic needle.

"I never drive my car to work," he told a visitor. "You didn't drive up here, did you?" Then he added: "I'd sell this business in a minute, even at a loss. But nobody wants it."

Mrs. Sarahlyce Dabney, director of the Bethany Family Circle, a community organization that works with the poor of Hunts Point, had her purse snatched just after 5 P.M. last April 1. Some men stopped the purse snatcher, for which she was grateful. But nobody would be her witness against the man in court.

"They all said they were too busy working," she said, amused at the excuse since 80 per cent of the people in her neighborhood are on welfare. "Everybody," she said, "is afraid."

Ex-addicts from Odyssey House have taken over the operation of 1007 Simpson from a landlord who doesn't want it. They call tenants' meetings twice a week. They want to motivate the people in the building. But they can't even motivate the people to come to the tenants' meetings. "Nobody cares," said one of the former addicts, Alton Johnson. "They are afraid."

"Afraid of what?" he was asked.

"Of everything," he replied.

The Rev. Louis Gigante, assistant pastor of St. Athanasius, has advocated the formation of defense groups to "confront" addicts and drive them from the neighborhood. But he can't find anyone willing to do the confronting.

"These people do not think of the streets as theirs, but as somebody else's," he said. "They are afraid of their problems. They want somebody else to solve them—the city, the police, even the parish priest."

Unlike Puerto Ricans on the Lower East Side, residents of Hunts Point are not "turf"-oriented. They tend to be older, more submissive, more unclear as to what they should expect from life in New York and less inclined to defend their neighborhood against junkie invaders.

In Hunts Point, they look fearfully toward abandoned buildings and complain about drug addicts, who emerge periodically to get fixes and to prey on the community. But nobody talks about getting them out. They are waiting for the police.

A visitor entered 999 Simpson Street at 8:30 P.M. last July 17 to determine whether the tenement was as empty as it appeared from the street.

Inside, he found a young man and his girl. Both were Puerto Rican. He was 22 and had recently completed a stay in a facility of the State Narcotic Addiction Control Commission. "They let me out when I was cured," he said. The girl was 19 and had recently served two weeks in jail for prostitution.

The young man was cooking heroin in a bottle cap, held over a small candle with twisted wire. He frowned as the stranger approached.

"You the man [police]?"

"No."

"Then why you here?"

"I want to know about the drug problem here."

"That's good," the young man said, intently watching the heroin. "We got a terrible problem here. Lotta kids getting hooked."

The heroin had cooked; he pulled some of it up into his hypodermic needle and matter-of-factly injected it into his girl's shoulder. He did not give it to her in a vein (mainlining), but just through the skin (skin-popping). "She ain't ready for no mainlining yet," he said.

Then he tied a piece of rubber tubing around his arm, and whirled his arm around to make his veins bulge. "Everybody keep still," he warned, "or I mess this up." The needle went in. Immediately his head began to nod. "Youuuuu ain't the mannnnn," he said from another world. His girl was still unaffected.

"It'll take a while," she said, "but in an hour, we'll be together. Don't you understand?"

STUDY QUESTIONS

1. How may "blight conditions" cause drug addiction?
2. Is the presence of police effective in curbing junkie activities?
3. How do nonaddicts live in this neighborhood? Who are they?
4. What is the significance of the fact that a convicted murderer is employed to "protect" a building?
5. Is there anything odd about the neighborhood reaction to a shoot-out?
6. What is the neighborhood real-estate situation? Is it surprising?
7. What varieties of addiction are discussed in the article?

8. Is the story about Mrs. Hajos effective in its context? Why?
9. Do the citizens of Hunts Point take an active role in law enforcement?
10. What are some of the proposals made to cure the ills of Hunts Point?

SUGGESTIONS FOR WRITING

1. Of all the deaths recorded in Hunts Point over a short period of time, not one was from suicide. A similar sample from any "normal" community would have included at least one suicide. What do you think accounts for this? Why do junkies and alcoholics kill themselves with their addiction, but rarely kill themselves with a gun? Are there any clues to the answer to this question in their life style?

2. Using just the evidence offered in this article, what do you feel has been the role of the police in this neighborhood? Assemble the evidence the article presents and develop a reasonable conclusion.

3. What can be done for a community like this one? If you were the mayor of New York or the borough president in charge of this area, what specific steps would you take to change Hunts Point? What would be your goals? What would be your expectations? Do you think you could really establish an effective program?

4. What do you think is the most awful aspect of life in Hunts Point? If you had to live there what would most frighten or enrage you? What would you do about it?

5. Many social critics have said that the American dream was built by business on the principle of the inviolability of private property. If this is true—or even possible—what should the role of business and property owners be? What is their responsibility? Should landlords in this community pay their taxes? Why?

BLACK CRIME: THE LAWLESS IMAGE

Fred P. Graham

The demand for "law and order" has never been heard more loudly in America. What it is usually taken to mean is: more police to curb black crime. In this article the author offers us some of the facts concerning the black crime rate.

Every nation has its equivalent of the mythical emperor who wore no clothes. In the fable, nobody could bring himself to believe what he saw until a child blurted out the truth, and then everyone had a laugh at the emperor's expense. In the United States the naked emperor was for years the high Negro crime rate; the boy who broke the spell was George Wallace, and nobody laughed.

In his campaign for President, Governor Wallace did not shout that the emperor had no clothes; a politician with his segregationist credentials could make his point without calling a spade a spade. Instead, he preached incessantly about rising crime. Everyone knew that it was Negro crime that was being deplored.

Wallace's early strength forced his rivals to talk tough about crime, too. Soon, so many politicians had vowed that they weren't necessarily criticizing Negroes when they demanded "law and order" that everybody understood that the term really was a racial slur of sorts.

Once established, this issue provided a nice vehicle for those candidates who wished to purify their liberal credentials; several pledged solemnly to call for "order with justice" instead. Vice President Humphrey did this, but he also mentioned Negro crime, stressing that most of the victims were Negroes. Richard Nixon tried "law and order with justice" in his speeches as a compromise, but the phrase did not sing; the "with justice" got lost in the final weeks of his winning campaign.

In mid-September of 1968, when the law-and-order flapdoodle was at its height, Attorney General Ramsey Clark testified before the National Commission on Causes and Prevention of Violence. After a few introductory remarks, Clark made this statement:

> Negroes, 12 per cent of the total population, were involved in 59 per cent of the arrests for murder: 54 per cent of the victims were Negro. Nearly one-half of all persons arrested for aggravated assault were Negro and the Negro was the primary victim of assault. Forty-seven per cent of those arrested for rape were Negro and again studies show the Negro is the primary victim. Sixty-one per cent of all arrested for robbery were Negro. Less than one-third of the persons arrested for property crime are Negroes.

This paragraph was dropped into the statement without elaboration or recommendations, and since Clark also locked horns that day with J. Edgar Hoover over the issue of police violence (which Clark deplored and Hoover excused), the racial reference passed unnoticed by the news media. But the spell was broken; a high government official had, apparently for the first time, talked publicly and in some detail about high Negro crime.

The long-standing national myopia about Negro crime has been a remarkable public exercise in whistling past a graveyard. It involved the Federal Bureau of Investigation, which buried the shocking statistics of Negro crime in its annual publications and said nothing; the press, which ignored Negro crime in its reports of the FBI's crime statistics; the Negro community, which suffered most but feared to be tarred by the lawlessness of the few; the professional criminologists, who saw what was happening but failed to make themselves heard outside academia; and officialdom, which operated under the premise that if nothing were said perhaps the problem would go away.

Rather than going away, it got worse—and while the national tendency continued to be to whistle and not look back, George Wallace saw to it that the phenomenon of Negro crime could never again be simply ignored. Events have shown that Wallace was a symptom and not the disease. His innuendos rang bells because many listeners had begun to suspect, through newspaper and word-of-mouth reports, that Negro street crime was indeed getting worse.

Since then, evidence has come to light to show that they were right. A spate of recent statistical studies by criminologists had suggested that the already high Negro crime rate had begun to accelerate; this phenomenon has now been confirmed by a national statistical survey that bears the imprimatur of the Federal Bureau of Investigation and the National Commission on the Causes and Prevention of Violence. The Violence Commission obtained from the FBI the most complete figures ever assembled on race and crime—figures that show Negro arrest rates for violent crimes in the cities to be twelve times that of whites across the board, as much as eighteen times that of whites for some offenses, and still climbing—especially among young people. The ultimate result of this realization can be constructive or corrosive, depending upon how the public reacts—but it seems inevitable that race and crime will become firmly linked in the public mind, and that the Supreme Court and other institutions that are caught up in the crime crisis will be affected by it.

Of those who had a clear view of the Negro crime situation all along but said nothing, Hoover's FBI has been the most oblivious. Its annual statistical roundup of crime, a tall volume entitled *Crime in the United States*, contains neat tables supported by detailed discussions of the figures. These discussions range from tedious flyspecking about trivia to disapproving comments on such subjects as the high recidivism rate among probationers and parolees, but there has never been an analysis of the lopsided arrest figures for Negroes that the tables show.

For instance, the FBI tabulations for 1967 disclosed—to those determined few who penetrated the columns of fine print—that more Negroes than whites were arrested for murder, robbery, carrying concealed weapons, prostitution, and gambling. Only the total number of arrests for each racial group is given for each offense, but since Negroes made up 12 per cent of the population, simple arithmetic would show that for the FBI's "index" crimes, the national arrest rate for Negroes was five times the arrest rate for whites, and for some violent crimes it was more than ten times as high. (When the FBI refined these data for the Violence Commission, it showed that Negro arrest rates in the cities were about double the national ratios. Sociologists despair because the FBI's failure to refine routinely its published racial data obscures facts such as this.)

Race has never been mentioned in the publicity releases that the Bureau issues with its figures, and because the 1967 racial statistics were dished out cold turkey in the FBI's tables, the disparity was not mentioned by the wire services' reports of the year's crime. As far as anyone can remember, neither the Associated Press nor the United Press International has ever reported the Negro arrest rates, although the wire services report the FBI's figures each time they are released.

Negro spokesmen were equally silent until the rhetoric of the 1968 political campaign broke the spell. "The fact that George Wallace said it doesn't mean it isn't true," said a leader of the National Association for the Advancement of Colored People's influential New York chapter, as his group came out, a few weeks after the election, for a tough policy against crime. The NAACP chapter declared that "the reign of criminal terror [in Harlem] must be stopped now." Its demands were almost four-square with the long-standing suggestions of J. Edgar Hoover—more police protection and tighter bail and probation restrictions.

The most curious lapse was the failure of the academicians to communicate with anyone but each other about the worsening situation. Since the 1920s sociologists have been writing in their scholarly journals about the high Negro arrest rates. If anybody on the outside noticed, for the most part they felt it best not to pass the information along. This was of little importance until the late 1960s, when Negro crime began to accelerate in an alarming pattern—there was a tendency toward more violence, by younger Negroes, more often directed at whites. The academicians called attention to the danger signs, but accurate word of what is happening has never reached the public beyond the readers of their own academic journals.

The motives behind the Negro crime taboo were obvious. Virtually every sociologist who has studied the subject agrees that the crime rate among blacks is far higher than that of the rest of the population, even after allowing for the blacks' generally low economic status. This is the ultimate product, most experts feel, of the economic and cultural ravages of a segregated system that has been presided over by whites. Thus to dissect the problem would expose flaws in the performances of both races. Moreover, as high as the Negro crime rate has gone, it still represents only a small minority of black people. In a recent year there were 2,923 arrests for "index" crimes for each 100,000 Negroes in the population, and although that is much higher than the white rate of 607, nobody wanted to tar the law-abiding majority of Negroes with a lawless image they did not deserve.

Yet with the racial disparities as wide as they are, the subject has been unpleasant enough to remind government officials and scholars of the ancient tradition that the messenger who brought bad news forfeited his head. That is apparently why nobody brought the statistics to the public's attention and into perspective when Negro arrest rates began to rise sharply in the mid-1960s—a silence that created a climate favorable for the likes of George Wallace. Under the assumption that nobody has suffered for exposing the crime statistics for the Federal Bureau of Investigation, the Violence Commission's staff decided to break the spell by asking the FBI to compile the most comprehensive report ever made of relative Negro and white arrest statistics and trends. What the FBI did was to take the urban arrest data for 1964 through 1967, relate them to the ages and racial characteristics of the arrestees, and arrive at the first reliable statistics of racial crime trends across the country.

The results showed that Negroes' arrest rates for violent crime were far higher than whites' rates—higher than most experts had guessed in their gloomiest moments. The gap was widening for murder, rape, and robbery, where the already high rates for blacks were climbing faster than the whites' rates. Most ominous of all, soaring rates among young blacks promised more of the same for the future.

Robbery presented the gloomiest picture: where Negroes had been arrested five times more often than whites in the country as a whole in 1950, the FBI's figures showed the Negro urban robbery rate to be sixteen times greater in 1967, and for the coming generation— those from ages ten to seventeen—the Negro rate was twenty times the white rate. In terms of arrest rates (the number per 100,000 persons per year), the national robbery rates in 1950 were 12.7 for whites and 68.8 for Negroes. By 1967 this had risen in the cities to 22.8 for whites and 368.9 for Negroes. Among the younger group, it was 27 for whites and 549.7 for young Negroes. It is this skyrocketing robbery rate among young Negroes that worries the experts most.

The FBI's study was only slightly less bleak for violent crimes other than robbery. For murder, the Negro arrest rate was eighteen times that of whites for persons of all ages. The rape rate among Negroes was eleven times that of whites of all ages, and twelve times the white rate in the younger group. For aggravated assault, the overall Negro rate was ten times that of whites, but unlike the other three types of violent crime, the whites' assault rate was rising faster. Surprisingly, the FBI found overall violent crime rates for young whites to have risen very little over that period, indicating that the much-discussed rising crime rate among young people could be largely a reflection of soaring crime among young blacks.

The Violence Commission experts knew that these figures tended to underscore black criminality, because only crimes of violence were included, and these have always been prevalent among nonwhites. If white-collar offenses and other middle-class crimes had been cranked in, the picture would not have been so stark. The experts were aware that the President's National Crime Commission had concluded that the Negro rates for burglary, larceny, and auto theft (the three property crimes in the FBI's crime index) increased by 33 per cent, while the white rate rose almost as fast, by 24 per cent.

White Americans were also known to be narrowing the gap in a few crimes other than assaults, notably in the area of narcotics offenses.

But what struck the Violence Commission with such force was that urban violence was much more a Negro phenomenon than people had known (or at least, had been able to prove), and that these trends were so pronounced among young blacks that the situation was almost certain to grow much worse in the future. The final blow was that all of this bore the imprimatur of the Federal Bureau of Investigation, which assured that it would strike public opinion with the force of holy writ.

The impact of this was such that the Negro members of the commission, Patricia Harris and Judge A. Leon Higginbotham, at first insisted that the study not be made public. Mrs. Harris, particularly, saw no reason to give ammunition to segregationists. Others on the Commission balked at suppressing the study, but they were torn, as others have been, between the desire to keep racists from exploiting such information and the need to inform society and encourage efforts to correct the conditions that breed crime.

They compromised by disclosing in the final Commission report that reported violent crime arrest rates for blacks of all ages were far higher than for whites. But no mention was made of the even higher rates of criminal violence found among the upcoming generation of young blacks, and there was no hint that disturbing new information about crime and race had been produced by the revered crime statistics machinery of the Federal Bureau of Investigation. The staff also agreed to strike from its task force report its conclusion that violent crime levels probably are much higher for blacks than for whites, and to substitute the statement that the arrest figures that have suggested this fact are probably reliable.

The Commission disbanded last fall, having published all of its task force reports except one—the one on individual acts of violence that contained the FBI's racial data. The indications were that a dearth of funds was largely responsible for the delay, and that at some future time the data would be published in a form that would enlighten scholars but would probably not reach the general public. The outcome was one that all concerned could accept, and it had the virtue of not adding a new public controversy to an already grim situation. But that did not change the fact that the findings themselves indicate that severe strains will probably come to bear on the Supreme Court, as "street crime" comes to be increasingly associated with one group—young blacks.

Criminologists find it particularly ominous that robbery is becoming so rampant among young Negroes. Robbery includes all thefts carried out by the use or threat of force—which generally means muggings and armed stickups. Thus it is considered a bellwether crime, the one that most accurately indicates people's willingness to use force against strangers. Apparently, young Negroes are becoming more ready to use force, and against whites; a recent study of Philadelphia revealed a growing tendency among Negroes to rob whites and an increase in the use of violence by Negroes against whites in the course of these crimes.

A straw in the wind came in a 1968 robbery in Washington, D.C. A police radio alert, broadcast at 4:12 P.M. on November 9, after a holdup at a movie theater just three blocks from the White House, alerted all police units to be on the lookout for two Negro males, each four feet tall and weighing about 80 pounds. The cashier at the theater estimated their ages at ten or eleven. Both carried guns. They took $80. One shouted, "I'll kill you," as they ran away.

Criminology studies abound with explanations for the traditionally high Negro crime rate, but the experts are mystified by the further recent jump in Negro crime. The long-term picture and the recent rise are almost inconsistent; most experts feel that the Negroes' low economic status is an important factor behind their history of criminality—yet the recent crime spurt came at a time of economic gain among black people.

One possible explanation is that the recent statistical rise in Negro crime is more apparent than real, that the lawlessness was there all along and that society is only now realizing it. Criminologist Marvin Wolfgang sees this as partially responsible for the current crime scare. The unprecedented exposure of traditional slum crime to white society is largely to blame, Wolfgang believes:

> Throughout history—on the Left Bank of Paris, in the slums of London, and in the worst neighborhoods of every city—there were murders and violence and crime, and society pushed it into the background and ignored it. Now the Negro is pushing out of his old boundaries and moving about in areas where some whites are still living. They are committing more crimes, and more crimes against white people—and, for the first time, society is aware of it. I think we're bound to go through a period of transition, in which the Negro crime rate will go higher.

A more psychological explanation for the recent upsurge is given by Professor Walter B. Miller of the Joint Center for Urban Studies at Cambridge. Dr. Miller is known for his belief in economic class as the predominant factor in determining criminality, a theory that underwent severe strains in the late 1960s, when Negro crime rose during a time of economic upswing for many Negroes. His studies in the 1950s of juvenile crime in low-income Boston neighborhoods showed that when black and white families of similar incomes and job status were compared, the arrest rates of their children were about the same. He concluded that white youngsters even turned up in court slightly more often than did black children on the same socio-economic level.

But in 1967, Professor Miller returned to the same neighborhoods and found that in that year the black youngsters' rates of arrest almost doubled that of whites—a rise that he blamed on civil-rights militancy and the current climate of defiance of authority among young blacks. "Young Negroes were provided incentives to violate the law by civil-rights militancy and the riots," he concluded.

> Suddenly there was an ideological justification for crime—to compensate for injustice, to punish white society. Because you have been deprived for so many centuries, you have a right to take back what is yours. You help your race when you oppose the police "pigs."

This will pass, Miller believes, just as the riot phase seems to have peaked. He notes that Negro migration from the South into the cities also seems to have begun to decline, and he feels that the current public anxiety about Negro crime will soon be remembered as a passing concern, like the excitement about youth gangs in the 1950s.

In the meantime, the evidence is mounting that crime by ghetto Negroes has reached levels that explain the public's receptivity to the law-and-order appeals during the 1968 campaign. Studies of robbery in Philadelphia and Chicago at about that time showed that blacks' arrest rates were about eighteen times that of white people in those cities—approximately double the disparity between Negroes and whites for the whole country. In Philadelphia, Negroes were charged with rape at twelve times the rate of white men, while the national Negro/white rate was much lower. In Stamford, Connecticut, the same pattern—to a less pronounced degree—was found in a racial analysis of all criminal offenses.

Finally, a study detailing 10,000 Philadelphia juveniles by Marvin Wolfgang and Thorsten Sellin corroborated the national urban figures produced by the FBI's study, which showed that city Negroes' arrest rates are about double the national Negro rates, and far and away higher than the whites'. They believe that the currently booming Negro crime rate may be a product of the shift of the Negro population from the rural South to the city slums, but this does not resolve the uncertainty that exists over the root causes of the historically higher Negro criminality.

No respectable sociologist believes that crime is a racial trait of Negroes. "That the serious criminality of the Negro American is greater than that of the white American is an established fact," says Professor Sellin, "but sociological studies have shown that this is due to no inborn racial trait but to the economic, educational, and social conditions of the Negro."

The catch comes when sociologists try to establish which conditions of the Negro contribute most to his high crime rate—his generally low economic status, or the cultural isolation and resentment that come from being trapped in a black slum in a white man's world.

"What the high figures for Negro arrests really show is that low-status people commit more crimes," Professor Miller says. "Eighty per cent of the Negroes in the country are in what we would call the lowest class. Only 30 per cent of the whites are. That's the difference."

Most sociologists believe that there is much more to it than poverty. The unwholesome mix of circumstances that more often than not accompanies criminality is likely to be the lot of anyone who is born poor, but these circumstances seem to weigh heaviest on those who are also black. As Marvin Wolfgang puts it:

> Thrust any child, white or colored, from the womb to a world that offers the rewards of status and success. With a moat of discrimination cut him off from the mainland so that there are few or no opportunities to achieve those rewards. Let him continue to wish for the same things the mainlanders desire, but make him move around much more, lose a father to death or desertion and a mother to work and dependency. Give him less knowledge to absorb, less money than the mainlander receives for the same tasks. Surround him with examples of unlawful achievers, and make him fight to protect the mainland without fully participating in the rules to govern it. Shorten his length of life, expose him to disease, treat him as if he were biologically inferior and call him nasty names to convince him of it. Even if the mainlanders value the service he gives them and the feeling of importance his contrast offers, he is lost.

The question of causation is far more than academic; if Negroes commit proportionately more crimes because poor people tend to break the law and most Negroes are poor, then there is hope in anti-poverty programs and other economic measures. But if segregated urban living breeds increasing crime, despite better wages and education for the people who have to live that way, then the prospects for future tranquillity are bleak. According to the President's Commission on Urban Problems, the Negro population of the big-city slums will almost double by 1985 (the national nonwhite population is expected to rise from 12 to 16 per cent by then), which could create a situation resembling the "apartheid society" that the National Advisory Commission on Civil Disorders warned about.

One of the first good comparative studies of crime by Negroes and white persons of similar economic status was conducted by Professor Earl R. Moses of Johns Hopkins University in Baltimore in 1940. It produced a bleak conclusion that is still accepted, widely but reluctantly, by most criminologists—that if Negroes and whites of the same socioeconomic levels are compared, the Negro crime rates are still higher.

More recently, Morris A. Forslund, gathering material for his Ph.D. dissertation at Yale, found that the overall crime rate among Negroes in Stamford, Connecticut, was about six times that of the city's whites. By comparing the frequency of crime among various age and income groups of both races, he concluded that the Negro rate was inflated by about 15 per cent because so many Negroes were young and thus statistically more likely to get into trouble. Further comparisons showed that another 30 per cent of the Negro crime total was due to the fact that so many were poor, and like all poor people, more likely to run afoul of the law. His conclusion: if age and poverty factors could be eliminated, Negroes would still commit three times more crime than whites. This he attributed to resentment by Negroes at white society, plus a ghetto culture that encourages criminal behavior.

The most impressive evidence that money and job status are not the overriding factors was turned up by Professors Wolfgang and Sellin in their study in Philadelphia. When they sorted the white and Negro boys into groups according to their families' earnings and job levels, they found the Negroes' delinquency rates higher for every income bracket. The boys from high-income Negro families, who had the lowest Negro arrest rates, had higher rates than the white boys in the highest-crime, lowest-income bracket. The professors concluded that psychological and cultural influences outweighed economic ones in fostering criminality.

This theory gained further credence when Negro crime was found to have accelerated between 1964 and 1967, while the economic lot of Negroes was improving. The number of nonwhites who lived below the government's statistical "poverty line" dropped from 10.9 million to 8.3 million during that time. The inevitable conclusion is that "wars on poverty" even if wildly successful (and some of the increase in Negro income must be credited to the economic stimulus of war in Vietnam) will not greatly sap the growth of Negro crime.

Because these impressions about high criminality among blacks are based upon arrest rates—conviction statistics are almost nonexistent —the argument has been made that they reflect police discrimination, a tendency to haul in Negroes more readily than whites. There are hints in the FBI's statistics that this is partially so. For years the police have arrested far more Negroes than whites for gambling and prostitution, consensual offenses that involve so much selectivity on the part of arresting officers that some experts have urged that they should not even be published by the FBI. In general, arrests across the country have declined for these consensual crimes, indicating that the police are tending to live and let live. But the prostitution arrests of Negro women have continued to climb while arrests of white women have declined. Negroes also constitute the bulk of those arrested for carrying concealed weapons, a statistic that could be partially attributable to the police's reputed readiness to "stop and frisk" Negroes when whites would be let alone.

One development that runs counter to this argument is the change in narcotics arrests over the past two decades. In the early 1950s there were always more narcotics arrests of Negroes each year than whites. This changed. Middle-class whites started smoking marijuana, and the police started arresting them for it. The narcotics arrest rate of Negroes is still high, but for the past few years more whites than Negroes have been arrested on narcotics charges and there is no evidence that race ever affected the situation, either way. Negroes also have extremely high arrest rates for murder (murder is so frequent among both male and female Negroes fifteen to twenty-five years old that it is their second-ranking cause of death), robbery, and felonious assault. Murder, and, to a lesser extent, robbery, do not lend themselves to selective enforcement by the police because the body or the empty cash register cannot be winked at, regardless of the color of the people involved. If anything, the police have traditionally been lax in arresting Negroes for aggravated assault because the victims are usually black.

Most experts believe that selective arresting probably does inflate the Negro crime rate in certain categories, especially when juveniles are the offenders. But they agree almost unanimously that the crime disparity between the races is real and would still be wide, even if the police always applied evenhanded enforcement.

As the Negro crime problem has begun to come out from under wraps, some whites have sought to blunt the backlash with a "don't worry, the victims are only Negroes" approach. The assertion is true, but the argument has not been very reassuring to Negroes. The vast majority of people who get murdered, assaulted, or raped are attacked by someone they know—relatives, acquaintances, or spouses. Even the great bugaboo of interracial crime—the Negro raping a white woman—is relatively rare. One study in Philadelphia showed that interracial rape is more likely to involve a white man and a black victim. Relatively few violent crimes cut across racial lines, with the exception of robbery. There a slim—but apparently growing—majority of the victims of Negro robbers are white. Murder, rape, aggravated assault—offenses that tend to symbolize "crime" to the average man—involve people of the same race about nine times out of ten.

Whatever consolation it is to the suburbanite to be assured that if he is murdered or his wife is raped it will be done by a white person, to hear white leaders stress the point makes Negro leaders uneasy. Sterling Tucker, an Urban League official who has a reputation for weighing his words with care, complained that Vice President Humphrey was doing the Negroes no favor by trying to take the edge off the "law and order" issue in this way. In a speech at the 1968 convention of the American Bar Association in Philadelphia, Mr. Sterling Tucker charged that this psychology could eventually give the white "keepers of the keys of the cities" an excuse to resort to apartheid to contain crime. Ultimately, he said, whites could decide "to seal ghettos off and keep the blacks in enslavement . . . instead of coming to grips with this in all of its ugliness."

It is this danger—that white society will come to see Negro crime as a thing apart, to be contained only through extraordinary measures —that poses the most serious threat to rule of law. An example has already been seen in Wilmington, Delaware, where heavily armed National Guard troops were sent into the Negro neighborhoods to control the rioting and looting that broke out in April of 1968, following the assassination of Dr. Martin Luther King, Jr. Negro resentment ran so deep that officials were afraid to remove the troops, and almost a year passed before they were withdrawn. A somewhat similar incident took place in Miami, where the Chief of Police sent officers equipped with shotguns and dogs into the Negro district to deal with "young hoodlums" who, he said, had taken advantage of the civil-rights campaign. "We don't mind being accused of police brutality," he said; "they haven't seen anything yet." There were echoes of this in the campaign promises of George Wallace and Richard Nixon to use all the police presence necessary to stanch the crime rise in the capital city.

Thus the phenomenon of unusually high Negro crime has its mirror image in extraordinary police response; with Negro robbery rates already sixteen times that of whites in the cities and still rising, there is every possibility that efforts to contend with Negro crime will increasingly be viewed as exercises in urban pacification. (After the New York NAACP issued its demand for harsher measures against criminals, a *New York Times* reporter found Harlem merchants urging the removal of young junkies to camps upstate—a proposal similar to South Vietnam's indoctrination camps for young Vietcong.) The most notable example so far is the plan being worked out in the District of Columbia for pretrial "preventive detention" of what President Nixon has called dangerous hard-core criminals. Other signs have been the increased use of curfews to cool ghetto unrest and occasional broad-scale searches for weapons in Negro areas. The ultimate direction of events may well have been foreshadowed when a high police official of the Washington, D.C., area's whitest and wealthiest Maryland suburb, distraught over the spillover of crimes committed in his community by criminals from the predominantly black city, felt free to suggest to Senator Joseph D. Tydings that "if you want to help us you should build a forty-foot chain link fence along the District line and put barbed wire on top."

For the Supreme Court, this trend creates special pressures that run counter to its recent rulings on criminal law. "Tension between the police and the judiciary has always been fundamental to our constitutional system," Nicholas deB. Katzenbach has said. "It is intentional and healthy and constitutes the real difference between a free society and a police state." Yet there are aspects to the Supreme Court's recent doctrines toward police power that make the Court as well as its new doctrines especially vulnerable to the tensions created by rising crime and racism.

Back when the Court read the Constitution to tolerate conduct by police that conformed with the flexible principle of "fundamental fairness," judges had discretion to limit their intervention in police affairs to those circumstances that they could expect to control. The Warren Court changed that when it laid down procedural rules that are supposed to be followed by police in all instances. Yet the temptation for the police to break the rules, and for the majority of whites to approve of their actions, may be on the rise—at a time when the flexibility of the courts has been reduced. And so a coincidence of events has heightened the traditional tensions between the forces of enforcement and of justice, and has greatly increased the likelihood of a constitutional crisis somewhere down the line.

STUDY QUESTIONS

1. How is the story of the emperor who wore no clothes related to Graham's subject? Is it a useful image in national politics?
2. How did politicians respond to George Wallace's threat?
3. Did the FBI trumpet the statistics about black crime? Why?
4. How significant are the statistical differences between crime by whites and blacks?
5. The NAACP has reacted strongly to the statistics now available. What has been their stand?
6. Why was the failure of the academicians so curious?
7. What do statistics project for the future?
8. Why are sociologists particularly disturbed and perplexed by the recent rise in the black crime rate?
9. What are some of the reasons for the current increase in black crime?
10. How effectively do the "class" arguments explain the differences in the crime rates of blacks and whites?

SUGGESTIONS FOR WRITING

1. The Violence Commission actually suppressed some of the statistics that showed the imbalance between the black and white crime rates. The Commission was motivated by a desire to deny bigots or segregationists more ammunition for their attack on blacks. Do you think their position was a reasonable one? Is there any chance that publication of all the facts would have helped blacks?
2. What uses can you envision for the information presented in this article? Obviously, it will be put to different uses by different groups. Consider how the following groups might use the statistical data: segregationists, the police, black militants, the average black citizen, the average white citizen, politicians.
3. Is it possible to detect where Graham's own sympathies lie? Does he in any way reveal his prejudices about black crime? Study his style, his manner of presenting evidence, and come to a convincing conclusion.
4. If poverty, social status, and lack of opportunity are ruled out as causes of higher crime rates among blacks, what is the hope for

the future? Resentment of white society and a ghetto climate conducive to criminal behavior seem serious, if not primary factors. What kinds of actions could be taken to alter those factors?

5. What is your own reaction to this article? Do you find yourself resenting it? Why?

HOW THE POLICE WORK IN WESTERN EUROPE AND THE U.S.

George Berkley

We tend to put our police in a difficult situation. We equip them with weapons designed to kill but we often wind up accusing them of using too much force. In European countries, where the concept of police work is very different, the question of force is settled beforehand: policemen are not "licensed to kill."

When it comes to police work, the democracies of Western Europe still strike any American observer as foreign countries. The gap between Old World and the New is illustrated by their different approaches to the use of deadly force. In the United States, a policeman carries as standard equipment a .38 special revolver and an 18-inch wooden truncheon. Some augment this with "sap" gloves (gloves loaded with lead), extra-heavy magnum revolvers, and, for riot-duty, yard-long wooden clubs. In Great Britain and Norway, policemen are not issued guns and carry them only on very rare occasions. Elsewhere in Scandinavia, policemen are issued guns but often leave them in their lockers when on daytime assignments. In virtually no European democracy do they carry guns when off-duty.

The standard firearm used in European police forces is the equivalent of our .32 automatic. It is not only much lighter than the .38 specials worn by our police, but is even less powerful than the .32 regulars carried by policewomen in New York City. Police truncheons in Europe are usually made of hard rubber: they break no bones and leave no scars. Sap gloves, magnum revolvers, elongated wooden billy clubs are very rare.

The European policeman is not only more lightly armed than his American counterpart but is more restricted in his right to use what

HOW THE POLICE WORK IN WESTERN EUROPE AND THE U.S.   Reprinted by permission of *The New Republic*, © 1969, Harrison-Blaine of New Jersey, Inc.

he has. In most European countries, a policeman cannot fire a gun for any purpose other than to protect life, his own or some one else's. Even if attacked, he is often not to shoot unless the attack endangers his life. French police regulations, for example, state that "resistance to an attack which does not expose anyone to a serious danger, but only to an act of violence or assault, does not in itself justify the use of a gun."

A German policeman *does* have the right, under certain circumstances, to fire at a fleeing felon. He must, however, aim at the arms or legs. Every two months, he is tested to determine whether he can shoot this well. He fires at an escaping criminal on a movie screen, and if he hits him in the back or head he flunks the test. The American policeman not only has the right but, in some cases, even the obligation to shoot fleeing felons. In some jurisdictions, he is forbidden to fire warning shots first. The cardboard silhouette figures used on police firing ranges in this country place the bulls-eye on the main body area.

As a result of these differences in their "armaments" policies, European and American police forces show contrasting ratios in civilian deaths to police deaths. According to the President's Crime Commission, the number of civilians killed by the police in this country is more than three times the number of policemen who lose their lives while on the job. In most European countries, many more policemen die in the line of duty than do civilians as a result of police activity. In Sweden, four policemen have been killed by civilians during the past four years. The Swedish police, meanwhile, have been responsible for only two civilian deaths during the past 13 years.

In all the upheavals that have rocked European countries lately, only one civilian has died as a consequence of police action—in Berlin in 1967, and the policeman responsible was promptly arrested, brought to trial. When 10,000 protesters rioted outside the US Embassy in London in March 1967, the police sustained 117 casualties compared to 44 for the demonstrators. Actually, the police were the more lightly armed, since they had only their truncheons while the demonstrators had poles and fireworks. In a student riot in Berlin on November 4, the ratio of injured policemen to rioters was on the order of four to one.

While European policemen tend to be less aggressive than their American colleagues in the use of force, they are often more enterprising in other ways. The German police have perhaps shown the most initiative here. They put on puppet shows for young children, conduct traffic kindergartens for slightly older children, give bicycle courses for still older ones. Most of these programs are carried on at police stations. To serve adults, the German police operate crime prevention clinics, aid distressed motorists and give bus tours to elderly citizens, pointing out traffic hazards. Some have even given annual parties to traffic offenders they have fined "to show them that the police aren't mad at them!" Swedish police also run traffic kindergartens, instruct older children in legal responsibility and even hold family auto rallys. Swedish patrol cars are equipped with extra spark plugs, gasoline, etc., to help motorists in trouble. Swedish policemen also sponsor and lead over 20 hobby clubs for young people. In Denmark, in addition to carrying out similar activities, the police operate a "re-socialization center" for homeless men. Even the French police have begun taking steps in this direction. In addition to running traffic kindergartens, the *Sureté* now operates some 40 summer vacation camps for young people, all staffed completely by policemen.

Such programs are not unknown in America: the first positive youth program in the history of police work was New York City's Police Athletic League. However, we look upon such efforts as public relations gestures, peripheral to the police function. Policemen assigned to such tasks are usually those men who are considered, and who consider themselves, to be outsiders within the department. In many cases, policemen themselves don't run the programs. New York's Police Athletic League itself is now largely a non-police organization with its own civilian staff.

German and Scandinavian police departments call their juvenile delinquency squads "youth protection squads," and they refer to juvenile delinquents as "endangered youth." Policemen assigned to this function work closely with social workers, often going on joint patrol. The hobby clubs run by policemen in Scandinavia are generally designed for young people who show a penchant for getting into trouble. In Germany, the police sometimes take juvenile delinquents out for trips in police boats or for rides on police horses.

Most European policemen have discarded the practice of swooping down on a suspect in a predawn raid. When the Swedish police went to arrest the Russian espionage agent, Sven Wennerstrom, in 1963, they waited until he was crossing a bridge on his way to work. Two police cars then drove up and blocked the bridge at both ends. The officer in charge got out, introduced himself and shook hands with the Soviet spy before placing him under arrest. German police customarily wait for the breakfast hour before knocking on the suspect's door with an arrest warrant. When Dortmund police went to arrest five suspected communist agents last summer, they arrived at such a respectable hour that all but one of the suspects had left for work.

Even the police killer is often accorded a modicum of humane treatment. In September 1966, police in Gothenburg, Sweden, received a tip that Clark Olafsson, a thug who a few weeks previously had shot and killed a policeman, was seated on a ledge outside the city. Olafsson was known to be armed. Instead of going after him with guns blazing, the police sent out two unarmed members of the force to bring him in. The two athletic constables disguised themselves as track runners and ran several laps around the unsuspecting murderer before seizing him. In the ensuing tussle, Olafsson managed to produce his gun and fire it twice, slightly wounding one of his captors. But Olafsson himself did not have a scratch on him when he was brought into police headquarters.

In keeping with this behavior pattern, Europeans have shown much less resistance to the growing emphasis on civil liberties, a trend which has swept many of their judicial systems as it has our own. Germany revised its penal code three years ago, requiring the police to inform all suspects of their right to remain silent or to have a lawyer. There was no loud outcry, as the equivalent US Supreme Court decision evoked from the American police.

France revised its penal code in 1962, setting much stricter limitations on the power of the police to detain and interrogate suspects. It produced remarkably little grumbling. Sweden has long had rules governing the rights of suspects, and the Swedish police officials I met seemed proud, rather than resentful, of them. The British, meanwhile, have operated uncomplainingly for over half a century under the famed Judges Rules, which stipulate that a policeman must caution a person charged with a crime of his right to remain silent and that he must not question anyone taken into custody.

Although corruption has always been a nagging problem for many, if not most, American police departments, it is insignificant in Europe. Even in France, where hostility to the police is endemic, imputations that the police take bribes almost never arise. Not only do German policemen give traffic tickets to each other, but a Hamburg patrolman once made his wife pay a fine for beating their carpets outdoors. A Cologne policeman who found himself late for a court appearance in 1966 parked illegally and gave himself a parking ticket. (This didn't keep him from receiving a reprimand from his superiors.)

This picture of European policemen is subject to qualifications. Abuses have occurred and doubtless will again. Nevertheless, European policemen do tend to view their role differently. Why?

For one thing, European police departments place much more emphasis on education. Police recruits receive three to four years of training in Germany, two years and nine months in Italy, one full year in Sweden, six months in France and thirteen weeks in Great Britain. While the British lag behind most other European countries in this respect, their recruit education period still compares favorably with that of the United States. California, which has the highest police education standards in America, requires only 370 hours of education for municipal policemen. New York State requires only eight weeks.

The curricula of most continental police schools devote considerable time to nontechnical subjects, including legal instruction plus a good deal of political science, applied psychology, and similar studies. Some 20 to 25 percent of the German recruit's first-year training and 15 percent of his second year is devoted to the social sciences. He is taught to avoid all prejudices and generalizations about classes or types of people, to be mindful of the frustrations of motorists and act accordingly, and to keep his sense of humor.

Government, psychology and "social medicine" (which includes alcoholism and the problems of handicapped people), make up 10 percent of the Swedish police recruit's classroom instruction. The text used for the course in government stresses minority rights and warns of the dangers of a police state. In 1964, French police schools inaugurated a 30-hour course in which the recruit is told he should make more use of his pen, his knowledge and his "human qualities," than of his physical force and weapons. It is pointed out that his duties are "first those of a citizen, secondly those of a civil servant and thirdly those of a policeman."

When it comes to grooming men for positions as officers or detectives, this discrepancy between police education in Europe and here markedly increases. In the US, the passing of a simple written examination, usually consisting of multiple-choice or true-false questions, is nearly always sufficient for advancement to command positions. Promotion to the detective force may come simply on the recommendation of a superior officer or a political connection. In Europe, such steps up the career ladder almost invariably require additional schooling, usually lasting from six months to a year. In Sweden, officers-in-training are taken on tours of psychiatric hospitals, alcoholism centers, prisons and other institutions.

Sweden earmarks some 300 of its top positions for lawyers who are recruited directly into the upper ranks. France recruits half of its lieutenant candidates from among civilians with a baccalaureate degree and half of its inspector candidates from law school graduates. German police forces are allowed to recruit 10 percent of their detective forces from the legal profession; applicants to the regular police who possess the *arbitur*—roughly equivalent to two years of higher education in this country—are allowed to apply for officer training three years earlier than can their less educated colleagues. England last year launched a new program under which a university graduate can advance from patrolman to officer at a fast pace.

European police forces also make more extensive use of women. They hold nearly five percent of all constabulary positions on the London police force. Some German states have set aside 10 percent of their detective positions for women. Scandinavian countries sometimes use policewomen for regular patrol work.

The recruitment of women and better-educated men gives the police force a broader base and makes it more representative of the population. So does the use of civilians, who make up over 20 percent of the total departmental personnel rosters in England and Sweden. Civilians do not just oversee but actually run most European police departments. Most of the top executive posts in Sweden, including the positions of police chief in the larger cities, are held by lawyers. A former judge directs the entire police operation, while a former teacher of French heads the main police academy in Stockholm. In Germany, not only are all police commissioners civilians, but so are most of their division heads, including the heads of the criminal police or detective forces. German police commissioners, as well as many of their division heads, usually hold doctorates in law. Half of the executive-level posts in the newly unified French police are held by civilians; the overall director of the national police is a former chief of staff at the Ministry of Education.

England has a more decentralized system than do the continental countries, and most police chiefs come up from the ranks. However, the commissioner of the largest and most important police force, the Metropolitan Police of Greater London, is more often a civilian than not. At least half of his division heads are nonpolicemen, including the assistant commissioner in charge of the famed Criminal Investigation Division. The Home Secretary in the British Government, meanwhile, issues rules and regulations covering the whole police force and can veto the appointment of, as well as require the removal of, any local police chief.

It was once customary in the United States, at least in the larger cities, to appoint a civilian as the police commissioner. Today, these positions are usually given to professional policemen. When Mayor

Lindsay tried to exert authority over the New York City police in 1966, his efforts were met with fierce resistance and were branded as "interference" by "outsiders."

The fact that civil servants tend to run European police departments tends to make these departments much more bureaucratic than ours. But interestingly enough, this may also produce democratic patterns of police behavior. Stripped of its negative connotations, bureaucracy implies, in essence, a system built on formal and standardized rules and procedures. The bureaucratic policeman is thus more likely to be impartial, less likely to be arbitrary in discharging his duties. The Berlin policeman I saw bending over an ill-clad drunk lying in the street and asking him in formal, polite German, "Where do you live, please?" illustrates my point. The same rules and manner apply to everyone.

With a civilian-controlled and bureaucratically oriented administrative structure, many European police systems are permitting their employees to share in decision-making. Nearly one out of every ten Swedish policemen sits on a joint-management board charged with working in some problem area. German policemen elect representatives to employee councils, which handle internal complaints and frequently have some say in the management of the force. Rank-and-file French policemen choose from their ranks nearly half the members of all police disciplinary and promotion boards. British police have representatives on the Police Council of Great Britain, which advises and negotiates with the Home Secretary. The result is greater understanding and acceptance of such key values as accommodation, patience and consultation. More important, such participation affords the policeman an outlet for his grievances. If nothing else, administrative devices such as these serve as a safety valve for a group which is always under pressure.

Trade unionism also tends to further these ends and most policemen in Western Europe are members of a union. The police unions provide additional opportunities for ventilating grievances and for taking part in such democratic processes as electing officers and approving decisions. The union provides a two-way communications link between the police and society. The union's spokesmen and publications offer the public better access to the policeman's point of view. At the same time, these spokesmen and publications are channels for receiving and transmitting to its members ideas from the nonpolice world. To the extent that the union brings the police closer to the trade union movement generally, it may also help offset right-wing tendencies, which seem so natural to the protectors of law, order and property.

Another practice permitted in some continental countries may do even more to keep the police in the political mainstream. They are permitted in Scandinavia and Germany to take part directly in political activity and are even allowed to run for office. Denmark customarily has four or five policemen sitting in its parliament, German state legislatures are sprinkled with policeman-lawmakers, and a small town in southern Sweden has actually elected all four of its policemen to its town council. Since policemen are essentially lower- and middle-echelon civil servants, they tend to run for office as members of working-class parties.

If policemen in some European countries take an active part in legislative work, legislative bodies also take an active interest in police work. (In contrast, our city councils, state legislatures and, when it comes to the FBI, even Congress are loath to interfere.) Here are some examples of zealous legislative oversight:

A Scottish patrolman knocked down and gave a nosebleed to a persistently pesky teen-age boy who refused to let him alone. The incident produced such an outcry in Parliament that Prime Minister Macmillan (this was in '59) had to set up a high-level tribunal to assess charges of police brutality.

In the summer of 1966, the Swedish parliament was outraged when policemen were seen taking pictures of some anti-American demonstrators. Police Director Persson hastened to assure the irate lawmakers that the picture-taking was done by the criminal police and not the security police, and was done only to have evidence in the event any laws were broken. (In a previous demonstration, the participants had burned an American flag, and it is against Swedish law to mutilate the flag of a country recognized by the government.)

A German customs officer shot and killed a fleeing smuggler in 1964. The state legislature of North Rhineland-Westfallen staged a two-day debate on the question of firearms use by policemen.

A Paris policeman shot and killed a motorist who was resisting arrest. The emasculated French parliament resounded with cries for more stringent controls over the police. (The Paris police union expressed regrets over the incident and asked that policemen be given increased education to prevent such an occurrence from happening again.)

In addition to legislative bodies, there are other agencies exercising control over the police. Sweden's ombudsman keeps a close eye on the cops and does not wait for a complaint before taking action. In

Germany, all detectives are officially classified as assistants to the public prosecutors of their respective states. Thus, they are directly supervised by the judicial branch. The French have a *juge d'instruction* or examining magistrate who oversees the entire conduct of a criminal investigation. In England, judges make up one-third of the watch committees (the other two-thirds are elected by the people) which have local supervision of the police.

The most important control mechanism, however, is the police themselves. Here, too, European countries seem far ahead of the United States. Drunkenness on the job in most European countries will bring a suspension of many months. Drunken driving, to say nothing of corruption or brutality, will bring prosecution in court and usually a jail sentence. A policeman's conduct off the job is supposed to be exemplary. An off-duty constable in England who threw a clod of earth at a cat that was tearing up his newly planted seedlings received an official reprimand.

Although in Sweden most complaints from the public go to the ombudsman, the Stockholm police have a civilian lawyer who checks out all complaints that come to the police themselves. German police departments set up special booths at public events, asking visitors to make such complaints. The number of complaints against policemen in such cities as London and Berlin far exceeds the number filed against policemen in New York City. And a much higher ratio of complaints in these cities is sustained, nearly 20 percent in West Berlin.

The police do not create a political culture; they reflect it. They behave in a way the society they serve expects them to behave. Thus, if European systems operate in a manner more consistent with democratic norms and values than do ours, it should tell us something about American democracy, and what it tells us should give us cause for some concern if not alarm.

STUDY QUESTIONS

1. What is the significance of the difference in the weapons carried by United States and European police?
2. When can the policeman in Europe use his gun? How does this differ from the United States?
3. How are German policemen trained to shoot at fleeing felons?
4. What are some of the unusual services offered by European police? Are such things unknown in the United States?

5. How are juvenile delinquents treated in Europe? How do you react to this approach?

6. Has the trend toward greater civil liberties for suspected criminals developed in Europe as it has in America? What are the differences?

7. Do you think education has much to do with the differences between European and United States police?

8. What roles do women play in European police forces?

9. Is bureaucracy a totally undesirable element in police matters?

10. What are some of the benefits of police unionization in Europe?

SUGGESTIONS FOR WRITING

1. Which of the differences in the behavior of U.S. and European police do you think is the most crucial? How do you think law enforcement in the United States would be changed if American police followed the example of their European counterparts in this one regard? Why is this difference more crucial than the others?

2. On the basis of this article, which changes in police tactics and instruction would you want to make in your own force if you were given the chance to be the chief of a police force in a major city? How well received do you think your alterations would be? What kind of a fight would you have on your hands—and with whom?

3. If it is true that "the police do not create a political culture; they reflect it," what do the differences in police behavior in Western societies really indicate? Can the behavior of police really be taken as an indication of the nature of a political culture?

4. Examine Berkley's method of presenting evidence in this article. If you were a critic of his position, with what statements would you take issue? Is his manner of dealing with evidence reasonable? Is his evidence of the best sort? Does his research seem thorough? Are his judgments the ones you think the evidence demands?

5. If everything Berkley said were true and all his judgments were the only ones to accept, would there still be any arguments for our police staying fully armed and using lethal force to protect life and property? What are the differences between American and European life styles that demand we have police who behave as ours do?

THE NARCOTICS TRADE: BIG BUSINESS

The Editors of *Forbes*

It may well be that one of the reasons for the overwhelming success of the narcotics trade in the United
States is that it is run with all the efficiency of a major
corporation. Some of the details are rather amazing.

It's an industry that runs to nearly $3 billion a year in the
U.S. alone. Worldwide? It's anybody's guess.

It's a real growth industry, expanding in the U.S. at 10% or more
yearly. The U.S. and the Far East are still the largest markets, but
they may not be for long; the European market is exploding. Yet,
nowhere in the world does the industry spend a dime on advertising.

Profitable? Incredibly so. Ten kilos (roughly 22 pounds) of the
raw material costs $350. Processed and packaged, it can bring in
anywhere from $280,000 to $500,000, with profits of perhaps 15% to
1,000% for everyone along the line. Naturally, there are risks: Whoever heard of a high-profit industry without them?

Of course, all figures on the industry are estimates. Hard statistics
are impossible to come by. For not only is the industry large, growing
and profitable, it's also illegal.

The industry is the manufacture and sale of heroin.

Heroin addiction is, of course, a plague. It started in the slums of
the nation's larger cities, but now rages unchecked almost everywhere
in the U.S., including upper-middle-class suburbia. It has crossed the
Atlantic to Italy, to France, where it was once almost unknown, and
even to England, which boasted for years that it had the problem
under control. It has destroyed the lives of nobody knows how many
hundreds of thousands. It is responsible for three deaths a day in New
York City alone.

THE NARCOTICS TRADE: BIG BUSINESS   From the April 1, 1970 issue of *Forbes*
Magazine. Reprinted by permission of *Forbes* Magazine.

A plague, yes. But it's an industry, too. In fact, such a plague would not exist if thousands of people were not profiting from it.

One thing few law-abiding citizens understand is that a criminal enterprise obeys the same economic laws as any other business, including the law of supply and demand. Like any legitimate industry the heroin industry has its bankers, its exporters and importers, its manufacturers, jobbers, retailers, salesmen. Like legitimate businessmen, moreover, the merchants of heroin strive constantly to diversify, and with a good deal of success. Heroin has financed many another enterprise.

Anyone going into a business must first analyze his market. In the U.S., the market for heroin consists of about 100,000 men, women and children in New York City and 100,000 more elsewhere. This is a conservative estimate. Some experts put the number of heroin addicts in the U.S. at 250,000, and some say there could be as many as 250,000 users in the New York metropolitan area alone.

The Justice Department's Bureau of Narcotics and Dangerous Drugs keeps a record of known narcotics addicts. On Dec. 31, 1968, the most recent date for which figures are available, they numbered 64,011; of these, over 60,000 were heroin addicts. Obviously, the vast majority of heroin addicts in the U.S. escape detection. A spokesman for the Bureau of Narcotics and Dangerous Drugs says it is therefore not unreasonable to multiply the number of known addicts by three or four to get the total number of addicts. This would mean that on Dec. 31, 1968 there were somewhere between 180,000 and 240,000 *heroin* addicts in the nation.

Also, assume that the number of known addicts increased by more than 25,000 in 1969. That would put the total addict population at somewhere between 220,000 and 280,000 on last New Year's Eve, [1969]. Therefore, 200,000 on heroin does not seem an unreasonable figure.

Let's accept the estimate of 100,000 addicts in New York City. Heroin is less expensive in New York than in many parts of the U.S., and for a simple reason: Most heroin enters the country by way of New York because New York is the biggest port of entry for both planes and ships. According to Deputy Chief Inspector John P. McCahey, head of the New York City Police Narcotics Bureau, the average junkie in New York spends $35 a day for heroin. Some addicts spend as much as $100 a day, but teenagers just acquiring the habit may be able to get along on as little as $7 to $15.

Let's accept the estimate of $35 a day on the average. This means that every day in New York City addicts spend $3.5 million for heroin. That's $1.3 billion a year.

As heroin moves south and west, it naturally becomes more expensive. McCahey estimates that, in the country as a whole outside New York, the average junkie has to spend $40 a day. That's $4 million a day, or close to $1.5 billion a year.

The heroin industry, like every other, starts with a raw material, in this case a flower called *papaver somniferum*, the "poppy of sleep." It can be grown in many parts of the world, but most of the poppies used in making heroin for the U.S. are grown in Turkey. The main reason is that, by international agreement, growing the flower of sleep is legal in Turkey. It yields a brown gum, opium, the base of codeine and morphine, which the medical world needs.

Under the international agreement, the Turkish government is supposed to buy up all the opium produced in the country. It pays about $120 for each ten kilos. However, the men who traffic in heroin pay as much as $350; and Turkish farmers are very poor.

Despite the Turkish government's efforts to prevent it, some 7% of the Turkish crop is diverted to opium brokers for the heroin industry. The brokers sell the opium for $400, a markup of nearly 15%, to dealers in Istanbul or Aleppo, Syria, or Beirut, Lebanon, getting it there by such bizarre means as having camels swallow rubber bags stuffed with opium. A camel has three stomachs, and, for that reason, takes a long time to digest anything.

Next the raw opium is converted chemically, by a relatively simple operation, into morphine base, a brown powder. This reduces the ten kilos to one, but makes that one kilo worth between $700 and $800. The converter sells the morphine base to a heroin laboratory, probably in France, adding $50 to $100 for the cost of shipping. Apparently by tacit agreement among the men in the heroin industry, the laboratories are run by Corsicans. There are heroin laboratories in Lebanon, the Far East and Mexico, but U.S. importers prefer the heroin made in France.

Converting morphine into heroin is a complicated process, requiring chemical skill, some equipment and several days' time. Three to seven people run each laboratory, usually on a profit-sharing basis. There are profits aplenty to share. The kilo of morphine base that cost, say, $850, including transportation, is worth anywhere from $3,500 to $15,000 when converted into heroin. (The price fluctuates.)

Now the U.S. importer enters the picture. He must have a bankroll, not only to pay for the heroin but also because the cost of transporting heroin from Europe to New York is about $1,000 a kilo. That is supposed to cover the bribes and the risks.

One practice is for the importer to pay 50% in cash before shipment. Then, if the heroin is seized, he and the exporter will lose equally. Suppose the importer buys 100 kilos at $5,000 a kilo, plus $1,000 a kilo for transportation. To put up half that amount would take $300,000 cash.

Very few people have that much ready cash, which is why the heroin industry needs people to do for it what bankers do for legitimate business. Where do narcotics bankers get the money? From gambling, loan-sharking, extortion—and previous heroin imports. Where else?

Getting the heroin into the U.S. takes a great deal of ingenuity. The smugglers use circuitous routes, traveling by land, sea and air. They constantly are thinking up new ways to hide the heroin. Last December Customs and New York City police discovered heroin hidden in the bottoms of two five-litre wine bottles under a glass partition with wine on top of the partition. The bottoms were hidden by raffia wrapping. This particular shipment came from Santiago, Chile.

Once the heroin is safely in the U.S., the money really starts rolling in. Says William Durkin, New York City regional director of the Bureau of Narcotics and Dangerous Drugs and a veteran of 20 years in narcotics work:

> The heroin comes in 85% to 95% pure. The importer sells it, still pure, to one, two, three, five Number Two men in ten- to 20-kilo lots for anywhere from $12,000 to $22,000 a kilo, depending on the market. The latest quotation is $12,500. The Number Two men then resell it, still pure, in one- and two-kilo lots to maybe ten or 15 Number Three men, just now at a price of around $22,000.
>
> The Number Three men have several choices: They can sell the stuff to Number Four men in half- or quarter-kilo lots for $28,000 to $29,000. Or they can short-weight, selling, say, a ninth of a kilo as an eighth. Or else, they can dilute the heroin; pretend it's pure and charge the full price for it.

The Number Four men are the cutters. Their factories usually are one room in a slum apartment, where they employ eight or ten people to dilute the heroin. The preferred dilutant is quinine, but they also use Mennite laxative or milk sugar though they have also been known to use roach powder. The resulting mixture is roughly 14% to 15% heroin. It could be more; it could be less. One ounce is worth $600 to $700 on today's market.

The mixture is packed in glassine bags, selling for $5 each. How much heroin in the bag depends on the going price of pure heroin—the higher the price of the pure stuff, the less heroin. At present, the bags contain roughly 100 milligrams each, about one three-hundredth of an ounce.

People who sell the $5 bags on the street are called "pushers." Most are themselves addicts, who sell the stuff in order to make the money to buy it. To those in narcotics, this is the beautiful part about the industry. Almost every customer is, in effect, a salesman. They don't need Madison Avenue. Addicts feel comfortable only among addicts, and therefore push to get their friends on dope.

Given the variations in the quantity and quality of heroin a $5 bag contains, estimates of how much a kilo of pure heroin is worth when cut, packaged and sold at retail vary all the way from $225,000 to $500,000. In a time of panic, real or contrived, the worth will increase sharply. This from $350 worth of poppy juice.

Who runs the industry? Until a few years ago, this was an easy question: The Mob, the Mafia, La Cosa Nostra, the organized gangsters of Sicilian extraction in the U.S. Now the picture is cloudy.

An international consortium of Spanish-speaking criminals (Spaniards, Cubans, Puerto Ricans and South Americans) clearly has entered the business of smuggling heroin into the U.S. and distributing it. And some experts believe there are now small entrepreneurs in the business.

Has La Cosa Nostra quit the heroin industry? On this, the experts disagree. Some argue that it has. The risks became too great, they say, after the conviction of La Cosa Nostra boss Vito Genovese in 1959 for narcotics conspiracy violation.

Says New York City's Deputy Chief Inspector McCahey:

> La Cosa Nostra is probably not any longer in the mainstream of drugs. For one thing, those arrested and investigated now are in the Spanish group, not La Cosa Nostra. No Italians have been arrested in New York City in the past three or four years. For another, the Spanish-speaking group active in heroin aren't being retaliated against by La Cosa Nostra.

A more convincing argument comes from federal officials, particularly in the Bureau of Narcotics and Dangerous Drugs and the Bureau of Customs, which spends about 75% of its energies fighting the narcotics traffic. Sure, they say, The Mob no longer operates on the lowest (and riskiest) levels of the heroin industry, but it continues to run the industry from on high.

Two men who argue this view are Albert W. Seeley and Edward T. Coyne, senior Customs special agents. When interviewed, they kept interrupting and amplifying each other, so they can be quoted as one:

> Narcotics is now organized worldwide mainly by three language groups—Italian, French and Spanish. Previously, there were only the Italians, in Italy and the U.S. They dealt with the French Corsicans. They permitted the Spanish-speaking group to get into the business only **within** the U.S. and only after the import stage and only well down the profit ladder between wholesaler and retailer. Beginning in 1963—although we didn't get this information until 1968—the Mafia gave permission to the French Corsicans to deal directly with the Spanish, provided the Corsicans gave it a portion of the profit they made from their Spanish sales. Now the Spanish have these international contacts, play importer and, within the U.S., handle their own business from the top level all the way down to the retailer.
>
> Meanwhile, the Mafia takes its cut, yes, but makes still more from its own participation. It continues to import, and in large quantities like 50 kilos and up, and then handles its own distribution, at least at the top level and maybe down to the middle, too.

Seeley and Coyne believe The Mob directly controls more than half the heroin supply in the U.S.; directly and indirectly, about 85%. Only it stays away from the actual "retail" level. It is the banker and the wholesaler.

What makes narcotics agents believe this? Like all detectives, they uncover a clue and make a judgment. In July 1968, Customs seized a cache of heroin on a TWA plane that had just arrived at Dulles International Airport from Frankfurt, Germany. Investigation disclosed that it had been shipped by a kind of criminal United Nations, consisting of French-speaking, Italian-speaking and Spanish-speaking hoods. This gang had been smuggling 100 kilos of heroin into New York every month, for enough profit to deposit $1 million every month in Swiss banks.

The heroin was being smuggled in black and brown cotton socks, linked like sausages. Seeley and Coyne say the heroin in the brown socks was for Italian customers; in the black socks, for Spanish-speaking customers. The route to New York was by way of Washington, Denver and San Francisco. The delivery man to the Italians in New York was one Jean-Marc Montoya, a French national, who is now languishing in prison.

Coyne and Seeley say the Mafia mobsters were charged $7,500 a kilo; the Spanish-speaking, $11,000. "Whom do you charge a lower price for something?" Coyne asks. "Your biggest and best customer, of course."

Coyne adds: "As long as there's a Mafia organization, they'll never get out of narcotics. It's just too profitable."

In that final sentence, Coyne spelled out the whole problem of heroin addiction: For those who use heroin, the stuff is death. For those who merchandise this death, it's money. As the risks become greater, so do the profits. And there always are those willing to accept great risks for great profits.

Think about that next time you wonder why the governments haven't been more effective in stamping out the heroin plague.

STUDY QUESTIONS

1. How did you react to the tone of the opening paragraphs of the article? Did they frighten you?
2. Why is heroin addiction called a "plague"?
3. How impressive are the estimates on the number of heroin addicts in the United States?
4. Is it reasonable to describe the heroin trade as a truly international operation? What are the implications of that description?
5. How much cooperation on the part of officials may be involved in the smuggling of heroin into this country?
6. Why don't the dealers in the industry need advertising? How do they get new customers?
7. Who runs the heroin business in this country?
8. Why do officials believe that the Mafia or La Cosa Nostra is no longer in the heroin business? What other views are possible?
9. What arguments are there for insisting that the Mafia is still very much in the trade?
10. Why do you think the heroin trade is such an international operation?

SUGGESTIONS FOR WRITING

1. One of the basic premises of this article is that the heroin trade exists for one principal reason: high profits. An inexpensive raw material yields enormous profits, so the trade flourishes. If you

accept that premise, how would you go about destroying the trade?

2. Make a rough estimate of how many people are involved in the production, processing, and selling of heroin in a given year. Why do you think there are so few arrests for heroin smuggling, processing, and so on, if so many people are involved? Does this seem strange to you?

3. What is the value of seeing the narcotics problem as a business problem? Is the title of this article just a cruel joke, or is there something serious to be learned from applying its message? If so, what is it? Why has society refused to take this approach?

4. How could our government immobilize the narcotics trade overnight? Could it simply take over the trade by flooding the market and reducing prices to a point where the underworld could no longer compete? What are the problems involved in this "solution"?

5. What kind of international measure could be taken to combat the trade without getting the government into the business of selling heroin? How effective would such measures be? Are agreements among governments a guarantee of success?

THE MOON LANDING

C. P. Snow

The moon landings are undoubtedly a marvelous achievement for science. But, as in so many cases, proving the nation's technological skill seems to be their principal aim. Must we meet every scientific challenge regardless of the results? A great writer and scientist suggests that we reconsider taking further steps into space.

We have seen a wonder. There has never been one quite like it. What first steps in human history would one have chosen to witness, if one could travel in time? The Vikings coming ashore wherever they did come ashore—Newfoundland?—in North America? Or the first little boat from Columbus' ship scraping the land under her keel? Yet all of that, or any other bit of geographical discovery, we should be seeing with hindsight. On the spot, it must have seemed much more down-to-earth. People getting out of boats must have looked (and felt) very much like people getting out of boats anywhere at any time.

No, we have had the best of it. We have seen something unique. It is right that it should have looked like something we have never seen before. In science-films, perhaps—but *this was real*. The figure, moving so laboriously, as though it was learning, minute by minute, to walk, was a man of our own kind. Inside that gear there was a foot, a human foot. Watch. It has come, probing its way down—near to something solid. One expects to hear (there is no air, one could hear nothing) a sound. At last, it has come down. Onto a surface. Onto the surface of the moon.

Well, we have seen a wonder. We ought to count our blessings.

This is the time when we might try to clear our minds about the whole project. There will never be a better time. If the landing had

THE MOON LANDING   From the August 26, 1969 issue of *Look* Magazine. Reprinted by permission of John Cushman Associates, Inc. Copyright © 1969 C. P. Snow.

failed, we shouldn't have been in a mood to be even moderately detached. But now we are happy, admiring and basking in a kind of reflected moonlight. If we can't ask sensible questions now, we never shall.

It is important to ask the right questions, though. For instance, I don't think it's realistic to wonder whether a moon landing should ever have been attempted. It may have been wasteful: it may have taken up energies and resources that neither of the superpowers could comfortably afford. We will consider that in a moment. But once the project was technically feasible at all—and no one has doubted that for a good many years—then *it was bound to be attempted*. Not for any of the highfalutin reasons that we have all bandied about.

Some of them existed, but they were rationalizations to make the decision seem more praiseworthy. Just as when people wanted to climb Everest or trek on foot to the South Pole, there was a lot of talk about the scientific results to be obtained: the great polar expeditions before the First World War got financed in the name of science. That was nonsense. The scientific achievements were minimal. The scientific results of the moon landing aren't minimal, but they wouldn't justify the project, and they weren't the ultimate reason for it. Nor were the military possibilities, though credulous persons in both the U.S. and the Soviet Union presumably at times thought they were. That bogey can be disposed of later.

National prestige was more like a genuine reason, but it didn't have to be proved to a reflective outsider that both the superpowers—once they became committed to space exploration—would emerge approximately equal, sometimes one leapfrogging the other, and vice versa. For technology doesn't speak either English or Russian, and—in a competitive activity, war or space or anything you like—no technological lead is ever held for long.

No, the project was bound to be attempted for a much deeper or more primitive reason. If there is a chance for men to put their feet where other feet have never been, they will try it. The answer of George Mallory, the English mountaineer, has become a tedious cliché, but like a lot of clichés, it is true. Why do you want to climb Everest? Because it is there.

Well, the moon was there. The moment there was a chance to get on it, someone was bound to try. The process was accelerated by national rivalries, but it would have happened even if the U.S. or the Soviet Union alone had had a monopoly of rocketry. For any great country has a supply of brave and spirited men who would have been ready for any adventure technology might give them. That is grand:

it makes one proud of belonging to the same species. But there is something else that is perhaps not so grand, that is unarguable and also sinister. That is—there is no known example in which technology has been stopped being pushed to the limit. Technology has its own inner dynamic. When it was possible that technology could bring off a moon landing, then it was certain that sooner or later, the landing would be brought off. However much it cost in human lives, dollars, rubles, social effort.

I do not find this reflection consoling. So far, the space project has not done practical harm. In money, it has cost a great deal, as well as in social effort. In human lives, so far as we know for certain, it has cost just four, three American and one Russian—a good many less than were lost before Everest was climbed (Mallory himself died there) or the South Pole expeditions got home. That is something to be thankful for. But it would be reassuring to find one case in which technology was called off: when human sense and will said, yes, that feat could certainly be done, but it isn't worth doing. When that happens, it will be a sign that we are gaining some hold on our destiny. At present, we are letting technology ride us as though we had no judgment of our own. There were a good many possible justifications for space exploration, and this wouldn't have been a good place to stop technology in its tracks.

But one can't—or at least I can't—say the same for the faster-than-sound passenger aircraft. Up to the present moment, billions of dollars have been spent by the U.K., France, the Soviet Union, the U.S., developing these machines. America can probably afford it. Britain can't. The Anglo-French *Concorde* is an extraordinary example of conspicuous waste. The time-saving in air journeys will be trivial, especially as the ground traffic to airports gets worse. Yet here again, the demon of progress in technology is making us all behave as though we had our brains amputated.

Of course, the moon landing and space exploration in general have cost the U.S. and Soviet Union prodigious amounts. There have been times when I might have said—and in fact did say once or twice—that the money could have been better spent. But now I have had second thoughts, and I believe that I was wrong. I was making what I said at the beginning was the mistake we have to avoid, that is of asking the wrong question. If one asks, could the money spent on space exploration have been used for something more valuable? then the answer is *of course*. But it is not the right question. The real question is—would the money, if diverted from space exploration, have actually been used for something more valuable? And there the answer is, almost certainly not.

Imagine that big rockets had proved unworkable, so that we couldn't project ourselves outside the earth's gravitational field. In that case, NASA wouldn't have existed; and in theory, a gigantic sum of money would have been free for other purposes. Does anyone really believe that most of it, or even a good share of it, would have gone to worthy, down-to-earth purposes, like making cities inhabitable once more? If anyone does believe that, he doesn't know how politics in our kind of society works. It is equally implausible to imagine that the money would have been devoted to increasing the food supply, and decreasing the population growth, in the poor countries of the world. Ask Robert S. McNamara—who, as president of the World Bank, is living with this nightmare problem—whether that could conceivably have happened. The only cause that might have seized the American imagination on a big scale is cancer research. A little of the investment might have been diverted in that direction. But, curiously enough, it would be quite impossible to spend the vast NASA funds on any pure or applied research in molecular biology or some other area immediately valuable to man. Even for nuclear physics, the most expensive of researches, there is, by the standard of military or space budgets, a fairly low saturation limit. It is singularly difficult to spend really big sums on entirely benevolent practical projects: either the projects can't absorb the money, or they have no political sex appeal. It isn't in the nature of politics for people to make themselves think ten years ahead—which is why we are running into a population-food crisis without sacrificing one night's sleep. The space project is probably—apart from military things—the only spender of big money that could have collected majority support from politicians and public. So we are misleading ourselves—and flattering ourselves—if we call it a waste.

Much the same seems to have been true in the Soviet Union. The budgeting is performed in a different fashion from ours: it is more completely centralized, and is of course not argued about in public. Nevertheless, similar considerations apply. The Soviet Academy of Sciences is allotted a massive bloc grant that it divides up among research projects—including many that we should think of as development. (This is as though the National Academy of Sciences in Washington was given funds to finance all research in all American universities and elsewhere.) But the space expenditure, like the military expenditure, must have been decided at a still higher level—one would guess in the Politburo itself. No doubt some of the Soviet academicians, like their American opposite numbers, complained that the money could have been used more sensibly, in particular on their own pet subjects. But their complaints got nowhere, and couldn't have got anywhere in America either.

There is one theoretical difference. If the space money in both countries had suddenly become available for other purposes, it is conceivable that the Soviet bosses would have found the problem easier to handle. Concentration on specific large-scale projects is something they are well adapted for: which, incidentally, is why they have done so well in space. But whether they could have used their equivalent of NASA funds on, say, housing or the rapid development of the Siberian mines is very doubtful. Political systems differ, but the difficulties of going faster than natural cussedness permits stay much the same.

The question of waste of money and effort becomes more misty the longer one looks. So does the military significance of space, though no doubt influential persons on both sides took it seriously almost until the present day. It is characteristic of the human tendency to become bedazzled by gadgets. Influential persons think, one more gadget, one more bright idea or piece of hardware, then we have an overwhelming military advantage. *Very fortunately*, the world is not so unstable as that: if it were, we should all be fastening our seat belts into futurity every hour of the day. The world is not so unstable, and even modern technological war is a good deal simpler, and looks as though it will remain so for the rest of the century. Once both sides had sent a rocket round the moon—and probably, to those who kept their heads, long before that, as far back as the first satellites—it was all exaggeratedly simple, as simple as the Mosaic laws. If you can send a rocket round the moon, you can take out Moscow or, alternatively, New York. You can take out (I apologise for using this inhuman jargon) any town anywhere on earth. Nothing can stop you. It is as simple as that. Simpler than neolithic warfare used to be. That is the balance under which we live. *Very fortunately*, it is a balance difficult to perturb. Whatever afflictions we run into, and there may be many, thermonuclear war between the superpowers is perhaps the most unlikely.

In the face of this cataclysmic simplicity, it is rather odd that people get excited about space landing platforms and so on. It is perfectly true that they could be used for discharging missiles: but that could be done much more conveniently from earth. It is also perfectly true that they could be used as sources of surveillance or spying; so could existing satellites at disproportionately less cost. Further, there are five or six different methods of getting military information, much more efficient and much cheaper: the U.S. and the Soviet are thoughtfully using them upon each other every day of the week. But responses to spying aren't at all rational: people blissfully ignore the really effective methods, and then get feverish about the James Bonds and Le Carre's heroes, who could disappear without making one cent's worth of difference.

People also get feverish, and feel a sort of superstitious horror into the bargain, at the thought of being watched from above. It doesn't merit all that fuss. No position in space is going to affect the balance of deterrence by one percent.

In fact, the competition in space between the U.S. and the Soviet Union has done no harm, or singularly little. There has been a difference of emphasis: the U.S. in the Kennedy Administration set its sights upon the moon, and the Soviet Union has been thinking in addition about planetary trips. But neither side would have been impelled to go so fast if the other hadn't existed. That speed has certainly used a lot of money and a lot of very rare skills, in which there would have been economies if the two countries, instead of competing, had cooperated. But, granted the history in which we have lived, it seems inevitable that the two sides would have competed somewhere. If not in space, then somewhere else. Quite possibly, more probably than possibly, somewhere more harmful. Granted that there was going to be a competition, it would have been moderately difficult to invent one more innocent. (Imagine that the two countries had settled on association football as the chief test of national prestige: the expenditure would have been less, but, to judge from international experience, the loss in temper, rancor and even life would have been significantly greater.)

Most of the questions about the moon landing (taken to be the symbol and emblem of the entire space project) don't seem, then, to be very realistic. They are the wrong questions. But there are a few questions really worth asking. One is, have we gained anything, and, if so, what? And what effect is the landing going to have on us? Will it change our lives? How, and to what extent?

As for the first, yes, we have gained something. The most important part of it is a moral gain—if men do something wonderful, then it ought to be and often is, a source of hope for the rest of us. We are compelled to spend so much time in this jagged century looking at the worst in other people and ourselves. We should be stupid and guilty if we didn't. But it is just as well that we should have the occasional spectacle forced upon us of men being clever, competent and brave.

Human beings are imitative animals. They imitate crime—not only the addiction to crime, but the way it is performed—with the utmost enthusiasm. It is a blessing when we are given something else to imitate: the technological and organizational skill of the whole NASA team, as well as the cool professional courage of Neil Armstrong and his colleagues.

There is also a clear scientific gain. We now know beyond doubt a good deal about the constitution of the moon; soon, we shall know more. This means that before long, we shall solve some tough scientific problems about how the solar system was formed. Further, we shall before long be able to erect laboratories on the moon or a space platform. That doesn't sound dramatic, but the result may be very dramatic. At the moment, cosmogonists are arguing and guessing about the nature of the universe. Observation outside the earth's atmosphere should tell us some of the answers. So the immediate human gain is large, and the scientific gain considerable. So far, so good. But will the landing have an effect on us? Will it change our lives?

I am afraid it will. I am afraid that in the long run, perhaps a generation, perhaps longer, it will have a bad effect. It will give us the feeling, and the perfectly justified feeling, that our world has finally closed in. This is forever the end of the mortal frontier.

I dislike saying what I have just said, and am going on to say. No one is fond of stating a negative opinion. Too many such opinions, even by men we consider tremendously wise, have turned out to be wrong. On that account alone, no responsible person would put forward a flat negative opinion unless he was unusually convinced.

Further, it is no fun putting forward any sort of opinion, positive or negative, unless you can see it checked one way or the other. This one can't be, in my lifetime and for far longer, maybe for hundreds of years. Yet I feel it would be cowardly not to speak my mind. There are some things on which we deceive ourselves very easily. Science presents us with many horizons to which we can't see the end. Fine. That doesn't mean that all horizons are infinite. I am sure this one isn't. (Yes, I know all about tachyons, those hypothetical particles moving faster than the speed of light.) The horizon is limited because of the size of the universe and the shortness of a human lifetime.

This is the only point on which I flatly disagree with the space enthusiasts. They speak as though reaching the moon (and the other possible spots in the solar system) is going to liberate the human imagination as the discovery of America did. I believe the exact opposite, that the human imagination is going to be restricted—as to an extent it was when the last spots on the globe had been visited, the

South Pole and the summit of Everest. Nowhere on earth for adventurous man to go. Very soon, there will be nowhere in the universe for adventurous man to go.

The analogy with the discovery of America is a very bad one. The Spaniards and Portuguese found riches, marvels, above all, people, in the American land. When Armstrong trod on the moon, he found lumps of inorganic matter, as he might have done at the South Pole. The South Pole is a pretty accurate analogy.

John Donne, writing his poem in the early 17th century, when the discovery of America was still fresh in English minds, rhapsodized about his mistress as, "O my America! my new-found land." Can anyone imagine him comparing the girl to the South Pole or the bleak and desert moon?

The trouble is, the solar system is a desperately disappointing place. Scientists have known this for a long time; it is now being confirmed in concrete, only too concrete, fact. Our planet is a peculiar fluke in a dead system. Before the end of the century, Americans and Russians will have landed on Mars. It is conceivable that they will discover traces of primitive organic life. Scientifically, that will be exciting. But that is the very most that we can anticipate. A little lichen on a barren world.

Where else can we go? One can tick off the possibilities on the fingers. One or two of the minor planets, perhaps. Just imaginably, but only just, one or two of the moons of Jupiter. Those, we can predict, will be more barren lumps of inorganic matter. Then we come to the end. That is the frontier. There is nowhere else in the entire universe where man can ever land, for so long as the human species lasts.

This has been scientifically obvious for long enough. The solar system is dead, apart from our world: and the distances to any other system are so gigantic that it would take the entire history of mankind from paleolithic man to the present day to traverse—at the speed of Apollo 11—the distance to the nearest star. So that the frontier is closed. We can explore a few lumps in our system, and that is the end. This has been, as I say, scientifically obvious for a good many years. But it sometimes takes a long time for scientific certainties to reach the public, even the educated public (think of the singular ignorance about human genetics). It takes the evidence of eyes and hands and feet—the eyes, hands and feet of Armstrong and his successors—to translate the scientific certainties into common knowledge. In the domain of space travel, I reckon that this will take from 30 to 100 years. Then disappointment, the sense of confinement, a kind of cosmic claustrophobia will set in.

We had better be prepared for it. It is no use holding out the prospect of limitless horizons when the horizons are certain to turn out only too desolately limited. Science-fiction writers (at least those who have scientific knowledge and insight, of whom there are plenty) have been fighting a rearguard action against the inevitable. But they will get tired of postulating relativistic biology and relativistic speeds. In fact, one of the casualties of the moon landing will be science fiction, at least as applied to space travel. You can write scientifically about what you know to be improbable, but you can't write scientifically for long about what you know to be impossible. Science-fiction writers will be driven inward, not outward, and will turn their attention to human biology and psychology. There is plenty to occupy them there for more than a hundred years.

Nevertheless, they will be driven inward. So will the imaginations of the rest of us. It is a paradox. The greatest exploration—that pioneers have been looking forward to so long. The greatest exploration. The pioneers weren't to know the realization that would afterward gradually dawn upon us. The realization that, as well as being the greatest exploration, it was very near the final one.

That is a pity. We badly need something to take us out—not constantly but for part of our time—out of this, our mundane life. The naïve idea of heaven did that for generation after generation, when people could believe that heaven was somewhere above us, up there beyond the sky. It was a naïve idea but very powerful, and nothing more sophisticated has been so powerful. To secular minds, the prospect of space, other worlds to find, other lives to meet, has been a substitute. To many, a substitute of almost equal power. Now that will fail us too. As a result of supreme technological skill and heroism, we are faced not with the infinite but with the immovable limits. The limits of our practical condition. We now know that the only lives we shall ever meet turn out to be our own.

STUDY QUESTIONS

1. Why was the first moon landing unique among "firsts"?
2. How much did science benefit from the moon walk?
3. What are some of the primitive reasons for our having decided to go to the moon in the first place?
4. How does Snow talk about technology? Do you agree with his feelings?

5. Would Snow have wanted technology halted before a lunar landing?
6. What does Snow think would have been done with the NASA funds if we had not undertaken a lunar-landing project?
7. Why does Snow think that thermonuclear war between the superpowers is unlikely?
8. What are the military advantages of space?
9. What does Snow mean when he says we will ultimately understand that we have reached the limits of the "mortal frontier"?
10. Is there reason to say that the solar system is a dead system?

SUGGESTIONS FOR WRITING

1. Snow makes a comparison between heaven and space, suggesting that for many people the idea of heaven and the idea of space have about the same value. Moreover, he suggests that for many of us the quest for space has actually supplanted the contemplation of heaven. How do you react to this notion? Does it seem feasible to you? Do you agree or disagree with it?
2. The basic hypothesis of the article is that the exploration of space will end on a profoundly depressing note and man will experience "a kind of cosmic claustrophobia." Offer an argument that defends or attacks this theory.
3. One of Snow's views is that we need something to take us out of "our mundane life"—not all the time, he says, but part of the time. Does this impress you as an accurate observation concerning mankind? In general, does your experience show that human beings try to take themselves out of their "mundane" lives? What are some of the most significant results of those attempts?
4. One of the most controversial statements Snow makes is that he would be grateful for the time when mankind recognizes a feat that is technologically possible but ultimately decides it is not worth achieving. If you are in accord with this view, offer some arguments that may persuade someone who does not agree with you. If you disagree with the view, explain why you oppose it.
5. Snow is very blasé about the supposed advantages of space exploration to the Russians and the Americans. In essence, he suggests there is no military significance to it for either nation. Nonetheless, he feels that the competition is necessary and harmless. Should we accept this thinking? Construct a sound argument to convince someone that Snow may be wrong.

"NOW WE ARE ALL SONS-OF-BITCHES"

William L. Laurence

The men who transported our world into the nuclear age were once considered heroes. They had surmounted one of the great boundaries of man's knowledge. Now that we more fully understand the implications of living in the shadow of nuclear destruction, their heroism is often questioned.

To the few of us on the desert near Alamogordo, N. Mex., that morning of July 16, 1945, the world, as we knew it, was never to be the same again. We watched that world explode in a fraction of a millionth of a second and a new world born in its ashes. We all knew that we had been privileged to be present at the birth of a new age— the Atomic Age.

Those moments that dismal, drizzly July morning are just as fresh in my memory as though they were just happening. Once again I hear the voice of gentle Sam Allison, assistant director of the Los Alamos Atomic Laboratory, intoning what was then the first countdown over the radio network, first at periods of minute intervals, beginning at "twenty minutes to Zero," and then the last ten seconds at intervals of one second.

I remember only too well the atmosphere of doubt that pervaded the scientists up to the last minute of the test. On the one hand, they were haunted by the fear that their "gadget," the product of the greatest concentration of brainpower in history, might turn out to be a "fizzle," which meant either a complete dud or the equivalent of no more than a few ordinary blockbusters in terms of TNT. On the other hand there were many, including some of the elite among them, who feared that man, like Sorcerer's Apprentice, may have started something beyond his control.

One day, when confidence in the successful outcome was very low,

"NOW WE ARE ALL SONS-OF-BITCHES"   From the July 11, 1970 issue of *Science News*. Reprinted by permission of Newspaper Enterprise Association.

someone composed a doggerel which became known as the "Los Alamos Blues":

> *From this crude lab that spawned the dud*
> *Their necks to Truman's axe uncurled*
> *Lo the embattled savants stood*
> *And fired the flop heard round the world.*

On the other hand, there were those who feared that the test would liberate a Frankenstein monster. After all, no such force had ever before been liberated on earth, and no one among the scientists, not even the great Enrico Fermi himself, was willing to guarantee that no such thing as the ignition of the atmosphere, either in the vicinity of the explosion, or even over the entire globe, might not take place.

"If the bomb fails to go off," Fermi said on the day before the scheduled test,

> then Oppie (Dr. Robert Oppenheimer) and the laboratory would have proved the system impossible and that would be the best of good news for man. On the other hand, there is the more remote possibility of atmospheric ignition.

"I invite bets," he said,

> first, against the destruction of all human life, and second, just that of human life in New Mexico.

One of the younger scientists was so unnerved that he was removed from the scene on the advice of the psychiatrists whom Gen. Leslie R. Groves had brought down to calm down the physicists. As it turned out, some of the psychiatrists had to calm down each other.

As a matter of fact, I had already prepared, at the request of Gen. Groves, a set of press releases, one of which reported that Dr. Oppenheimer and a number of other distinguished physicists, chemists and educators, who had visited Oppie's ranch in New Mexico, had lost their lives in an accidental explosion of an Army ammunition dump. But when Gen. Groves heard of Fermi's apocalyptic speculation he decided Fermi was making a bad joke, though a good many of the senior physicists did not feel that Fermi was merely joking.

Allison spoke into two microphones linking the control station by wire and radio to the other observation points.

"Twenty minutes to Zero!" Allison announced.

"Fifteen . . . ten . . . five minutes to Zero!"

Dr. Joseph L. McKibben, University of California physicist, was in charge of the control panel that would actually fire off the bomb. Not far from him stood young Dr. Donald Hornig, in charge of a reserve switch that would stop the operation at a command from Dr. Kenneth T. Bainbridge, Harvard physicist, the field commander, in case anything went wrong.

Turning to Oppenheimer, who was just passing by, young Hornig, who later became Special Assistant to the President for Science and Technology, asked: "What if I just say this can't go on and stop it?"

Oppenheimer looked at the young face grinning at him in the glare. "Are you all right?" he asked. Just then Allison's voice was heard again.

"Four minutes to Zero!"

"Three . . . two . . . fifty-five seconds to Zero!"

At forty-five seconds McKibben turned on the automatic timer. Allison kept counting off the seconds.

"Ten . . . nine . . . eight . . . seven . . ."

Like many in the group Allison had his doubts. What if Fermi's qualms were right? In a few more seconds, as I count them off, we may release on earth 1,000 billion curies of radiation, the equivalent of a million tons of radium, an unimaginable quantity never released before on this earth, a quantity possibly great enough to set the atmosphere on fire and extinguish all life on earth. Do I have the right to participate in an experiment that might kill off the human race?

"Three . . . two . . . one . . ." It was the voice of doom tolling off the world's last seconds.

And then, after an agonizing interval, the voice from the clouds shouted "ZERO!" and at that instant, as I recorded soon after that morning, there rose from the bowels of the earth a light not of this world, "brighter than a thousand suns," lighting up earth and sky with a dazzling luminosity. Up it went, a great ball of fire, changing colors as it kept shooting upward, expanding and rising, rising and expanding, an elemental force freed from its bonds after being chained for billions of years. A giant mountain was born in a few seconds instead of millions of years, quivering convulsively.

Then out of the great silence came a mighty thunder. It was the blast from thousands of blockbusters going off simultaneously. The thunder reverberated all through the desert, bounced back and forth from the Sierra Oscuro Mountains, echo upon echo. The ground trembled under our feet as in an earthquake.

The big boom came about one hundred seconds after the great flash—the first cry of a newborn world.

That morning, while still in a state of semi-consciousness, I wrote:

> *On that moment hung eternity;*
> *Time stood still,*

Space contracted into a pinpoint.
It was as though the earth had opened
And the skies had split;
One felt as though he had been privileged
To witness the Birth of the World;
To be present at the Moment of Creation
When God said: "Let there be Light!"

But Prof. George B. Kistiakowski, Russian-born Harvard chemist, saw an entirely different vision. "It was the nearest to Doomsday," he told me that morning, "that one could possibly imagine. I am sure that at the end of the world, in the last millisecond of the earth's existence, the last man will see something very like to what you and I have seen."

A little later I ran into Prof. Ernest O. Lawrence, inventor of the cyclotron, who was one of my neighbors at the desert that morning. "I'll never forget what you said," he exclaimed. Since I had forgotten, he reminded me.

"You said that it was like watching the Second Coming of Christ!" Later still I asked Dr. Oppenheimer, the intellectual head of the project, what his first thoughts had been at the Zero moment. "At that moment," I heard him say, and his voice sounded as though it came from far away, "there flashed into my mind a passage from the Bhagavad-Gita: 'I am become Death, the shatterer of worlds!'" It was the line in which Krishna had reassured a reluctant royal swordsman that he was both the slayer and the slain. But the most down-to-earth reaction came from young Prof. Bainbridge: "Now," he said, "we are all sons-of-bitches!"

I watched the "shatterer of worlds" a little more than three weeks later as I witnessed the duplicate of the "gadget" tested in the desert, the second atomic bomb made of the man-made element, plutonium, dropped from a B-29, half a mile in front of the B-29 in which I was riding, over the city of Nagasaki. The vision that I then saw was entirely different from the one I saw in the desert. And here, in brief, is what I recorded on the spot in the only eyewitness account of what I saw, written by one half awake like one recording a nightmare seen in broad daylight.

Awe-struck, I watched a pillar of purple fire shoot upward, becoming ever more alive as it climbed skyward through the white clouds. It was no longer smoke, or dust, or even a cloud of fire. It was a living thing, a new species of being, born right before our incredulous eyes.

At one stage of its evolution, covering millions of years in terms of seconds, the entity assumed the form of a giant square totem pole, its base about three miles long . . . It was a living totem pole, carved with many grotesque masks grimacing at the earth.

There came shooting out of the totem pole's top a giant mushroom, even more alive than the pillar, seething and boiling in a white fury of creamy foam, sizzling upward and then descending downward, a thousand geysers rolled into one. It kept struggling in an elemental fury, like a creature in the act of breaking the bonds that held it down. In a few seconds it had freed itself from its gigantic stem and floated upward with tremendous speed, its momentum carrying it into the stratosphere to a height of about 60,000 feet.

But at that instant another mushroom, smaller in size than the first, began emerging out of the pillar. It was as though the decapitated monster was growing a new head.

We could still see the giant totem pole and its mushrooms when we last gazed at them from a distance of about two hundred miles. The pillar was a giant mountain of jumbled rainbows in travail. I knew that much living substance had gone into the making of those rainbows.

The quivering top of the pillar was protruding to a great height through the white clouds, giving the appearance of a monstrous prehistoric creature with a ruff around its neck, a fleecy ruff extending in all directions, as far as the eye could see.

STUDY QUESTIONS

1. How many people witnessed the first atomic blast? Were they aware of its significance?
2. Did the scientists have full confidence in their "gadget"?
3. What is "atmospheric ignition"?
4. Does it seem reasonable that psychiatrists were on the scene at Alamogordo?
5. What was the significance of the bets Fermi made?
6. Why was the vision of the bomb exploding over Nagasaki so different from the explosion in New Mexico?
7. How much time passed between the first test of the atomic bomb and its first use on humans? Is the interval surprising?

SUGGESTIONS FOR WRITING

1. Examine the language Laurence uses to describe the dropping of the bomb on Nagasaki. It is a very metaphoric passage. Analyze it in specific terms to see what is suggested by the passage. Is it in any way disturbing to you?

2. Laurence poses one of the questions asked by physicists at the test: "Do I have the right to participate in an experiment that might kill off the human race?" Answer that question on the basis of your own feelings as well as the information presented in this article. Did the scientists in this project have the right to do what they did?

3. What do the differences of opinion—extremely wide in some instances—among these well-informed scientists tell you about the work that went into developing the atomic bomb? What do they tell you about science in general?

4. How do you feel about the "gift" these scientists gave man? Do you think the freeing of nuclear power was like the creation of a kind of Frankenstein monster? Give your reasons as carefully and in as much detail as possible.

TOWARD A UNIVERSAL BIOLOGY:
THE SEARCH FOR LIFE ON MARS

Dietrick E. Thomsen

The next phase of space research will be directed toward Earth's neighboring planets. Both Russia and America will be studying Venus and trying to determine whether there is life on Mars. The efforts that each country will be making in order to answer that question promise to be extraordinary.

Biology is a provincial science. The only examples of life known so far are those found here on earth. Yet earth is dwarfed to insignificance by the rest of the universe and scientists generally agree that the existence of life elsewhere is almost a certainty.

But biologists, limited for now to only the forms on earth, are hindered in making generalizations about life. Discovery of living organisms in other places—or proof of the absence of life on certain other planets—would vastly expand the biologists' perspective. The immediate target in the search for extraterrestrial life is the planet Mars.

In the words of Dr. Wolf Vishniac, chairman of the department of biology and associate director of the Space Science Center at the University of Rochester, biologists could be happy if they find life on Mars and they could be happy if they do not find life on Mars. "If we find living organisms on Mars," he says, "it will be a great discovery." It will precipitate a rush "to see whether the proteins are the same," and otherwise to compare terrestrial and Martian forms.

There are some biologists, Dr. Vishniac says, "who would prefer not to find living organisms on Mars." They are intrigued by the idea of

TOWARD A UNIVERSAL BIOLOGY: THE SEARCH FOR LIFE ON MARS   Reprinted, with permission, from the July 24, 1971 issue of *Science News*, the weekly news magazine of science and the applications of science, copyright 1971 by Science Service, Inc.

two planets of similar size and shape, one with life, one without. In that case one planet would be the experiment, one the control. In either case, biologists would understand a good deal more about life on earth by studying Mars.

Programs to investigate the possibility of life on Mars are being pursued by both the Soviet Union and the United States. They were described in June in Seattle at the . . . Plenary Meeting of the Committee on Space Research of the International Council of Scientific Unions.

In all cases experiments are planned on the assumption that wherever life exists, its chemistry is based on the same elements—carbon, oxygen and nitrogen—as on earth. The sandmen of science fiction, whose existence is based on silicon chemistry, are not being seriously considered.

The expectation of carbon-based life is the simplest way to begin, and, says Dr. Vishniac, the discovery in the last few years that organic compounds like those on earth populate the interstellar dust clouds enhances the expectation by showing that compounds of this type form readily in various parts of the universe. Whether or not the origin of life is in the interstellar dust clouds, the discovery of organic compounds there, he says, makes "biology very much a part of cosmology."

Because microorganisms are the most basic forms of life, the Mars experiments are all directed to the discovery of microorganisms inhabiting the Martian soil. Large plants and animals cannot exist without a flourishing microflora in the soil, but microflora can exist without larger forms of life.

If the microflora is there, one of the questions is who will be first to find it. There is much speculation about whether the Russian vehicles now moving toward Mars carry biological experiments. The craft are large enough to contain landers, and landers might carry biological experiments. The Russians aren't saying yes or no, but knowledgeable Americans tended to conclude that the current Mars probes do not carry such experiments after hearing negative-sounding reports on the subject by Russian investigators. (On the other hand, the Russians could be saving other reports till after their probe lands.)

All that the Russians presented at Seattle were results of preliminary experiments in which certain terrestrial life forms were grown under simulated Martian conditions. They took bacteria from the Nubian Desert and from Arctic soil and grew them in simulated Mars soil under very low humidity. They then attempted to detect the presence of life in the cultures by the sort of sensors that can be sent on an automated Mars probe.

To detect life in such cultures, one might begin by looking for the energy-releasing compound adenosine triphosphate (ATP), but the Russians reject this with the remark that ATP may be synthesized spontaneously, and therefore its presence does not necessarily indicate life.

Another way is to introduce radioactively labeled organic compounds to the organisms as food. An example would be glucose that contained carbon 14. One then measures the radioactive carbon dioxide given off. But the Russians did not have good luck with this approach. They found that the evolution of $C^{14}O_2$ depends on the humidity, and that not very much of it is produced in a dry atmosphere such as Mars is supposed to have.

Russian pessimism notwithstanding, American scientists are going ahead with the preparation of experiments to be carried on the two Viking Mars landers scheduled for launch in August and September 1975. Congress recently authorized the first funds for the Viking project.

Viking's biological effort was described for the meeting by Dr. Harold R. Klein, director of life sciences at the National Aeronautics and Space Administration's Ames Laboratory at Moffett Field, Calif. First of all, he says, the lander will carry cameras for a close-up view of the terrain, and, he laughs, "we may see some Martians." More likely the cameras would show temporal changes in the color or other aspects of the soil brought about by the activity of microflora.

Another general experiment that may show evidence of life will sample the chemical content of the Martian atmosphere. If it should find oxidized and reduced gases together—carbon dioxide and methane for example—this coexistence could mean that organisms were producing them since in the usual procedures of inorganic chemistry oxidized and reduced gases should cancel each other out.

The heart of the biological effort is four experiments that will attempt direct detection of microorganisms in the Martian soil in four different ways. Dr. Klein calls this "shotgun effort" advisable because some Martian organisms may like it dry and some may like it wet. Some may like to eat the same food as terrestrial organisms; some may prefer native Martian nutrients.

The experimental package will have four chambers into which scoops will drop Martian soil. Different things will happen in each chamber.

The first experiment will attempt to find living matter by burning it out of the soil. Martian soil will be incubated in an atmosphere containing carbon dioxide and carbon monoxide labeled with carbon 14. After incubation the sample will be heated to 600 degrees C. to drive off remaining radioactive gas. Then it will be heated to 700 degrees, at which point organic matter in the soil should be oxidized. Any radioactive carbon oxides found after the second heating should represent carbon ingested by the organisms.

A dry regime is planned for the second chamber which will incubate Martian soil with very small amounts of nutrient (0.2 milliliter to a cubic centimeter of soil). The medium is still not decided; a mixture of carbon 14-labeled formate, lactate, glycine and glucose has been used in exploratory studies. Gas exchange in the atmosphere of the incubator would be monitored for evidence of life.

Organisms that like it wet will enjoy the third chamber, where they will be incubated in a very wet nutrient medium, a broth consisting of water, amino acids and other simple organic substances. A gas chromatograph would measure the uptake or release of hydrogen, oxygen, nitrogen, methane and carbon dioxide.

Lovers of native Martian cuisine will be at home in the fourth experiment, which will incubate Martian soil in distilled water but will not introduce any terrestrial nutrients. It will then examine the water for changes in optical properties brought about by the suspension of microorganisms in it.

Breadboard models of some of these experiments already exist, says Dr. Klein. The finished versions must go into a space 9.5 by 10 by 11.5 inches and weigh 20 pounds. Engineers assure him it can be done.

The two Viking spacecraft will consist of orbiters and landers coupled together. After the orbiters are established in an orbit around Mars, they will dispatch the landers. Data taken by the landers will be automatically recorded and sent to earth by automatic telemetry. The landers are planned to have a lifetime of 90 days, and each of the biological experiments is supposed to process several soil samples during this time. The results will be eagerly awaited by the world biological community—unless the Russians upstage the missions.

STUDY QUESTIONS

1. In what way is biology a "provincial" science?
2. What are some of the reasons for assuming there is life elsewhere in the universe?

3. Why will some scientists be pleased if we find there is no life on Mars?
4. Why is the expectation of carbon-based life the simplest way to begin the search for life on Mars?
5. Why are scientists so interested in finding microflora on Mars?
6. Could the Russian vehicles now headed toward Mars be carrying equipment designed to discover life?
7. Why is ATP not wholly reliable as an indicator of the presence of life?
8. When will the United States begin its Mars probes?
9. What four experiments will the United States perform in its effort to discover life on Mars?

SUGGESTIONS FOR WRITING

1. Does it really matter whether there is life on Mars? Could it be considered a waste to invest so much of our energy and resources in a search for Martian microorganisms?
2. How would you react if scientists discovered that not only flora but fauna exist on Mars? What would be the implications if they found that the planet was "peopled" by small animals the size of chipmunks? How do you think others would react?
3. Let us assume that life was found not to exist on Mars or on the other planets in our solar system. What do you think would be the reactions of governmental and intellectual leaders around the world? Would it have any practical effect on their behavior? Could it have?
4. Do you think the methods scientists are using are as comprehensive as they might be? Are they as sophisticated as you would have expected? If you were a biologist, how would you want to go about conducting these experiments?
5. What major problems do you see in this approach to finding out whether there is life on Mars? How much chance of success do you think it has?

GOVERNMENT AND SCIENCE

Francis D. Wormuth

The distinction between science and government in most modern societies is not as simple to make as it would seem. Science makes modern government possible in the United States, and the government reciprocates by giving science massive grants and assistance. This arrangement may not always operate in the best interest of the people.

The current involvement of government in science and technology has already produced, or threatens to produce, not merely dangers but certain injury of great magnitude. Aboveground tests of atomic weapons, underground tests, and nuclear power plants have already caused poisoning and pollution from radioactivity and will cause more. Nuclear power plants will continue to produce thermal pollution. The supersonic jets which are to be developed with federal funds will cause what is being called noise pollution on a nationwide scale.

The federal government has repeatedly tested such poisons as nerve gas in the open air, and it is sheer luck that only the sixty-four hundred Skull Valley sheep have thus far been killed. It has paid out large sums to breed new diseases. Sometimes it has even released these biological weapons experimentally, as in the seeding of part of the Dugway base with anthrax and the release of infected animals at Dugway. Recently, the Defense Department reluctantly admitted that it had released tularemia in Alaska. This action was followed by a belt of cases southeastward across Canada and seventy cases, the first in history, in Vermont in 1968. The Interior Department licensed the extraction of oil off Santa Barbara under circumstances that made it

GOVERNMENT AND SCIENCE   Reprinted, with permission, from the March 1970 issue of *The Center Magazine,* a publication of the Center for the Study of Democratic Institutions in Santa Barbara, California.

likely that what did occur would occur: the destruction of birds, sea lions, seals, and fish.

Other injuries are inflicted by private action. In some cases the federal government supervises the activity; in others Congress has ignored steadily increasing evils. According to a 1968 report to Congress by the General Accounting Office, federal enforcement of pesticide-control laws already on the books has been lax. Although DDT may be brought under control before it destroys the streams and oceans altogether, air and water pollution from a variety of other sources will cause irreversible damage to the atmosphere and the water unless arrested.

It is not, then, simply a matter of the death of a fraction of the human population. The ecological damage is cumulative and could destroy the very conditions of life.

While it is impossible to halt the technological revolution, it is imperative to control it. Controlling it requires that experiments which threaten to produce harmful effects be evaluated in advance, and prohibited if there is reasonable ground to anticipate harm. It is necessary to put an end to the damaging processes and employment of harmful products of technology.

Recently, President Nixon renounced chemical and biological warfare: presumably some hazardous experiments will be discontinued. But CBW is only one source of concern. In other fields, experimentation goes on without effective supervision or evaluation. Congress cannot perform these tasks. It cannot master the details involved in the authorization of experiments; only in the case of total success or total disaster can it evaluate an experiment even after the fact.

Legislative regulation is a primitive device. In the past, in establishing control of activities which Congress desired not merely to permit but to regulate, Congress has had to create administrative agencies and delegate rule-making power to them. This arrangement should be adapted to the control of science. There is greater readiness to accept a proposal to deal with new problems if familiar tools are employed, and rightly so. These familiar forms have an established place within the legal order, whereas the relation of new techniques to the rest of the legal order would be in doubt. Moreover, we know what kinds of behavior to expect from established institutions, and can take that into account in extending the administrative structure.

Some aspects of our present system of administrative law have virtues other than that of familiarity. In particular, any extension or rectification of the administrative structure should reflect the prudent considerations underlying the rule against the delegation of legislative power and the requirement that government observe due process. Congress may authorize an administrative agency to make rules applying a general policy prescribed by Congress, but it must specify the purpose and the means and set boundaries to administrative discretion; otherwise, there is an unconstitutional delegation of legislative power. This formula is imprecise and is easily manipulated. For this reason some students of administrative law think it serves no useful purpose. In fact, however, it expresses a fundamental political principle. With all its faults, Congress, which embodies a variety of interests, concerns, and points of view, is dependent upon—and to some degree responsive to—the citizenry. On the other hand, an administrative agency tends to get caught up by narrow and exclusive interests. Decisions on fundamental policy should be made after the broadest review. In some cases, Congress does do this well.

We must take into account, however, that in science Congress does not, and in the nature of things cannot, perform this function well. A single appropriation supports a large variety of activities and experiments, many of which are not even formulated at the time the act is passed and none of which is properly evaluated in the time available to Congress. Comprehensive evaluation cannot be supplied by specialists chosen merely for technical proficiency. Their proposals should be subjected to the scrutiny of other interests. This is not to say that the scientific interest must necessarily yield; it does mean that all relevant considerations should be canvased. Before legislating, Congress ordinarily holds hearings and at least undertakes to give the impression that it solicits conflicting views.

In 1935, in *Panama Refining Company vs. Ryan,* the Supreme Court said the due process clause requires that executive rule-making be preceded by fact-finding. The Court has withdrawn somewhat from this position, but in the Administrative Procedure Act of 1946, Congress required advance notice of most administrative actions, whether rule-making or adjudication, if they affected conventional private interests. If administrative decisions on matters of purely private import, such as licensing, require the assistance of the adversary method, surely this method is indispensable in arriving at sound judgments about the fateful questions raised by modern science and technology.

If these considerations—the desirability of evaluating a proposal from many points of view and, as a means to this end, the use of adversary procedure—are to be given full scope, we should reorganize our administrative agencies. In the typical case, regulation of an industry or a practice—rule-making, adjudication, licensing, dispensing, inspection—is entrusted to a single agency. This came about by an historical accident. However, a rationale has been invented for it. It is now said that effective regulation requires expertise. If a single agency deals with all facets of a problem, it acquires much more information than if only one facet were dealt with.

During the second Administration of Franklin D. Roosevelt, the American Bar Association mounted a sustained attack against the practice of uniting in a single agency the function of investigating and initiating complaints with that of adjudicating. The A.B.A. argued that an agency which performed both functions was simultaneously prosecutor and judge; what it decided in a judicial capacity would therefore have been prejudged. Defenders of the system claimed that the commissioners who sat as judges took no part in the preparation of the prosecution. Yet it was true that on many occasions a commission itself had initiated the cases it later decided. The A.B.A. abandoned its campaign with the death of the New Deal. Nevertheless, the possibility of abuse is apparent and extends into other government areas as well. In 1954, when the Attorney General told his hearing board that an alien should be deported, and the board duly confirmed this judgment, the Supreme Court held that the Attorney General had unlawfully influenced the judgment of his subordinates (*United States ex rel. Accardi vs. Shaughnessy*).

The A.B.A. objected only to agencies making decisions as to the illegal conduct or culpability of individuals or corporations, but the device of the independent commission is subject to other objections. A commission tailored to a particular industry and possessing wide regulatory authority over it is likely to be converted from policeman to protector. In part, this is a natural consequence of continual intimate association. In part, no doubt, it results from the agency's feeling of responsibility for the industry. Since its decisions spell health or decline for the industry, the agency feels obligated to maintain it in good health. The indulgence and favoritism shown by the Interstate Commerce Commission for the railroads are well known. It has discriminated against pipelines and water carriers in order to benefit the railroads.

This identification of the regulator with the regulated is much less likely to occur with a commission that is assigned to prohibit a given practice throughout the business world, such as the Federal Trade Commission, which has attempted to enforce the antitrust laws through much of its history. Yet, when the F.T.C. has been given more particularized assignments, comparable to that of the Interstate

Commerce Commission, it has shown, at least according to some ob-
servers, great partiality toward these associations. The Food and
Drug Administration has had a checkered history. For a long time it
had a very friendly relationship with the pharmaceutical industry,
which it regulates; only in recent years has it become more strict. This
has evoked loud protests from the drug industry.

The principal federal agencies that deal with science are not regulatory; they are themselves engaged in operations—like the Atomic
Energy Commission and the Defense Department—or in subsidizing
the activities of others, like the National Institutes of Health. These
agencies are charged with specific tasks in carrying out public policy.
To a much greater degree than is the case with the Interstate Commerce Commission, the narrower, more immediate concern blots out
the larger and more remote.

This is strikingly illustrated in the Atomic Energy Commission's
infatuation with atomic energy. It has no responsibility for delivery
systems, but only for producing explosives. It has produced enough of
these to destroy the world many times over, but continues its tests to
refine the bomb. It grants licenses to construct nuclear power plants
without considering the possibility of thermal pollution; in fact, its
spokesmen deny that this is even a relevant consideration. It is so
anxious to find new uses for atomic energy that it is carrying on a
series of explosions to release natural gas, although each such explosion appears to violate two provisions of the Atomic Energy Act.
While there is authorization for explosions to research "the military
application of atomic energy," no provision of the act appears to
authorize explosions for non-military purposes, although research
which employs atomic by-products may be licensed by the A.E.C.
The other provision forbids the interstate transportation of explosive
devices. There are certain exceptions but they do not include non-
military use.

There are several reasons for the grim enthusiasm of the A.E.C.
The career aspirations of men in any enterprise hang on the continuance and extension of the enterprise. In the case of scientific experimentation, there is the added factor of scientific curiosity. It is an
article of faith that the pursuit of scientific truth cannot do harm. In
the face of rapidly accumulating evidence to the contrary, it is still
supposed by scientists as well as laymen that every advance of scientific knowledge must contribute, in the language of Francis Bacon, to
"the relief of man's estate."

In any agency created to carry out operations of a highly specialized
sort, there is another danger probable enough to amount almost to a

certainty. In the A.E.C. the personnel are chosen because of their competence in nuclear science. Such competence is indispensable. But a lifetime of specialization means that the staff will have not only an official and institutional commitment but a personal one to the extension of a single probing finger of science. In all probability the price they have paid for competence in this narrow branch of science is unfamiliarity with other branches, such as genetics and ecology, though these ought to be highly relevant to the agency's activities. If by chance the nuclear scientist is aware that the findings of these sciences raise doubts about the wisdom of a particular experiment, nevertheless his personal involvement in his special field is likely to cause him to attach greater weight to the chance of extending knowledge of the atom than the chance of adverse consequences.

The division of opinion between nuclear scientists and geneticists on the propriety of projected tests, as well as the consequences of past ones, illustrates the bias that a discipline gives to its practitioners. To entrust to nuclear scientists decisions on questions involving not only the behavior of the atom but the very continuance of life on earth is like taking as one's sole medical adviser a surgeon who has no tool other than his knife.

It may well be that the heads of operating agencies—the Secretary of Defense or the commissioners of the A.E.C.—are not themselves scientists. In this case they will not have personally experienced the fanatical devotion to a single area of inquiry that characterizes the scientific specialist—Edward Teller, for example. But this does not improve the situation; it may even make it worse. The non-professional director has an institutional commitment to the work of his agency. He depends on the specialists on his staff for advice, but is unable to evaluate their advice. The specialists, however, having no authority over the final decision, feel far less responsibility for it. They are likely to fall into a partisan posture in dealing with their superior; they envisage their role as one of advocacy rather than judgment. Consequently, the agency may undertake rash action which the specialists themselves would not have endorsed if they bore official responsibility for the decision.

When those who are engaged in experimentation are the sole judges of the question whether experiments should be undertaken, other considerations are likely to receive short shrift. During the nineteen-fifties, the A.E.C. regularly assured us that its open-air tests could cause no physical injury. But in the April, 1969, issue of the *Bulletin of the Atomic Scientists*, Dr. Ernest J. Sternglass offered statistical evidence—the only kind the case admits of, and as conclusive as evi-

dence of that kind can be—that these tests caused three hundred and
seventy-five thousand infant deaths between 1951 and 1966 and are
still producing thirty-four thousand deaths a year. (His findings
seemed to have been confirmed by the inadequate criticisms offered
by A.E.C. partisans in the October and December issues of the
Bulletin.)

The power to make rules should not be entrusted to those who will
be governed by those rules. In order to justify projected tests, the
A.E.C. revised its level of tolerance of radioactivity upward. The
power to do that should have been assigned to an independent agency
whose staff of experts would be in no way involved in the operation
of the A.E.C. If such an agency had no other function than to super-
vise the A.E.C., it might well develop a paternal concern such as the
I.C.C. has for the railroads. But if it were given the task of supervising a number of operating agencies (if it were patterned after the
F.T.C. rather than the I.C.C.), this would be less likely.

Let us postulate a large administrative agency—like the French
Council of State, staffed by scientific generalists who are supported by
specialists in all fields—which would be given jurisdiction over a
number of operating agencies; let us call it the Public Science Council.

The Public Science Council would have power to make rules for the
A.E.C. and the other operating agencies which it supervises. It would
review particular tests or activities before they were undertaken, and,
governed by a general standard enacted by Congress, its rule-making
and authorization of tests would occur only after a hearing in which
adversary procedure was employed.

A successful evaluation of competing considerations, common to
rule-making and to the authorization of individual experiments, can
be made only if all the arguments pro and con are presented in their
most persuasive form to the Public Science Council. The A.E.C. and
other agencies are qualified to present their case, but there should also
be an agency whose official duty would be to offer countervailing arguments. (A comparable function is performed in Indiana by the public
counsel who argues for rate reductions before the Public Service Commission.) This adversary agency might be called the Public Safety
Council. Its staff should include scientists particularly knowledgeable
about biology and environmental science, and capable of evaluating
the projects of operating agencies. To this end, the Public Safety
Council should have cordial relations with university departments in
the fields of conservation and ecology and should administer whatever grants-in-aid are given in these fields.

It is not likely, however, that all the interests that should be heard would be represented on the Public Safety Council. Voluntary groups and the residents in an area which may suffer local injury from an atomic explosion or the testing of gases or diseases should also be allowed to present their cases. Conservation groups may wish to offer arguments which are not merely scientific.

Like the A.E.C., the Defense Department conducts experiments; the present level of its biological and chemical experiments is obscure. Its tests should be administered under general rules established by the Public Science Council and, unless there is compelling reason for secrecy, should be subject to challenge by the Public Safety Council. Since the justification offered for developing chemical and biological weapons was to deter other countries from employing them, there seems to have been no reason for secrecy; a weapon is no deterrent unless potential enemies know that it exists.

Hearings before the Public Science Council should be conducted under the general rules of administrative law. This would require the Council to make findings of fact on two questions: the case for the proposed action—the probability of success, the utility of the probable result, and the need for the action, considering here not only the need for the anticipated result but the availability of alternative and preferable routes to the same end; and the case against the action—the probability of substantial injury to both private and public interests in health, physical environment, conservation, and aesthetics. The project should be approved only if the Public Science Council finds that there is reasonable ground for undertaking the experiment and no reasonable ground for expecting harmful results.

Even the decisions of a Public Science Council, however, might need further scrutiny. A substantial body of opinion opposes judicial review of administrative decisions on the theory that these are founded in administrative expertness and that the courts, lacking this skill, ought not to upset them. But the courts, in reviewing the decisions of administrative agencies, bring to bear not only the values of the administrative process but the values of other branches of the law, those of constitutional law, the law of property, and the law of civil rights, for example. In reviewing scientific decisions, one would expect the courts to give weight to the values of the individual in society, which usually receive summary treatment at the hands of scientists. Administrative decisions should not be made solely with reference to scientific values, no matter how scrupulously they are administered. They should be reviewed in the context of the whole legal order. It therefore seems desirable that the decisions of a Public Science

Council be reviewed by the Court of Appeals of the District of Columbia. They should be reversed for error of law, or if there is not substantial evidence of that, then on the basis of the whole record that the proposed action will meet the affirmative standards specified above, or if there is substantial evidence on the basis of the whole record that the proposed action will harm the private or public interest. The Supreme Court might then review by *certiorari*. In particular cases, other forms of judicial review may also be available. Where the doctrine of constitutional fact applies, there is a right to trial *de novo* in the District Court. There may also be cases in which even the members of an operating agency may be personally suable in an injunction proceeding or a tort action.

The considerations that apply to the supervision of governmental operations, such as those of the A.E.C. and the Defense Department, apply equally to the supervision of private action. The Food and Drug Administration licenses new drugs for distribution. The testing of these drugs is carried out by the manufacturers, who have a strong financial interest in launching them, but the F.D.A. acts on the basis of the manufacturers' reports without any confirming tests of its own. Probably the tasks of carrying out independent tests and approving new drugs should be transferred to the Public Science Council, which would also enact general rules for the industry concerning testing and eligibility for licensing. A Public Science Council, furthermore, would be less vulnerable to the importunities, the badgering, and the political attacks that have been leveled against such regulatory bodies as the Bureau of Standards and the F.D.A. We know of cases in which these tactics on the part of industry have failed, but one supposes that there are unreported cases in which they have succeeded.

An enormous amount of scientific research is supported by the federal government. The appropriation is made to a governmental agency without adequate specification of the project for which it is to be spent. The agency—one of the National Institutes of Health, for example—then distributes the money to universities or other contractors for research projects. Sometimes the research project is initiated by the governmental agency; in other cases, as with many contracts of the National Institutes of Health, they are proposed by individuals and grants awarded in the manner of a prize contest. The abandon with which money has been spent is incredible. Between 1940 and 1967, the annual federal appropriation for science increased from one hundred million dollars to seventeen billion dollars. This occurred, as Michael D. Reagan pointed out in the April, 1968, *Bulletin of the Atomic Scientists,* entirely without the establishment of priorities even on the part of the scientific sponsors of research; it occurred by the simple aggregation of requests.

The physicist Charles Schwartz once said that when he was with the Institute of Defense Analyses the house rule was that any weapon that cost less than ten per cent of the G.N.P. was worth working on. A university esteems a faculty member in proportion to the size of the grants he wins; accordingly, the expense of a project, rather than its intrinsic merit, is likely to determine the professor's choice of a research problem. As one might expect, the contracting agency, the dispenser of benefits, takes a benevolent interest in its protégés and applies no harsh standard of evaluation. In addition, since it awarded the contract, it has a selfish interest in concealing its errors of judgment.

Congress should scrutinize the purpose for which it appropriates money for research, but it may be utopian to expect this much. Except where military secrecy precludes this, every proposed contract for research should be submitted to a panel of the Public Science Council, with the Safety Council once again representing the public interest.

There remains the function of evaluation. The General Accounting Office evaluates some of the activities of executive agencies for financial misconduct (some are exempted from its authority) but it is inadequately staffed to audit all the activities falling within its jurisdiction. It does have the power to refuse settlement; and it reports its findings to Congress, where they are usually ignored. The G.A.O. should be enormously enlarged by the addition of members who are able to evaluate all the scientific and technological adventures of the national government, and report to Congress the success or failure of experiments. To finance this supervision, five per cent of every appropriation for research should go to the General Accounting Office. The G.A.O. could duplicate the skills of the Public Science Council and the Public Safety Council. This would not be wasteful; if checks and balances are needed anywhere, it is in controlling the ills that spill from Pandora's box.

These proposals arise from a consideration of federal activities already undertaken. Vast areas remain which should be brought under administrative control. The distribution of insecticides should be subjected to the scrutiny of the Public Science Council. Water and air pollution still go largely uncontrolled. The Public Safety Council should be given the task originally assigned to the National Resources Committee (which more than thirty years ago issued a warning against water pollution) of preparing studies that will inform the public of these dangers.

STUDY QUESTIONS

1. Why does Wormuth start by talking about pollution?
2. How do you feel about our research with nerve gas and "exotic" diseases?
3. Does Wormuth think our current situation is serious? Do you?
4. What is the relationship Wormuth sees between science and technology?
5. How effective is legislative regulation of new experiments?
6. What are Wormuth's reasons for thinking Congress could be effective in controlling unbounded research? Do you agree?
7. What are some of the weaknesses of the governmental commissions?
8. Why are specialized regulatory agencies sometimes likely to be lax?
9. Wormuth calls the Atomic Energy Commission flagrantly one-sided in its practices. Why?
10. How does the A.E.C. react to the claim that open-air testing of atomic bombs caused 375,000 infant deaths between 1951 and 1966?

SUGGESTIONS FOR WRITING

1. Analyze Wormuth's argument. What is he in favor of and what exactly is he arguing against? What are the basic weaknesses of his argument? What are the principal strengths? How effectively do you think he uses his evidence? If he has convinced you, what do you think was most significant in winning you over? Could it be your own prejudice?
2. Wormuth says, "It is an article of faith that the pursuit of scientific truth cannot do harm." How do you react to this statement? Can you defend it? How would you attack it? Take either stand and develop it clearly.
3. Wormuth talks a great deal about government strengthening itself to effectively handcuff science. Is there any possibility that the sciences could get together and handcuff government? What are the promising features of such action by the sciences? What are the bad features?
4. Examine the author's references to instances when science and

government seem to merge in their interests. What seems to happen then? Are the best interests of the public usually served? Are science and government, when they join forces, really worried about serving the larger interests of the public? Review the article carefully before answering.

5. Suppose government took no special interest in science at all. What do you think the results would be? Would you and people you know well benefit from such a situation, or would you suffer? Use details from the article and be as explicit as possible.

ALL ABOUT ECOLOGY

William Murdoch and Joseph Connell

Ecology is a relatively new word in the popular vocabulary. Until recently it was used primarily by scientists to describe the delicate balance of life that exists between plants and animals, including man. Today, with that balance severely threatened, the term also suggests our attempts to save ourselves from doom.

The public's awakening to the environmental crisis over the past few years has been remarkable. A recent Gallup Poll showed that every other American was concerned about the population problem. A questionnaire sent to about five hundred University of California freshmen asked which of twenty-five topics should be included in a general biology course for non-majors. The top four positions were: Human Population Problems (85%), Pollution (79%), Genetics (71.3%), and Ecology (66%).

The average citizen is at least getting to know the word ecology, even though his basic understanding of it may not be significantly increased. Not more than five years ago, we had to explain at length what an ecologist was. Recently when we have described ourselves as ecologists, we have been met with respectful nods of recognition.

A change has also occurred among ecologists themselves. Until recently the meetings of ecologists we attended were concerned with the esoterica of a "pure science," but now ecologists are haranguing each other on the necessity for ecologists to become involved in the "real world." We can expect that peripatetic "ecological experts" will soon join the ranks of governmental consultants jetting back and forth to the Capitol—thereby adding their quota to the pollution of the atmosphere. However, that will be a small price to pay if they succeed

ALL ABOUT ECOLOGY   Reprinted, with permission, from the January 1970 issue of *The Center Magazine*, a publication of the Center for the Study of Democratic Institutions in Santa Barbara, California.

in clearing the air of the political verbiage that still passes for an environmental policy in Washington.

Concern about environment, of course, is not limited to the United States. The ecological crisis, by its nature, is basically an international problem, so it seems likely that the ecologist as "expert" is here to stay. To some extent the present commotion about ecology arises from people climbing on the newest bandwagon. When the limits of ecological expertise become apparent, we must expect to lose a few passengers. But, if only because there is no alternative, the ecologist and the policymakers appear to be stuck with each other for some time to come.

While a growing awareness of the relevance of ecology must be welcomed, there are already misconceptions about it. Further, the traditional role of the expert in Washington predisposes the nation to a misuse of its ecologists. Take an example. A common lament of the socially conscious citizen is that though we have enough science and technology to put a man on the moon we cannot maintain a decent environment in the United States. The implicit premise here seems clear: the solution to our ecological crisis is technological. A logical extension of this argument is that, in this particular case, the ecologist is the appropriate "engineer" to resolve the crisis. This reflects the dominant American philosophy (which is sure to come up after every lecture on the environment) that the answer to most of our problems is technology and, in particular, that the answer to the problems raised by technology is more technology. Perhaps the most astounding example of this blind faith is the recent assurance issued by the government that the SST will not fly over the United States until the sonic boom problem is solved. The sonic boom "problem," of course, cannot be "solved." One job of the ecologist is to dispel this faith in technology.

To illustrate the environmental crisis, let us take two examples of how the growth of population, combined with the increasing sophistication of technology, has caused serious problems which planning and foresight could have prevented. Unfortunately, the fact is that no technological solutions applied to problems caused by increased population have ever taken into consideration the consequences to the environment.

The first example is the building of the Aswan High Dam on the upper Nile. Its purposes were laudable—to provide a regular supply of water for irrigation, to prevent disastrous floods, and to provide electrical power for a primitive society. Other effects, however, were simply not taken into account. The annual flood of the Nile had brought a supply of rich nutrients to the eastern Mediterranean Sea, renewing its fertility; fishermen had long depended upon this annual cycle. Since the Aswan Dam put an end to the annual flood with its load of nutrients, the annual bloom of phytoplankton in the eastern Mediterranean no longer occurs. Thus the food chain from phytoplankton to zooplankton to fish has been broken; and the sardine fishery, once producing eighteen thousand tons per year (about half of the total fish catch), has dropped to about five hundred tons per year.

Another ecological effect of the dam has been the replacement of an intermittent flowing stream with a permanent stable lake. This has allowed aquatic snails to maintain large populations, whereas before the dam was built they had been reduced each year during the dry season. Because irrigation supports larger human populations, there are now many more people living close to these stable bodies of water. The problem here is that the snails serve as intermediate hosts of the larvae of a blood fluke. The larvae leave the snail and bore into humans, infecting the liver and other organs. This causes the disease called schistosomiasis. The species of snail which lives in stable water harbors a more virulent species of fluke than that found in another species of snail in running water. Thus the lake behind the Aswan Dam has increased both the incidence and virulence of schistosomiasis among the people of the upper Nile.

A second example we might cite is the effect of DDT on the environment. DDT is only slightly soluble in water, so is carried mainly on particles in the water for short distances until these settle out. But on tiny particles in the atmosphere it is carried great distances; it may even fall out more heavily in distant places than close to where it was sprayed. DDT is not readily broken down by microorganisms; it therefore persists in the environment for many years. It is very soluble in fats so that it is quickly taken up by organisms. Herbivores eat many times their own weight of plants; the DDT is not broken down but is accumulated in their bodies and becomes further concentrated when the herbivores are eaten by the carnivores. The result is that the species at the top of the food chain end up with high doses of it in their tissues. Evidence is beginning to show that certain species of predators, such as ospreys, are being wiped out as a result of physiological debilities which lead to reproductive failure, all caused by accumulations of DDT.

The reproduction of top carnivores such as ospreys and pelicans is being reduced to negligible amounts, which will cause their extinction. No amount of technological ingenuity can reconstruct a species of osprey once it is extinct.

The tendency of DDT to kill both the herbivorous pest as well as its predators has produced some unpredicted consequences. In natural circumstances, herbivores are often kept at rather low numbers by their predators, with occasional "outbreaks" when there is a decrease in these enemies. Once spraying is started, and both the pests and their natural enemies are killed, the surviving pests, which have higher rates of increase than their predators, can then increase explosively between applications.

Before pesticides were applied to North American spruce and balsam forests, pest populations exploded once every thirty years or so, ate all the leaves, and then their numbers plummeted. Since spraying began, the pests, in the absence of a balancing force of predators, are continually able to increase between sprayings. In two instances, in cotton fields in Peru and in cocoa plantations in Malaysia, the situation became so bad that spraying was stopped. The predators returned and the damage by pests was diminished to the former tolerable levels. Another consequence of spraying has been that any member of the pest population which happens to be physiologically resistant to an insecticide survives and leaves offspring; thus resistant strains are evolved. Several hundred of these resistant strains have evolved in the last twenty years.

Because DDT is not present in concentrated form in the environment, it does not represent an energy resource common enough to support microorganisms. None has yet evolved the ability to break it down, even though it has been used as a pesticide for twenty-five years. Chlorinated hydrocarbons may even reduce drastically the plant productivity of the oceans. These plants are not only the base of the ocean food chain but also help maintain the oxygen supply of the atmosphere.

In sum, the indiscriminate use of DDT throughout the world, its dispersal by the atmosphere, its property of killing both pests and their enemies, and the evolution of resistant strains, have combined to create a crisis in the environment. The reaction has been to stop spraying some crops and to ban the use of DDT in some countries. Probably the correct solution, though, is to use pesticides carefully, applying them very locally (by hand if possible) to places where pest outbreaks are threatening, and to introduce or encourage enemies of the pests. This is called "integrated control." It is the hope of the future.

Since this article concerns pure ecology, it is probably worth distinguishing between pure and applied ecology. Applied ecologists are concerned with such problems as controlling pests and maximizing the yield from populations. Pure ecologists study interactions among individuals in a population of organisms, among populations, and between populations and their environments. (A population is a more or less defined group of organisms that belong to the same species.)

A brief indication of how some ecologists spend their time may be in order here. One of us (Connell) became interested in discovering what determines the distribution on the rocky seashore of a species of barnacle. He made frequent visits to the shore, photographed the positions of barnacles, counted their numbers at different levels on the shore at different life stages, noted the density and positions of predators, other barnacle species, and so forth. He developed hypotheses (in one area, that the limit to distribution is set by the presence of another barnacle species; in another, that beyond a certain height on the seashore a snail species eats them all) and tested the ideas by various experiments such as placing cages on the shore to exclude predators or removing the competing species. This work went on for several years and has now firmly established the two hypotheses.

Murdoch spent the past three years in the laboratory examining an idea about predators. The idea was that predators keep the numbers of their various prey species stable by attacking very heavily whichever species is most abundant. (The idea is a bit more complicated than that, but that is approximately it.) This entailed setting up experiments where different predators were offered different mixtures of two prey species at a variety of densities, and then counting the number eaten of each species. These experiments led to others, in order to test different sub-hypotheses. The conclusion was that predators would "switch" only under very particular conditions.

Other ecologists spend long periods in the field trying to measure what happens to the vegetable material in a field. How much is produced and what percentage goes to rabbits, mice, insects? What percentage of the total weight of mice produced (biomass) is eaten by weasels and how efficient are weasels at converting mouse biomass to weasel biomass? Such work takes a great deal of time, estimates are rough, shaky assumptions have to be made, and in the end we have only approximate answers.

Other ecologists try to build mathematical models which might suggest how a community or some subset of a community comes to have the structure which our rough measurements tell us it may have. In pursuing all these activities they hope to build models of how nature works. The models, while not being copies of nature, should catch the essence of some process in nature and serve as a basis for explaining the phenomena that have been observed. They hope these models will be generally, though not necessarily universally, applicable. They study particular systems in the hope that these systems are not in all respects, or even in their major aspects, unique. Thus the aspirations of ecologists are not different from those of any other scientists.

Ecologists face problems which make their task difficult and at times apparently insurmountable. It is a young science, probably not older than forty years; consequently, much of it is still descriptive. It deals with systems which are depressingly complex, affected by dozens of variables which may all interact in a very large number of ways. Rather than taking a census of them, these systems must be sampled. Ecology is one of the few disciplines in biology in which it is not clear that removing portions of the problem to the laboratory for experimentation is an appropriate technique. It may be that the necessary simplification this involves removes exactly the elements from the system which determine how it functions. Yet field experiments are difficult to do and usually hard to interpret. Ecology, moreover, is the only field of biology which is not simply a matter of applied physics and chemistry. The great advances in molecular biology resulted from physicists looking at biological systems (such as DNA), whose basic configuration is explicable in terms of the positions of atoms. But the individual or the population is the basic unit in ecology. It seems certain, then, that a direct extension of physics and chemistry will not help ecologists.

Finally, there is the problem that each ecological situation is different from every other one, with a history all its own; ecological systems, to use a mathematical analogy, are non-Markovian, which is to say that a knowledge of both the past and the present is necessary in order to predict the future. Unlike a great deal of physics, ecology is not independent of time or place. As a consequence, the discipline does not cast up broad generalizations. All this is not a complete list of the general problems ecologists face, but it may be enough to provide a feeling for the difficulty of the subject.

Ecologists, though, do have something to show for forty years' work. These are some of the general conclusions they have reached. (Not all ecologists, by any means, would agree that they are generally applicable—and those who do agree would admit that exceptions occur—but they are the kind of basic conclusions that many ecologists would hope to be able to establish.)

———Populations of most species have negative feedback processes which keep their numbers within relatively narrow limits. If the species itself does not possess such features, or even if it does, the community in which it exists acts to regulate numbers, for example, through the action of predators. (Such a statement obviously is not precise, e.g., how narrow are "relatively narrow limits"? A measure of ecology's success, or lack of it, is that, in forty years, there are no more than a half-dozen populations in which regulation has been adequately demonstrated; and the basis for belief in regulation is either faith or very general observations, such as the fact that most species are not so abundant that they are considered pests.)

———The laws of physics lead to derivative statements in ecology. For example, the law that matter cycles through the ecosystem, to be used again and again. Or the law that energy from the sun is trapped by plants through photosynthesis, moves up the food chain to herbivores and then to carnivores as matter, losing energy at each successive conversion so that there is generally less energy and biomass in higher food levels than in lower ones. Ecologists have tried to take such truths from physics and construct more truly ecological generalities from them. Thus, to stay with the same example, it appears likely that there are never more than five links in any one chain of conversions from plant to top predator.

———It is probably true, on a given piece of the earth and provided that the climate doesn't change, that a "climax" ecosystem will develop which is characteristic of the area's particular features and that places with similar features will develop similar ecosystems if left undisturbed. Characteristically, a "succession" from rather simple and short-lived communities to more complex and more persistent communities will occur, though there may be a reduction in the complexity of the final community. We use "final" to mean that a characteristic community will be found there for many generations. We might go further and say that during the period of development disturbances of the community will result in its complexity being reduced. (Again, such statements will certainly arouse the dissent of some ecologists.)

———Finally, most ecologists would agree that complex communities are more stable than simple communities. This statement illustrates the difficulties faced by theoretical ecologists. Take some of its implications: What is complexity and what is stability in an ecological setting? Charles Elton embodied the idea in a simple, practical, and easily understood way. He argued that England should maintain the hedgerows between its fields because these were complex islands in a simple agricultural sea and contained a reservoir of insect and other predators which helped to keep down pest populations. The idea here seems quite clear. Ecologists, though, want a more precise exposition of the implications of the statement. What kind of complexity? What is stability?

Physical complexity, by providing hiding places for prey, may increase stability. Certainly biological complexity in general is thought to lead to stability—more species or more interspecific interactions, more stability. But we may ask, more species of what sort? Here a variety of answers is available. It has been suggested that complex communities are stable, i.e. able to resist invasion by species new to the area, by having all the "niches" filled. Thus sheer numbers of kinds of organisms in all food levels were considered the appropriate sort of complexity. To keep the numbers of prey stable, the most likely candidates are predators. Now other questions arise: Do we just want more species of predators? Do we want more species of predators which are very specific in the prey they eat, implying that prey are stabilized by having many species feed on them? Do we want predators which are very general and attack many prey species, so that we still have a large number of interspecific interactions which are made up in a different way? The answer is not obvious, and indeed there is disagreement on it. Furthermore, if one studies the way some predators react to changes in the numbers of their prey, their short-term responses are such as to cause *instability*. Thus only some types of biological complexity may produce stability.

What do we mean by stability? In the examples cited, we have meant numerical constancy through time, but this is by no means the only meaning. It has even been suggested that numerical *in*constancy is a criterion for stability. Stability might also mean that the same species persist in the same area over long periods, showing the same sort of interspecific interactions (community stability). A community or population might be considered stable because it does not change in response to a great deal of environmental pressure, or because it changes but quickly returns to its original state when the disturbing force is removed. It is worth noting that if a population or community is observed merely not to change, we cannot tell whether this is owing to its ability to resist perturbing factors or merely to the absence of such factors. If we want to know about the *mechanisms* which might lead to the truth of our original statement, "complexity leads to stability," all the above points are important.

This general statement about complexity and stability rests upon the kind of observation readily apparent to most intelligent laymen.

Thus simple agricultural systems seem to be much more subject to outbreaks of herbivores than the surrounding countryside. Ecosystems in the tropics appear to be more stable than in the simpler temperate zone. In turn the temperate zone seems to be more stable than the Arctic. This seems to be mainly an article of faith. However, even this classic sort of evidence is questioned—for example, small mammals may actually be more unstable numerically in the United States than in the much simpler Arctic environment. Other evidence comes from the laboratory. If one takes small species of prey and predator—for example, two single-celled animals or two small mites—and begins culturing them together, the numbers of prey and predators fluctuate wildly and then both become extinct quickly, for the predators exhaust their food source. "Simple" predator-prey systems tend to be unstable. There is some evidence that if physical complexity is added the system may become more stable. From these examples of the generalizations ecologists have arrived at, an important question emerges. Even if we dispense with the idea that ecologists are some sort of environmental engineers and compare them to the pure physicists who provide scientific rules for engineers, do the tentative understandings we have outlined provide a sound basis for action by those who would manage the environment? It is self-evident that they do not.

This conclusion seems to be implied in a quotation from an article published in *Time* on the environment, which underlines the point that application of the ecologist's work is not the solution to the environmental crisis. According to *Time*:

> Crawford S. Holling was once immersed in rather abstract research at the University of British Columbia—mathematical models of the relationship between predators and their prey. "Three years ago, I got stark terrified at what was going on in the world and gave it up." Now he heads the university's interdepartmental studies of land and water use, which involve agriculture, economics, forestry, geography, and regional planning. "What got me started on this," says Holling, "were the profound and striking similarities between ecological systems and the activities of man: between predators and land speculators; between animal-population growth and economic growth; between plant dispersal and the diffusion of people, ideas, and money."

The "rather abstract research" was ecology. Holling's testimony is that it would not provide a solution. Yet, by and large, ecologists are concerned and probably have the best understanding of the problem.

We submit that ecology as such probably cannot do what many

people expect it to do; it cannot provide a set of "rules" of the kind needed to manage the environment. Nevertheless, ecologists have a great responsibility to help solve the crisis; the solution they offer should be founded on a basic "ecological attitude." Ecologists are likely to be aware of the consequences of environmental manipulation; possibly most important, they are ready to deal with the environmental problem since their basic ecological attitude is itself the solution to the problem. Interestingly enough, the supporting data do not generally come from our "abstract research" but from massive uncontrolled "experiments" done in the name of development.

These attitudes and data, plus obvious manifestations of physical laws, determine what the ecologist has to say on the problem and constitute what might be called environmental knowledge. Some examples of this knowledge follow, though this is not to be taken as an encapsulation of the ecologist's wisdom.

———Whatever is done to the environment is likely to have repercussions in other places and at other times. Because of the characteristic problems of ecology some of the effects are bound to be unpredictable in practice, if not in principle. Furthermore, because of the characteristic time-dependence problem, the effects may not be measurable for years—possibly not for decades.

———If man's actions are massive enough, drastic enough, or of the right sort, they will cause changes which are irreversible since the genetic material of extinct species cannot be reconstituted. Even if species are not driven to extinction, changes may occur in the ecosystem which prevent a recurrence of the events which produced the community. Such irreversible changes will almost always produce a simplification of the environment.

———The environment is finite and our non-renewable resources are finite. When the stocks run out we will have to recycle what we have used.

———The capacity of the environment to act as a sink for our total waste, to absorb it and recycle it so that it does not accumulate as pollution, is limited. In many instances, that limit has already been passed. It seems clear that when limits are passed, fairly gross effects occur, some of which are predictable, some of which are not. These effects result in significant alterations in environmental conditions (global weather, ocean productivity). Such changes are almost always bad since organisms have evolved and ecosystems have developed for existing conditions. We impose rates of change on the environment which are too great for biological systems to cope with.

———In such a finite world and under present conditions, an increasing population can only worsen matters. For a stationary population, an increase in standard of living can only mean an increase in the use of limited resources, the destruction of the environment, and the choking of the environmental sinks.

There are two ways of attacking the environmental crisis. The first approach is technology; the second is to reverse the trends which got us into the crisis in the first place and to alter the structure of our society so that an equilibrium between human population and the capacities of the environment can be established.

There are three main dangers in a technological approach to the environmental crisis. The first threatens the environment in the short term, the second concerns ecologists themselves, and the third, which concerns the general public attitude, is a threat to the environment in the long term.

Our basic premise is that, by its nature, technology is a system for manufacturing the need for more technology. When this is combined with an economic system whose major goal is growth, the result is a society in which conspicuous production of garbage is the highest social virtue. If our premise is correct, it is unlikely we can solve our present problems by using technology. As an example, we might consider nuclear power plants as a "clean" alternative to which we can increasingly turn. But nuclear power plants inevitably produce radioactive waste; this problem will grow at an enormous rate, and we are not competent to handle it safely. In addition, a whole new set of problems arises when all these plants produce thermal pollution. Technology merely substitutes one sort of pollution for another.

There is a more subtle danger inherent in the technological approach. The automobile is a blight on Southern California's landscape. It might be thought that ecologists should concern themselves with encouraging the development of technology to cut down the emission of pollutants from the internal combustion engine. Yet that might only serve to give the public the impression that something is being done about the problem and that it can therefore confidently await its solution. Nothing significant could be accomplished in any case because the increasing number of cars ensures an undiminishing smog problem.

Tinkering with technology is essentially equivalent to oiling its wheels. The very act of making minor alterations, in order to placate the public, actually allows the general development of technology to proceed unhindered, only increasing the environmental problems it causes. This is what sociologists have called a "pseudo-event." That is, activities go on which give the appearance of tackling the problem; they will not, of course, solve it but only remove public pressure for a solution.

Tinkering also distracts the ecologist from his real job. It is the ecologist's job, as a general rule, to oppose growth and "progress." He cannot set about convincing the public of the correctness of this position if in the meantime he is putting his shoulder behind the wheel of technology. The political power system has a long tradition of buying off its critics, and the ecologist is liable to wind up perennially compromising his position, thereby merely slowing down slightly or redirecting the onslaught of technology.

The pressures on the ecologist to provide "tinkering" solutions will continue to be quite strong. Pleas for a change of values, for a change to a non-growth, equilibrium economy seem naive. The government, expecting sophistication from its "experts," will probably receive such advice coolly. Furthermore, ecologists themselves are painfully aware of how immature their science is and generally take every opportunity to cover up this fact with a cloud of obfuscating pseudo-sophistication. They delight in turning prosaic facts and ideas into esoteric jargon. Where possible, they embroider the structure with mathematics and the language of cybernetics and systems analysis, which is sometimes useful but frequently is merely confusing. Such sophistication is easily come by in suggesting technological solutions.

Finally, there is always the danger that in becoming a governmental consultant, the ecologist will aim his sights at the wrong target. The history of the Washington "expert" is that he is called in to make alterations in the model already decided upon by the policymakers. It would be interesting to know what proportion of scientific advice has ever produced a change in ends rather than in means. We suspect it is minute. But the ecologist ought not to concern himself with less than such a change; he must change the model itself.

We should point out that we are not, for example, against substituting a steam-driven car for a gas-driven car. Our contention is that by changing public attitudes the ecologist can do something much more fundamental. In addition, by changing these attitudes he may even make it easier to force the introduction of "cleaner" technology, since this also is largely a *political* decision. This certainly seems to be so in the example of the steam-driven car.

We do not believe that the ecologist has anything really new to say. His task, rather, is to inculcate in the government and the people basic ecological attitudes. The population must come, and very soon, to appreciate certain basic notions. For example: a finite world cannot support or withstand a continually expanding population and technology; there are limits to the capacity of environmental sinks; ecosystems are sets of interacting entities and there is no "treatment" which does not have "side effects" (e.g. the Aswan Dam); we cannot continually simplify systems and expect them to remain stable, and once they do become unstable there is a tendency for instability to increase with time. Each child should grow up knowing and understanding his place in the environment and the possible consequences of his interaction with it.

In short, the ecologist must convince the population that the only solution to the problem of growth is not to grow. This applies to population and, unless the population is declining, to its standard of living. It should be clear by now that "standard of living" is probably beginning to have an inverse relationship to the quality of life. An increase in the gross national product must be construed, from the ecological point of view, as disastrous. (The case of underdeveloped countries, of course, is different.)

We do not minimize the difficulties in changing the main driving force in life. The point of view of the ecologist, however, should be subversive; it has to be subversive or the ecologist will become merely subservient. Such a change in values and structure will have profound consequences. For example, economists, with a few notable exceptions, do not seem to have given any thought to the possibility or desirability of a stationary economy. Businessmen, and most economists, think that growth is good, stagnation or regression is bad. Can an equilibrium be set up with the environment in a system having this philosophy? The problem of converting to non-growth is present in socialist countries too, of course, but we must ask if corporate capitalism, by its nature, can accommodate such a change and still retain its major features. By contrast, if there are any ecological laws at all, we believe the ecologists' notion of the inevitability of an equilibrium between man and the environment is such a law.

We would like to modify some details of this general stand. Especially after the necessary basic changes are put in motion, there *are* things ecologists as "experts" can do: some of them are sophisticated and others, in a very broad sense, may even be technological. Certainly, determining the "optimum" U.S. population will require sophisticated techniques. Ecologists, willy-nilly, will have to take a central role in advising on the management of the environment. They already are beginning to do this. The characteristics of ecology here determine that this advice, to be good, will be to some extent sophisticated to fit particular cases. Thus good management will depend on long-term studies of *particular* areas, since ecological situations are both time-dependent and locale-dependent. These two features also ensure that there will be a sizable time-lag between posing the question and receiving the ecological advice, and a major job of the ecologists will be to make the existence of such lags known to policymakers.

Ecologists sometimes will have to apply technology. As one instance, integrated pest control (that is, basically biological control with occasional small-scale use of pesticides) will surely replace chemical control, and integrated pest control can be considered biological technology. In this area there is some promise that sophisticated computer modeling techniques applied to strategies of pest control may help us design better techniques. The banning of DDT, for example, could no doubt be a laudable victory in the war to save the environment, but it would be disastrous to mistake a symbolic victory like this for winning the war itself.

STUDY QUESTIONS

1. What is the relationship between environment and ecology?
2. Is the ecological crisis limited to any specific part of the globe?
3. What are the fallacies in the thinking of those who feel we can "solve" our ecological problems?
4. What effect has the Aswan Dam had on sardines in the Mediterranean?
5. In what way is DDT a mixed blessing?
6. What are the dangers of spraying pesticides in large areas?
7. What is the distinction between pure and applied ecology?
8. Why are complex communities more stable than simple communities?
9. What are the implications of saying "the environment is finite"?
10. Should ecologists become governmental consultants?

SUGGESTIONS FOR WRITING

1. The authors say again and again that the idea that technology may be able to get us out of our ecological mess should be discouraged: the public would begin to believe there is an imminent solution. How do you feel about this advice? Does it seem desirable to discourage faith in technology?

2. One of the subjects of the article is the relationship between science (ecologists) and government. Analyze the authors' case, decide precisely what they understand that relationship to be, and then offer alternatives to it. How might ecologists be involved in government without harm being done to the public?

3. "Our contention," say the authors, "is that by changing public attitudes the ecologist can do something . . . fundamental." They suggest that changing public opinion would be much more effective than winning government over or making new laws. Do you agree?

4. The authors also say that the only solution to growth is not to grow. Why is this concept so difficult for most people to accept? How can we overcome the public prejudice that favors the opposite view? Write a brief essay on the importance of stopping rampant growth.

5. If the ecologists convince government that our population must be controlled, and if ecologists are named government consultants, recommending specific controls at specific times, what would the moral implications of being an ecologist actually be? Is there any kind of training that would adequately develop his moral awareness? Explain.

POPULATION: A PERSONAL PERSPECTIVE

Anne Funkhouser

The population explosion is not something we must look for in the future: it is here now. The famines have not yet begun but, given our present rate of population growth, they are predicted for late 1975. If we have taken no other measures by then, famine will prove an effective—though somewhat involuntary—means of population control.

With increasing frequency we are being exposed to the grim statistics of population increase and its attendant consequences of famine, social unrest, pollution of air, water, soil and animal life (including humans), and irretrievable loss of natural resources. Biologists have long been aware of the basic principle of population increase whereby under appropriate conditions a population increases in a logarithmic fashion—the rate of increase is slow at first, but becomes progressively more rapid. Regardless of the date we choose for the beginning of man, his rate of increase has been slow until the last hundred years. World population did not reach one billion until about 1850, but by 1950 it had reached two-and-a-half billion, and at this rate will at least double its present three-and-a-half billion by the year 2000.

The reason lies partly in one of man's most humane efforts—his concern for decreasing the death rate. Under natural conditions, predation, lack of food, and disease will take their toll to keep population size more or less stable. Until recently man had famine and plagues to keep his numbers in check. The more people you save from disease, the more people will be around to have babies. People are not reproducing more; there are simply more of them surviving in each generation.

POPULATION: A PERSONAL PERSPECTIVE   Reprinted from the October 1969 issue of *Journal of the American Association of University Women* by permission of *Journal of the American Association of University Women.*

Now the possible consequences of man's numbers have become so awesome as to be almost unbelievable. Aside from the obvious crowding and environmental pollution there are subtle, even more catastrophic possibilities. For example, we are threatening photosynthetic activity (our *only* source of oxygen) to such an extent that the oxygen content of the atmosphere may actually decrease. The effect, if it does not occur suddenly (as has been suggested), would be the same as moving everyone to higher and higher altitudes, which would increase death rates from a variety of cardiac and respiratory disorders. This would not be my choice of a means for alleviating the population crisis.

Just as we have been bombarded with the unhappy "facts" of the population problem, so we are also exposed to the eternal optimists with "solutions." However, even casual examination of most of these solutions shows them to be specious—there is just so much arable land in the world and it can produce just so much food; there is just so much water; we can use just so much fertilizer and pesticides without endangering the environment; the notion of "farming the seas" is so far from practicality at present that it is not worth consideration; and the idea of "colonizing space" is downright silly. *The only means of averting extinction by overpopulation lies in equalizing the birth and death rates.*

Because women have babies and raise them, and because women are particularly concerned about the fate of their babies, there are certain aspects of this problem which are of special importance to women. Although the United States is certainly a developed country, we are by no means immune from overpopulation. Since most of us must limit our activities to the country and community in which we live, I would like to examine one particular proposal for dealing with U.S. population, and make some tentative suggestions as to areas of interest to women and in which their action could be particularly effective.

In January 1969, the President's Commission on Population and Family Planning issued a report which urged immediate policies to begin resolution of problems of population increase. Some of these recommendations have been acted upon, and there is every reason to believe that more will be in the near future. In the face of constant reminders of the inevitable results of our exploding human population, we may be cheered that the government is finally going to "do something about it." But should we be so optimistic? Does the answer to the problems of our exploding population lie in expanding "family planning" programs to make information available to "all American women who want but cannot afford it"? What are the assumptions upon which the Commission's report is based? What are the facts to substantiate these assumptions? Is American population growth based only on the fertility of the poor and uneducated? Are "family planning" programs the most effective means of reducing our population growth? Most important, will making "family planning" information available to all segments of the population significantly reduce the U.S. birth rate?

To designate the poor and uneducated as the recipients of this program assumes that they desire small families but lack the means of achieving them. A massive amount of data clearly indicates that families in the lower socio-economic levels have larger families because they want larger families. Differences in *desired* family size are correlated with both educational level and economic status, and those differences have existed as long as such information has been available. The poor and uneducated *want* larger families than the more affluent and better educated.

In addition, the percentages of both men and women in lower socio-economic groups who approve birth control is lower than among the better educated and more affluent. Those who are supposed to need this information most are least in favor of a policy which would make it available.

A 1966 Gallup Poll question: "Do you think birth control pills should be made available free to all women on relief who are of child-bearing age?" asks directly about the policy of birth control for the poor. Among women, the percentages of those in favor drop from 75% for the college educated to 59% for those of grade school education, and for men from 82% for those with a college education to 38% for those with no more than a grade school education. A program which is unacceptable to those for whom it is designed can hardly be expected to meet with overwhelming success.

A number of inferences can be drawn from the inverse correlation between acceptability of birth control and socio-economic level. Almost all of us have grown up with the idea that progress is equated with growth, and our economy has been devoted to the notion of increase. At the present time, we have difficulty accepting the fact that a halt, or even a decrease, in population size may not only be "good," but may be the only means of averting disaster. Is it possible that among the less well educated, the older virtues of "increase" have not given way to the realization that some kinds of growth are harmful, simply because these people have never encountered the arguments against growth? It is hard enough to convince a college freshman of the consequences of logarithmic increase, of the fact that his or her third child will adversely affect population as a whole, of even a few of the far-reaching results of indiscriminate reproduction. Perhaps education plays more of a role in halting population increase than the Commission report has suggested.

The Commission report emphasizes "family planning" (which is nothing but a euphemism for contraceptive information), rather than population control which has too many unpleasant connotations. All that "family planning" involves is allowing families to choose the number of children they want, and give them the means of spacing these children if they so desire. Although lower income families tend to choose slightly larger families than the more affluent, the most frightening statistics are those relating to desired family size regardless of socio-economic level. In the U.S. from 1952 to the present, *the average ideal family size desired by all non-Catholic women was more than three children.* Any discussion of population must lead to a goal of zero population growth because any growth continued long enough will use up the life supporting resources of the earth. Only by reducing the average family size to one less than that desired by the highest socio-economic group can we expect to achieve population stability. (I am assuming that no reasonable person or nation would deliberately choose wars, plagues or famine as a means of controlling population.) One is left to wonder if education in the simple arithmetic of the results of three children per family should not immediately be presented to all socio-economic levels.

Furthermore, by emphasizing *family* planning the Commission report automatically excludes the unmarried. It is particularly unfortunate that no provision is made for very young women because government statistics show that 41% of the illegitimate babies born in the United States are to women 19 years of age and younger. To reduce this number requires a strong program of sex education in junior and senior high schools. We are all aware that this would meet with strong opposition from many sides, and the degree of this opposition can be judged by answers to another 1966 Gallup Poll question: "Do you think they (the pills) should be made available to teen-age girls?" Only slightly more than 30% of college educated men in the upper income levels approved, and only 13% of those in lower educational and economic levels. The *highest* percentage of approval from women was only about 15%.

Providing birth control pills for young women involves far more than is usually implied in "family planning," and of course implies more than is usually meant by sex education. However, the magnitude of the problem is such that no reasonable avenue of assistance should be disregarded for outmoded reasons. Our culture depends too strongly on sex-oriented roles to accept the notion that young, unmarried women may actually need contraceptive devices. It is pointless to belabor the idea that in our society young women are not expected to require contraceptive information until marriage, and once married they are under strong pressure to have a family, usually to the exclusion of a career. But it is patently obvious that teen-age girls *do* have babies and so *do* need contraceptive devices and information on why and how to use them. Our attitudes on this subject need reordering to bring them more in keeping with reality. I am well aware that this may be simply stated, but will require enormous personal and societal readjustment.

This is not the place to more than suggest that the amount of variation allowed within sex roles is rather narrowly restricted by society. All persons are expected to conform to certain ranges of "normality" and deviations are ostracized. As long as this direct and indirect coercion includes reproduction, we are compounding our problem by adding unnecessarily to population growth. With an outlook prejudiced by my discipline, I have felt that variation from the usual sex role was biologically inconsistent. But arguments based on the biology of lower animals are not necessarily applicable to man, and I am forced to ask what is really "wrong" with a female sex role that does not follow the reproductively-oriented pattern of lower animals? In addition, pressure on women to fulfill a reproductive occupational role at the expense of a career is an even more potent force increasing population. Despite the enormous strides made in recent years, the usual training of girls does not emphasize creative satisfactions outside of motherhood; job opportunities for women are not equal to those for men and salary scales for the same jobs are often discriminatory. Society's rewards for women are still geared to homemaking and motherhood, and so long as this is true it is unreasonable to expect women to reduce the number of their children and so deliberately reduce this area of socially acceptable satisfaction. Any program of population control must include means for broadening the occupational roles of women.

The logical extension of the idea of a baby "only when you want it and if you want it" would allow a woman to choose not to have a baby if she finds herself pregnant. No currently known birth control method is 100% effective. Even in the most "planned" family, accidents may happen, and the only way to avoid these unnecessary and unwanted additions to the population is to make abortion readily available to all who wish it. Our abortion laws and the sickly overlay of "morality" that surrounds them are in the same category as objections to sex education and resistance to provision of contraceptive devices to the unmarried. The number of people on the earth today has quite suddenly made these laws and the reasons for them outdated and actually dangerous to our continued existence.

However, assuming that all segments of the population are exposed to the highest level of education in all aspects of the population crisis and that a wide variety of contraceptive methods is available to everyone, there will still be accidents which may not be terminated by abortion and there will still exist a discrepancy between those who may have and not want children, and those who want but cannot have them. A subject often overlooked in discussions of population is that of adoption. Although they vary significantly from state to state, our adoption laws in too many areas seem designed to prevent adoption. An argument against birth control which may be of great cogency to some women is that they simply love children and would not be satisfied with only two. I cannot deny the validity of this argument. But if adoption laws were less rigid, and most important, if the misplaced distinction between biological and adoptive children were diminished, such women could find fulfillment in as many children as the family felt it could afford simply by adopting them. The biological and psychological effects of malnutrition and of inadequate human interaction on very young children (under one year) have been abundantly documented. Either of those conditions can produce permanent impairment of normal human functioning. Our adoption laws may have been designed to protect children, but in operation they may insure that the child cannot develop his full human potential by preventing him from joining a family at the earliest possible age.

The facts are incontrovertible—human reproduction is in excess of human death and the numbers of human beings are increasing more rapidly than the means of feeding them. We are past the point where we can sit back in idleness hoping for a technological solution. The scope of the problem is such that there is no single solution, certainly no technological solution. At first glance, human reproduction may appear to be a bio-medical problem, but simply because we are human beings rather than some other animal, any program dealing with population must extend into the realms of psychology, sociology, politics, economics, education—virtually all aspects of human endeavor.

Many women have a feeling of hopelessness in the face of such enormity and imagine they can do nothing as individuals. But until we exterminate ourselves, it is my personal conviction that we must consider the individual as the ultimate focus of our attention, and the actions of each individual as vitally important to survival. There is a host of possibilities for action: in politics, even if this is no more than writing letters to those in a position to make decisions; in education, even if we only educate our children and grandchildren; in becoming aware of the consequences of overpopulation and encouraging the addition of this material to school curricula at all levels; in promoting long overdue changes in abortion and adoption laws; in fighting for the preservation of what we still have in natural resources; in educating ourselves and not being afraid to change our minds about such things as sex education, abortion and the Pill for everyone who may need them regardless of age or marital status; in making such a difficult personal decision as not to have a third child because this dooms someone else's child to death by starvation.

Women have a very special role in combating population increase. They are fighting not only for their own lives, but for a decent life for the children they are raising. Inertia will inevitably bring a horrible kind of defeat. We need courage and luck. I wish us both.

STUDY QUESTIONS

1. What are the population predictions for the year 2000?
2. Why is oxygen a factor in population control?
3. The author is skeptical about the optimists who have counseled us not to be alarmed. Why? Is she right?
4. In the United States, is population control in any way linked to socio-economic status?
5. Why is the term "family planning" preferable to "population control"?
6. Is sex education a factor in family planning?
7. The author makes some references to the "lower animals" when talking about the female sex role. Why?
8. Why does the author defend abortion as a method of birth control?
9. Why does the author speak directly to women? Is she justified?
10. What are the author's positions on adoption?

SUGGESTIONS FOR WRITING

1. How do you feel about the idea of giving birth control pills to all girls when they reach puberty? Write an essay that defends or attacks this proposition. Take into account the major moral, religious, emotional, and populational factors.
2. The author says that soon one of the most important and difficult decisions a woman will have to make is not to have a third child. If a woman bears more than two children, she will be condemning another woman's already born child to starvation. How do you react to this? Would you be willing to make that decision? Would most other people? Base your judgment of the public's reaction on details from the article and from your general experience.
3. The different social classes have different attitudes on the subject of population control. The lowest socio-economic classes seem to resent all forms of birth control except abstention. Try to explain why this difference exists. Do you see any indications that class attitudes and behavior are changing?
4. A tremendous emphasis is placed on convincing individuals to adopt certain views and practices voluntarily. Is it possible that population control is no longer a voluntary matter? Is it possible that government ought to be regulating the number of children we may have, as well as the number of cars we may use and the number of pollutant chemicals we may utilize?
5. In this article, abortion is treated as just another form of birth control. The author deplores the "sickly overlay of 'morality' that surrounds" our abortion laws—which generally prevent abortion even for those who wish it. What do you think is right in this instance? Should an abortion be freely available for anyone who wishes it? Should abortions be mandatory in some instances? Or should they never be permitted?

THE ENVIRONMENTAL CRISIS: FIVE FACTORS

Kenneth E. F. Watt

Understandably, discussions of the environmental crisis are prone to complexity. In this article, however, the author boils the issues down to five areas of concern. Although simply stated, his indictment of such capitalistic principles as competition and the profit motive suggests that some very difficult changes must be made.

1.   A basic measure of success in a free enterprise capitalistic economy is profit. All investors, myself included, evaluate alternative investment strategies on the basis of their prospective growth in profitability. Profit, in turn, is simply the difference between the gross income from any activity, and the overhead incurred as a consequence of conducting that activity. Thus, if the nature of the game is to maximize profit, then this can be achieved simply by minimizing the overhead required to earn a unit of profit.

What never seems to have been spelled out clearly are the implications of the profit motive for the management of resources and the preservation of the environment. Consider a situation in which a resource will last 60 years if we do not exploit it intensively, or 20 years if we exploit it intensively. Suppose that the equipment to harvest that resource lasts only 20 years. Suppose, further, that we have the option of using up the resource in 20 years, or in 60 years. Clearly, if we use the resource up in 20 years, our overhead will only include the cost of purchasing one set of equipment; if we take 60 years to use up the resource, the equipment must be replaced twice, which increases the overhead.

This is, of course, a highly oversimplified abstract example, but in general, the most profitable way to exploit any resource is to use it up just as quickly as possible. The only reason that this principle has

THE ENVIRONMENTAL CRISIS: FIVE FACTORS   Reprinted from the April–May 1970 issue of *Motive* by permission of *Motive*, copyright 1970.

rarely been pointed out is that it has never been technologically feasible to wipe out a resource extremely quickly.

Now is the foregoing simply nonsense, or does the historical record in fact indicate that resources are exploited as fast as they can possibly be used? There are a large number of instances in which the historical record shows that a resource was used up just as quickly as it could possibly be used, completely without regard for making the resource last. Indeed, the historical record shows that, in many instances, a resource was not only used up as quickly as it could possibly be exploited, but also there was an immense waste involved in the exploitation.

This has been true for the whaling industry, the sealing industry, the buffalo hunting in the American West and the petroleum industry. In the case of the buffalo, only 75 pounds of meat was actually eaten from most buffalo that were used for food after being shot. In the case of petroleum, there is no imaginable technique that humanity could devise to burn it up faster. We use large, unnecessarily inefficient engines in our cars—engines delivering low mileage per gallon —and we ride one person per car, instead of 80 per bus wherever possible. Just as a herd of 80 million buffalo was reduced to a few dozen animals in 88 years, the world supply of petroleum will be used up in about 130 years (beginning about 1880).

In other words, a key element in the profit motive is that it doesn't provide humanity with any motive to save anything. Some legal, governmental and institutional innovations are therefore necessary to protect us from the free operation of the profit motive, so that enough of everything is left on earth to allow humanity to survive. This may sound like an extreme statement, but a little thought will show that there is nothing in the profit motive by itself that will guarantee the survival of anything; guaranteeing survival of anything is not the reason for the profit motive. The failure of the profit motive to allow survival of any resource is a principle that shows up repeatedly in a large number of historical scenarios.

In looking for solutions to these problems, the following possibilities seem feasible. First, we need a modification of the capital gains tax system under which income derived from investments held over six months is taxable as capital gains. It turns out that a very high proportion of all stocks are sold shortly after six months. Thus, the six-month period is far too short; if it were extended to ten years, for example, investors would be encouraged to take the long view and would not invest in corporations following self-destructive policies (such as elimination of the resources they exploit).

A second method of conserving the environment is through rigidly enforced quota systems on resources taken from such common property resources as the oceans. If we had a system of international law which would govern the oceans, and if all nations adhered to the law, and it was enforced, the blue whales would not now be almost extinct.

Third, we need a system of land banks, in which certain land parcels are set aside for perpetuity for a certain purpose, with no subtractions from these banks under any circumstances. For example, land parcels with superb scenic value and beachfront property would be set aside for recreational use, prime agricultural land would be set aside for agricultural use, and so on. At present, prime agricultural and recreational land is being converted to urban use, when hillsides would be better sites for urban centers. Each part of the world should decide on its optimum population, then set aside enough prime agricultural land to guarantee agricultural self-sufficiency for that population for perpetuity. Any part of the world which plans on having its food needs supplied by some other part will be in for a rude surprise if it turns out that many parts of the world are operating on this same strategy.

2.   Another fundamental problem with our relationship to the environment is that the human population, unlike all other populations, does not function as a self-regulating system which maintains itself with some equilibrium of population density. Rather, the human population operates as a system which is constantly going out of control. Consider a city. If the city were a living organism, or a population of organisms, it would function as follows: When the city grew too large for the surrounding resources (farmland), natural forces would operate to make the city contract in population size and area until it could be supported by the surrounding resources. This would happen, in the case of a natural population, by a decrease in the birth rate and an increase in the death rate which, in combination, would produce a sharp reduction in the population size.

However, in the case of the human population in a city, if it becomes too large for the present area of the city, zoning and taxation systems are manipulated until the farmers owning the farmland adjacent to the city find it uneconomic to continue farming and sell their land for tract housing developments. This process has worked in many places to this point in history, because the city could purchase food from some other farmland located a greater distance away from the city. However, two processes are now converging to trap us in a vise. On the one hand, as the population grows larger, there is an increasing need for food; on the other hand, as the urban population grows and cities expand, about two tenths of an acre of prime farmland are converted from agricultural to urban use for each person added to the urban population. In modern America, one person added to the population means one person added to the urban population, because there is a constant migration away from rural America.

This problem can be dealt with by tightening up the system of zoning and taxation, so we cut down on rezoning of farmland at the urban perimeter. Also, we need master land plans for each state and a system of land banks, as previously mentioned.

3. Another important environmental problem is that all planning is done by agencies which have a vested interest to proceed with some project. Thus, highway departments evaluate highway plans, the Army Corps of Engineers evaluates its own plans, and so on. A fundamental institutional decision-making defect is hidden in this process. In any objective evaluation of alternative strategy decisions, in which long-term costs and benefits are assigned to each option and the most attractive option chosen on that basis, one of the most important options is taking no action at all.

That is, if a highway department is considering building a freeway down the length of a valley or over a mountain, one of the options considered should be not to build the highway. It often turns out that no action is the best action. For example, if the planners for the Aswan High Dam had considered not building the dam at all, they would have seen that, over a period of one or more centuries, this was the option with the most attractive benefit/cost ratio.

The difficulty at present is that, for many kinds of decision-making, the only staffs with the expertise to make professional evaluations of different options are in those organizations which are already committed to action. Thus, all the people involved in making decisions are in fact a vested interest group. Many recent historical examples show very clearly that vested interest groups can be something less than totally objective about decision-making. The decisions of the Central Intelligence Agency and the military with respect to the Bay of Pigs and Vietnam are two examples.

One solution to this difficulty is to set up a new agency, with an adequate budget and a large staff of experts, to serve as an environmental ombudsman. This agency would have to review and approve all plans for any activity in the environmental area. Thus, the decision to go ahead with the S.S.T., offshore drilling at Santa Barbara and similar projects would be scrutinized by this group.

4. Many people have the notion that since there is so much public discussion about the environment at the moment, the government, with all its vast resources, must be taking the appropriate action to clean up the situation. Specifically, if one thinks through the implications of the preceding statement, it implies that the government is (1) collecting the data necessary to serve as the basis for taking intelligent actions, (2) analysing the data, to determine the appropriate course of action and (3) funding the remedial action implied by the data analysis. In fact, the government in many instances has not yet begun with the first step, let alone thought about the second or the third.

For example, there has been considerable discussion of the possibility that the buildup in global air pollution would lead to serious geophysical effects, such as overheating the world by the "greenhouse effect," which cuts down on escape of heat from the earth, or chilling the world by having too high a proportion of the incoming solar radiation bounce off the surface of high altitude smog particles. One would suspect that because of all this discussion, the government has gone to great effort to find out exactly what the concentration of smog particles is at very high altitudes and has tried to determine how much of this smog accumulation is due to manufacturing and transportation activity, and how much is due to volcanic eruptions. The fact is, such an effort would cost only a few million dollars—trivial by comparison to a moon landing. But no such effort has been made. Thus, there is a critical misranking of national scientific priorities. It is imperative that these priorities be re-examined immediately with a critical eye for the vested interests—such as concern for an ever-increasing GNP—which manipulate corporate functioning in government as well as private industry. Following such a re-examination of priorities, the government must begin critically needed, creative actions.

One such action would be for the government immediately to create a new type of catastrophe warning institution which collects facts, either on its own or from various governmental organizations, analyzes those facts and makes the necessary recommendations to the people. Our present level of ignorance with respect to a wide variety of obviously important phenomena is simply inexcusable, particularly in the face of the rapid rates of change.

5.   An extremely important factor in the environmental crisis is due to the relationship between competition and demand. Where a resource is becoming exhausted, instead of trying to conserve it, the exploiting agencies each become nervous that, if they do not maintain the exploitation rate right up to the time of total resource exploitation, they will not get their fair share. Thus, the fact that there is competition between them helps to sustain and even inflate demand.

An extremely clearcut instance of this was the blue whale industry, in which the technical advisors to the International Whaling Commission advised the whaling nations that if they did not cut their rate of whaling of blue whales down to a mutually agreed-upon quota, which would be set by the advisors, the blue whales would soon be extinct. In the face of this advice, the whaling nations decided not to drop their exploitation rate down to the quota. The same scenario has been re-enacted many times in history, and the most important current instance is the world stock of crude oil. I estimate that this will be all gone by about 2010, which will probably come as a shock or be interpreted as nonsense by most petroleum geologists. However, my predictions are based on analysis of trends in demand.

First, world crude oil demand has been increasing at about 7 per cent per annum for a long time. This is an amazing sustained rate of increase. Furthermore, all signs point to a maintenance of this extraordinary rate of increase. More and more categories of demand are coming into the world economy which have a growth rate far in excess of 7 per cent. For example, world growth in passenger-miles flown in commercial airliners will probably increase during 1970 by 14 per cent. The governments of the world are doing everything imaginable to increase this rate. The S.S.T. aircraft is an example. Careful study of the decision to go ahead with the S.S.T., so that the U.S. has a 500-plane fleet by the fall of 1978, shows that this decision is similar to the decision of the whaling nations to wipe out the whales. The U.S. does not need the S.S.T., but we must have it because the French, British and Russians have it.

The fundamental issue here is what Garrett Hardin calls the tragedy of the commons. No one has a vested interest in protection or conservation of a common property resource that belongs to no one but that everyone can use. Thus, under the present scheme of things, the whole planet will quickly turn into a desolate waste, with the human survivors carefully picking through the remaining scraps of living material to try to find enough edible material to survive.

A solution to this final class of problems is to have firmly adhered-to agreements among all users with regard to rate of use of resources, and firm enforcement of that rate. Also, there must be mutually agreed-to price fixing to slow down use rate. For example, the price of all petroleum products should be tripled immediately, all over the world. This would produce no hardship over the long run because engine and automobile manufacturers would simply produce products three times as efficient. The high pricing would also be the greatest thing that ever happened to urban rapid-transit systems, which can move people much more quickly and easily and at lower cost in space and energy per passenger-mile.

Each of the solutions to the five major problems directly involves the federal government which, as we've pointed out, has not yet begun serious research, let alone taken significant actions. But the sheer enormity of the ecological crisis necessitates the federal government's moving, with knowledge, speed and force, into the problem-solving side of things. Anything less will not be enough.

STUDY QUESTIONS

1. Why does the author begin by talking about the profit motive?
2. Why is it cheaper to consume a resource immediately than to use it up over a long period of time?
3. When will the world's supply of petroleum be used up?
4. Is there a relationship between the profit motive and savings?
5. Who owns the oceans? Why does it matter?
6. What are the natural methods of population control the author mentions?
7. How serious is the problem of having agencies with vested interests established to regulate industries?
8. Why is the option of doing nothing an important option?
9. Has the government taken prompt action in response to the environmental threats?
10. What is the "tragedy of the commons"?

SUGGESTIONS FOR WRITING

1. What is your solution to the problem of competition? The competitive spirit has been praised as the backbone of America. Is there a good chance that we have begun to suffer from environ-

mental hazards partly because we allowed the competitive spirit to run rampant? What are the alternatives to competition?

2. The author talks about only one aspect of the profit motive, though it is a telling one. Can you think of other aspects of the profit motive that might either reinforce the author's position or actually weaken it?

3. Is the author's suggestion that we immediately triple the price of all petroleum products really a good one? Consider the short-term and the long-term effects. Would the petroleum companies go along with this idea even if they were convinced it was good? Should they be forced to comply?

4. Examine the solutions Watt offers to the problems as he enumerates them. Do they seem like viable and reasonable solutions to you? Evaluate each of them in terms of its likelihood of producing the desired effects.

5. The author says "there is nothing in the profit motive by itself that will guarantee the survival of anything." Assuming this is true, or at least highly possible, is there any way to maintain the profit motive and at the same time make it more concerned with the survival of all living things?

THE CHANGING SIGNIFICANCE OF FOOD

Margaret Mead

Americans produce, eat, and waste more food than they need. Most of us recognize the relationship between food and personal health, but few realize that food has great political and cultural importance. In the coming decade, when many other nations will find themselves unable to feed their people, America will discover that its food excesses represent an agonizing responsibility.

We live in a world today where the state of nutrition in each country is relevant and important to each other country, and where the state of nutrition in the wealthy industrialized countries like the United States has profound significance for the role that such countries can play in eliminating famine and providing for adequate nutrition throughout the world. In a world in which each half knows what the other half does, we cannot live with hunger and malnutrition in one part of the world while people in another part are not only well nourished, but over-nourished. Any talk of one world, of brotherhood, rings hollow to those who have come face to face on the television screen with the emaciation of starving children and to the people whose children are starving as they pore over month-old issues of glossy American and European magazines, where full color prints show people glowing with health, their plates piled high with food that glistens to match the shining textures of their clothes. Peoples who have resolutely tightened their belts and put up with going to bed hungry, peoples who have seen their children die because they did not have the strength to resist disease, and called it fate or the will of God, can no longer do so, in the vivid visual realization of the amount and quality of food eaten—and wasted—by others.

Through human history there have been many stringent taboos on watching other people eat, or on eating in the presence of others.

THE CHANGING SIGNIFICANCE OF FOOD   Reprinted from the March/April 1970 issue of *American Scientist* by permission of the author and *American Scientist*.

338

There have been attempts to explain this as a relationship between those who are involved and those who are not simultaneously involved in the satisfaction of a bodily need, and the inappropriateness of the already satiated watching others who appear—to the satisfied—to be shamelessly gorging. There is undoubtedly such an element in the taboos, but it seems more likely that they go back to the days when food was so scarce and the onlookers so hungry that not to offer them half of the little food one had was unthinkable, and every glance was a plea for at least a bite.

In the rural schools of America when my grandmother was a child, the better-off children took apples to school and, before they began to eat them, promised the poor children who had no apples that they might have the cores. The spectacle of the poor in rags at the rich man's gate and of hungry children pressing their noses against the glass window of the rich man's restaurant have long been invoked to arouse human compassion. But until the advent of the mass media and travel, the sensitive and sympathetic could protect themselves by shutting themselves away from the sight of the starving, by gifts of food to the poor on religious holidays, or perpetual bequests for the distribution of a piece of meat "the size of a child's head" annually. The starving in India and China saw only a few feasting foreigners and could not know how well or ill the poor were in countries from which they came. The proud poor hid their hunger behind a façade that often included insistent hospitality to the occasional visitor; the beggars flaunted their hunger and so, to a degree, discredited the hunger of their respectable compatriots.

But today the articulate cries of the hungry fill the air channels and there is no escape from the knowledge of the hundreds of millions who are seriously malnourished, of the periodic famines that beset whole populations, or of the looming danger of famine in many other parts of the world. The age-old divisions between one part of the world and another, between one class and another, between the rich and the poor everywhere, have been broken down, and the tolerances and insensitivities of the past are no longer possible.

But it is not only the media of communication which can take a man sitting at an overloaded breakfast table straight into a household where some of the children are too weak to stand. Something else, something even more significant, has happened. Today, for the first time in the history of mankind, we have the productive capacity to feed everyone in the world, and the technical knowledge to see that their stomachs are not only filled but that their bodies are properly nourished with the essential ingredients for growth and health. The progress of agriculture—in all its complexities of improved seed, methods of cultivation, fertilizers and pesticides, methods of storage, preservation, and transportation—now make it possible for the food that is needed for the whole world to be produced by fewer and fewer farmers, with greater and greater certainty. Drought and flood still threaten, but we have the means to prepare for and deal with even mammoth shortages—if we will. The progress of nutritional science has matched the progress of agriculture; we have finer and finer-grained knowledge of just which substances—vitamins, minerals, proteins—are essential, especially to growth and full development, and increasing ability to synthesize many of them on a massive scale.

These new twentieth-century potentialities have altered the ethical position of the rich all over the world. In the past, there were so few who lived well, and so many who lived on the edge of starvation, that the well-to-do had a rationale and indeed almost a necessity to harden their hearts and turn their eyes away. The jewels of the richest rajah could not have purchased enough food to feed his hungry subjects for more than a few days; the food did not exist, and the knowledge of how to use it was missing also. At the same time, however real the inability of a war-torn and submarine-ringed Britain to respond to the famine in Bengal, this inability was made bearable in Britain only by the extent to which the British were learning how to share what food they had among all the citizens, old and young. "You do not know," the American consul, who had come to Manchester from Spain, said to me: "you do not know what it means to live in a country where no child has to cry itself to sleep from hunger." But this was only achieved in Britain in the early 1940s. Before, the well-fed turned away their eyes, in the feeling that they were powerless to alleviate the perennial poverty and hunger of most of their own people and the peoples in their far-flung commonwealth. And such turning away the eyes, in Britain and in the United States and elsewhere, was accompanied by the rationalizations, not only of the inability of the well-to-do—had they given all their wealth—to feed the poor, but of the undeservingness of the poor, who had they only been industrious and saving would have had enough, although of course of a lower quality, to keep "body and soul together."

When differences in race and in cultural levels complicated the situation, it was only too easy to insist that lesser breeds somehow, in some divinely correct scheme, would necessarily be less well fed, their alleged idleness and lack of frugality combining with such matters as sacred cows roaming over the landscapes—in India—or nights spent in the pub or the saloon—at home in Britain or America—while fathers drank up their meager pay checks and their children starved. So righteous was the assumed association between industriousness and food that, during the Irish famine, soup kitchens were set up out of town so that the starving could have the moral advantage of a long walk to receive the ration that stood between them and death. (The modern version of such ethical acrobatics can be found in the United States, in the mid-1960s, where food stamps were so expensive, since they had to be bought in large amounts, that only those who had been extraordinarily frugal, saving, and lucky could afford to buy them and obtain the benefits they were designed to give.)

The particular ways in which the well-to-do of different great civilizations have rationalized the contrast between rich and poor have differed dramatically, but ever since the agricultural revolution, we have been running a race between our capacity to produce enough food to make it possible to assemble great urban centers, outfit huge armies and armadas, and build and elaborate the institutions of civilization and our ability to feed and care for the burgeoning population which has always kept a little, often a great deal, ahead of the food supply.

In this, those societies which practiced agriculture contrasted with the earlier simpler societies in which the entire population was engaged in subsistence activities. Primitive peoples may be well or poorly fed, feasting seldom, or blessed with ample supplies of fish or fruit, but the relations between the haves and the have-nots were in many ways simpler. Methods by which men could obtain permanent supplies of food and withhold them from their fellows hardly existed. The sour, barely edible breadfruit mash which was stored in breadfruit pits against the ravages of hurricanes and famines in Polynesia was not a diet for the table of chiefs but a stern measure against the needs of entire communities. The chief might have a right to the first fruits, or to half the crop, but after he had claimed it, it was redistributed to his people. The germs of the kinds of inequities that later entered the world were present: there was occasional conspicuous destruction of food, piled up for prestige, oil poured on the flames of self-glorifying feasts, food left to rot after it was offered to the gods. People with very meager food resources might use phrases that made it seem that each man was the recipient of great generosity on the part of his fellows, or on the other hand always to be giving away a whole animal, and always receiving only small bits.

The fear of cannibalism that hovered over northern peoples might be elaborated into cults of fear, or simply add to the concern that each member of a group had for all, against the terrible background that extremity might become so great that one of the group might in the end be sacrificed. But cannibalism could also be elaborated into a rite of vengeance or the celebration of victories in war, or even be used to provision an army in the field. Man's capacity to elaborate man's inhumanity to man existed before the beginning of civilization, which was made possible by the application of an increasingly productive technology to the production of food.

With the rise of civilizations, we also witness the growth of the great religions that made the brotherhood of all men part of their doctrine and the gift of alms or the life of voluntary poverty accepted religious practices. But the alms were never enough, and the life of individual poverty and abstinence was more efficacious for the individual's salvation than for the well-being of the poor and hungry, although both kept alive an ethic, as yet impossible of fulfillment, that it was right that all should be fed. The vision preceded the capability.

But today we have the capability. Whether that capability will be used or not becomes not a technical but an ethical question. It depends, in enormous measure, on the way in which the rich, industrialized countries handle the problems of distribution, of malnutrition and hunger, within their own borders. Failure to feed their own, with such high capabilities and such fully enunciated statements of responsibility and brotherhood, means that feeding the people of other countries is almost ruled out, except for sporadic escapist pieces of behavior where people who close their eyes to hunger in Mississippi can work hard to send food to a "Biafra." The development of the international instruments to meet food emergencies and to steadily improve the nutrition of the poorer countries will fail, unless there is greater consistency between ideal and practice at home.

And so, our present parlous plight in the United States, with the many pockets of rural unemployment, city ghettos, ethnic enclaves, where Americans are starving and an estimated tenth of the population malnourished, must be viewed not only in its consequences for ourselves, as a viable political community, but also in its consequences for the world. We need to examine not only the conditions that make this possible, to have starving people in the richest country in the world, but also the repercussions of American conditions on the world scene.

Why, when twenty-five years ago we were well on the way to remedying the state of the American people who had been described by presidential announcement as "one third ill-housed, ill-clothed, and ill-fed," when the vitamin deficiency diseases had all but vanished, and a variety of instruments for better nutrition had been developed, did we find, just two short years ago, due to the urgent pleading of a few crusaders, that we had fallen so grievously behind? The situation is complex, closely related to a series of struggles for regional and racial justice, to the spread of automation and resulting unemployment, to changes in crop economies, as well as to population growth and the inadequacy of many of our institutions to deal with it. But I wish to single out here two conditions which have, I believe, seriously contributed to our blindness to what was happening: the increase in the diseases of affluence and the growth of commercial agriculture.

In a country pronounced only twenty years before to be one third ill-fed, we suddenly began to have pronouncements from nutritional specialists that the major nutritional disease of the American people was overnutrition. If this had simply meant overeating, the old puritan ethics against greed and gluttony might have been more easily invoked, but it was overnutrition that was at stake. And this in a country where our ideas of nutrition had been dominated by a dichotomy which distinguished food that was "good for you, but not good" from food that was "good, but not good for you." This split in man's needs, into our cultural conception of the need for nourishment and the search for pleasure, originally symbolized in the rewards for eating spinach or finishing what was on one's plate if one wanted to have a dessert, lay back of the movement to produce, commercially, non-nourishing foods. Beverages and snacks came in particularly for this demand, as it was the addition of between-meal eating to the three square, nutritionally adequate meals a day that was responsible for much of the trouble.

We began manufacturing, on a terrifying scale, foods and beverages that were guaranteed not to nourish. The resources and the ingenuity of industry were diverted from the preparation of foods necessary for life and growth to foods nonexpensive to prepare, expensive to buy. And every label reassuring the buyer that the product was not nourishing increased our sense that the trouble with Americans was that they were too well nourished. The diseases of affluence, represented by new forms of death in middle-age, had appeared before we had, in the words of Jean Mayer, who has done so much to define the needs of the country and of the world, conquered the diseases of poverty—the ill-fed pregnant women and lactating women, sometimes resulting in irreversible damage to the ill-weaned children, the school children so poorly fed that they could not learn.

It was hard for the average American to believe that while he struggled, and paid, so as not to be overnourished, other people, several millions, right in this country, were hungry and near starvation. The gross contradiction was too great. Furthermore, those who think of their country as parental and caring find it hard to admit that this parental figure is starving their brothers and sisters. During the great depression of the 1930s, when thousands of children came to school desperately hungry, it was very difficult to wring from children the admission that their parents had no food to give them. "Or what man is there of you, whom, if his son ask bread, will he give a stone?"

So today we have in the United States a situation not unlike the situation in Germany under Hitler, when a large proportion of the decent and law-abiding simply refuse to believe that what is happening can be happening. "Look at the taxes we pay," they say, or they point to the millions spent on welfare; surely with such quantities assigned to the poor, people can't be really hungry, or if they are, it is because they spend their money on TV sets and drink. How can the country be overnourished and undernourished at the same time?

A second major shift, in the United States and in the world, is the increasing magnitude of commercial agriculture, in which food is seen not as food which nourishes men, women, and children, but as a staple crop on which the prosperity of a country or region and the economic prosperity—as opposed to the simple livelihood—of the individual farmer depend. This is pointed up on a world scale in the report of the Food and Agriculture Organization of the United Nations for 1969, which states that there are two major problems in the world: food deficits in the poor countries, which mean starvation, hunger, and malnutrition on an increasing scale, and food surpluses in the industrialized part of the world, serious food surpluses.

On the face of it, this sounds as foolish as the production of foods guaranteed not to nourish, and the two are not unrelated. Surpluses, in a world where people are hungry! Too much food, in a world where children are starving! Yet we lump together all *agricultural* surpluses, such as cotton and tobacco, along with food, and we see these surpluses as threatening the commercial prosperity of many countries, and farmers in many countries. And in a world politically organized on a vanishing agrarian basis, this represents a political threat to those in power. However much the original destruction of food, killing little pigs, may have been phrased as relieving the desperate situation of little farmers or poor countries dependent upon single crop exports, such situations could not exist if food as something which man needs to provide growth and maintenance had not been separated from food as a cash crop, a commercial as opposed to a basic maintenance enterprise. When it becomes the task of government to foster the economic prosperity of an increasingly small, but politically influential, sector of the electorate at the expense of the well-being of its own and other nations' citizens, we have reached an ethically dangerous position.

And this situation, in the United States, is in part responsible for the grievous state of our poor and hungry and for the paralysis that still prevents adequate political action. During the great depression, agriculture in this country was still a viable way of life for millions. The Department of Agriculture had responsibility, not only for food production and marketing, but also for the well-being from the cradle to the grave, in the simplest, most human sense, of every family who lived in communities under 2,500. Where the needs of urban man were parceled out among a number of agencies—Office of Education, Children's Bureau, Labor Department—there was still a considerable amount of integration possible in the Department of Agriculture, where theory and practices of farm wives, the education of children and youth, the question of small loans for small landowners, all could be considered together. It was in the Department of Agriculture that concerned persons found, during the depression, the kind of understanding of basic human needs which they sought.

There were indeed always conflicts between the needs of farmers to sell crops and the needs of children to be fed. School lunch schemes were tied to the disposal of surplus commodities. But the recognition of the wholeness of human needs was still there, firmly related to the breadth of the responsibilities of the different agencies within the Department of Agriculture. Today this is no longer so. Agriculture is big business in the United States. The subsidies used to persuade farmers to withdraw their impoverished land from production, like the terrible measures involving the slaughter of little pigs, are no longer ways of helping the small farmer on a family farm. The subsidies go to the rich commercial farmers, many of them the inheritors of old exploitive plantation traditions, wasteful of manpower and land resources, often in the very counties where the farm workers, displaced by machinery, are penniless, too poor to move away, starving. These subsidies exceed the budget of the antipoverty administration.

So today, many of the reforms which are suggested, in the distribution of food or distribution of income from which food can be bought, center on removing food relief programs from the Department of Agriculture and placing them under the Department of Health, Education, and Welfare. In Britain, during World War II, it was necessary to have a Ministry of Food, concerned primarily in matching the limited food supplies with basic needs.

At first sight, this proposal is sound enough. Let us remove from an agency devoted to making a profit out of crops that are treated like any other manufactured product the responsibility for seeing that food actually feeds people. After all, we do not ask clothing manufacturers to take the responsibility for clothing people, or the house-building industry for housing them. To the extent that we recognize them at all, these are the responsibilities of agencies of government which provide the funds to supplement the activities of private industry. Why not also in food? The Department of Health, Education, and Welfare is concerned with human beings; they have no food to sell on a domestic or world market and no constituents to appease. And from this step it is simply a second step to demand that the whole system of distribution be re-oriented, that a basic guaranteed annual income be provided each citizen, on the one hand, and that the government police standards, on behalf of the consumer, on the other.

But neither of these changes, shifting food relief programs from Agriculture to Health, Education, and Welfare, or shifting the whole welfare program into a guaranteed income, really meet the particular difficulties that arise because we are putting food into two compartments with disastrous effects; we are separating food that nourishes people from food out of which some people, and some countries, derive their incomes. It does not deal with the immediacy of the experience of food by the well-fed, or with the irreparability of food deprivation during prenatal and postnatal growth, deprivation that can never be made up. Human beings have maintained their dignity in incredibly bad conditions of housing and clothing, emerged triumphant from huts and log cabins, gone from ill-shod childhood to Wall Street or the Kremlin. Poor housing and poor clothing are demeaning to the human spirit when they contrast sharply with the visible standards of the way others live.

But food affects not only man's dignity but the capacity of children to reach their full potential, and the capacity of adults to act from day to day. You can't eat either nutrition or part of a not yet realized guaranteed annual income, or political promises. You can't eat hope. We know that hope and faith have enormous effects in preventing illness and enabling people to put forth the last ounce of energy they have. But energy is ultimately dependent upon food. No amount of rearrangement of priorities in the future can provide food in the present. It is true that the starving adult, his efficiency enormously impaired by lack of food, may usually be brought back again to his previous state of efficiency. But this is not true of children. What they lose is lost for good.

What we do about food is therefore far more crucial, both for the quality of the next generation, our own American children, and children everywhere, and also for the quality of our responsible action in every field. It is intimately concerned with the whole problem of the pollution and exhaustion of our environment, with the danger that man may make this planet uninhabitable within a short century or so. If food is grown in strict relationship to the needs of those who will eat it, if every effort is made to reduce the costs of transportation, to improve storage, to conserve the land, and there, where it is needed, by recycling wastes and water, we will go a long way toward solving many of our environmental problems also. It is as a responsible gardener on a small, limited plot, aware of the community about him with whom he will face adequate food or famine, that man has developed what conserving agricultural techniques we have.

Divorced from its primary function of feeding people, treated simply as a commercial commodity, food loses this primary significance; the land is mined instead of replenished and conserved. The Food and Agriculture Organization, intent on food production, lays great stress on the increase in the use of artificial fertilizers, yet the use of such fertilizers with their diffuse runoffs may be a greater danger to our total ecology than the industrial wastes from other forms of manufacturing. The same thing is true of pesticides. With the marvels of miracle rice and miracle wheat, which have brought the resources of international effort and scientific resources together, go at present prescriptions for artificial fertilizer and pesticides. The innovative industrialized countries are exporting, with improved agricultural methods, new dangers to the environment of the importing countries. Only by treating food, unitarily, as a substance necessary to feed people, subject first to the needs of people and only second to the needs of commercial prosperity—whether they be the needs of private enterprise or of a developing socialist country short of foreign capital—can we hope to meet the ethical demands that our present situation makes on us. For the first time since the beginning of civilization, we can feed everyone, now. Those who are not fed will die or, in the case of children, be permanently damaged.

We are just beginning to develop a world conscience. Our present dilemma is due to previous humanitarian moves with unanticipated effects. Without the spread of public health measures, we would not have had the fall in infant death rates which has resulted in the population explosion. Without the spread of agricultural techniques, there would not have been the food to feed the children who survived. The old constraints upon population growth—famine, plague, and war—are no longer acceptable to a world whose conscience is just barely stirring on behalf of all mankind. As we are groping our way back to a new version of the full fellow-feeling and respect for the natural world which the primitive Eskimo felt when food was scarce, so we are trembling on the edge of a new version of the sacrifice to cannibalism of the weak, just as we have the technical means to implement visions of responsibility that were very recently only visions.

The temptation is to turn aside, to deny what is happening to the environment, to trust to the "green revolution" and boast of how much rice previously hungry countries will export, to argue about legalities while people starve and infants and children are irreparably damaged, to refuse to deal with the paradoxes of hunger in plenty, and the coincidences of starvation and overnutrition. The basic problem is an ethical one; the solution of ethical problems can be solved only with a full recognition of reality. The children of the agricultural workers of the rural South, displaced by the machine, are hungry; so are the children in the Northern cities to which black and white poor have fled in search of food. On our American Indian reservations, among the Chicanos of California and the Southwest, among the seasonally employed, there is hunger now. If this hunger is not met now, we disqualify ourselves, we cripple ourselves, to deal with world problems.

We must balance our population so that every child that is born can be well fed. We must cherish our land, instead of mining it, so that food produced is first related to those who need it; and we must not despoil the earth, contaminate, and pollute it in the interests of immediate gain. Behind us, just a few decades ago, lies the vision of André Mayer and John Orr, the concepts of a world food bank, the founding of the United Nations Food and Agriculture Organization; behind us lie imaginative vision and deep concern. In the present we have new and various tools to make that vision into concrete actuality. But we must resolve the complications of present practice and present conceptions if the very precision and efficiency of our new knowledge is not to provide a stumbling block to the exercise of fuller humanity.

STUDY QUESTIONS

1. How does Margaret Mead relate the rich nations to the poor? Is she being realistic or overdramatic?
2. What are some of man's food taboos?

3. How have the mass media made it less easy for the rich to be comfortable while many of the poor are starving?
4. Do we have the technology to feed everyone in the world?
5. How has technology affected our ethical situation?
6. Has the history of America been one of consistently responding to the needs of the ill-fed?
7. Why does Margaret Mead bring up the subject of cannibalism?
8. What emotional effect do diet foods have on Americans?
9. Is it reasonable to say that we produce *too much* food?
10. How does the economy of farming relate to this problem?

SUGGESTIONS FOR WRITING

1. Margaret Mead constantly stresses the ethical problems of food and food distribution. Take a stand on this issue. What is your view concerning your responsibility to provide food for those who are poor and starving? Do you have an ethical or moral obligation to the poor? Write what you feel, not what you think you *should* feel.
2. The article mentions the government's subsidy payments to farmers, which are larger than welfare payments. What is your view on the desirability of such subsidies? Must we continue them? What would happen if we stopped? How could we reasonably adjust them?
3. Assume that we have enough extra food to rescue another nation from starvation. If India, China, and Nigeria each suffered a famine at the same time, how would you decide which one should be saved? How ethical is your judgment?
4. What precisely is Margaret Mead's position? What is she arguing for and how effectively does she argue? What is it that weakens or strengthens her position for you? Are you convinced? Try to analyze the reasons for your own position on the matter.
5. Margaret Mead says we "are just beginning to develop a world conscience." Is this true? Do you see any evidence of that fact in public affairs? In this article? What does it mean to develop a world conscience, and what good would it do? Would a world conscience be a totally unmixed blessing? Do some of the points the author makes suggest that it might even be somewhat dangerous?

THE NEW WOMAN: OUT TO FINISH WHAT THE SUFFRAGETTE STARTED

Caroline Bird

In the late 1960s the spirit of the suffragette was rekindled and the movement we call Women's Lib achieved public recognition. Like the efforts women made to get the vote early in this century, the goals of the Women's Liberation Movement have been controversial and its tactics have often been ridiculed. The movement has certainly not succeeded in obtaining full rights for women, but it has definitely inspired a mood for changes in that direction.

Just four years ago, the successful women I interviewed were spending a lot of energy proving that their husbands and children were not neglected, demonstrating their "femininity" by tottering around in frilly clothes and insisting that they liked men better than women. They could say that they envied this or that privilege of men, if they smiled or shrugged when they said it. But not many dared to say that they wished they were male, that they preferred to be single or childless or that they liked the company of women better than that of men.

Today, a surprising number of women all over the country are daring to say precisely these things. These four years, in fact, have ushered in—almost incredibly—an entirely new era for American women. Consider what has been happening:

New York State has stopped inquiring into a woman's reasons for wanting an abortion and California into her reasons for wanting a divorce. Some colleges have abandoned all responsibility for the private lives of women students. Many newspapers have given up the

THE NEW WOMAN: OUT TO FINISH WHAT THE SUFFRAGETTE STARTED   From the July–August 1970 issue of *Think* Magazine. Reprinted by permission from the author and *Think* Magazine, copyright 1970 by International Business Machines Corporation.

attempt to classify job ads by sex. Women are admitted to scores of clubs, restaurants, colleges and jobs formerly closed to them, and every Ivy League college has women students on some basis or other. Congress has removed the legal barrier to women generals and admirals. The venerable Protestant Episcopal Church has abolished its women's division and is presently considering the elevation of women to the priesthood.

Women are also gaining at work. Favorable court decisions are striking down the state labor laws which had "protected" factory women from the hours and duties which led to promotion and competition with union men. The proportion of women in graduate school is rising, and the gap between the starting salaries of men and women college graduates is narrowing.

Quite clearly, too, women are more assertive of their rights. They are filing charges of discrimination on the basis of sex with the Equal Employment Opportunity Commission and government agencies charged with eliminating discrimination from the civil service. The Equal Rights Amendment forbidding legal distinction of any kind between male and female citizens has attracted support from women who just a little while ago had judged it "too far out" to be worth political effort. When Senator Birch Bayh announced hearings on the amendment, 100 witnesses asked to testify, mostly for it. Virtually everybody in the women's rights movement has moved to new, more radical ground.

But the most startling innovation since 1966 has been the appearance of a new kind of woman, more alien to American tradition than the flapper of the 1920s, the man-suited, career spinster of the 1930s, or the Rosie who riveted the bombers during World War II. Virtually non-existent in 1966, the new, liberated woman can today be found on every college campus and in every sizable American city.

The American woman she most resembles is a character successful women had patronized as necessary, perhaps, in her time, but thankfully needed no more: the politically alert, fiercely autonomous and sometimes man-hating suffragette who won the vote for women at the end of World War I by militant hunger strikes and street demonstrations. Well-educated, privileged, the new liberated woman is often attractive and almost always young—seldom over 25. She is, in addition, idealistic, intense but soft-spoken. And she is furious. Men can't believe her even when they see her. In their book, she's an impossibility: a beautiful or potentially beautiful woman who is deliberately throwing away the advantages of her sex.

She is not fighting to liberate herself from sex repressions. In her privileged circles, her mother and sometimes her grandmother accomplished that. Nor is she out to broaden her horizons to include man's world. The new women scorn requesting, politely or otherwise, that men please move over and give them a piece of the action (the middle-of-the-road New Feminism of the National Organization for Women). They want to remake the world men have created, from top to bottom.

All the new women don't see eye to eye. Still, a majority could probably be mustered for the following platform:

Love is the most important human relationship and is available to any two or more individuals of any sex who care deeply for each other and are committed to contributing to each other's personal growth. Love may or may not include sexual relationships and should not be confused with *romantic love*, a put-up job they think is utilized to trap women into giving up their own identities.

Home and family (including the cooking, cleaning and shopping) must be an egalitarian institution to which all contribute equally. It can comprise any combination of adults and children, whether related by blood or sexual ties, who find it rewarding to live together. New forms of home and family must be developed by personal experimentation.

Children must be a fully optional responsibility for both men and women. Women must have the right to terminate any pregnancy for any reason, and no loss of prestige should attach to any person who chooses not to reproduce. The rearing of children shall be the equal responsibility of mother and father and shall not be considered a full-time job for anyone, or the source of any woman's identity.

Divorce must be available to either partner without fault.

Alimony degrades a wife by assuming that she has been supported in return for sexual favors and is entitled to severance pay when she is jilted.

Jobs must be available to both sexes on the basis of individually determined capacity, without presumption that the required capacity is more likely to occur in a member of one sex than the other.

Consumer goods shall not be promoted as contributors to masculinity or femininity or by exploiting the sexual attraction of women employees or images.

Media shall not brainwash women and girls into accepting a limited, domestic role.

Schools—ditto.

Sex differences in ability and responses which can be proven by objective testing must be ascribed to the way boys and girls are brought up, until they can be specifically attributed to anatomical differences.

Sex roles based on a division of labor between men and women are not inevitable in the world of the future just because they have been universal in the past.

Psychoanalysis has crippled women by attempting to "adjust" them to a feminine role unacceptable to free human beings.

Freud made the mistake of assuming that Victorian marriage and family arrangements which subordinated women to men were inevitable and desirable.

Marx saw that the bourgeois family enslaved women by making them the private property of their men.

None of these thoughts is really new. What *is* new is that they have been welded together into a coherent philosophy on the basis of which women can make personal decisions on husbands, jobs, schools, birth control methods, alimony, child-rearing and politics. The Women's Liberation Movement (WLM), more familiarly known as Women's Lib, is, if anything, overorganized. At the Second Congress to Unite Women held in New York this past May, 600 women represented scores of the shifting new groups which were turning up with names like Bread and Roses, The Feminists, the Media Women, Redstockings, OWL (Older Women's Liberation), SALT (Sisters All Learning Together), as well as WITCH (Women's International Terrorist Conspiracy from Hell).

The movement began with bright, white girls from privileged homes who were free to join the student movement for Negro rights in college because they weren't pushed to marry well or earn money. When they went South for the movement, they found themselves identifying with the blacks more easily than the white boys. They knew how it felt to shut up; take a back seat; accept segregation, exclusion from clubs, restaurants and meetings; lower their sights to work which was "realistically" open to them; cope with imputations of natural inferiority; and see themselves portrayed in print and picture as stereotypes rather than individuals.

In 1967 it began to dawn on the girls who had gone into the radical movement fulltime after graduation that they were toting coffee and typing, like office girls in business establishments. Those who had joined the movement to escape suburban domesticity found themselves making beds and washing dishes like their legally married mothers. Not taken seriously, refused an opportunity for more substantial participation, these movement women who were "feminists" concluded in 1968 that they couldn't really be liberated unless they did it all by themselves, and while most hoped to rejoin men after their liberation, most excluded men. (The Feminists of New York actually limit to one-third the number of members who may be formally or informally married.)

Women's Liberation made its national debut in September 1968 by halting—if only for a few seconds—the television crowning of Miss America at Atlantic City. They picketed the contest with signs "Let's Judge Ourselves as People." They brought "freedom trash baskets" into which they proposed to dump hair curlers, false eyelashes, girdles, bras and other devices for making themselves over into the standard sex object. They crowned a live sheep. They threw a stink bomb. They chanted, "We Shall Not Be Used."

Women saw the point, even when they violently, and somewhat defensively, denied that they felt "used." The pageant had long made women feel uneasy, but few had verbalized or even admitted the discomfort they experienced at the spectacle of women parading in a competition to determine which one was most attractive to men. It was hard to say anything against a beauty contest without sounding envious or hostile. The rhetoric of revolution removes this embarrassment by making the notion that women are against each other a myth perpetrated by men to keep women from joining together against their "oppression."

The Miss America protest was a model of what the Communists used to call "agit-prop," or the art of making revolutionary capital out of a current event. It was also the proving ground for what they thought was a brilliant new rationale for dealing with a hostile press. The protesting women made the media carry the message by laying down their own ground rules for press coverage. They refused to talk to male reporters. They refused to identify a leader. And they insisted on speaking as an anonymous group. Radicals have sometimes refused to identify their leaders in order to protect them from arrest, but Women's Lib did so in part to refute the notion that women are unable to cooperate. In the revolutionary vocabulary, group action is a "zap."

Zap, used still, is maddening to the media. So, too, is the attitude of Women's Lib. No group has ever treated the press so disparagingly. But it has worked. Caught off guard, intrigued, or merely stunned, the print media have given Women's Lib more space than the brassiest press agent could possibly hold out to the most gullible potential client.

Even more innovative is the solution Women's Lib has developed to the gut problems of any social action: how to recruit new members. The technique is "consciousness raising." A consciousness-raising session is informal, intimate. Ideally, a dozen or more women get together to talk about their experiences *as women*, to call to mind the little slights, frustrations and hangups they have put out of mind as inevitable.

There is, say the feminists, a well of anger hidden somewhere inside the gentlest women. Consciousness raising lets the genie out of the bottle. Once a woman admits to herself how she has been victimized, she can never go back to the Garden of Eden. She gets angrier and angrier and she infects the women around her. Every woman who admits she is a victim makes it that much harder for the next woman to pretend she isn't a victim. The anger feeds on itself, and it is contagious. That's what Women's Lib is all about. It is less a movement than a revolutionary state of mind. But is it, really, a revolution?

According to the article on Revolution in the *New Encyclopedia of Social Science*, revolutions are most likely to occur when the old order is breaking down, the despots are reforming themselves, the condition of the oppressed is improving, widening education has created a "revolution of expectations" and a war complicates the work of the ruling class. Read "men" for the powers that be, "women" for the oppressed, and paragraphs of the essay take on new and striking sense.

The old order, the patriarchal system *is* breaking down: more women are single or divorced, more wives are self-supporting, more children are born out of wedlock, more sex is extramarital. The despots are reforming themselves: more men, particularly younger men, treat women as companions rather than sex objects. The condition of women *is* improving, but perhaps not as fast as widening education is raising expectations. Finally, a war *is* distracting attention from domestic reforms that would improve the status of women, not the least of which is the establishment of child care centers.

The analogies go even further, to the characteristics of the movement itself. Like political revolutions, Women's Lib is afflicted with schisms, exhausting ideological debate, suspicion of charismatic leaders and experts or professionals who have earned their credentials under the established system. Many of the younger groups are not particularly eager, for instance, to be lectured by authors like Betty Friedan or Caroline Bird. They want and need to speak for themselves, in their own idiom. And like other revolutionaries, they are almost pathologically afraid—as well they might be—that in a general upheaval, some sister (comrade, brother) might feather her own nest.

This fear, plus the need for solidarity among the oppressed, explains to some degree why they need consensus decisions.

For all the similarities to classical revolutions, there is one great divide: women can't revolt against society in quite the same way that workers or blacks can revolt. Sex lines cut across class lines. As a bitter feminist has put it, women are the only oppressed class that lives with the master race. They cannot, like the black separatists, really secede from society. For the most part, men are part of the daily lives of even the most fire-breathing feminist.

What is actually happening, I think, is something that carries a wider meaning even than the status of women, trying as that status may be to those concerned about it. The notion of women as an oppressed group has surfaced in every revolution of modern history. The "demands" of the Congress to Unite Women would not have surprised Mary Wollstonecraft, who wrote *A Vindication of the Rights of Women* in 1791, the year before the French revolutionaries deposed Louis XVI. They would have delighted Elizabeth Cady Stanton, whose Seneca Falls "Declaration of Principles" demanded the vote for women at a time when the issue of slavery threatened the survival of the United States.

Women's Liberation is spreading because American society is in a comparable state of revolution. It reflects not only the revolt of the black separatists, whose rhetoric it follows so closely, but the general loss of credibility in all constituted authority—political, educational, intellectual, religious, even military.

Where will women come out? If previous revolutionary periods are any guide, the answer is: "Better—at least so far as their status as women is concerned." Beyond that, and just as importantly, the answer has to be: "No better than the society as a whole comes out."

STUDY QUESTIONS

1. How has the self-image of women been different in the last few years than it was in the previous decade?
2. What effect has the Equal Rights Amendment had on women?
3. Has female militancy had a good or a bad effect on women's rights?
4. Why does the author make a point of describing the new woman as "a beautiful or potentially beautiful woman"?

5. What's wrong with "romantic love"?
6. Why is alimony thought to degrade a woman?
7. Why do women object to Freud?
8. How did working in the South help liberate some white women?
9. What does the Miss America pageant have to do with the movement?
10. How has Women's Liberation treated the press?

SUGGESTIONS FOR WRITING

1. For you, what is the most startling tactic used by the Women's Liberation Movement? Why is it startling, what is its effect, and how do you think it affects others?
2. Near the end of her article, Caroline Bird suggests that "The condition of women *is* improving, but perhaps not as fast as widening education is raising expectations." Do you agree with this judgment, or do you think it overlooks the facts?
3. One often hears the argument that women have made astounding progress and that perhaps they are moving too fast. Is there any reason to agree with this position? To disagree?
4. There is no question but that the author links the Women's Liberation Movement with a general radicalism or revolutionary tendency in American life. Do you agree with this view? Is there evidence for or against such a judgment? If it is true, what will happen to Women's Liberation as the urge to revolution cools in our society?
5. The nuclear family is the target of many of the protests Women's Liberationists make against American society. They feel, for instance, that housework and child-raising should be shared equally by husband and wife instead of being performed almost exclusively by the woman. How would such an arrangement contribute to the liberation of women in America? Do you think that the sharing of household duties would strengthen the average nuclear family, or destroy it?

WOODSTOCK AND BEYOND—WHY?

Edwin Kiester, Jr.

For the thousands of young people who were there it
was like a religious experience. For those who missed it,
it was thoroughly covered by the news media and later
celebrated on records and on film. Woodstock started
as a music festival, survived the bad weather and bad
drugs, and through the media and a touch of something
almost mystical, became a unique temporary city and an
important cultural symbol.

Suddenly, last summer, came Woodstock—and it left an impact on both sides of the generation gap that persists today.

True, there had been rock-pop-folk music festivals before. Newport, Rhode Island, had been holding them for almost 20 years. Only
a week or two earlier, 15,000 rock fans had overrun Newport Beach,
California, and a few days later, Denver, Colorado. But then one
sunbaked August weekend, 300,000 or 400,000 or 500,000 young people, swarming like lemmings crossing Arctic tundra, converged on the
rolling farmfields of New York's Catskill Mountains, clogging every
major artery as they came. Under a blue haze of smoke, drenched by a
series of cloudburst rains, they established for three days the third
largest city in New York State—or its greater disaster area, depending
on who you talked to. They smoked pot, dropped acid, swam nude,
made public love, slept in the mud, and utterly overwhelmed every
facility for water, sanitation, public health, and even food the sponsors had provided.

From the first, Woodstock achieved among the young the status of
instant myth, the kind of once-in-a-lifetime experience to be recalled
and embellished forever. The audiences poked each other and exclaimed with wonder, "Did you hear? We're a disaster area!" or

WOODSTOCK AND BEYOND—WHY?   From the July 1970 issue of *Today's Health*,
published by the American Medical Association. Reprinted by permission of the
author and *Today's Health*.

"Wow! I never dreamed there were so many of us!" Performer Arlo
Guthrie burbled happily before his appearance, "The whole damned
New York Thruway is closed down! You know that? The whole
damned New York Thruway!" Afterward, "Were you at Woodstock?" became a cultural watchword, separating the insiders from the
crowd. *Woodstock: The Movie* opened to rave reviews and played to
exuberant audiences everywhere despite its three-hour length. Yippie
leader Abbie Hoffman hopped aboard the bandwagon—he proclaimed
himself a citizen of what he called "The Woodstock Nation," and
said it had just declared war on "The Pig Nation." Promoters of rival
festivals capitalized on Woodstock's fame with slogans like, "Better
than Woodstock," and newspaper and television interest in festivals
quickened.

For much of the older generation, however, Woodstock was less
hallowed myth than disturbing mystery. "When my contemporaries
were asked what it was all about," wrote anthropologist Margaret
Mead, "they were puzzled." They could not picture themselves en-
during the broiling sun, torrential rains, viscous mud, teeming crowds,
and earsplitting sounds the young people thrived on. A few were
amused by the spectacle—"Look at that," said one woman, pointing
to a newspaper photograph, "400,000 nonconformists!"—but the majority of elders could only be described as concerned, troubled, or terrified. "My God!" you heard again and again. "What are things coming to?"

This year there will be no happening at Woodstock. But there will
be plenty of other "Woodstocks" to keep the controversy crackling
among both young and old. Festivals this summer are popping up
everywhere, like dandelions after a May rain. Each one flaunts anew
all the Woodstock hallmarks, from drugs to nudity, and each again
raises the hackles of an alarmed adult community.

But is alarm justified? Are festivals dangerous to health and morality? Are they really rife with drugs, spiced with sex, prone to violence?
Why in the world do young people press together into such jams of
humanity? What do they get out of it? Does the mood last? And,
most important, are festivals a fad—or will they have significant impact on society?

Adults certainly didn't get clear answers from the young. "It was
beautiful," they say of Woodstock, but when they try to explain further, they cannot. "Like we could all groove together, you know?" was
the best one could stammer. "I mean it was real human being to human being. You weren't like, alone, and you knew you weren't. I
mean, you were *somewhere*."

Physicians and others who are specialists in the study of human behavior have opinions about the festivals, too.

"My enthusiasm for such festivals is very limited," says Dana Farnsworth, M.D., director of student health services at Harvard. "Too many young people get exploited in the process."

"I seem to recall people acting the same way about Frank Sinatra in the 40's and Benny Goodman in the 30's," says Howard Rome, M.D., chief of psychiatry at the Mayo Clinic. "And not very long ago, people were screaming about the Beatles."

"It is no fad, but a desperate move to form a temporary community against a society that is hassling them all the time," declares Edgar Z. Friedenberg, Ph.D., professor of social foundations at the State University of New York at Buffalo, and author of a book called *Coming of Age in America*.

"Rock festivals seem to me fundamentally a religious phenomenon," says Paul Goodman, Ph.D., the sociologist and author who criticized the American philosophy of child rearing in *Growing Up Absurd*. "Traveling to a place is very important in it, like the religious pilgrimages of the Middle Ages."

"Woodstock marks the end of the United States of America as a Protestant, up tight, New England type of country," states Amitai Etzioni, Ph.D., of Columbia University, a sociologist who took an active part in student-faculty negotiations during his university's disorders.

> The new style implies a reaction against the traditional Puritan thinking on work versus fun, individual values versus those of large groups, being "cool" versus expressing feelings spontaneously, and representative democracy versus mass participation.

On one point, however, virtually everyone agrees: There is a great deal more to rock festivals than simply a large army of feckless kids sitting in the grass and listening to music.

Unquestionably, of course, music is the festival's original magnet. The Woodstock sponsors offered perhaps the greatest array of rock talent ever seen anywhere—Arlo Guthrie, Joan Baez, Joe Cocker, Richie Havens, Country Joe and the Fish, Sha-na-na, the Jefferson Airplane, and a host more whose names mean little to most adults but a great deal to rock cultists. When *The New York Times* interviewed six Woodstockers after the event, one of the girls told what had attracted her to the festival: "They had the most fantastic lineup of stars I'd ever heard about, more than any place, better than Newport."

A moment later, however, she was explaining how she felt about the festival, and the following dialogue took place.

"Was that feeling before you heard the music?"

"Oh, I never made it to the concert. I never heard any music at all."

"*The whole weekend?*"

"The whole weekend."

The assumption that music is the dominant theme of such gatherings is a false one, according to Lewis Yablonsky, Ph.D., professor of sociology at San Fernando Valley State College in California and author of *The Hippie Trip.*

> Music is the backdrop. It serves, as in all cultures, to validate, reinforce, and illuminate the culture.
>
> But the real purpose of a festival is a gathering of the tribe, a getting together of people of like mind. Essentially, it is no different from a meeting of the American Sociological Association. People at festivals don't hold seminars on how to smoke pot better, or how to handle an abortion naturally, or how to deal with the fuzz, but they communicate constantly, in a more random way, about how to live another life style within the framework of society. The tribal gathering validates the size of the movement—makes it visible. It is important for a person who feels all alone, smashed down, on the wrong track, to find others who share his position, share his attitude toward dope, sex, and the "obscene plastic society." He comes away revitalized, spiritually happy, ready for another year,

sociologist Yablonsky explains.

Older people often forget, Columbia's Etzioni says, that few people of any age group attend a cultural event simply for the sake of the cultural event. There are almost always social trappings, formal or informal, that accompany it. For younger people on such occasions, there may be dating, games, picnics, flirting, and camaraderie. In this sense, Woodstock is not much different from the spelling bees of frontier times or, say, performances of Shakespeare in Central Park today. Festivals *are* different in one way, however, sociologist Etzioni says: "The young people come not as a matter of social form, but for 'content'—because they hope to get new attitudes and ideas."

Is the rock festival part of a political movement?

Abbie Hoffman contends it is the opening skirmish in a revolution of the new society against the old.

"He has to say that," declares Edward R. Guy, M.D., a Bryn Mawr, Pennsylvania, psychiatrist who himself writes rock music and whose two daughters went to Woodstock. "That's what Hoffman wants people to believe."

Author-sociologist Goodman, who appeared at a rock festival held at Cornell University in support of the Rev. Daniel Berrigan, the Jesuit priest-poet convicted of destroying draft records, found the audience strikingly nonpolitical despite the festival's purpose. "When anyone had a message of nonviolence, sweetness, kindness, Christian ethics, particularly if he expressed it with good humor—well, he got fantastic attention and applause. It was a sharp distinction, surprising, and a little touching. It was a festival of peace."

Another sociologist, Kurt Lang, Ph.D., of the State University of New York at Stony Brook, participated in last November's Viet Nam Moratorium Day in Washington. He likens rock festivals to that demonstration. "Mainly, it was a big thing that everyone wanted to be part of," he says. "Obviously it had a political message that grew out of real concern, but the gathering itself was more social than revolutionary." Sociologist Etzioni notes that few youth gatherings are violent, and that in civil rights and other demonstrations, extremist attempts to foment violence are generally unsuccessful.

Certainly, however, festivals have what many older people would consider a political and even revolutionary atmosphere. Their mood is anti–Viet Nam, antidraft, anti-Nixon, antidiscrimination, down-with-the-Establishment. At Woodstock, Joan Baez mentioned her husband's jail sentence for draft resistance and drew prolonged applause. Country Joe and the Fish launched into the antiwar song "*Vietnam Rag*"—the crowd joined in with gusto. An Army "medevac" helicopter appeared at the scene, and the crowd cheered when the master of ceremonies told them, "They're with us, not against us!"

Still, the political portents of festivals can hardly be written off. Sociologist Etzioni, for instance, sees them as part of a turning point in U.S. politics: "The Woodstock-type gathering implies mass-event politics versus the one-vote, one-signature type of politics of the past." Hippie expert Yablonsky agrees: "Whether it is a battle in the sense that Abbie considers it one or not, the movement helps to crystallize a lot of inarticulate feeling, mood, and structure, and shows these people their massiveness and power. That certainly has political implications."

For most parents whose offspring want to attend the 1970 festivals, the disquieting judgment of those consulted by *Today's Health* is that the most worrisome conditions to adults—the widespread use of drugs, uninhibited sex, public nudity, obscenity, indiscriminate throwing together of the sexes, and public health problems—all will very likely crop up again. "I think they are intrinsic to the problem," says Hollis Ingraham, M.D., New York State Commissioner of Public Health, whose department was charged with supervision of health conditions at Woodstock. Since Woodstock, drug use and nudity have become barometers of a festival's success—like champagne on New Year's Eve. For instance, much of the disrobing at Woodstock was impromptu—a response to the hot sun, pelting rain, and omnipresent mud. Two weeks later, a Texas festival was held in cool, dry weather—and people took their clothes off anyway.

Actually, the drug-and-sex scene at Woodstock may have been overrated, according to both witnesses and experts. The young people contend they were "stoned about 102 percent of the time" on marijuana, but psychiatrist Rome of Mayo Clinic, for one, doesn't consider this extreme—"Pot is the mark of the times, like the flapper's cigarette, or the Depression's bathtub gin." Hard drugs and hallucinogens like mescaline and LSD seem to have been used only by a peripheral group. Proselytization for drugs, persons urging others to try them, occurred, but apparently was not widespread. Often, veteran drug users kept a careful eye on first-time users to prevent bad trips.

As for sex, some young people contend there was no more in the hills of New York State than in the vicinity of the average college campus. Besides, said one boy, "Most people were discreet. They always waited for night."

The breakdown of public health arrangements at Woodstock has since spurred passage of a state law governing future "residential gatherings." Sponsors of any event expected to attract 5000 or more persons over three days must satisfy health officials that proper provision has been made for water supply, sewerage, toilet facilities, refuse disposal, campgrounds, foods, fire protection, and public health. The facilities must be completely approved 15 days in advance.

In the view of State Health Commissioner Ingraham, the Woodstock sponsors made adequate provisions for daily crowds of 50,000—the estimated daily attendance based on advance ticket sales. Assisted by health department sanitary engineers, they set up fully equipped campgrounds with public spigots, portable toilets, and refuse disposal facilities. But the large turnout quickly swamped the setup, and spread into new areas where no facilities had been established. Storms and jammed access roads complicated the problem. Service trucks were delayed by traffic and then bogged down in the mud when they arrived. A counterpoint to the rock music was the insistent whine of spinning wheels.

However, says Doctor Ingraham, there never was much danger of a serious outbreak of disease. "The people were young and healthy,"

Doctor Ingraham says, "and unless you have a contaminated water supply or a contaminated central food supply, both of which we tried to keep close tabs on, you are not likely to have a health problem in the short run."

The emergency medical care setup at Woodstock was extensive. Dr. William J. Abruzzi, a Wappingers Falls, New York, physician, who previously had organized medical programs for civil rights marches and demonstrations, was in charge. He enlisted 18 physicians, 36 nurses, and 27 medical assistants, and established two "emergency rooms" in trailers, a 30-bed hospital tent, and two standby ambulances. When Doctor Abruzzi realized that attendance would far outstrip estimates, he quickly recruited more medical and nursing personnel, established a full-fledged 100-bed hospital in nearby Monticello High School, and alerted every ambulance in Sullivan County. Army helicopters from Stewart Air Force Base in Newburgh, New York, were brought in to airlift patients from festival grounds to county hospitals.

During Woodstock's three days, Doctor Abruzzi reported later, his medical team treated 5162 persons, the greatest number for foot lacerations, puncture wounds, and infections caused by going without shoes. They saw 87 cases of exhaustion, 64 of exposure, and 57 of heat prostration. There were 797 "bad trips" from drugs, but only 72 were severe enough to require medical attention, and only 28 of those received medication. Twenty miscarriages and threatened miscarriages occurred. Three persons died—one in a tractor accident and two by drug overdoses. But not one person was treated for injuries that might have been received by fighting.

Indeed, most older persons associated with rock festivals have only praise for the peacefulness of the audiences. "These are the best kids in the country," exulted one father after a Midwestern festival. Demographically, they certainly are—the Woodstock audience, for example, was almost exclusively white, upper-middle-class, upper-income, and well-educated. There were few black faces and few persons over 30. The ages of the audience members dipped as low as 15, but the majority were in their late teens and early 20's. "This is right in the tradition of youth asserting its independence," says psychiatrist Rome. "When they get older they will join the Kiwanis and the Rotary Club."

But some festival goers seem to be doing more than sowing youthful wild oats. Says sociologist Goodman: "They seem to be looking for some kind of solace and temporary joy, as if they are suffering from a terrible uprootedness and anxiety and need to be happy for a few minutes." Sociologist Lang agrees with him: "They seem to wish to stand on the threshold of the beyond."

Perhaps one reason that Woodstock and its successor festivals have been nonviolent is that authorities, faced with overwhelming numbers of law violators, simply ignore the violations. Written and unwritten laws are suspended for the duration. At Woodstock, pot reportedly was hawked like hotdogs at a football game. Anything went in dress, behavior, and language. If police had been hard-nosed about indecent exposure laws at Woodstock, for example, they might have filled every jail in Sullivan County.

"The festival becomes virtually a nation of its own," sociologist Yablonsky says.

> There is a gut-level thrust toward drowning out the external society. The small society takes over completely, establishes its own laws and morality. It becomes normative and "legal" to smoke pot, denude, and "do one's thing." The police are handcuffed and the external society disabled.

Doctor Ingraham, the man who was faced by 300,000 pot smokers and a handful of police at Woodstock, says, "I'm an old conservative, and I don't believe in the law being consciously or continuously broken, but this was a new and unusual situation, and we acted according to what seemed most sensible."

The young people say that the festivals prove something: that when restrictions on pot-smoking and other ways of doing one's thing are taken off, a peaceable society results. If the third largest city in New York State can remain peaceful for three days, they say, other cities could do the same. "The kids would like to believe that and so would I," says psychiatrist Rome. "But there are other peaceful short-time gatherings. It happens at football games all the time." Would Woodstock itself have remained quiet had it continued longer? "One cannot comment," says sociologist Etzioni, "on what did not happen."

Although they disagree about the scope of the change, most of those consulted by *Today's Health* believe festivals are symptomatic of a marked worldwide shift in attitudes and values among the young. Religious, social, political, and personal standards are in a state of flux. The upcoming generation will believe and feel differently from their elders, and will inhabit a different type of society. Rock festival behavior itself will not become the norm but many of the trends it signifies will. Stony Brook's sociologist Lang thinks the shape of these changes is already clear.

"Freud," he says,

> pictured the id, the life force of man, as antirational and primitive. Only the superego, the rational spirit of man, he said, made us human and civilized.
>
> But now the young people are saying that real humanity lies in the id, that rationality has estranged man from his "humanness." They say that technological civilization and ideas of rationality have gone about as far as they can go, or maybe even too far. They are saying "Good-bye to progress, good-bye to rationality—it's time to get back to basic feelings." And that's what they're doing at festivals.

The dissenters are psychiatrist Rome and Herbert H. Hyman, Ph.D., a sociologist, of Wesleyan University. "This is not as unique as some would have us believe," says psychiatrist Rome, repeating his belief that festivals are just today's form of youthful rebellion.

> When I was at the University of Pennsylvania, we used to have what they called "Rowbottoms." Some one would shout into the Quad, "Rowbottom!" Then every window would open and people would hurl whatever could be hurled. At Harvard, they have the same thing. They call them "Rineharts." It's just a latter-day Dionysian Festival. Youth has always done this collective thing.

Sociologist Hyman agrees that the movement is simply old wine in new bottles. "Anybody who studies such matters realizes that youth is the most unstable basis for a social movement of any kind. The only things which produce abiding loyalty are social organizations and class interests. Youth, after all, grow up!"

Nonetheless, the rock festival phenomenon holds many lessons for older persons, the experts all agree. "I can't imagine," psychiatrist Rome says,

> any group of people over 30 comporting themselves in this way in these numbers. There is no reason for adults to click their tongues or lament some of the circumstances of the festivals. Adults could learn greater acceptance of other points of view. They could learn to be a little more elastic in their expectations.

Many of the experts consulted by *Today's Health* themselves have offspring in the rock festival age group, and, expertise or no expertise, they experience some of the same fears and feelings of less aware parents about them. Sociologist Lang, for instance, has a college-age daughter, who did not attend Woodstock. If she wanted to go to a festival this summer, what would he say? "I'd probably tell her, 'It's crazy. It'll be mobbed, you'll spend all your time on the road, you won't get to hear anything. What do you want to do that for?' If she insisted, of course, I'd probably say, 'Well, it's your own damned business.'"

"Of course," he adds, "my wife might have different ideas. She's the worrier."

Psychiatrist Guy of Bryn Mawr watched daughters Nancy, 18, and Susan, 16, head for Woodstock last August. Susan, after camping out on the New York Thruway, was felled by heat prostration and treated by Doctor Abruzzi's medical crew. She returned home halfway through the weekend because of the illness, the general discomfort, and because her food ran out. Nancy started from home early, made more provisions, and thoroughly enjoyed the whole experience. Their father, in view of Susan's experience, doesn't know if he'd want them to go again. Like sociologist Lang, however, he says he'd probably say yes—if they insisted. He adds: "But I have very definite misgivings about the way young people make doing nothing the purpose of life."

Many who go to festivals, of course, are beyond the age of parental consent or even guidance. They live away from home, or on college campuses, and decide for themselves whether to attend festivals and how to behave when they get there. For parents who do worry, however, the consensus advice seems to be, "Don't!" Quote the ever-comforting psychiatrist Rome: "All in all, it's good for them. Most of them, anyway."

Quote Nancy Guy of Bryn Mawr, disagreeing with her father: "People don't want to be nowhere doing nothing. They want to be somewhere, doing something." And her sister Susan adds, "You guys make too much of it. I'm glad I went to Woodstock, but it's not a for-ever and ever thing."

STUDY QUESTIONS

1. What made Woodstock so noticeably different from other music festivals?
2. How have older people reacted to Woodstock? Why do many of them fail to understand its implications?
3. What are some of the theories used to explain the Woodstock phenomenon?
4. Was the music played at Woodstock the central and most important aspect of the festival? How many of the young people who came actually heard the music?

5. What are the political implications of Woodstock? What are its religious implications?
6. What seems to have been the prevailing attitude on sex and drugs at the festival?
7. How does a festival like Woodstock tend to "change" the law? Why does the author describe it as a "nation unto itself"?
8. What are "Rowbottoms" and "Rineharts"? How are they similar to Woodstock?
9. Why is it hard to imagine people over thirty behaving as the people at Woodstock did?
10. What do you make of the kinds of medical problems doctors faced during the festival?

SUGGESTIONS FOR WRITING

1. One commentator felt worried "about the way young people make doing nothing the purpose of life." What does the commentator seem to mean? Is this true? Is there any evidence in or out of the article that might prove it false?
2. What do you think was the most valuable benefit of having gone to Woodstock? If another Woodstock festival was planned, would you want to be there? Why? Try to be as specific as possible and imagine that your essay is intended for someone your own age who has said he definitely would not want to go.
3. It is said that one important aspect of Woodstock is that there was no fighting, no criminal violence on the part of those who were there. The implied conclusion is that sex, dope, and music are the keys to human peace, if not to human happiness; they are the keys to stabilizing the social order. Is this true? Can you defend or attack this premise coherently?
4. Do you really think that such "festivals are symptomatic of a marked worldwide shift in attitudes and values among the young"? Most of those consulted by the author think so. Take a stand and give the most positive argument you can devise to defend your position.
5. Even if it is true that Woodstock was peaceful for as long as it lasted, do you think it would have remained peaceful if it had continued for months or, perhaps, not ended at all? What would the problems have been if Woodstock had not ended but, receiving the land as a gift, had accepted the challenge of building a permanent city?

DEMISE OF THE DANCING DOG

Cynthia Ozick

Some of the inequities women suffer in employment—
such as lower pay for equal work and discrimination in
hiring and promotion—are easily demonstrated. As a
result of the Women's Liberation Movement, these
wrongs are beginning to be remedied. But many aspects
of the discrimination women face in their work are
somewhat more subtle, and their remedy will require
fundamental changes in our way of thinking.

I have just emerged from a year of Examining the Minds of the
Young. It was a curious experience, like going into theatre after theatre in a single night, and catching bits of first acts only. What I saw
of all those beginnings was extraordinary: they were all so similar. All
the characters were exactly the same age, and most had equal limitations of imagination and aspiration.

"I have never in all my various travels seen but two sorts of people,
and those very like one another; I mean men and women, who always have been, and ever will be, the same," wrote Lady Mary Wort-
ley Montagu in the middle of the eighteenth century. Human nature
is one.

The vantage-point from which I came to these not unusual conclusions was not from reading the great philosophers, or even from
reading Lady Mary—it was from a job. I was hired by a large urban
university to teach English to freshmen: three classes of nearly a
hundred young men and young women, all seventeen, some city-born,
some suburban, some well-off, some only scraping by, of every ethnic
group and of every major religion but Hindu. Almost all were
equipped with B high school averages; almost all were more illiterate
than not; almost all possessed similar prejudices expressed in identical
platitudes. They were identically uneducated, and the minds of the

DEMISE OF THE DANCING DOG   Reprinted from the March–April 1969 issue of
Motive by permission of the author.

uneducated young women were identical with the minds of the uneducated men.

Now this last observation was the least surprising of all. I had never doubted that the human mind was a democratic whole—that it was androgynous, epicene, asexual: call it what you will. It had always seemed axiomatic to me that the minds of men and women were indistinguishable.

My students confirmed this axiom to the last degree. You could not tell the young men's papers from the young women's papers. They thought alike (badly); they wrote alike (gracelessly); and they believed alike (docilely). And what they all believed was this: that the minds of men and women are spectacularly unlike.

They believed that men write like men, and women like women; that men think like men, and women like women; that men believe like men, and women like women. And they were all identical in this belief.

Still, to teach at a university is not simply to teach; the teacher is a teacher among students, but he is also a teacher among teachers. He has colleagues, and to have colleagues is to have high exchanges, fruitful discourses, enlightening quarrels. Colleagues, unlike students, are not merely literate but breathtakingly literary; not merely educated but bent under the weight of multitudinous higher degrees; not merely informed but dazzlingly knowledgeable; not merely unprejudiced but brilliantly questing.

And my colleagues believed exactly what my students believed.

My colleagues were, let it be noted, members of a Department of English in the prestige-college of an important university. I was, let it be revealed, the only woman instructor in that Department. Some years before, the college had been all-male. Then the coeds were invited in, and now and then in their wake a woman was admitted, often reluctantly, to the faculty. I was in touch with novels, poetry, essays, enlarging meditations; but of "the world," as it turned out, I apparently knew little.

I came to the university in search of the world. I had just finished an enormous novel, the writing of which had taken many more years than any novel ought to take, and after so long a retreat my lust for the world was prodigious. I wanted Experience, I wanted to sleep under bridges—but finding that all the bridges had thickly trafficked cloverleafs under them, I came instead to the university. I came innocently. I had believed, through all those dark and hope-sickened years of writing, that it was myself ("myself"—whatever that means for each of us) who was doing the writing. In the university, among my colleagues, I discovered two essential points: (a) that it was a "woman" who had done the writing—not a mind—and that I was a "woman writer"; and (b) that I was now not a teacher, but a "woman teacher."

I was suspect from the beginning—more so among my colleagues than among my students. My students, after all, were accustomed to the idea of a "woman teacher," having recently been taught by several in high school. But my colleagues were long out of high school, and they distrusted me. I learned that I had no genuinely valid opinions, since every view I might hold was colored by my sex. If I said I didn't like Hemingway, I could have no *critical* justification, no *literary* reason; it was only because, being a woman, I obviously could not be sympathetic toward Hemingway's "masculine" subject-matter—the hunting, the fishing, the bullfighting, which no woman could adequately digest. It goes without saying that among my colleagues there were other Hemingway dissenters, but their reasons for disliking Hemingway, unlike mine, were not taken to be simply ovarian.

In fact, both my students and my colleagues were equal adherents of the Ovarian Theory of Literature, or, rather, its complement, the Testicular Theory. A recent camp-follower (I cannot call him a pioneer) of this explicit theory is, of course, Norman Mailer, who has attributed his own gift, and the literary gift in general, solely and directly to the possession of a specific pair of organs. One writes with these organs, Mailer has said in *Advertisements for Myself*; and I have always wondered with what shade of ink he manages to do it.

I recall my first encounter with the Ovarian Theory. My students had been assigned the reading of *Wise Blood*, the novella by Flannery O'Connor. Somewhere in the discussion I referred to the author as "she." The class stirred in astonishment; they had not imagined that "Flannery" could connote a woman, and this somehow put a different cast upon the narrative and their response to it. Now among my students there was a fine young woman, intelligent and experimental rather than conforming, one of my rare literates, herself an anomaly because she was enrolled in the overwhelmingly male College of Engineering. I knew that her mind usually sought beyond the commonplace—she wrote with the askew glance of the really inquisitive. Up went her hand.

"But I could *tell* she was a woman," she insisted. "Her sentences are a woman's sentences." I asked her what she meant and how she could tell. "Because they're sentimental," she said, "they're not concrete like a man's." I pointed out whole paragraphs, pages even, of un-

sentimental, so-called "tough" prose. "But she *sounds* like a woman
—she has to sound that way because she is," said the future engineer,
while I speculated whether her bridges and buildings would loom
plainly as woman's work. Moreover, it rapidly developed that the
whole class now declared that it too, even while ignorant of the author's sex, had nevertheless intuited all along that this was a woman's
prose; it had to be, since Flannery was a she.

My second encounter with the idea of literature-as-physiology was
odder yet. This time my interlocutor was a wonderfully gentle, deeply
intellectual young fellow-teacher—he was going to *prove* what my
freshmen had merely maintained. "But of *course* style is influenced by
physical make-up," he began in his judicious graduate-assistant way.
Here was his incontrovertible evidence: "Take Keats, right? Keats
fighting tuberculosis at the end of his life. You don't suppose Keats's
poetry was totally unaffected by his having had tuberculosis?" And he
smiled with the flourish of a young man who has made an unanswer-
able point. "Ah, but *you* don't suppose," I put it to him cheerfully
enough, "that being a woman is a *disease?*"

But comparing literary women with having a debilitating disease
is the least of it. My colleague, after all, was a kindly sort, and stuck
to human matters; he did not mention dogs. On the other hand,
almost everyone remembers Dr. Johnson's remark upon hearing a
woman preacher—she reminded him, he said, of a dog dancing on its
hind legs; one marvels not at how well it is done, but that it is done at
all. That was two centuries ago; wise Lady Mary was Johnson's contemporary. Two centuries, and the world of letters has not been
altered by a syllable, unless you regard the switch from dogs to disease as a rudimentary advance. Perhaps it is. We have advanced so
far that the dullest as well as the best of freshmen can scarcely be distinguished from Dr. Johnson, except by a bark.

And our own Dr. Johnson—I leave you to guess his name—hoping
to insult a rival writer, announces that the rival "reminds me of nothing so much as a woman writer."

Consider, in this vein, the habits of reviewers. I think I can say in
good conscience that I have never—repeat, *never*—read a review of a
novel or, especially, of a collection of poetry by a woman which did
not include somewhere in its columns a gratuitous allusion to the
writer's sex and its supposed effects. The Ovarian Theory of Literature
is the property of all society, not merely of freshmen and poor Ph.D.
lackeys: you will find it in all the best periodicals, even the most
highbrow.

Reviewers must take merit as their point of concentration, not the flap of skirts, not the glibbest of literary canards. Still, the canards are, in their way, great fun, being as flexible and fragile as other toys. A collection of canards is bound to be a gaggle of contradictions. When, for instance, my bright engineering student identified Flannery O'Connor as "sentimental," she was squarely in one-half of a diluvial, though bifurcated, tradition. Within this tradition there are two hoary views of woman. One: she is sentimental, imprecise, irrational, over-emotional, impatient, unperseveringly flighty, whimsical, impulsive, unreliable, unmechanical, not given to practicality, perilously vague, and so on. In this view she is always contrasted with man, who is, on the other hand, unsentimental, exact, rational, controlled, patient, hard-headed, mechanically gifted, a meeter of payrolls, firm of purpose, wary of impulse, anything but a dreamer.

Description Number One accounts for why, throughout her history, she has been a leader neither of empires nor of trades nor of armies. But it is also declared that, her nature having failed her in the practical world, she cannot succeed in the world of invention either: she is unequipped, for example, for poetry, in that (here is Description Number Two) she is above all pragmatic, sensible and unsentimental, unvisionary, unadventurous, empirical, conservative, down-to-earth, unspontaneous, perseveringly patient and thus good at the minutiae of mechanical and manipulative tasks, and essentially unimaginative. In short, she will wander too much or she will wander not at all. She is either too emotional or she is not emotional enough. She is either too spontaneous or she is not spontaneous enough. She is either too sensitive (that is why she cannot be president of General Motors) or she is not sensitive enough (that is why she will never write *King Lear*).

But none of this is to imply that woman is damned, and damned from every direction. Not at all. The fact is that woman *qua* woman is more often celebrated. If she cannot hear the Muse, says Robert Graves, what does it matter? She *is* the Muse. *Man Does, Woman Is*, is the title of Graves's most recent collection of poetry. If we are expected to conclude from this that woman is an It rather than a Thou, why deplore it? The Parthenon, too, is beautiful, passive, inspiring. Who would long to *build* it, if one can *be* it?

And even this is unfair, for it is simultaneously true that woman is frequently praised as the more "creative" sex. She does not need to make poems, it is argued, she has no drive to make poems, because she is privileged to make babies. A pregnancy is as fulfilling as, say,

Yeats's *Sailing to Byzantium*. Here is an interesting idea worth examination. To begin with, we would have to know what it cost Yeats—I am speaking physically—to wring out a poem of genius. Perhaps we cannot know this. The writing of great and visionary literature is not a common experience, and is not readily explorable. Yeats himself spoke of the poet living amid whirlwinds. Virginia Woolf, a writer of a kind of prose very near poetry in tone and aspiration, was racked in the heat of composition by seizures of profoundly tormenting headaches. Isaac Babel called himself a "galley slave." Conrad was in a frenzy for weeks on end—

> I turn in this vicious circle and the work itself becomes like the work in a treadmill—a thing without joy—a punishing task . . . I am at it day after day, and I want all day, every minute of a day, to produce a beggarly tale of words or perhaps to produce nothing at all . . . One's will becomes the slave of hallucinations, responds only to shadowy impulses, waits on imagination alone.

Dostoyevsky said plainly: "*I worked and was tortured.*"

That is what "creativity" is. Is a pregnancy like that? The fact is, given health, the condition of pregnancy is—in the consciousness— very nearly like the condition of non-pregnancy. It is insulting to a poet to compare his titanic and agonized strivings with the so-called "creativity" of childbearing, where—consciously—nothing happens. One does not will the development of the foetus; one can be as dull or as active, as bored or as intense, as one pleases—anything else is mere self-absorption and daydreams: the process itself is as involuntary and as unaware as the beating of one's own heart. Of course, it is a miracle that one's heart goes on beating, that the foetus goes on growing—but it is not a human miracle, it is Nature's miracle.

To call a child a poem may be a pretty metaphor, but it is a slur on the labor of art. Literature cannot be equated with physiology, and woman through her reproductive system alone is no more a creative artist *than* was Joyce by virtue of his kidneys alone, or James by virtue of his teeth (which, by the way, were troublesome). A poem emerges from a mind, and mind is, so far as our present knowledge takes us, an unknowable abstraction. Perhaps it is a compliment to a woman of no gifts to say of her in compensation, "Ah, well, but she has made a child." But that is a cheap and slippery mythology, and a misleading one.

All this is, one would think, almost stupefyingly obvious. It is embarrassing, it is humiliating, to be so obvious about the quality either of literature or of woman. She, at any rate, is not a Muse, nor is she on the strength of her womb alone an artist. She is—how stupidly obvious!—a person. She can be an artist if she was born talented. She can be a Muse if she inspires a poet, but she, too (if she was born talented), can find her own Muse in another person. Mme. de Sévigné's Muse was her daughter, and what male Muse it was who inspired Emily Brontë's Heathcliff, history continues to conjecture. The Muse —*pace* Robert Graves—has no settled sex or form, and can appear in the shape of a tree (cf. *Howards End*) or a city (the Paris of *The Ambassadors*) or even—think of Proust!—a cookie.

Yet in our culture, in our country, much is not obvious. With respect to woman and with respect to literature, ours is among the most backward areas on earth. It is true that woman has had the vote for forty-five years, and she has begun to enter most professions, though often without an invitation. We are far past the grievances Virginia Woolf grappled with in *A Room of One's Own* and *Three Guineas* —books which are still sneered at as "feminist." In 1929, when Virginia Woolf visited Oxford (or was it Cambridge? she is too sly to say which), she was chased off a lawn forbidden to the feet of women. By then, of course, our colleges were already full of coeds, though not so full as now. And yet the question of justification remains.

Only a few months ago, in my own college, a startling debate was held—"Should a Woman Receive a College Education?" The audience was immense, but the debaters were only three: an instructor in Anthropology (female), a professor of History (male), and a fiercely bearded professor of Psychology (ostentatiously male). According to the unironic conventions of chivalry, the anthropologist spoke first. She spoke of opportunities and of problems. She spoke of living wholly and well. She did not ignore the necessities and difficulties of housekeeping and child-rearing; she spoke of the relations of parents, children, and work-in-the-world; she talked extensively about nursery-schools.

She took as her premise not merely that women ought to be fully educated, but that their education should be fully used in society. She was reasoned and reasonable; she had a point of view. Perhaps it was a controversial point of view, perhaps not—her listeners never had the chance of a serious evaluation. Her point of view was never assailed or refuted. It was overlooked. She spoke—against mysterious whispered cackles in the audience—and sat. Then up rose the laughing psychologist, and cracked jokes through his beard. Then up rose the laughing historian, and cracked jokes through his field—I especially remember one about the despotism of Catherine the Great: "That's what happens when a woman gets emancipated." Laughter from all sides.

Were the historian and the psychologist laughing at the absurdity of the topic the callow students' committee had selected for debate? An absurd topic—it deserves to be laughed out of court, and surely that is exactly what is happening, for here in the audience are all these coeds, censuring and contradicting by their very presence the outrageous question. Yet look again: the coeds are laughing, too. Everyone is laughing the laughter of mockery. They are not laughing at the absurdly callow topic. They are laughing at the buffoonery of the historian and the psychologist, who are themselves laughing at the subject of the topic: the whole huge room, packed to the very doors and beyond with mocking boys and girls, is laughing at the futility of an educated woman. *She* is the absurdity.

The idea of an educated woman is not yet taken seriously in American universities. She is not chased off the campus, she is even welcomed there—but she is not taken seriously as a student, and she will not be welcomed if she hopes to return as a serious life-long scholar. Nor will she be welcomed afterward in the "world." A law firm may hire her, but it will hide her in its rear research offices, away from the eyes of clients. The lower schools will receive her, as they always have, for she is their bulwark; their bulwark, but not their principal, who is a man. We have seen her crawling like Griselda through the long ordeal of medicine: she is almost always bound to be a pediatrician, for it is in her nature to "work with children."

I will not forget the appalling laughter of the two mocking debaters. But it was not so appalling as the laughter of the young men and the young women in the audience. In the laughter of the historian and the psychologist I heard the fussy cry—a cry of violated venerable decorum, no doubt—of the beadle who chased Virginia Woolf off the grass in 1929. But what of that youthful mockery? It was hideous; it showed something ugly and self-shaming about the nature of our society and the nature of our education—and by "our education" I do not mean the colleges, I mean the kindergartens, I mean the living-rooms at home, I mean the fathers and the mothers, the men and the women.

In this country the women, by and large, are at home. Why? Well, plainly because they belong there. They are there to rear the children, and if they have a whole lot of children, there will usually be a helpless baby. The mother is at home to take care of the helpless baby. That is right and reasonable. Everyone agrees—Nature agrees, the father agrees, Society agrees.

Society agrees? That is very interesting. That, too, is an idea worth examination. It is very useful for society to have the mother at home. It keeps her out of the way. If, say, she stopped at only two children—but if she stopped at only two, she would be in danger of reducing the birthrate, which now rivals India's—if she stopped at two, those two might be half-grown, and safely shut up in a school building most of the day, by the time she is thirty-five. And if she were thirty-five—a young, healthy, able, educated thirty-five—with no helpless baby to keep her at home, and most of the day free, what would she do?

Society shudders at the possibility: she might want to get a job. But that would never do. Why, if you counted up all the young, healthy, able, educated, free women of thirty-five, it might come to nearly half the population! And, as things stand now, there are not even enough jobs for the other half of the population, the truly bread-winning half. And what about all those three-quarters-grown persons we call adolescents? Society shudders at them, too: the economy is an inn with no room for adolescents and women. But if it will not allow adolescents and women to share in its work (how can it? so much of the work is done by machines), society must at least provide something else to keep the adolescents and women occupied, if only artificially. So, out of the largesse of its infinitely adaptable lap, it gives women knitting and adolescents transistor radios to dance to. (And for the adolescents of even mediocre capacities—here, there is no discrimination by sex—it comes up with colleges, and fraudulent debates, and more dancing.)

Society provides a complete—and in essence custodial—culture for each group it is forced to keep out of the way. It is a culture of busy-work and make-believe and distraction. Society is very clever, and always has been. Once upon a time, before machines, women and adolescents *were* needed and used to the last degree in the economy. Women were not educated because an unautomated house requires a work-horse to maintain it, and a woman who cannot read or write is somehow better at hauling water in from the pump than one who can. (Why this should be, only the experience of society can explain.) But now society—so long as we fail to renovate it—can furnish work for only a quarter of the population, and so the rest must be lured into thinking it is performing a job when it is really not doing anything beyond breathing.

That is why there are in our society separate minority cultures for

adolescents and for women. Each has its own set of opinions, prejudices, tastes, values, and—do not underestimate this last—magazines.
You and I are here concerned only with the culture of women. Society, remember, is above men and women; it acts *in* men and
women. So you must not make the mistake of thinking that the culture of women is the conspiracy of men. Not in the least. That is an
old-fashioned, blue-stocking view of the matter, and it is erroneous.
The culture of women is believed in by both men and women, and it
is the conspiracy of neither, because it is the creature neither of men
alone, nor of women alone, but of society itself—that autonomous,
cunning, insensitive sibling of history.

The culture of women consists of many, many things—products as
well as attitudes, but attitudes mostly. The attitudes generate the
products, and the products utilize the attitudes. The most overriding
attitude is summed up in a cult-word: "Home." (Notice that builders
do not sell houses, they sell "homes"—a case of attitude and product
coalescing.) But what does "Home" mean? It means curtains, rugs,
furniture, a boiler in the cellar, magazines with dress patterns and
recipes and articles full of adulterated Freud, a dog, a box of cereal-
bones for the dog, a kitchen floor that conscience insists must be
periodically waxed, and so forth: but mostly, of course, it means
"Children." And "Children" are not regarded as incomplete or new
persons, as unformed destinies, as embryo participants in the society
—above all, they are not regarded simply as *children*: they are a
make-believe entity in themselves, a symbol of need and achievement,
just as the dog-biscuits (not real bones) are a make-believe entity in
themselves (does the dog think they are real?). "Children" as a concept have, in their present incarnation, a definite function, which is
to bolster the whole airy system of make-believe. "Children" are there
to justify "Home"; and "Home" is there to justify a third phantom
entity—the heroine of the fairy-tale, also an invention and an abstraction, the "Homemaker."

This is our "problem"—the problem of a majority's giving its credence and its loyalty to a daydream. And it is a bigger problem than
any other we know of in this country, for the plain and terrifying
reason that we do not even consider it to be a problem. Whenever the
cliché-question is put, "What is the Number One problem in America today?" the cliché-answer comes: "Civil rights—the Negro Revolution." Scarcely. The solution to *that* problem is *there*—we have only
to catch up to it, and with all our might. If the debate at my college
had dealt with civil rights, it would have been serious and passionate

and argumentative. We had a Vietnam teach-in: *it* was serious and passionate and argumentative. But no one will be serious and passionate and certainly no one will be argumentative, concerning attitudes about and of women. Once a problem has been articulated, the answer is implicit; the answer is already fated. But this problem is never articulated; there is no answer, because no one asks the question. It is a question that has not yet found its Malcolm. Its substance is, on every level, the stuff of primitive buffoonery.

Well, what *is* the question? Who will formulate it? "Feminists" will not, because it is not a feminist question. It is not a group question or a special-interest question or a conspiratorial question. It is a humanist question. (And yet note how questions that long ago began as purely "feminist," such as birth control with Margaret Sanger, eventually become the foremost and profoundest of humanistic concerns. One has only to read Julian Huxley's essays on evolution in relation to population expansion to grasp this.) Nor will documents formulate it—I am thinking of a recent very popular document, a tract called *The Feminine Mystique*. It was, as tracts go, a superb one, but tracts give answers, somewhat mechanically, and here the question has not yet been put. Besides, it is poets, and never sociologists (still less those even more amorphous persons called "social thinkers"), who are traditionally the formulators and articulators of those seminal questions to which the majority is deaf: the prophets were artists and not lecturers, and so were the composers of our spirituals.

Virginia Woolf is the artist-pioneer, the Margaret-Sanger-as-bard, so to speak, of this social question. Among artists, she has no successor. Not until art has seized and possessed and assimilated this question will it begin to interest the scientist-humanists.

But what are the components of the question? Here they are: no great female architects, painters, playwrights, sailors, bridge-builders, jurists, captains, composers, etc., etc.

Here I think of a curious analogy. Say what you will about the gifted Jews, they have never, up until times so recent that they scarcely begin to count, been plastic artists. Where is the Jewish Michelangelo, the Jewish Rembrandt, the Jewish Rodin? He has never come into being. Why? Have oppression and persecution erased the possibility of his existence? Hardly. Oppression and persecution often tend to reinforce gifts; to proscribe is more effective than to prescribe. Where, then, *is* the Jewish Michelangelo? Is it possible that a whole people cannot produce a single painter? And not merely a single painter of note, but a single painter *at all*? Well, there *have* been artists among the Jews—artisans, we should more likely call them, decorators of trivial ceremonial objects, a wine-cup here, a scroll-cover there. Talented a bit, but nothing great. They never tried their hand at wood or stone or paint. "Thou shalt have no graven images" —the Second Commandment—prevented them. And it is not until a very, very little while ago, under the influence of a movement called "Emancipation," or "Enlightenment," that we begin to see creeping in a Chagall, a Modigliani, an Epstein, who have ceased to believe that art insults the Unity of God. It will be a long, long time before the Jews have their Michelangelo. Before a "David" can happen, a thousand naked Apollos must be hewn. (And Apollo *did* insult the Unity of God.) There must be a readied ground, a preparation—in short, a relevant living culture to frame the event.

The same, I think, with our problem. Gifts and brains are not transmitted, like hemophilia, from the immune sex to the susceptible sex. Genius is the property of both sexes and all nations alike. That is the humanist view. The Jews have had no artists not because they have had no genius for art, but because their image of themselves as a culture inhibited the exercise of the latent gift. And all those non-existent female Newtons and Bachs and Leonardos and Shakespeares —they have had no more chance of leaping from the prison of their societal fates than any Greek slave, or a nomad's child in Yemen today.

The emancipation of women is spectacularly new. As with what we now call the Black Revolution, it is clear that emancipation does not instantly result in achievement. Enlightenment must follow. And the enlightenment has, for women, and especially by women, not yet occurred.

It has not yet occurred even at the most expressive point of all—in the universities. It is the function of a liberal university not to give right answers, but to ask right questions. And the ultimate humanist question, as we have seen, has not yet been expressed (my students had never in all their lives heard it put); the components of the un-realized question, as we have seen, are the experiences and needs and omissions and premises of a culture. A culture can have a seemingly unchanging premise, and then suddenly it will change; hence, among the Jews, Chagall and Modigliani and Epstein; hence, in literature, the early epistolary artists—Mme. de Sévigné and Lady Mary—and then, close on their heels, the genius novelists, Jane and George. Literature was the first to begin it, since literature could be pursued privately and at home.

Cultivation precedes fruition. Perhaps we cannot have our great women architects, painters, playwrights, sailors, bridge-builders, jurists, captains, composers, and so forth, until we have run-of-the-mill women in these roles, until all that is a commonplace—until, in short, women enter into the central stream of mankind's activities, until woman-as-person becomes as flat and unremarked a tradition as man-as-person. Reproduction, trick it out as you will in this or that myth, is still only reproduction, a natural and necessary biological function—and biology, however fancied up with tribal significance and mystical implication, is not enough. Unless you are on the extreme verge of death, it is never enough just to keep on breathing.

Even woman's differing muscular capacity—much is made of this, unsurprisingly—is, in the age of the comprehensive machine, an obstacle to almost no pursuit. The machine widens experience for everyone, and equalizes the physical endurance of men and women. A long journey is no longer a matter of muscle, but of jet-schedules. Presumably, it will become harder and harder to maintain that novelists who are women are condemned to a narrower focus than that of men because their lives are perforce narrower.

The question is, then, I believe, a question touching at least peripherally on art. Not merely literary art, but all the human arts, including those we call science. And I have ventured that the question must be formulated as a humanistic issue, not a sectarian one, not a divisive one. Art must belong to all human beings, not alone to a traditionally privileged segment; every endeavor, every passion, must be available to the susceptible adult, without the intervention of myth or canard.

Woman will cease solely to be man's Muse—an It (as she is, curiously, for writers as disparate as Graves and Mailer, as she was for Freud)—and will acquire Muses of her own when she herself ceases to be bemused with gaudy daydreams and romances—with lies reinforcing lies—about her own nature. She limits—she self-limits—her aspirations and her expectations. She joins the general mockery at her possibilities. I have heard her laughing at herself as though she were a dancing dog. You have seen her regard her life as a disease to be constantly tended and pacified. She does not yet really believe that she is herself accessible to poetry or science: she wills these into her sons, but not into her daughters. She surrounds herself with the devices and manipulations of an identity that is not an identity. Without protest she permits the intractable momentum of society to keep her from its worthinesses and larger adventures, from its expressive labor. She lives among us like a docile captive; a consuming object; an accomplice;

an It. She has been successfully persuaded to work for and at her own imprisonment.

If one were to bow to the tempting idea that her role has come about through a conspiracy (as it could not have, for custom is no plot), it would appear as though it were a conspiracy of sluggish women, and never of excluding men. The fervor and energies of the women who are not lazy, those rare activist personalities who feel the call of a Cause, are thrown pragmatically into the defense of that easy and comfortable role; the barricades of the pleasant prison are manned —no, womaned—by the inmates themselves, to prevent the rebels from breaking out.

But the rebels are few.

That is because, among us, no one rebels, no one protests, no one wants to renovate or liberate, no one asks any fundamental questions. We have, alas, the doubtful habit of reverence. Above all we respect things-as-they-are. If we want to step on the moon, it is not to explore an unknown surface or to divine a new era, but to bolster ourselves at home, among the old home rivals; there is more preening than science in that venture, less boldness than bravado. We are so placid that the smallest tremor of objection to anything at all is taken as a full-scale revolution: a bunch of college students sit down, and university presidents at commencements all over the country begin en masse to chirp out alarmed and startled strictures on the subject of rashness, failing discipline, the threat to civil peace. Should anyone speak up in favor of the obvious, it is taken as a symptom of the influence of the left, the right, the pink, the black, the hippie. An idea for its own sake— especially an obvious idea—has no respectability.

Among my last year's students—let us come back to *them,* for they are our societal prototypes—all of this was depressingly plain. That is why they could not write intelligibly—no one had ever mentioned the relevance of writing to thinking, and thinking had never been encouraged or induced in them. By "thinking" I mean, of course, not the simple ability to make equations come out right, but the devotion to speculation on that frail but obsessive distraction known as the human condition. My students—male and female—did not need to speculate on what goals are proper to the full life; male and female, they already knew their goals. And their goals were identical. They all wanted to settle down into a perpetual and phantom coziness. They were all at heart sentimentalists—and sentimentalists, Yeats said, are persons "who believe in money, in position, in a marriage bell, and whose understanding of happiness is to be so busy whether at work or play, that all is forgotten but the momentary aim." Accordingly, they had all opted, long ago, perhaps at birth, for the domestic life, the enclosed life, the constricted life—the life, in brief, of the daydream, into which the obvious must not be permitted to thrust its scary beams.

By the "obvious" I mean, once again, the gifts and teachings and life-illuminations of art. The methods of art are variegated, flexible, abstruse, and often enough mysterious. But the burden of art is obvious: here is the world, here are human beings, here is childhood, here is struggle, here is hate, here is old age, here is death. None of these is a fantasy, a romance, or a sentiment, none is an imagining; all are obvious. A culture which does not allow itself to look clearly at the obvious through the universal accessibility of art is a culture of tragic delusion, hardly viable; it will make room for a system of fantasy Offices on the one hand, and a system of fantasy Homes on the other, but it will forget that the earth lies beneath it all.

Such a culture will turn out role-playing stereotypes (the hideousness of the phrase is appropriate to the concept) instead of human beings. It will shut the children away from half the population. It will shut aspiration away from half the population. It will glut its colleges with young people enduringly maimed by illusions learned early and kept late. It will sup on make-believe. But a humanistic society— you and I do not live in one—is one in which a voice is heard: "Come," it says, "here is a world requiring architects, painters, playwrights, sailors, bridge-builders, jurists, captains, composers, discoverers, and a thousand things besides, all real and all obvious. Partake," it says, "live."

Is it a man's voice or a woman's voice? Students, colleagues, listen again: it is two voices. "How obvious," you will one day reply, and if you laugh, it will be at the quaint folly of obsolete custom, which once failed to harness the obvious; it will not be at a dancing dog.

STUDY QUESTIONS

1. What does the author mean by "Human nature is one"?
2. How does the author describe college freshmen? Does the description irritate you?
3. Why does the author worry about the ways in which so many freshmen think alike?
4. What did the author's students and colleagues have in common?

5. Do men and women write differently?
6. How is the "dancing dog" related to the point of the article?
7. What does sentimentality have to do with the concept of a "woman writer"? How do you feel about the female engineering student's response?
8. Is childbirth comparable to creating a great work of literature?
9. Do you think the "idea of an educated woman is not yet taken seriously in American universities"?
10. Is it true that "among us, no one rebels, no one protests"?

SUGGESTIONS FOR WRITING

1. How do you stand on the first question Cynthia Ozick raises: do men think like men and women think like women? Is such a distinction really plausible, or do you feel you could defend quite a different proposition? Are there fundamental intellectual and emotional differences between men and women that affect their ways of thinking?
2. The author describes her freshman students as being "identically uneducated, and the minds of the uneducated young women were identical with the minds of the uneducated men." Do you think this is a reasonable evaluation of freshmen in general? How would you attack or defend such a statement?
3. The article presents a range of arguments directed at the theory that women are somehow basically different from men. Which of these arguments do you think is the most impressive? How could you strengthen it?
4. Do you think there is a basic difference between male and female writers—that is, a difference detectible in their writing? Take examples from this book, or any others, and try to show whether there is a perceptible difference.
5. If you think that this essay presents an unacceptable argument, attack it. But be sure that you find solid grounds on which to base your attack. Do not initiate any of the fallacious ways of thinking that Cynthia Ozick exposes. If you find her argument convincing, how do you imagine a critic would begin to attack it? How would you defend it against such an attack?

RACISM AND ANTI-FEMINISM

Shirley Chisholm

Shirley Chisholm is female, black, and one of the most
distinguished politicians in the country. In this statement
on anti-feminism and its relationship to racism, she
speaks with the authority only personal experience can
provide. Her hope is that women will soon break out of
their traditional stereotypes and pursue their quest for
equal rights in the manner associated with history's
great revolutionaries.

Women take an active part in society and in particular do they
take a part in the present social revolution. And I find the question,
do women dare to liberate themselves, as much of an insult as I would
the question, "Are you, as a black person, willing to fight for your
rights?"

America has been sufficiently sensitized as to whether or not black
people are willing to both fight and die for their rights to make the
question itself asinine and superfluous. America is not yet sufficiently
aware that such a question applied to women is equally asinine and
superfluous.

I am both black and a woman. That is a good vantage point from
which to view at least two elements of what is becoming a social
revolution: the American Black Revolution and the Women's Liberation Movement. But it is also a horrible disadvantage. It is a disadvantage because America, as a nation, is both racist and anti-feminist.
Racism and anti-feminism are two of the prime traditions of this
country.

For any individual, challenging social traditions is a giant step, a
giant step because there are no social traditions which do not have
corresponding social sanctions, the sole purpose of which are to protect the sanctity of the traditions.

RACISM AND ANTI-FEMINISM   Reprinted from the January–February 1970 issue
of the Black Scholar by permission of the author and the Black Scholar.

Thus when we ask the question "Do women dare?" we are not asking if women are capable of a break with tradition so much as we are asking, "Are they capable of bearing with the sanctions that will be placed upon them?"

Coupling this with the hypothesis presented by some social thinkers and philosophers that in any given society the most active groups are those that are nearest to the particular freedom that they desire, it does not surprise me that those women most active and vocal on the issue of freedom for women are those who are young, white, and middle-class; nor is it too surprising that there are not more from that group involved in the Women's Liberation Movement.

There certainly are reasons why more women are not involved. This country as I said is both racist and anti-feminist. Few, if any, Americans are free of the psychological wounds imposed by racism and anti-feminism.

A few weeks ago while testifying before the Office of Federal Contract Compliance, I noted that anti-feminism, like every form of discrimination, is destructive both to those who perpetrate it and to their victims; that males with their anti-feminism, maim both themselves and their women.

In *Soul on Ice* Eldridge Cleaver pointed out how America's racial and sexual stereotypes were supposed to work. Whether his insight is correct or not, it bears close examination.

Cleaver, in the passage "The Primeval Mitosis," describes in detail the four major roles. There is the white female who he considers to be "Ultra-feminine" because ". . . she is required to possess and project an image that is in sharp contrast to . . ." the white male's image as the "Omnipotent Administrator . . . all brain and no body."

He goes on to identify the black female as "Subfeminine" or "Amazon" by virtue of her assignment to the lowly household chores and those corresponding jobs of tedious nature. He sums up the role of the black male as the "Supermasculine Menial, all body and no brain," because he was expected to supply society with its source of brute power.

What the roles and strange interplay between them have meant to America, Cleaver goes on to point out quite well.

What he does not say and what I think must be said is that because of the bizarre aspects of their roles and the influence that non-traditional contact among them has on the general society, blacks and whites, males and females, must operate almost independently of each other in order to escape from the quicksands of psychological slavery. Each—black male and black female, white female and white male—must escape first from their own historical trap before they can be truly effective in helping others to free themselves.

Therein lies one of the major reasons that there are not more women involved in the Women's Liberation Movement. Women cannot, for the most part, operate independently of males because they often do not have sufficient economic freedom.

In 1966 the median earnings of women who worked full-time for the whole year was less than the median income of males who worked full-time for the whole year. In fact, white women workers made less than black male workers, and of course, black women workers made the least of all.

Whether it is intentional or not women are paid less than men for the same work, no matter what their chosen field. Whether it is intentional or not, employment for women is regulated still more in terms of the jobs that are available to them. This is almost as true for white women as it is for black women.

Whether it is intentional or not, when it becomes time for a young high-school girl to think about preparing for her career, her counselors, whether they be male or female, will think first of her so-called "natural" career—housewife and mother—and begin to program her for a field with which marriage and children will not unduly interfere.

That is exactly the same as the situation of the young blacks or Puerto Ricans whom the racist counselor advises to prepare for service-oriented occupations because he does not even consider the possibility of their entering the professions.

The response of the average young lady is precisely the same as the response of the average young black or Puerto Rican—tacit agreement—because the odds do seem to be stacked against them.

This is not happening as much as it once did to young minority-group people. It is not happening because they have been radicalized and the country is becoming sensitized to its racist attitudes and the damage that it does.

Young women must learn a lesson from that experience!

They must rebel—they must react to the traditional stereotyped education mapped out for them by the society. Their education and training is programmed and planned for them from the moment the doctor says, "Mr. Jones, it's a beautiful baby girl!" and Mr. Jones begins deleting mentally the things that she might have been and adds the things that society says that she *must* be.

That young woman (for society begins to see her as a stereotype the moment that her sex is determined) will be wrapped in a pink blanket (pink because that is the color of her caste) and the unequal segregation of the sexes will have begun.

Small wonder that the young girl sitting across the desk from her counselor will not be able to say "No" to educational, economic, and social slavery. Small wonder, because she has been a psychological slave and programmed as such since the moment of her birth!

On May 20th of last year I introduced legislation concerning the equal employment opportunities of women. At that time I pointed out that there were three and one-half million more women than men in America but that women held only two percent of the managerial positions; that no women sit on the AFL–CIO Council or the Supreme Court; that only two women had ever held Cabinet rank and that there were at that time only two women of Ambassadorial rank in the Diplomatic Corps. I stated then as I do now that this situation is outrageous.

In my speech on the Floor that day I said:

> It is true that part of the problem has been that women have not been aggressive in demanding their rights. This was also true of the black population for many years. They submitted to oppression and even co-operated with it. Women have done the same thing. But now there is an awareness of this situation, particularly among the younger segment of the population.
>
> As in the field of equal rights for blacks, Spanish-Americans, the Indians and other groups, laws will not change such deep-seated problems overnight. But they can be used to provide protection for those who are most abused, and begin the process of evolutionary change by compelling the insensitive majority to re-examine its unconscious attitudes.

The law cannot do it for us, we must do it ourselves. Women in this country must become revolutionaries. We must refuse to accept the old—the traditional—roles and stereotypes.

We must reject the Greek philosopher's thought, "It is thy place, women, to hold thy place and keep within doors." We must reject the thought of St. Paul who said "Let the woman learn in silence." And we must reject the Nietzschean thought "When a woman inclines to learning, there is something wrong with her sex apparatus."

But more than merely rejecting we must replace those thoughts and the concepts that they symbolize with positive values based on female experience.

A few short years ago if you called most Negroes black it was tantamount to calling them niggers. But now black is beautiful and black is proud. There are relatively few people, white or black, who do not recognize what has happened.

Black people have freed themselves from the dead weight of the albatross of blackness that once hung around their neck. They have done it by picking it up in their arms and holding it out with pride for all the world to see. They have done it by embracing it—not in the dark of the moon but in the searing light of the white sun. They have said "Yes" to it and found that the skin that was once seen as symbolizing their shame is in reality their badge of honor.

Women must come to realize that the superficial symbolisms that surround us are negative only when we ourselves perceive and accept them as negative. We must begin to replace the old negative thoughts about our femininity with positive thoughts and positive actions affirming it and more.

But we must also remember that that will be breaking with tradition and we must prepare ouselves—educationally, economically and psychologically—in order that we will be able to accept and bear with the sanctions that society will immediately impose upon us.

I am a politician. I detest the word because of the connotations that cling like slime to it but for want of a better term I must use it.

I have been in politics for twenty years and in that time I have learned a few things about the role of women in politics.

The major thing that I have learned is that women are the backbone of America's political organizations. They are the letter-writers and envelope-stuffers, the telephone-answerers; they are the campaign-workers and organizers. They are the speech-writers and the largest numbers of potential voters.

Yet they are but rarely the standard-bearers or elected officials. Perhaps it is in America, more than any other country, that the inherent truth of the old bromide "The power behind the throne is a woman" is most readily apparent.

Let me remind you once again of the relatively few women standard-bearers on the American political scene. There are only ten United States Representatives. There is only one Senator and there are no Cabinet members who are women. There are no women on the Supreme Court and only a small percentage of lady judges at the Federal Court level who might be candidates.

It is true that at the state level the picture is somewhat brighter just as it is true that the North presents a surface that is somewhat more appealing to the black American when compared with the South. But even though in 1967 there were 318 women in various state legislatures, the percentage is not good when compared with the fact that in almost all fifty states there are more women of voting age than there are men; and that in each state the number of women of voting age is increasing at a greater rate than the number of men. Nor is it an encouraging figure when compared with the fact that in 1966 there were not 318 but 328 women in the state legislatures.

Secondly I have learned that the attitude held by the high school counselors that I mentioned earlier is a general attitude held by political bosses. A few years ago a politician remarked to me about a potential young female candidate, "Why invest all the time and effort to build up the gal into a household name when she's pretty sure to drop out of the game to have a couple of kids at just about the time we're ready to run her for mayor?"

I have pointed out time and time again that the harshest discrimination that I have encountered in the political arena is anti-feminism —both from males and brainwashed "Uncle Tom" females.

When I first announced that I was running for the United States Congress last year, both males and females advised me, as they had when I ran for the New York State Assembly, to go back to teaching, a woman's vocation, and leave the politics to the men.

One of the major reasons that I will not leave the American political scene—voluntarily, that is—is because the number of women in politics is declining.

There are at least two million more women than men of voting age but the fact is that while we get out the vote we often do not get out *to vote.* In 1964, for example, 72 percent of registered males voted while only 67 percent of registered females voted. We seem to be a political minority by choice.

I believe that women have a special contribution to make to help bring order out of chaos because they have special qualities of leadership which are greatly needed today. These qualities are the patience, tolerance and perseverance which have developed in many women because of their suppression. If we can add to these qualities a reservoir of information about techniques of community action we can indeed become effective harbingers of change. Women must participate more in the legislative process because, even with the contributions that I have just mentioned, the single greatest contribution that women could bring to American politics would be a spirit of moral purpose.

But unfortunately women's participation in politics is declining, as I have noted. Politics is not the only place that we are losing past gains, though. Columnist Clayton Fritchey in a column *Woman In Office*, noted that "although more women are working, their salaries keep falling behind men's. Some occupations are (still) closed by law to women. Key property laws favor men. In 1940 women held 45 per cent of all professional and technical positions as against 37 per cent today."

The decline is a general one. But it is because it is a decline that I believe that the true question is not whether or not women dare to move. Women have always dared! The question which now faces us is, "Will women dare move in numbers sufficient to have an effect on their own attitudes toward themselves and thus change the basic attitudes of males and the general society?"

Women will have to brave the social sanctions in great numbers in order to free themselves from the sexual, psychological, and emotional stereotyping that plagues us. Like black people we will have to raise our albatross with pride.

It is not feminine egoism to say that the future of mankind may very well be ours to determine. It is simply a plain fact. The softness, warmth, and gentleness that are often used to stereotype us are positive human values; values that are becoming more and more important as the general values of the whole of mankind slip more and more out of kilter.

The strength that marked Christ, Gandhi, and Martin Luther King was a strength born not of violence but of gentleness, understanding and genuine human compassion.

We must move outside the walls of our stereotypes but we must retain the values on which they were built.

No, I am not saying that we are inherently those things that the stereotypes impute that we are; but I am saying that because of the long-enforced roles we have had to play we should know by now that the values are good ones to hold and I am saying that by now we should have developed the capacity to not only hold them but to also dispense them to those around us.

This is the reason that we must free ourselves. This is the reason that we must become revolutionaries in the fashion of Christ, Gandhi, King and the hundreds of other men and women who held those as the highest of human values.

There is another reason. In working toward our own freedom we can also allow our men to work toward their freedom from the traps of their stereotypes.

We are challenged now as we never were before. The past twenty years, with its decline for women in employment and government, with its status quo attitude toward the preparation of young women for certain professions, make it clear that evolution is not necessarily always a process of positive forward motion. Susan B. Anthony, Carrie Nation and Sojourner Truth were not evolutionaries. They were revolutionaries, as are many of the young women of today. More women and more men must join their ranks.

New goals and new priorities, not only for this country, but for all mankind, must be set. Formal education will not help us do that. We must therefore depend on informal learning.

We can do that by confronting people with their own humanity and their own inhumanity. Confronting them wherever we meet them —in the church, in the classroom, on the floors of Congress and the state legislatures, in bars and on the streets. We must reject not only the stereotypes that others hold of us but also the stereotypes that we hold of ourselves and others.

In a speech made a few weeks ago to an audience that was predominantly white and all female I suggested the following if they wanted to create change:

> You must start in your own homes, your own schools and your own churches . . . I don't want you to go home and talk about integrated schools, churches or marriages when the kind of integration you are talking about is black with white.
>
> I want you to go home and work for—fight for—the integration of male and female—human and human. Frantz Fanon pointed out in **Black Skins, White Masks** that the Anti-Semitic was eventually the Anti-Negro. I want to say that both are eventually the Anti-Feminist. And even further, I want to indicate that all discrimination is eventually the same thing—Anti-Humanism.

That is my challenge for us today, whether we are male or female.

STUDY QUESTIONS

1. What is the effect of calling racism and anti-feminism "traditions"?
2. From what social groups do most Women's Liberationists come? Why is Shirley Chisholm not surprised by that?
3. How do you react to Eldridge Cleaver's analysis of roles in America?
4. What is the "historical trap" each of us must avoid?

5. What is the current economic situation of women?
6. Why does society begin to stereotype a girl as soon as she is born?
7. How impressive are Shirley Chisholm's statistics concerning female employment in high government positions?
8. How has usage of "black" changed in recent years? Who changed it?
9. What does the author mean when she says that women are a "political minority by choice"?
10. To what extent is political participation by women declining?

SUGGESTIONS FOR WRITING

1. A suggestion for changing anti-feminist attitudes is to follow the example of black people who hold up their "albatross" with pride. How can this tactic of making a virtue of what formerly held one back be used by women?
2. Shirley Chisholm exhorts women to become revolutionaries in "the fashion of Christ, Gandhi, King." What does she mean? Do you agree? Can women really gain their liberation by becoming revolutionaries? Is there any other way?
3. One important point in the article is that if any gains are to be long lasting, new goals and new priorities must be set for the nation as a whole, not just for blacks and women. Is this true? What specific action would it entail? Who could set such goals?
4. One of the injustices the author cites is the fact that women often are paid less for the same job than men are. Do you think that this generally is the case? Should women get the same pay as men, or should they be paid less? What are the arguments for and against the situation as it now is?
5. What kinds of experiences have you actually had with anti-feminism? Are there people in your family, in your school, or at your job who are anti-female? Give some thought to the definitions of anti-feminism suggested by the article before you respond. Are you, in any way, an anti-feminist?

THE CULTURE OF CIVILITY

Howard S. Becker and Irving Louis Horowitz

The West Coast has long been called the bellwether for changes in America's life style and social attitudes. San Francisco, the home of the youth movement during the 1960s, continues to be especially conspicuous for its toleration of behaviors considered extreme in other parts of the nation. Becker and Horowitz examine that city's approach to drugs, homosexuality, prostitution, and pornography in an attempt to convey the unique spirit of accommodation that exists in San Francisco.

Deviants of many kinds live well in San Francisco—natives and tourists alike make that observation. The city's apparently casual and easygoing response to "sex, dope and cheap thrills" (to crib the suppressed full title of Janis Joplin's famous album—itself a San Francisco product) astounds visitors from other parts of the country who can scarcely credit either what they see happening or the way natives stroll by those same events unconcerned.

Walking in the Tenderloin on a summer evening, a block from the Hilton, you hear a black whore cursing at a policeman: "I wasn't either blocking the sidewalk! Why don't you motherfucking fuzz mind your own goddamn business!" The visiting New Yorker expects to see her arrested, if not shot, but the cop smiles good-naturedly and moves on, having got her back into the doorway where she is supposed to be.

You enter one of the famous rock ballrooms and, as you stand getting used to the noise and lights, someone puts a lit joint of marijuana in your hand. The tourist looks for someplace to hide, not wishing to be caught in the mass arrest he expects to follow. No need to worry. The police will not come in, knowing that if they do they will have to arrest people and create disorder.

THE CULTURE OF CIVILITY   Reprinted from the April 1970 issue of *Transaction* by permission of *Transaction*.

Candidates for the city's Board of Supervisors make their pitch for the homosexual vote, estimated by some at 90,000. They will not be run out of town; the candidates' remarks are dutifully reported in the daily paper, as are the evaluations of them by representatives of SIR, the Society for Individual Rights.

The media report (tongue in cheek) the annual Halloween Drag Ball, for which hundreds of homosexuals turn out at one of the city's major hotels in full regalia, unharassed by police.

One sees long-haired, bearded hippies all over the city, not just in a few preserves set aside for them. Straight citizens do not remark their presence, either by gawking, hostility or flight.

Nudie movies, frank enough to satisfy anyone's curiosity, are exhibited in what must be the largest number of specialty movie houses per capita in the country. Periodic police attempts to close them down (one of the few occasions when repression has been attempted) fail.

The items can be multiplied indefinitely, and their multiplicity demands explanation. Most cities in the United States refuse to let deviants indulge themselves publicly, let alone tolerate candidates who seek their bloc votes. Quite the contrary. Other cities, New York and Chicago being good examples, would see events like these as signs of serious trouble, omens of a real breakdown in law enforcement and deviance control, the forerunner of saturnalia and barbarian take-over. Because its politicians and police allow and can live with activities that would freak out their opposite numbers elsewhere, San Francisco is a natural experiment in the consequences of tolerating deviance. We can see from its example what results when we ignore the warnings of the custodians of conventional morality. We can see too what lessons can be learned about the conditions under which problems that perhaps lie deeper than matters of morals or life style can be solved to the satisfaction of all the parties to them.

We can summarize this low-key approach to deviance in the phrase "a culture of civility." What are its components, and how does it maintain itself?

San Francisco prides itself on its sophistication, on being the most European of American cities, on its picturesque cosmopolitanism. The picturesque quality, indeed the quaintness, rests in part on physical beauty. As the filling of the Bay and the destruction of the skyline by high-rise buildings proceeds to destroy that beauty, the city has come to depend even more on the presence of undigested ethnic minorities. It is as though San Francisco did not wish its Italians, Chinese or Russians to assimilate and become standard Americans, preferring instead to maintain a panoply of ethnic differences: religious, cultural and culinary (especially culinary). A sophisticated, livable city, in this view, contains people, colonies and societies of all kinds. Their differences create a mosaic of life styles, the very difference of whose sight and smell give pleasure.

Like ethnic minorities, deviant minorities create enclaves whose differences add to the pleasure of city life. Natives enjoy the presence of hippies and take tourists to see their areas, just as they take them to see the gay area of Polk Street. Deviance, like difference, is a civic resource, enjoyed by tourist and resident alike.

To enjoy deviance instead of fearing it requires a surrender of some common sense notions about the world. Most people assume, when they see someone engaging in proscribed activity, that there is worse to come. "Anyone who would do that [take dope, dress in women's clothes, sell his body or whatever] would do anything" is the major premise of the syllogism. "If you break one law or convention, who knows where you'll stop?" Common sense ignores the contrary cases around us everywhere: professional criminals often flourish a legion-naire's patriotism; housewives who are in every other respect conventional sometimes shoplift; homosexuals may be good family providers; some people who habitually use the rings from poptop cans to work the parking meter would not dream of taking dope, and vice versa. "Deviance," like conforming behavior, is highly selective. San Francisco's culture of civility, accepting that premise, assumes that if I know that you steal or take dope or peddle your ass, that is all I *know*. There may be more to know; then again, there may be nothing. The deviant may be perfectly decent in every other respect. We are often enjoined, in a generalization of therapeutic doctrine, to treat other people as individuals; that prescription comes nearer to being filled in San Francisco than in most places in the United States.

Because of that tolerance, deviants find it possible to live somewhat more openly in San Francisco than elsewhere. People do not try so hard to catch them at their deviant activities and are less likely to punish them when caught. Because they live more openly, what they do is more visible to straight members of the community. An established canon of social psychology tells us that we find it harder to maintain negative stereotypes when our personal experience belies them. We see more clearly and believe more deeply that hippies or homosexuals are not dangerous when we confront them on the street day after day or live alongside them and realize that beard plus long hair does not equal a drug-crazed maniac, that limp wrist plus lisp does not equal child-molester.

When such notions become embodied in a culture of civility, the citizenry begins to sense that "everyone" feels that way. We cannot say at what critical point a population senses that sophistication about deviance is the norm, rather than a liberal fad. But San Francisco clearly has that critical mass. To come on as an anti-deviant, in a way that would probably win friends and influence voters in more parochial areas, risks being greeted by laughter and ridicule in San Francisco. Conservatives who believe in law and order are thus inclined to keep their beliefs to themselves. The more people keep moralistic notions to themselves, the more everyone believes that tolerance is widespread. The culture maintains itself by convincing the populace that it is indeed the culture.

It gets help from public pronouncements of civic officials, who enunciate what will be taken as the collective sentiment of the city. San Francisco officials occasionally angle for the conservative vote that disapproves licentiousness. But they more frequently take the side of liberty, if not license. When the police, several years ago, felt compelled to close the first of the "topless joints," the judge threw the case out. He reasoned that Supreme Court decisions required him to take into account contemporary community standards. In his judgment San Francisco was not a prudish community; the case was dismissed. The city's major paper, the *Chronicle*, approved. Few protested.

Similarly, when California's leading Yahoo, Superintendent of Public Instruction Max Rafferty, threatened to revoke the teaching credentials of any San Francisco teacher who used the obscene materials listed in the standard high school curriculum (Eldridge Cleaver's *Soul on Ice* and LeRoi Jones' *Dutchman*), the City did not remove the offending books from its curriculum. Instead, it successfully sued to have Rafferty enjoined from interfering in its operation.

In short, San Franciscans know that they are supposed to be sophisticated and let that knowledge guide their public actions, whatever their private feelings. According to another well-known law of social psychology, their private feelings often come to resemble their public actions, and they learn to delight in what frightens citizens of less civil cities.

We do not suggest that all kinds of deviation are tolerated endlessly. The police try, in San Francisco as elsewhere, to stamp out some vices and keep a ceiling on others. Some deviance frightens San Franciscans too, because it seems to portend worse to come (most recently, users and purveyors of methedrine—"speed merchants" and "speed freaks"—whose drug use is popularly thought to result in violence and crime). But the line is drawn much farther over on the side of "toleration" in San Francisco than elsewhere. A vastly wider range of activities is publicly acceptable. Despite the wide range of visible freakiness, the citizenry takes it all in stride, without the fear and madness that permeates the conventional sectors of cities like Detroit, Chicago, New York, Washington, D.C. and similar centers of undaunted virtue.

How does a culture of civility arise? Here we can only speculate, and then fragmentarily, since so few cities in the United States have one that we cannot make the comparisons that might uncover the crucial conditions. San Francisco's history suggests a number of possibilities.

It has, for one thing, a Latin heritage. Always a major seaport, it has long tolerated the vice that caters to sailors typical of such ports. It grew at the time of the gold rush in an explosive way that burst through conventional social controls. It ceded to its ethnic minorities, particularly the Chinese, the right to engage in prostitution, gambling and other activities. Wickedness and high living form part of the prized past every "tourist" city constructs for itself; some minor downtown streets in San Francisco, for instance, are named for famous madames of the gold rush era.

Perhaps more important, a major potential source of repressive action—the working class—is in San Francisco more libertarian and politically sophisticated than one might expect. Harry Bridges' longshoremen act as bellwethers. It should be remembered that San Francisco is one of the few major American cities ever to experience a general strike. The event still reverberates, and working people who might support repression of others know by personal experience that the policeman may not be their friend. Trade unionism has a left-wing, honest base which gives the city a working-class democracy and even eccentricity, rather than the customary pattern of authoritarianism.

Finally, San Francisco is a town of single people. Whatever actual proportion of the adult population is married, the city's culture is oriented toward and organized for single people. As a consequence, citizens worry less about what public deviance will do to their children, for they don't have any and don't intend to, or they move from the city when they do. (Since there are, of course, plenty of families in the city, it may be more accurate to say that there are fewer white middle-class families, that being the stratum that would, if family-based, provide the greatest number of complaints about deviance. Black, chicano and oriental populations ordinarily have enough to worry about without becoming guardians of public morality.)

San Francisco is known across the country as a haven for deviants. Good homosexuals hope to go to San Francisco to stay when they die, if not before. Indeed, one of the problems of deviant communities in San Francisco is coping with the periodic influx of a new generation of bohemians who have heard that it is the place to be: the beatnik migration of the late fifties and the hippie hordes of 1967. But those problems should not obscure what is more important: that there are stable communities of some size there to be disrupted. It is the stable homosexual community that promises politicians 90,000 votes and the stable bohemian communities of several vintages that provide both personnel and customers for some important local industries (developing, recording and distributing rock music is now a business of sizeable proportions).

Stable communities are stable because their members have found enough of what they want to stay where they are for a while. If where they were proved totally unsatisfying, they presumably would move elsewhere, unless restrained. But no one forces deviants to live in San Francisco. They stay there because it offers them, via the culture of civility, a place to live where they are not shunned as fearsome or disgusting, where agents of control (police and others) do not regard them as unfortunate excrescences to be excised at the first opportunity. Because they have a place to stay that does not harass them, they sink roots like more conventional citizens: find jobs, buy houses, make friends, vote and take part in political activities and all the other things that solid citizens do.

Sinking roots stabilizes deviants' lives, as it does the lives of conventional citizens. They find less need to act in the erratic ways deviants often behave elsewhere, less need to fulfill the prophecy that because they are deviant in one respect they will be deviant in other, more dangerous ways. San Francisco employers know that homosexuals make good employees. Why not? They are not likely to be blackmailed by enterprising hustlers. The police seldom haul them off to jail for little reason or beat them because they feel like pushing some "queers" around. Homosexuals fear none of this in San Francisco, or fear it much less than in most places, and so are less given to the overcompensatory "camping" that gets their fellows into trouble elsewhere.

Police and others do not harass deviants because they have found,

though they may deny it for public relations purposes, that looking
the other way is sometimes a good policy. It is easier, when a Be-In is
going on, to turn your back on the sight of open marijuana smoking
than it is to charge into the crowd and try to arrest people who will
destroy the evidence before you get there, give you a hard time, make
a fool of you and earn you a bad press—and have no conviction to
show for it. At the same time, when you turn your back, nothing
worse is likely to happen: no muggings, no thefts, no rapes, no riots.
Police, more calculating than they seem, often choose to reach just
this kind of accommodation with stable deviant communities.

The accommodation works in circular fashion. When deviants can
live decent lives, they find it possible to behave decently. Furthermore,
they acquire the kind of stake they are often denied elsewhere in the
present and future structure of the community. That stake constrains
them to behave in ways that will not outrage nondeviants, for they
do not want to lose what they have. They thus curb their activities according to what they think the community will stand for.

The community in turn, and especially the police, will put up with
more than they might otherwise, because they understand that nothing else is forthcoming, and because they find that what they are confronted with is not so bad after all. If homosexuals have a Halloween
Drag Ball, the community discovers it can treat it as a good-natured
joke; those who are offended discover that they needn't go near the
Hilton while it is happening.

No doubt neither party to such a bargain gets quite what he would
like. Straight members of the community presumably would prefer
not to have whores walking the downtown streets, would prefer not to
have gay bars operating openly. Deviants of all kinds presumably
would prefer not to have to make any concessions to straight sensi-
bilities. Each gives up something and gets something, and to that
degree the arrangement becomes stable, the stability itself something
both prize.

What we have just described verges on the idyllic, Peace and Harmony in Camelot forever. Such a dream of perfection does not exist in
San Francisco, though more deviants there have more of the advantages of such a bargain, perhaps, than in any other city in the United
States. Nor is it clear that the system we described, even in its perfect
form, would be such an idyll.

In San Francisco, as everywhere, the forces of decency and respectability draw the line somewhere and can be every bit as forceful and

ruthless the other side of that line as the forces of decency and respectability anywhere else. When the Haight-Ashbury got "out of hand" with the overcrowded transiency of 1967, the city moved in the police Tactical Squad, the City Health Department and all the other bureaucratic weapons usually used to roust deviants. They did it again with the growth of violence in that area associated with the use and sale of methedrine. In general, the city has responded with great toughness to those deviants it believes will not be satisfied with something "reasonable." In particular, political dissent has sometimes been met with force, though San Francisco police have never indulged themselves on any large scale such as that which made Chicago police internationally detested.

The system has beauty only for those deviants who do not mind giving up some portion of their liberty, and then only if the portion they are willing to give up is the same as what the community wants given up. This no doubt is the reason an accommodative system works well with those whose deviant desires are narrowly circumscribed, and may have less utility with those whose wants can be accommodated only at the expense of others who will not easily give up their privileges. In fact, current political difficulties clearly result from the breakdown of accommodation.

These considerations indicate the more general importance of San Francisco's experiment in tolerating and accommodating to the minor forms of deviance encompassed in sex, dope and cheap thrills. How can a complex and differentiated society deal with variety and dissent and simultaneously with its own urges for centralized control? An accommodative relationship to difference, in which it is allowed to persist while it pays some minimal dues to the whole, is what San Francisco recommends to us, suggesting that the amount of the dues and the breadth of the license be set where both parties will, for the time being, stand still for it. The resulting working arrangement will be at least temporarily stable and provide for all concerned a tranquility that permits one to go about his business unharmed that many will find attractive.

But is this no more than a clever trick, a way of buying off deviant populations with minor freedoms while still keeping them enslaved? Beneath the rhetoric, the analysis is the same. The more radical statement adds only that the people who accept such a bargain ought not to, presumably because they have, if they only knew it, deeper and more important interests and desires which remain unsatisfied in the accommodative arrangement. So, of course, do those who hold them in check. Perhaps that is the ultimate lesson of San Francisco: the price of civilization, civility and living together peacefully is not getting everything you want.

It is tempting to think that an accommodation based on civility and mutual interest provides a model for settling the conflicts now wracking our urban areas. Our analysis suggests that this is a possibility, but no more than that. Peace can occur through accommodation, the example of the potheads and pimps tells us, only under certain not so easily attained conditions. Those conditions may not be present in the ethnic and political problems our major cities, San Francisco among them, are now experiencing.

Accommodation requires, as a first condition, that the parties involved prize peace and stability enough to give up some of what they want so that others may have their desires satisfied as well. But people take that point of view only when the accommodation leaves them enough of a share to want no more. Some urban groups no longer believe that they are getting that necessary minimum, either because they have learned to interpret their situation in a new light or because they have lost some advantages they once had.

Members of black communities may be no worse off than ever, but they are considerably worse off than whites and know it. For a variety of historical reasons, and as a matter of simple justice, some of them no longer regard the little they have as sufficient reason to keep the peace. All the discussion about how many blacks feel this way (is it 10 percent or 50 percent?) and how strongly they feel it (are they willing to fight?) is irrelevant to the main point: enough feel strongly enough to make a lot of trouble for the white community, thus changing the balance of costs to the whites and insisting on a new division of rights as the price of stability.

Some members of white communities probably are objectively worse off and may resent it sufficiently to give up peace and stability in an effort to raise the costs to others and thus minimize their losses. Many whites in civil service positions, in the skilled trades and in similar protected occupational positions have lost or are in danger of losing competitive job advantages as governments act to do something about the injustice that afflicts black communities. Without a general expansion of the economy, which is *not* what blacks demand, injustices inflicted on blacks can be remedied only by taking something away from more favorably situated whites. It may be possible to improve the education of poor black children, for instance, only by taking away some of the privileges of white teachers. It may be possible to give black youths a chance at apprenticeships in skilled trades only by removing the privileged access to those positions of the sons of present white union members. When whites lose those privileges, they may feel strongly enough to fracture the consensus of civility.

The deviant communities of San Francisco show us cases in which the parties involved agree in a way that leaves each enough. But that may only be possible when the interests to be accommodated involve morals and life styles. When those interests include substantial economic prizes, major forms of privilege and real political power, it may be that nothing less than a real-life assessment of relative intensities of desire and ability to inflict costs on others will suffice. That assessment takes place in the marketplace of conflict.

This suggests a second, more procedural condition for the achievement of urban peace through accommodation and civility. Mechanisms and procedures must exist by which the conflicting desires and resources for bargaining can be brought together to produce a temporarily stable working arrangement. The accommodations of enforcement officials and deviants typically occur in a host of minor bargaining situations. Hassles are settled by the people immediately involved, and settled "on their own merits"—which is to say, in a way that respects the strength of everyone's feelings and the amount of trouble each is prepared to make to have his way. The culture of civility works well because the myriad of separate local bargains respect and reflect what most of the involved parties want or are willing to settle for.

We do not allow ourselves this extreme degree of decentralized decision-making with respect to many important problems (though many critics have suggested we should). Instead, we allow federal, state or city bureaucracies to make general policies that inhibit local accommodation. While government might well intervene when circumstances make bargaining positions unequal, we know now that it is not ordinarily well equipped to reach accommodative agreements that will work at the grass roots. Unable to know what the people who inhabit local areas will want and settle for, officials turn to technocrats for solutions.

Thus, when we confront the problem of slums and urban renewal, we send for the planner and the bulldozer. But the lives of urban residents are not determined by the number or newness of buildings. The character of their relationships with one another and with the outside world does that. Planners and technocrats typically ignore those relationships, and their influence in shaping what people want, in constructing solutions. They define "slums" impersonally, using such impersonal criteria as density or deterioration, and fail to see how awakened group consciousness can turn a "slum" into a "ghetto," and a rise in moral repute turn a "ghetto" into a "neighborhood."

Too often, the search for "model cities" implies not so much a model as an ideology—a rationalistic vision of human interaction that implies a people whose consistency of behavior can nowhere be found. We already have "model cities": Brasilia at the bureaucratic end and Levittown at the residential end. And in both instances, the force of human impulses had to break through the web of formal models to make these places inhabitable. In Brasilia the rise of shantytown dwellings outside the federal buildings made the place "a city," whereas the Levittowners had to break the middle-class mode and pass through a generation of conformity before they could produce a decent living arrangement. To design a city in conformity to "community standards"—which turn out to be little more than the prejudices of building inspectors, housing designers and absentee landlords—only reinforces patterns of frustration, violence and antagonism that now characterize so many of America's large cities. To think that the dismal failure of large housing projects will be resolved by their dismal replacement with small housing projects is nonsense. Minibuildings are no more of a solution than maxibuildings are the problem.

In any event, centralized planning operating in this way does not produce a mechanism through which the mutual desires, claims and threats of interested groups can sort themselves out and allow a *modus vivendi*, if one exists, to uncover itself. The centralized body makes bargains for everyone under its influence, without knowing their circumstances or wants, and so makes it impossible for the people involved to reach a stable accommodation. But centralized planning still remains a major solution proffered for urban problems of every kind.

Accommodations reached through the mechanism of old-fashioned city political machines work little better, for contemporary machines typically fail to encompass all the people whose interests are at stake. Richard Daley demonstrated that when the Chicago ghetto, supposedly solidly under his control, exploded and revealed some people his famed consensus had not included. Lyndon Johnson made the same discovery with respect to opponents of the Vietnam War. Insofar as centralized decision-making does not work, and interested parties are not allowed to make bargains at the local level, accommodative stability cannot occur.

So the example of San Francisco's handling of moral deviance may not provide the blueprint one would like for settling urban problems generally. Its requirements include a day-to-day working agreement

among parties on the value of compromise and a procedure by which
their immediate interests can be openly communicated and effectively
adjusted. Those requirements are difficult to meet. Yet it may be that
they are capable of being met in more places than we think, that even
some of the knottier racial and political problems contain possibilities
of accommodation, no more visible to us than the casual tolerance of
deviance in San Francisco was thinkable to some of our prudish fore-
bears.

STUDY QUESTIONS

1. What activities do the San Francisco police try to stop on moral
   grounds?
2. Why do other cities worry about controlling deviants?
3. How do ethnic differences contribute to San Francisco's tolerance?
4. What does it mean to talk about the standards of the community
   in a city like San Francisco?
5. How does the working man contribute to the "culture of civility"
   of San Francisco?
6. How stable are stable communities?
7. What do the authors mean by "accommodation" when describing
   the ways in which deviants and straights get along?
8. What is the relationship between politics and "accommodation"?
9. What differences are there between a "slum" and "a ghetto"?
   Between a "ghetto" and a "neighborhood"?
10. How likely is it that San Francisco will be a model for tolerance
    across the country?

SUGGESTIONS FOR WRITING

1. Should a major city such as San Francisco permit so many kinds
   of deviation to flourish within its jurisdiction? Do you think that
   such permissiveness will ultimately harm San Francisco? What
   are your reasons? Use as much evidence from the article as possible.
2. Again and again the authors suggest that the culture they describe in San Francisco is a "culture of civility." What do they

mean by "civility"? Is it a useful term for us? Do you take exception to it? What might be a better term?

3. At one point in this article the authors assert that "the price of civilization, civility and living together peacefully is not getting everything you want." Is this true? Are you willing to give up some of the things you want in order to participate in civilization?

4. How much "freakiness" is your community willing to tolerate? Would the life of a deviant be bearable in your community? Should it be? Try to be utterly frank about the nature of your community and the reasons for its limits on tolerance. Would you like to see your community change in this regard?

5. Early in the essay the authors say, "The culture maintains itself by convincing the populace that it is indeed the culture." What, exactly, do the authors mean? Can you accept their statement based on the information in the article about life in San Francisco? Is this statement true for all communities? Is it verified by the experiences you have had in your own community?

B 2
C 3
D 4
E 5
F 6
G 7
H 8
I 9
J 0
1